The Victims of Crime

Robert A. Jerin
Endicott College

Laura J. Moriarty
Virginia Commonwealth University

Prentice Hall
Upper Saddle River, New Jersey
Columbus, Ohio

Library of Congress Cataloging-in-Publication Data

Jerin, Robert A.
   The victims of crime / Robert A. Jerin, Laura J. Moriarty. —1st ed.
     p. cm.
  ISBN-13: 978-0-13-502835-3 (alk. paper)
  ISBN-10: 0-13-502835-3 (alk. paper)
    1. Victims of crimes—United States. 2. Victims of crimes—Research—United States.
  3. Victims of crimes—United States—Statistics. 4. Crime—United States.
  5. Family violence—United States. I. Moriarty, Laura J. II. Title.
  HV6250.3.U5J467 2010
  362.880973—dc22

                                        2008035589

Editor-in-Chief: Vern Anthony
Acquisitions Editor: Tim Peyton
Editorial Assistant: Alicia Kelly
Media Project Manager: Karen Bretz
Director of Marketing: David Gesell
Marketing Assistant: Les Roberts
Production Manager: Wanda Rockwell
Creative Director: Jayne Conte
Cover Design: Lisbeth Axell
Cover Illustration/Photo: Getty Images, Inc.
Full-Service Project Management/Composition: Shiny Rajesh/Integra Software Services Pvt. Ltd.

Credits and acknowledgments borrowed from other sources and reproduced, with permission, in this textbook appear on appropriate page within text

Pearson Education Ltd., London
Pearson Education Singapore, Pte. Ltd
Pearson Education, Canada, Ltd
Pearson Education–Japan
Pearson Education Australia PTY, Limited

Pearson Education North Asia, Ltd., Hong Kong
Pearson Educación de Mexico, S.A. de C.V.
Pearson Education Malaysia, Pte. Ltd
Pearson Education Upper Saddle River,
  New Jersey

Prentice Hall
is an imprint of

www.pearsonhighered.com   ISBN-13: 978-0-13-502835-3
                                   ISBN-10:   0-13-502835-3

To Bev, my companion and confidant, Mike and Matthew, and Mom, Marjorie J. Jerin, for always believing and supporting me.

—Robert A. Jerin

To Luke, Max, Caleb, Kai, and Keira — the next generation of thoughtful and caring individuals. May you always know the value of a good education and have the compassion to help those in need.

—Laura J. Moriarty

Foreword

The transfer of knowledge gained from research and theory to practice is of critical importance in the field of crime victim services. With the publication of *The Victims of Crime*, Dr. Robert Jerin and Dr. Laura Moriarty help to equip us all with the tools we need to better understand and act in our respective areas of academic Victimology and direct victim services and advocacy. This important text presents a breadth of coverage that is not available in other publications and adeptly balances the traditional areas of victimological study with several leading-edge areas of inquiry that make this book extremely timely.

Jerin and Moriarty are both major figures in Victimology, not only due to the tremendous knowledge they bring from the academy side of the equation, but also because they have both "toiled in the fields" themselves, providing assistance to victims and survivors of criminal victimization. Their clear understanding of the practical utility of solid academic information is evident in the excellent mixture of key theoretical and empirical underpinnings that are presented with the specific implications for those who seek to assist victims.

After laying the major groundwork in the first section, Victimology, readers are guided through sections on Crime Victims and the Criminal Justice System, Interpersonal Victimization, and Stranger Victimization. Law, policy, case studies, evaluations, and other examples are used to demonstrate the imperative intersections of theory and practice, and all of this is based in research-based decision-making about which approaches warrant our support. Readers looking for up-to-date information on child abuse, sexual assault, intimate partner violence, and elder abuse will find an extremely relevant array of current information, while those looking for developments in newer areas of inquiry, such as the impact of economic violence or terrorism, or novel approaches in restorative justice that serve victims, offenders, and society-at-large, will find a comprehensive treatment of recent information in those areas.

As noted above, this text comes at an important time. Those in our field are aware of the fact that the Victims of Crime Act (VOCA) Crime Victims Fund has been for several years the target of significant attempts to reduce its funding capacity, with some proposals even zeroing-out all VOCA reserves, which would result in no federal funding for victim services. From its 1984–1985 collection of $68.3 million for distribution to victim services programs, the Crime Victim Fund has become a primary source of funding distributing in excess of $500 million currently with total deposits into the fund of approximately $9 billion from 1984 through 2007. As we know, though, this actually represents only a small fraction of the cost of crime to victims, which has been estimated in excess of $450 billion per year. With this as our backdrop, we all need to better equip ourselves with a powerful tool for victim advocacy, one that is effective on both the individual and larger policy-level, and that is knowledge. Jerin and Moriarty have brought us an excellent compilation of information for our advocacy toolkit. Whether a beginning student or seasoned practitioner, you will find very useful information here.

Mario Thomas Gaboury, J.D., Ph.D.
Professor and Chair of Criminal Justice
Oskar Schindler Humanities Foundation Endowed Professor
University of New Haven, West Haven, Connecticut
President, American Society of Victimology

Contents

SECTION III INTERPERSONAL VICTIMIZATION

Preface

The public is always the victim of crime, since crime is, by definition, an act regarded as injurious to the public.

—EDWIN H. SUTHERLAND 1924

The title of this book, "The Victims of Crime," pays homage to the first criminological study of crime victimization and to crime victims' issues by Edwin Sutherland in 1924. In Chapter III, "The Victims of Crime," of his revolutionary textbook, *Criminology*, he included the study of crime victimization. Although this initial victimological study was only 10 pages long (the shortest of any of the 25 chapters), his early insight into a major social issue has now blossomed into a unique discipline which encompasses an in-depth examination of crime victimization, its causes, the reactions to it, and its impact.

In this book we study crime victims, their victimizations, and their treatment by the criminal justice system. The authors have a wide variety of experiences working with victims and with the criminal justice system. We have between us worked as a legal advocate in the court for victims of abuse, a domestic violence victims' advocate, rape crisis and domestic violence counselor, a guardian ad litem, and a juvenile justice counselor. We have also participated in and led university-wide victim advocacy programs, community victimization surveys, and crime prevention/safety committees. We also belong to the international victimology organization, the World Society of Victimology; the national victimology organization, the American Society of Victimology; the national crime victims' advocacy organization, the National Organization for Victim Assistance; along with numerous other national and local victims' organizations. In addition to practical experience, we have over 40 years of academic experience where we have conducted many research projects studying crime victims' issues besides teaching numerous courses on Victimology, victims of crime, and crime prevention at both the undergraduate and graduate levels. We have also experienced crime victimization. This book incorporates all of our practical and academic experiences.

When we first decided to write this book, we purposefully identified issues and concerns students and professionals have voiced over the years. The organization of this book reflects the affect of those concerns. Materials included or excluded have been done so based upon what we found students and professionals needed to form an understanding of victims of crime and the justice system.

Overview of the Book

Section I, Victimology, which includes Chapters 1–3, provides a foundation for understanding the discipline of Victimology, the crime victims' movement, and the victim in the current justice system. Chapter 1 offers an overview of the historical treatment of crime victims by the justice system. Included in this presentation is our working definition of crime victims, an examination of crime victims' typologies, and legislation and programs affecting crime victims. Chapter 2 presents information on the measurement of crime victimization and theories of victimization. Information involving sources of victimization, current victimization data, and interpretations of that data are included within the chapter. Chapter 3 provides a comprehensive analysis of crime-prevention theory and programs. The issue of crime prevention versus crime control is examined, and various methods of crime prevention are also studied.

Section II, Crime Victims and the Criminal Justice System, which includes Chapters 4–6, presents an examination of the issues and programs crime victims find in the criminal justice system. Over these three chapters the crime victims' involvement with and treatment by the American justice system—police, courts, and corrections—is presented. In Chapter 4, the crime victim and law enforcement function is examined. Issues including how the police have historically related to crime victims, the impact that law enforcement can have on crime victims, police liability issues, and police-based victim witness programs are covered. Chapter 5 provides information on the American court system and its treatment of crime victims. Beginning with the historical treatment of victims, the chapter moves on and examines court-based victim witness programs and the personnel providing services to crime victims. Chapter 6 examines the correctional system and restorative justice policies found in the justice system. The history of the treatment of crime victims in corrections, the development, and the victim's participation in the parole process are presented. An in-depth presentation on the use of restitution and the restorative justice philosophy is also presented. The use of the crime victims–centered restorative justice system and its benefits provides a new avenue to crime victims as they try to recover from their victimizations.

Section III, Interpersonal Victimization, which includes Chapters 7–10, examines special classes of victims whose victimization is mostly caused by an acquaintance, an intimate partner, or relative. In Chapter 7, crimes associated with sexual violence and their consequences are presented. Definitions of sexual assault and rape, its prevalence, reporting issues, theories and myths concerning sexual violence, and its impact on victims is presented. Chapter 8 presents the issues associated with domestic violence. Theories of abuse, the psychological impact upon victims, and additional issues including marital rape are included. Additionally, the victimization created by sexual harassment is also provided. Chapter 9 examines the child victim. A definition of child abuse, its history, and the extent of the problem provide the foundation for this chapter. Programs for abused children, violence in schools, and ritual abuse are also included within this chapter. Chapter 10 examines violence against the elderly. This is a growing problem as our society ages. Areas including the definition of elderly abuse, the extent of abuse, theoretical explanations, and policy implications and programs are presented in this chapter.

Lastly, Section IV, Stranger Victimization, which includes Chapters 11–14, explores specific types of crime victimizations mostly committed by someone unrelated to the victims. Chapter 11 tackles the modern-day problems of economic victimizations. The topics of fraud, identity theft, corporate criminality, and other types of economic victimizations are studied. In Chapter 12, the issue of hate crimes and other crimes against special populations is studied. Definitions of hate crimes, their extent, and the theories associated with this violence are presented. Examples of this violence are presented for a clearer understanding of the field.

Chapters 13 and 14 provide an examination of terrorism, mass killings domestically, human trafficking, and genocide. Additionally, international crime victim recognition by the United Nations and victims services within specific foreign countries is also presented. In Chapter 13, the study of terrorism, both domestic and international, is presented. The tremendous impact of these horrific crimes is analyzed. Additionally, the crimes of school shooting, serial killing, and drunk driving are examined because of the tremendous impact these crimes have on survivors and on society. Chapter 14 begins with the actions of the United Nations on behalf of crime victims. Research on the international victimizations of genocide and human trafficking are also presented. The chapter also examines various foreign victims' programs including those found in New Zealand, Canada, Great Britain, and The Netherlands. The chapter concludes with an analysis and prediction of what lies ahead for the crime victims' movement into the next millennium. Legislative initiatives, victim services, and criminal justice policy issues are all presented.

The book is a comprehensive analysis of victims' issues, and we have tried to incorporate all the important topics that would fall into an overview of Victimology. We thank the reviewers for their insightful analysis of our work, and we acknowledge that we have tried to include all the recommendations that were provided by these individuals. Still, we know there might be some issues that we have not addressed and, as such, we invite and encourage comment, critique, and criticism of this work so that it may continue to evolve to better meet the needs of students and professionals in the field.

Acknowledgments

We would first like to thank all the dedicated victim services personnel who assist crime victim survivors every day as they try to put their lives back together. Additionally, a thank you to all of the criminal justice personnel who work tirelessly to protect, comfort, and provide services to crime victims. The information and encouragement provided by these professionals has been invaluable.

We would like to also thank the former teachers, peers, and current colleagues for their support, encouragement, and assistance in making this book a reality. Additionally, we would like to thank our former and current students who took Victimology courses with us. Their natural curiosity about victimization and their overall genuine concern for crime victims is inspiring to us.

There are also many individuals and organizations who have provided information, advice, and editorial critique of our manuscript who also must be recognized. We thank the following for reviewing the manuscript: Lisa M. Calderon, Metropolitan State College of Denver; Ron Davis, Mayland Community College; Natasha A. Frost, Northeastern University; Mike King, Salt Lake Community College and Weber State University; and Felicia Kolodner, University of Maryland at Shady Grove. We would like to also thank our colleagues who offered editorial comment on our manuscript, especially, Beverly Dolinsky, Patricia Grant, and members of the American Society of Victimology. The assistance of the reviewers of the manuscript was also invaluable. We would also like to thank Prentice Hall, especially Tim Peyton and Bob Mutchnick, for supporting this important project and our editor Alicia Kelly, who has been excellent in helping express our views in print.

Lastly, but most importantly, we would like to recognize the tremendous courage of the survivors of criminal violence; their fight for justice continues.

About the Authors

Robert A. Jerin is Professor of Criminal Justice at Endicott College. He received his Ph.D. in Criminal Justice from Sam Houston State University (1987), the Master of Criminology degree from Florida State University (1980), and the Bachelor of Criminal Justice degree from the University of New Haven (1975). He is a life member of the National Organization for Victim Assistance, the World Society of Victimology, and the American Society of Victimology. He is also a board member of the American Society of Victimology and a member of the National Center for Victims of Crime. In 2005, Dr. Jerin was the recipient of the John P. J. Dussich award from the American Society of Victimology for his contributions to the field of Victimology. He has published numerous books, chapters, and scholarly articles in such journals as the *American Journal of Police, Criminal Justice Policy Review, Journal of Criminal Justice and Popular Culture,* and *Tokiwa International Victimology Institute Journal.*

Dr. Jerin has worked as a juvenile detention officer and child care worker for the State of Connecticut, and volunteered in North Carolina as a crime victim's advocate and a battered women's and rape crisis hotline counselor. Dr. Jerin is the former Chair of the Law and Justice Department at Endicott College and a past Director of Criminal Justice Programs at Anna Maria College. Dr. Jerin is currently on the steering committee and educational curriculum committee for the Massachusetts' Victims' Assistance Academy. He also volunteers as a hotline counselor as well as a legal advocate for victims of domestic abuse in the Essex County (MA) court system.

Laura J. Moriarty is Professor of Criminal Justice and Vice Provost for Academic and Faculty Affairs at Virginia Commonwealth University. Her earned degrees include the Ph.D. from Sam Houston State University (1988), and the Master of Criminal Justice (1985) and the Bachelor of Criminal Justice (1984) degrees from Louisiana State University. Her research areas include victims of crime, victimology, fear of crime, and violent crime. She is the author, co-author, or co-editor of six books, with three in second editions. She has also published over 50 scholarly articles, book chapters, and non-refereed articles.

Dr. Moriarty started her career in criminal justice as a volunteer at the Louisiana Training Institute (LTI), an all-male juvenile detention center, where she mentored detainees. While pursuing the doctoral degree, she worked as a hotline volunteer for a women's shelter in Texas. When she started her first academic job in Cullowhee, NC, she was trained as a Guardian ad Litem, participating in child neglect cases, and she served on the Board of Directors for the local battered women's shelter. She, along with a colleague at Virginia Commonwealth University, received a Phi Kappa Phi grant to teach reading readiness to homeless children. She also has served on a Citizens' Advisory Committee to the Juvenile and Domestic Relations Court in Richmond, VA, where domestic violence petitions are considered.

SECTION I

Victimology

CHAPTER

The Victims of Crime: An Overview

INTRODUCTION

Crime victims are the essential component of the **criminal justice system**. Without the cooperation of crime victims, crimes may not be reported and if reported or discovered by authorities, the ability of the state to convict someone of a crime would be nearly impossible. Given this importance, you would believe that crime victims and how they are treated would be the number-one priority of the criminal justice system. However, the criminal justice system has for the most part ignored the needs and wishes of crime victims throughout modern history.

The study of crime victims, the reasons for their victimization, and the analysis of how they are treated by society, specifically by the criminal justice system, is known as **victimology**. While the most visible victimization is from street crime (such as murder, rape, armed robbery, or theft), white-collar, political, environmental, organized, and corporate criminality cost society as much financially, if not more (Moore and Mills, 1990). The media hypes up every murder or celebrity victimization, yet most victimizations are property crimes which happen to everyday people. Even the fear of crime affects the quality of everyone's life and a person's longevity (Brown, 1993). We also know that price fixing costs all consumers, corruption and bribery undermine our political system, and general violence can strike anyone at any time, either directly (such as being robbed) or indirectly (such as having a loved one killed by a drunk driver).

WHO ARE CRIME VICTIMS?

In legal terms, a **crime victim** is anyone who is injured (harmed) or killed due to a violation of the criminal law. Who then is a crime victim? In many ways everyone is. As **Edwin Sutherland** declared, "The public is always the victim of crime" (1924, 62). As the first criminologist to examine the victims of crime, Sutherland recognized the tremendous impact crime has on individuals and society. While the consequences may not be physical or even quantifiable, everyone is injured by crime. In the early 1900s, the estimates of the cost of crime was upwards of $6 billion (Sutherland, 1924). More recent estimates are that the public and private sectors spent $450 billion annually to pay for police departments, courthouses, prisons, and the personnel that operate our criminal justice system. Money is also spent to cover medical costs incurred directly and indirectly from crime victimization (Miller, Cohen, and Wiersema, 1996). Today, given the aftermath of September 11, it could easily be estimated that the costs of victimization are recognized to be in the trillions of dollars. Of this amount, billions are

1

spent on crime prevention programs, security equipment, and security personnel; in addition, many more dollars are lost each year in worker productivity due to absences or injuries resulting from crime victimization.

The crime victims most visible to the public in the criminal justice system are single victims of violent crime (such as Nicole Brown Simpson) or groups (such as victims of the September 11 terrorist attacks). Victims of crime can be directly or indirectly victimized, in their homes or outside of them, by strangers or people they know, at any time—day or night. Many crimes do not get reported to police, but many do. Crime victims can suffer various mental and physical injuries as serious as being killed or a continual fear that it will happen again (Smith and Hill, 1991). Crime victims may lose either thousands of dollars or only a few, and victims range in age from unborn fetuses to centenarians. Every age, sex, race, and ethnic group is a potential victim of crime. Additionally, many people become indirect victims of crime (such as families, friends, coworkers, and even strangers who witness the offenses).

Crime victims don't choose to be victims the way their offenders may choose to become criminals. However, they suffer, maybe for the rest of their lives, the effects of the violence and harm committed upon them. In an effort to better understand victims of crime and the differing effects of victimization, a description of crime victims' role in the criminal justice process is necessary. The term **victim of crime** is also used to describe a **survivor** of criminal victimization. While victims of homicides do not specifically fit this categorization, their families, loved ones, and associates do. The injuries these survivors incur can be physical, emotional, material, or monetary. Survivors never asked to be raped, swindled, or abused, and parents certainly didn't ask that their children be murdered. As long as a violation of the criminal law has taken place, the survivors of that violation may be classified as victims of crime.

The ultimate victim of all crime is society. The criminal laws establish society as the injured party because crimes "harm not only the individual, but the entire community, their commission being seen as a threat to the public order" (Greenbery, 1984, 5). This is why criminal cases are titled *The State of* _____ versus so and so or *United States of America* versus so and so. If a person violates a state criminal statute by killing someone, the state becomes the injured party.

TYPOLOGIES OF VICTIMS OF CRIME

Historically, authors have tried to distinguish between victims of crime by examining victim culpability with their own victimization. As a pioneer in the study of crime victims, **Hans von Hentig** (1948) established this trend in *The Criminal and His Victim*. Using psychological, social, and biological factors, he classified victims into various typologies which included the young, the female, the old, the mentally defective and mentally deranged, immigrants, minorities, dull normals, the depressed, the acquisitive, the wanton, the lonesome and heartbroken, tormentors, and blocked, exempted, and fighting victims (Schafer, 1981).

To von Hentig, the young become victims because they are weak and inexperienced. The likeliness of their being victimized is due to their vulnerability. Females become victims for similar reasons. Females are seen as weak and more likely to be victimized by male aggressors. The old are likely to become victims of property crimes because of their accumulation of wealth. Additionally, they are not able to defend themselves and are seen as having decreased mental alertness. The mentally defective and other deranged persons (such as alcoholics and drug addicts) are disabled and thus make easy targets. They suffer from various mental handicaps, which provides for greater susceptibility to victimization. Immigrants are also easy targets because they are adjusting to a new culture. Immigrants also face victimization because of prejudice and their lack of economic status. Likewise, minorities are affected by racial prejudice. Their economic status also requires them to live in high-crime areas. Dull normals can be easily swindled. von Hentig believed that their lessened intellectual abilities make them easy victims, especially to con games. The depressed lack the ability to fight off crime and can be seen as submissive. This group is both mentally and physically unable to prevent victimization. The acquisitive are the gamblers, the greedy persons who open themselves up to fraud and "get-rich- quick" schemes. This group can include both the poor and the rich, and those struggling to survive and those trying to make a quick buck. The wanton are unable to cope in society and are seen as promiscuous persons looking to be victimized. The lonesome and the heartbroken are potential victims because they seek companionship and are vulnerable. Widows and widowers fall into this category. Tormentors are people who set up their own victimization (such as a husband who beats his wife and is then killed by her at a later date). von Hentig's final category includes blocked, exempted, and fighting victims. The blocked and exempted don't fight back, like someone being black-mailed. Fighting victims are ones who resist but are overcome by their victimizers (Meadows, 2007).

Beniamin Mendelsohn, in his work *Rape in Criminology,* further classified crime victims by combining victim culpability and legal issues (Schafer, 1968). Mendelsohn is known as the father of victimology based upon his extensive research into victimization and the victim–offender relationship. Mendelsohn's focus on victim culpability provided the starting point for the study of crime victimization, or what is known as the science of victimology. His six graduated levels of victim complicity were the completely innocent victims, victims of minor guilt, victims as guilty as the offenders, victims more guilty than the offenders, most guilty victims, and imaginary victims.

The complicity of crime victims in their own victimization was based upon their contribution to the criminal act, whether knowingly or not. The completely innocent victims were those that did not facilitate their victimization either through actions or provocation. An example of this would be a person driving down the road, obeying all of the traffic laws and being killed by a drunk driver. Victims of minor guilt were found to have unknowingly or inadvertently contributed to their victimization. An example of this would be someone walking down a street at night in a strange city and getting mugged. The third level is victims as guilty as the offenders. An example of this would be someone seeking to buy drugs and then being assaulted or robbed. The category of victims more guilty than offenders is reserved for individuals who initiate or provoke the criminal act. A person who starts a fight in a bar and is beaten up matches this typology. The most guilty victim is reserved for the criminal who ends up becoming a victim. The abusive partner who is shot by the victim would be an example here. Lastly, the imaginary victims are those "victims" who claim to have been victimized when in reality no victimization ever took place. The runaway bride who claims to have been kidnapped, when in reality she just got cold feet and decided not to get married is an example of this type of "victim."

Stephen Schafer (1968) provided one of the first victim-oriented examinations of the offender–victim relationship in his book *The Victim and His Criminal.* Schafer was laying the foundation for the new study of crime victims and victimization, moving away from victim culpability and blame to effects of victimization and the harm done to crime victims (see Table 1.1). Schafer's seven categories included four in which there is no victim culpability: unrelated victims, biologically weak victims, socially weak victims, and political victims. **Unrelated victims** are the victims of crimes committed by strangers. Victims of bank robberies and car jacking fall into this category. **Biologically weak victims** are those who are victimized because they make easy targets due to certain physical or mental characteristics. Children and the elderly are but two groups that fit this category. **Socially weak victims** do not understand the customs of society, so they make tempting targets. Immigrants and minorities fit into this category. **Political victims** are those who suffer at the hands of political opposition and are trapped by political situations.

Two categories recognize some victim responsibility: provocative victims and precipitative victims. **Provocative victims** have done something to provoke a victimization, such

TABLE 1.1   Typologies and Definitions of Victim Responsibility

Typology	*Definition*	*Example*
No Victim Responsibility		
• Unrelated Victims	Victimization by a stranger. This is traditionally considered street crime.	Getting mugged in a city.
• Biologically Weak Victims	Elderly, disabled, and children. These individuals can't protect themselves and thus make themselves easy targets.	Abuse of the elderly in convalescent homes and cases of child abuse.
• Socially Weak Victims	Immigrants, tourists, and minorities. These individuals do not understand the culture and thus make themselves easy targets.	Economic criminal victimization of illegal immigrants who are afraid to go to authorities.
• Political Victims	War protesters, demonstrators, and economically disadvantaged. These individuals oppose those in power.	Being arrested for speaking out against war.
Some Victim Responsibility		
• Provocative Victims	These individuals have done something to incite victimization.	People who start fights and road rage participants.
• Precipitative Victims	These individuals tempt fate and seem to ask for victimization to happen.	People who get drunk and flash money around or walk down dark alleys late at night.
Total Victim Responsibility		
• Self-Victimizing	These individuals harm themselves by engaging in a criminal act.	Drug addicts, prostitutes, and alcoholics.

Source: Based on Schafer (1968).

as a man who sleeps with another man's wife and is assaulted as a result. **Precipitative victims** are those who tempt fate and seem to ask for a crime to happen. A person walking alone at night in the wrong end of town fits this category (Schafer, 1968). One more category of crime victim, according to Schafer, is totally responsible for their victimization: **self-victimizing** people who victimize themselves, such as drug abusers, alcoholics, and gamblers. All of these categories look at the responsibility of victims for their own victimization.

Ezzat Fattah (1967) also tried to establish a classification scheme for crime victims. His five major classifications are nonparticipating victims, latent or predisposed victims, provocative victims, participating victims, and false victims. Besides these main classifications, he suggested 11 subcategories. Although these categories are similar to those previously presented, they still fail to include all the different types of crime victims or affects of victimization (Schafer, 1981). Seriousness of the criminal violation is an additional method of classifying crime victims. The types of criminal violations that can occur are classified into two categories: felonies and misdemeanors. **Felonies** are crimes punishable by a year or more in prison and are considered the most serious offenses (such as murder and rape). **Misdemeanors** are crimes punishable by up to a year in jail and are not considered serious (such as petty theft).

The criminal justice system also defines and treats victims differently depending on whether the criminal event happened in a domestic or a nondomestic situation. Victims of domestic violence are usually viewed as having complicity in their victimization. Additionally, offenses are viewed as less serious if they occur in domestic situations. Examples of this would be spousal assault, spousal rape, and child abuse. Assaults upon women by their domestic partners have traditionally been ignored by the police, prosecution, and courts. For example, in many states, it was legal for a husband to rape his wife until recently (see Chapter 9). The first state to prohibit rape within marriage was Nebraska in 1976. North Carolina became the last state to criminalize marital rape in 1993 (National Organization for Victim Assistance, 1995a). In courtrooms across the United States, parents who physically and sexually abuse their children are offered treatment alternatives, while stranger assaults result in long prison sentences. In some states, domestic cases are handled by separate family courts instead of the regular criminal court.

Whether victims knew the offenders or not (stranger versus acquaintance crime) also affects how victims are treated in the criminal justice system, especially in rape and assault cases. Date rape or acquaintance rape is treated differently than sexual assaults by strangers. While the nature of the act and the injury to the victim may not differ, the way legislatures, police, prosecution, and the courts view the amount of harm done and the extent of responsibility the victim must share vary greatly. While it has been found that some prosecutors will not accept date rape cases because they feel it is nearly impossible to get convictions (LaFree, 1989), there are numerous successful prosecutions for acquaintance rape.

The characteristics of the victim are also an important part of the substantive criminal law (Dubber, 2002). The seriousness of the crime in many ways is determined by the victim. Age is a major factor in determining what criminal act, if any, occurred. Statutory rape is a perfect example. If it were not for the age of the victim, the act of a sexual relationship between such consenting individuals would not be a crime. Age also affects the punishment of offenders, especially if the victim is considered a senior citizen. Enhanced penalties for offenses against senior citizens are common. Even someone's occupation can impact the substantive law. A person who kills a police officer is guilty of a capital offense in states with the death penalty, whereas if the victim is a domestic partner, the charge would be much less serious.

Whether the victim is involved in a personal attack or has property stolen or damaged also affects how a crime victim is viewed by the criminal justice system. Property crimes are not as serious as personal victimizations. The chance of a property crime going to trial is remote. Most crime compensation programs reimburse a victim only for a physical injury or the associated losses sustained in a physical attack. While the trauma incurred by a crime victim may not differ between cases of getting mugged and having one's house robbed, the treatment of the victim by the criminal justice system does vary. This is because the criminal justice system looks at crime as a threat to society, and not at how one person is affected. Authorities will also refuse to provide support unless the victim reports the crime. The criminal justice system looks at its own needs first, then society's, and finally the victim's. Each of these categorizations provides a clearer picture of the social and legal view of the victim; however, none of these categories is mutually exclusive and multiple categorizations can apply to individual crime victims.

HISTORY OF CRIME VICTIMS AND THE JUSTICE SYSTEM

It is generally accepted that three eras define the crime victim's role within the criminal justice system: the Golden Age, the Dark Age, and the Reemergence of the Victim (Schafer, 1977; Polito, 1990; Parent, Auerbach, and Carlson, 1992). The **Golden Age** was a period of time in which crime victims were completely involved in the decision-making process concerning what needed to be done to the offenders. The offended or their survivors were responsible for bringing forth the charges, prosecuting the individuals, and deciding the disposition for offenders. They also received restitution from the offended for the harm incurred (Schafer, 1968).

An artifact of the Golden Age is the **Babylonian Code of Hammurabi**, dating back some 4,000 years. This early code recognized crime victims and the effects of the harm incurred from their victimization. It also recognized the responsibility of the state if it failed to apprehend a victim's offender. The code stated,

> If the robber is not caught, the man who has been robbed shall formally declare that ever he has lost before a god, and the city and the mayor in whose territory or district the robbery has been committed shall replace whatever he has lost for him. If it is the life of the owner that is lost, the city or mayor shall pay one maneh of silver to his kinsfolk (Parent, Auerbach, and Carlson, 1992, 54).

Here the state recognized its duty to innocent crime victims if offenders could not be apprehended or made to pay restitution or both. This ancient philosophy provided for some restoration of victims.

The **Dark Age** was a period from about the Middle Ages until the twentieth century, when the state assumed complete responsibility for arresting, prosecuting, and punishing the criminal offender. The government decided that crimes would no longer be against the victims but would be harms against the state. Crime victims no longer had a part in the decision process but were just other pieces of evidence. Crime victims were left to seek justice from offenders in civil court (Schafer, 1968).

In the United States, the treatment of crime victims by various criminal justice system components has ranged over the centuries from inclusion to exclusion, partnership to a dictatorship, and concern to ambivalence. Victims' involvement in the criminal justice process has taken various forms. In colonial times, victims were completely responsible for the apprehension, prosecution, and in many cases disposition of offenders. There were no public police agents, only sheriffs, who demanded a fee to make arrests. Prosecutors had to be hired to prosecute cases. The sanctions placed upon offenders could include triple damages to crime victims and other punishments as the victims saw fit (Johnson, 1987).

Once public prosecution and the expanded use of public police came into effect in the mid- to late nineteenth and early twentieth centuries, the role of crime victims was reduced to that of reporters of criminal events and, to a lesser extent, witnesses for the state, if needed. The criminal justice bureaucracy excluded victims from having any say in the proceedings and dispositions handed down by the government and excluded restitution to crime victims as part of the criminal justice process. Crime victims were restricted to the use of civil remedies at their own expense in order to have a say in their own victimization.

The **Reemergence of the Victim** is a very recent age. The recognition that crime victims, as people, deserve consideration by the system started in the 1950s (Schafer, 1968). The last 40 years have seen a complete reversal of the Dark Age, and a new and better Golden Age may be at hand. Some of the earliest references to crime victims in criminological literature occurred in the first well-known American criminology textbook, Edwin Sutherland's (1924) *Criminology.* In this text he included a chapter called "The Victims of Crime." This chapter examined the various ways crime victims were categorized or their typologies, the individual and social costs of crime, and the current extent of victimization. Sutherland's initial classification of crime victims first recognized the difference between the victimization of society as a whole and the victimization of individuals. Sutherland proposed that individual victimization occurred in one of two ways: direct victimization (being murdered, raped, etc.) or indirect victimization (having to pay taxes for the criminal justice system or paying higher prices for goods). Sutherland surmised that there were many more indirect victims.

Sutherland's examination of victims of homicide provides even more insight into analyses that are being undertaken today. Sutherland recognized the difference in rates based upon race, gender, age, and ethnic origin. He recognized the problem of domestic homicides and was also the first to report on the interracial nature of homicide. Sutherland found that "the victim and the offender generally belong to the same group, with reference to color, nationality, and age" (1924, 64). Even though this initial inclusion of the victims of crime occurred in the study of criminology, it would be another 50 or 60 years before the study of crime victims and related issues became part of mainstream criminology. While concern for crime victims emerged in the 1930s, seldom was concrete action taken. For example, a major governmental study of crime, the Wickersham Commission's Report of 1931, examined the problem of crime and the criminal justice system, but it offered little information concerning crime victims (Johnson, 1987).

In the 1940s, two European authors laid the foundation for the study of victims of crime during the mid-1900s. Beniamin Mendelsohn wrote *Rape in Criminology* (1940) and Hans von Hentig wrote an article, "Remarks on the Interaction between Perpetrator

TABLE 1.2   U.S. Rights Movements, 1950–present day

Social Movement	Time Period
Civil Rights	1950s–1970s
Social Welfare	1960s
Women's Rights	1960s–1980s
Grassroots/Survivors	1960s–2000s
Law and Order	1970s–2000s
Federal Activism	1980s–2000s

and Victim" (1941), and later produced a textbook, *The Criminal and His Victim* (1948). These studies focused attention on victim–offender relationships and the role of crime victims in their own victimization. These works provided the initial scientific study of crime victims, which today is known as victimology (see Schafer, 1981). The term *victimology* was first used in the United States in 1949 by Fredric Wertham. Building upon these foundations, American criminologist Marvin Wolfgang (1958) undertook a longitudinal study of homicide in Philadelphia that occurred from 1948 through 1952 (Doerner and Lab, 2006). Wolfgang's work was seminal in identifying three main factors found in victim-precipitated homicides: prior relationship, escalation of violence, and alcohol consumption. He also continued the focus on victim participation established by Mendelsohn and von Hentig.

Research based upon crime victims' perspective of criminal events had its beginnings in the 1960s. In 1965, the **President's Commission on Law Enforcement and Administration of Justice** initiated the first national survey of crime victimization called the **National Crime Survey (NCS)**. The results of these pilot studies were startling. The estimates of forcible rapes that occurred were almost four times as high as were being reported by the **Uniform Crime Reports (UCR)** (Inciardi, 1993). For the first time, it was demonstrated that the amount of crime known to the police was far less than what was occurring. A more detailed discussion of these data collection efforts and others are found in Chapter 2.

Stephen Schafer (1968) questioned the use of victim typologies that sought to blame victims as the foundation for victimology. Instead, he sought to establish the functional responsibility of victims as the basis for any typology. Schafer's (1981) analysis of the various typologies concluded that victimology must embrace the examination of criminals, victims, and their society as a singular comprehensive concept. Schafer is responsible for moving victimological research away from an assessment of victim-only risk factors and toward the criminal justice system's responsibility to both criminals and victims (Wallace, 1998). Schafer (1977) also called for recognition of certain fundamental rights of victims such as restitution and fair treatment by the criminal justice system. This precipitated a historic shift in the focus of the criminal justice system.

Additional publications in the field of victimology started to increase in the 1970s. Relying upon victimization statistics, the beginnings of victimological theory (see Chapter 2) started to develop (Williams and McShane, 1999). These theories presented the notion that victimization could be predicted based upon the actions of victims, not just offenders. The new theories examined why certain individuals were more likely than others to become victims of crime. The answer, they surmised, was that the

TABLE 1.3   Major Academic Publications in the Field of Victimology

1924	Edwin Sutherland	*Criminology*
1940	Beniamin Mendelsohn	*Rape in Criminology*
1948	Hans von Hentig	*The Criminal and His Victim*
1957	Margery Fry	*Justice for Victims*
1958	Marvin Wolfgang	*Patterns in Criminal Homicide*
1968	Stephen Schafer	*The Victim and His Criminal*
1971	Menachem Amir	*Patterns in Forcible Rape*
1975	Frank Carrington	*The Victims*
1978	Hindelang, Gottfredson, and Garofalo	*Victims of Personal Crimes*
1979	Cohen and Felson	*Social Changes and Crime Rate Trends*
1981	Galaway and Hudson	*Perspectives on Crime Victims*
1983a	Robert Elias	*Victims of the System*
1984	Andrew Karmen	*Crime Victims*
1993	Mawby and Walklate	*Critical Victimology*

"patterned activities, or lifestyles, of individuals lead to differential victimization rates" (Williams and McShane, 1999, 237). Larry Cohen and Marcus Felson (1979) put forth another theory based on the newly gathered victimization data—routine activities theory. This theory examined not only the precursors to the criminal event but also suggested prevention techniques.

A major step in the comprehensive understanding of crime victims occurred in 1981 with the publication of *Perspectives on Crime Victims* by Burt Galaway and Joe Hudson. This book brought together leading scholars in the field of victimology to provide a comprehensive assessment of the research available. It examined the victim's place in the criminal justice system, the costs of crime, the strengths and weaknesses of victim surveys, and issues of victim vulnerability, culpability, and involvement with the criminal justice system. Additionally, the book examined services for crime victims and studies assessing the quality of victim programs, a precursor to much of the current research.

Another type of examination of issues surrounding crime victims is called **critical victimology**, which studies the abuse of crime victims by the criminal justice system to further its own agenda (Elias, 1986; Mawby and Walklate, 1993). Critical victimologists criticize the false promises made by governments with compensation and other programs. To critical victimologists, victims are pawns used to validate and assist a broken criminal justice system. Instead of addressing the true causes of crime and victimization (such as inequality, poverty, and power differentials), the criminal justice system reacts after the fact and inadequately provides programs for crime victims.

EARLY SOCIAL MOVEMENTS AND THE ROLE OF GOVERNMENT

In the 1950s, society started examining the role of government in creating additional victimization. First, the **civil rights movement** questioned the institutionalization of racism by the local, state, and federal government. The right of all people to have a say in their governing and the operation of government structure became a central theme. Voting rights issues, segregation of public and private facilities, and the unequal treatment of individuals by bureaucratic institutions came to the forefront, laying the foundation for questioning the government operation of the criminal justice system. The passage of a comprehensive Civil Rights Act set the stage for scrutinizing crime victims' issues. More-over, Margaret Fry (1957) publicly questioned the government's duty to compensate its citizens for failing to prevent criminal injuries to innocent victims. Her call paved the way for new government policies beginning in the mid-1960s (Karmen, 1990).

Politically, the call for a social welfare state established under the Johnson Administration also enhanced victims' standing. In 1965, Congress authorized the first pilot study of crime victimization, which continues today as the **National Crime Victimization Survey (NCVS)** (Smith, 1988). Calling for more responsibility of government to its citizens and the idea of the "Great Society," the Johnson Administration laid the groundwork to provide money for victims' issues.

The **crime victims' movement** is a recent phenomenon in world history and has been active in the United States only in the last 40 years (see Appendix A) (Cuomo, 1978; Elias, 1986; Finn and Lee, 1987; Kelly, 1990; Jerin, 2004). Two movements emerged during the 1960s that provided the cornerstone of today's victims' agenda. First, the feminist movement (or **women's movement**) initiated most of the grassroots support for initial victims' programs. During the 1960s, feminists spoke out against the status quo that ignored the domestic abuse women faced, especially being made to feel like criminals in rape cases. Women sought to have more say in controlling their bodies and in making the criminal justice system more responsible for stopping the violence against them, especially in cases of rape and domestic violence. Issues of male violence against women and the way women were being revictimized by the criminal justice process gained national attention. Demonstrations, marches, and rallies were held to publicize the plight of women and to force changes in the operation of the current system (Dussich, 1986).

Second, and concurrently with the women's movement, the **law and order movement** also took national prominence. The law and order movement was a conservative ideology that believed that offenders had too many rights and we needed to become more punishment-oriented in dealing with criminals. During this time, increased riots occurred in major cities, the number of criminal acts increased due to the population explosion of the baby boomers, and the antiwar movement posed a perceived threat. As a reaction to the liberal policies of the Supreme Court during the 1960s, a large conservative populist movement developed that demanded stricter laws, tougher punishments, and equal rights for crime victims. This led to the federal government establishing the President's Commission on Law Enforcement and Administration of Justice, whose report, *The Challenge of Crime in a Free Society* (1967), highlighted many citizens' concerns over the crime problem and what should be done. As a result of this report, the federal government established the **Law Enforcement Assistance Administration (LEAA)**, which provided funds for improving the criminal justice system. Some of these funds helped establish several of the first victims' programs (Dussich, 1986).

Grassroots and Survivors' Movement

In the 1970s, the crime victims' movement took its first steps toward legitimacy. Like a young child starting to walk, the victims' movement moved at a quicker pace. More states provided **compensation programs**, and private grassroots operations using

LEAA's financial support started the first victim service programs. In 1972, the first rape crisis centers were established in San Francisco, Los Angeles, Washington, D.C., and Ann Arbor, Michigan. When these programs were first developed, they were usually staffed by former victims. In 1974, local district attorneys in Brooklyn, New York, and Milwaukee, Wisconsin, established the first victim/witness program, which provided assistance to crime victims who had to go to court. Even law enforcement–based victim assistance programs were established in Florida and Indiana (Dussich, 1986).

Another movement took place in the use of research undertaken during the 1970s. Research became focused on crime victims' services and rights. John Dussich (1976) provided some of the earliest analyses of crime victims' service needs and possible programs. John Stein (1977) advocated for greater victim services at all levels of the criminal justice system, and the legal analysis of Frank Carrington (1975) and Carrington and Nicholson (1984) regarding the commensurable rights of crime victims through civil action established a rich research tradition.

National crime victims' organizations also were founded by survivors of various victimizations and their supporters, including the **National Organization for Victim Assistance (NOVA)** in 1975, the **National Coalition Against Sexual Assault (NCASA),** the **National Coalition Against Domestic Violence (NCADV)**, and **Parents of Murdered Children (POMC)** in 1978. Even international organizations and conferences that focused on crime victims' issues were established. By 1979, with the founding of the **World Society of Victimology**, the crime victims' movement had begun to emerge as a force for the public recognition of crime victims' issues (National Organization for Victim Assistance, 1993).

Federal Activism Movement

Simultaneously, the federal government was also providing invaluable research on crime victims. Three major governmental reports specifically addressing victims' issues were published during the 1980s. The first, the final report from the President's Task Force on Victims of Crime (1982), provided a firsthand account of the impact of crime upon victims and their revictimization by the criminal justice system. Over the eight months of study, the Task Force heard from hundreds of crime victims, researchers, practitioners, and service providers concerning the treatment of crime victims by the criminal justice system and the private organizations from which they sought assistance. The report provided a "synthesis of information" (119) and recommendations for addressing the problems faced by crime victims.

The second major governmental report to be released was the U.S. Attorney General's Task Force on Family Violence (1984). This report built upon the information provided by Straus (1973) and Straus, Gelles, and Steinmetz (1980) and reported that the extent of domestic violence and the harm it caused were grossly underestimated. Additional research by Sherman and Berk (1984) on the use of mandatory arrests in domestic violence cases (see Chapter 4) and by Walker (1980) sparked major initiatives to change polices toward arresting the batterer.

The final major governmental report of the 1980s was from the President's Child Safety Partnership in 1987. This study examined child victimization in the United States and the quality of the programs available to protect children in both the public and private sectors. The report was the first comprehensive attempt to gather accurate information about the nature and extent of child victimization. The report concluded that a partnership was necessary between the public and private sectors to work toward protecting children and making sure that they are supported in every way.

Additionally, the 1980s saw the government elevate crime victims to important partners in its efforts to deal with crime by creating an **Office for Victims of Crime (OVC)** within the Office of Justice Programs. The office established a national resource center to provide information to crime victims and their supporters, help train professionals to work and treat victims, and develop model legislation to protect victims' rights.

In the 1990s, the federalism of the crime victims' movement continued. During the 1990s, the federal Crime Victims' Fund collected over $3 billion to distribute to federal crime victims' state compensation and local crime victims' programs. The first draft of a federal crime victims' constitutional amendment was proposed and supported by Senators Dianne Feinstein and John Kyl. The passage of the Community Notification Act (**Megan's Law**) required community members to be notified of the location of any convicted sex offenders. Congress was even responsible for establishing the National Domestic Violence Hotline, providing 24-hour crisis intervention and referral information to victims of domestic violence. During the 1990s, the federal government also recognized the national nature of the crimes of stalking and identity theft and passed legislation, making each a federal offense.

A major federal initiative for crime victims came in the 1990s with the publication of a comprehensive report from the Office for Victims of Crime, entitled *New Directions From the Field* (1998). This report reexamined how well governments, criminal justice agencies, communities, and professionals had implemented the original recommendations of the 1982 Presidential Task Force Report. This new document provided a comprehensive report on the accomplishments of the victims' movement and set forth a new set of recommendations on victims' rights and services to strive for as the country entered the twenty-first century. Many of these recommendations are included in this book as they relate to the various components of the criminal justice system and the community and what it can do to be more victim-friendly. The culmination of federal activism in the 1990s for crime victims came in early 2000 with the reauthorization of the **Violence Against Women Act**. This Act was signed into law by President Clinton and marked a continuing federal commitment to recognizing and protecting female victims of violence.

The new millennium began on a tragic note with the horrendous victimization that occurred on September 11, 2001. The federal response was swift and comprehensive, with the introduction of new policies and laws that sought to compensate the victims and survivors of the terrorist carnage. Passage of the September 11th Compensation Fund of 2001 not only provided for direct compensation to victims and survivors of the terrorist attacks but also established rights and procedures for future victims and to prevent future crimes. Another major piece of legislation passed in the wake of September 11 was the Uniting and Strengthening America by Providing Appropriate Tools Required to Intercept and Obstruct Terrorism **(USA PATRIOT) Act** of 2001, which provided greater police powers to law enforcement to investigate possible terrorists and to try to prevent any future acts of terrorism against the United States.

Crime Victims' Rights Movement

The **President's Task Force on Victims of Crime** (1982) attempted to change the U.S. Constitution with the addition of one simple sentence to the Sixth Amendment that would have guaranteed victims the right to be heard throughout their judicial proceedings (Young, 1996. This attempt failed; however, today most states have enacted their own constitutional amendments or state statutes that provide for victims' rights or guidelines for the treatment of crime victims by the criminal justice system. Further, in 1982, the federal government passed a provisional crime victims' Bill of Rights as part of the **Omnibus Victim and Witness Protection Act**. This act was expanded in the Crime Control Act: the Victims' Rights and Restitution Act of 1990 (42 U.S.C. 10606). In 1994, with bipartisan support, Congress passed the Violence Against Women Act (the VAWA), which federalized certain rights for women.

The greatest impact on the operation of the criminal justice system is occurring with the passage of crime victims' bills of rights and state constitutional amendments. This legislation specifically addresses procedures that criminal justice systems must follow. The influence of these bills of rights upon the criminal justice system is widespread. Most establish procedures for keeping crime victims informed of the progress of their cases, making sure they receive certain governmental services or information, allowing victims to have input into the sentencing phase of the criminal justice process, and even participating in the charging decision (National Organization for Victim Assistance, 1990).

The state legislatures have been the leaders in advancing the cause for crime victims' rights. An example of a model state constitutional amendment is the following one passed by 79 percent of Connecticut voters. The amendment (**XXIX**) to the Connecticut Constitution in November of 1996 states:

In all criminal prosecutions, a victim, as the General Assembly may define by law, shall have the following rights:

1. The right to be treated with fairness and respect throughout the criminal justice process;
2. The right to timely disposition of the case following arrest of the accused, provided no right of the accused is abridged;
3. The right to be reasonably protected from the accused throughout the criminal justice process;
4. The right to notification of court proceedings;
5. The right to attend the trial and all other court proceedings the accused has the right to attend, unless such person is to testify and the court determines that such person's testimony would be materially affected if such person hears other testimony;
6. The right to communicate with the prosecution;
7. The right to object to or support any plea agreement entered into by the accused and the prosecution and to make a statement to the court prior to the acceptance by the court of the plea of guilty or *nolo contendere* by the accused;
8. The right to make a statement to the court at sentencing;
9. The right to restitution which shall be enforceable in the same manner as any other cause of action or as otherwise provided by law; and
10. The right to information about the arrest, conviction, sentence, imprisonment and release of the accused. (http://www.jud.state.ct.us/crimevictim/crime-const-rights.htm. January 15, 2006)

In 1995, the National Victims' Constitutional Amendment Network (NVCAN) proposed the first draft of language for a federal victims' rights constitutional amendment. These efforts led to the introduction of a bipartisan amendment: The Constitutional Rights for Crime Victims (Senate Joint Resolution 44), sponsored by Senators Jon Kyl and Dianne Feinstein, was sent to the full Senate for its consideration in 1998. This legislation is modeled after the constitutional amendments that have been used in many states. This proposed amendment is still in legislative limbo, but the federal government has passed statutory rights for crime victims within the federal system. Summarizing these provisions, they include the following:

- The right to be treated with fairness and with respect for the victim's dignity and privacy.
- The right to be reasonably protected from the accused offender.
- The right to be notified of all court proceedings.
- The right to be present at all public court proceedings related to the offense.
- The right to be heard and submit a statement at all public proceedings relating to the crime.
- The right to confer with attorneys for the government in the case.
- The right to restitution.
- The right to information about the conviction, sentencing, imprisonment, and release of the offender.

Currently, 33 states have enacted crime victims' constitutional amendments. http://www.usdoj.gov/usao/ma/vicwit.html. January 15, 2006).

CRIME VICTIMS' LEGISLATION

By the 1980s, the crime victims' movement had established itself as a potent political and social force in the United States. Tremendous gains had been made for victims' organizations, programs, services, legislation, and funding on the federal, state, and local levels since the 1960s. The foundations of these changes were laws passed on the federal and state levels affecting the operation of the criminal justice system, the delivery of services by the states and federal government, and the role of the victim in the criminal justice system. Even though victims' legislation started very slowly in the 1960s, it has generated an avalanche of laws in the 1980s into the 1990s (National Organization for Victim Assistance, 1990). With the new millennium, crime victims' legislation is continuing to be at the forefront. (See Appendix A for a historical overview of the legislation and events relating to crime victims and the crime victims' movement.)

The explosion of legislation in the last 25 years due to the involvement of the federal government in pressing crime victim issues has had the greatest effect on the criminal justice system.(President's Task Force on Victims of Crime 1982; U.S. Department of Justice, 1985; Office for Victims of Crime, 1998; Jerin, 2004). Additionally, local and national grassroots organizations of crime victims and their supporters have been very active in seeking to get their message out. Researchers in the criminal justice field also helped to popularize crime victims' perspective with greater examination of crime victims' issues (Galaway and Hudson, 1981; Carrington and Nicholson, 1984; Elias, 1986; Moriarty and Jerin, 1998; Moriarty, 2003).

The new victims' legislation impacts three concerns of crime victims. The first concern is providing government-sponsored services and programs for victims. These programs include victim/witness programs and compensation programs. The second concern is the right of victims to be informed of and participate in the criminal justice process. The third area redefines or implements new criminal statutes and penalties that are more responsive to crime victims' perspectives (National Organization for Victim Assistance, 1990).

The first legislation to establish legislation for victims was the passage of California's victim compensation program in 1965 (Ramker and Meagher, 1982). The program sought to provide crime victims with an insurance policy against the expense of physical injury due to criminal acts. By the end of the 1960s, state-sponsored compensation programs began to take hold, with five additional states offering some level of compensation to victims of violent crimes. This number grew during the 1970s with more states establishing programs; however, many programs ran into funding and administrative problems that threatened to derail these valuable programs.

The rescue of victim compensation programs occurred in 1984 with the passage of the **Victims of Crime Act**. This federal legislation established consistent guidelines for states as to levels of compensation. It also provided states with an additional funding source for their compensation programs as well as other victim assistance programs. The **crime victims' fund** was made up of monies from federal criminal fines, penalties, and bond forfeitures and was used to support federal and state victim compensation and local victim service programs. Beginning in 1985, the fund had deposits totaling $68 million. By 2006, the deposits totaled $551 million (see Table 1.4). Because of the availability of federal funds, by 2002 all 50 states could offer some type of compensation program.

CRIME VICTIM COMPENSATION

Programs that compensate victims of crime are best thought of as "insurance systems of last resort" (National Organization for Victim Assistance, 1990, 1). The programs are set up as a safety net for crime victims and their families to cover costs due to victimization that cannot be recovered from offenders or other sources. Unlike restitution, compensation does not require that the offenders are caught, tried, or convicted. (See Appendix B for an example of an application for compensation.)

State government compensation to victims of crime was abandoned long before the modern era, and it wasn't until the 1950s that **Margery Fry**, an English magistrate and reformer, reintroduced the idea (Kutner, 1966; Carrow, 1980; Elias, 1984). She sought to resurrect the concept of state-sponsored compensation as a result of a case in which a person was blinded by two offenders. As a result of the injury, the crime victim was awarded restitution from the offenders. However, the payment schedule set up by the court would have taken the victim over 400 years to collect (Schafer, 1970). The court awarded 11,000 pounds (approximately $50,000) to the victim, and the two assailants were ordered to pay him 5 shillings weekly. Fry argued that the government should compensate innocent victims of crime (Fry, 1957). She believed in the social contract perspective, the idea that the government was responsible to its citizens for failing to protect them and not allowing them to protect themselves. Since crime victimization is a governmental failure, she argued, the government should offer its citizens insurance or compensation to restore them to their precrime state.

New Zealand and England led the way by enacting national programs in 1963 and 1964, respectively (Kutner, 1966). In the United States, Senator Ralph Yarborough of

Texas introduced the first victim compensation legislation in Congress; however, it would be another 19 years before any federal compensation legislation was enacted. State-sponsored crime victim compensation programs developed in the United States, beginning in California in 1965. By the end of the 1960s, five additional states (New York, Massachusetts, Maryland, Hawaii, and Georgia) had established their own programs (Ramker and Meagher, 1982). By the end of the 1970s, the number of states had grown to 30, and by the end of the 1980s, all but two states (Maine and South Dakota) had such programs. On April 6, 1992, Maine became the last state to provide a crime victim compensation program for crimes occurring within its borders (National Organization for Victim Assistance, 1992).

The establishment of a federal program to provide for victims of federal crimes and to provide additional funds to state compensation programs occurred with the passage of the Victims of Crime Act of 1984 (VOCA). The act was based upon recommendations put forth in 1982 by the President's Task Force on Victims of Crime, which called on Congress to enact legislation to provide federal funding to assist state crime victim compensation programs. The principle provisions of VOCA are:

- To establish a crime victims' fund in the Treasury for the purpose of funding annual grants to states for victim compensation programs.
- To provide grants to programs that provide services to victims of crime.
- To impose penalty assessments upon convicted federal defendants.
- To promote more uniform services among the states.
- To provide compensation to victims of federal crimes.

Congress initially established a cap of $100 million on the fund and a sunshine clause that authorized VOCA only until 1988. This cap on the funds VOCA could receive was raised in 1986 to $110 million. In 1988, VOCA was reauthorized, and the fund limit was raised to $125 million, which would go to $150 million by fiscal year 1994 (Parent, Auerbach, and Carlson, 1992). As can be seen in Table 1.4, the fund has grown tremendously since the early 1990s. The initial funding for VOCA came from penalty assessments. Initially, VOCA imposed a mandatory penalty assessment on all convicted federal defendants in addition to any fine or other sentence that was imposed by the court. The assessments were $25 on individual misdemeanants, $100 on other misdemeanants, $50 on individual felons, and $200 on other felons. These special assessment provisions applied to all federal convictions, including petty offense convictions. In addition to assessments, the fund also received monies from federal fines, bond forfeitures, and royalties from the sale of literary rights, the so-called "Son-of-Sam" provision (Parent, Auerbach, and Carlson, 1992). Fifty percent of the fund was to go to state victim compensation programs and 50 percent was to be given out in grants to eligible crime victim assistance programs. The impact the federal VOCA program has had on state crime victims' compensation and victim assistance programs is extensive.

To qualify for funds from the federal program, the states were required to meet certain criteria. Beginning in 1986, state programs were to

- Reimburse crime victims or their survivors for medical expenses resulting from physical injury as the result of a violent crime, including mental health counseling, lost wages, and funeral expenses.
- Promote victim cooperation with law enforcement agencies.

TABLE 1.4   Federal Crime Victims' Fund Deposits, 1985–2006

Year	Amount	Year	Amount
1985	$68 million	1996	$525 million
1986	$62 million	1997	$363 million
1987	$77 million	1998	$324 million
1988	$93 million	1999	$985 million
1989	$133 million	2000	$777 million
1990	$146 million	2001	$544 million
1991	$128 million	2002	$519 million
1992	$221 million	2003	$361 million
1993	$144 million	2004	$834 million
1994	$185 million	2005	$668 million
1995	$233 million	2006	$551 million

- Not use federal funds to supplant available state funds.
- Compensate victims who are nonresidents of the state on the same basis as resident victims.
- Compensate victims of federal crimes on the same basis as victims of state crimes.
- Provide other information and assurances reasonably requested by the attorney general. (U.S. Dept. of Justice, 1985, 2)

When VOCA came up for renewal in 1988, it was amended, and four additional requirements were added in order for state programs to receive federal funding. Beginning in 1991, state programs needed to also:

- Offer compensation to victims of drunk-driving accidents and domestic violence.
- Compensate residents who are victims in other states that do not have crime victim compensation programs.
- Establish rules formally establishing what constitutes "unjust enrichment" if the state denies claims on that basis.
- Meet procedural requirements—application, reporting, auditing—to qualify for VOCA grants. (Parent, Auerbach, and Carlson, 1992, 2–3)

Except for the criteria set forth by VOCA, each state is allowed to establish additional provisions, such as the maximum award, financial need requirement, minimum loss, filing deadlines, compensable crimes (excluding federal crimes, drunk driving, and domestic violence), and compensable losses. All states except New York have a cap on the maximum amount of benefits crime victims can receive. The range of awards for all other states is from $5,000 to $50,000. A large number of states require that crime victims suffer a minimum loss of at least $100 in order to file a claim. A vast majority of the states offer emergency awards to provide immediate assistance to crime victims whose victimization has created a sudden financial crisis. Only a few states offer compensation for property loss and for pain and suffering, for reasons of cost containment and the availability of insurance for property losses. States also require that crime victims cooperate with law enforcement and in the prosecution of offenders if possible in order to be eligible, which eliminates crime victims who fail to report crimes.

Another restriction on who can receive compensation is contributory misconduct rules. The purpose of these rules is to eliminate individuals who are injured while committing a crime or substantially contribute to their own victimization. Examples of this are drug dealers who are host when a deal goes bad and individuals injured in a bar fight that they started (National Organization for Victim Assistance, 1990; Parent, Auerbach, and Carlson, 1992).

States must provide some funding in order to receive the federal money. States use various means to fund their victim compensation programs including taxes, special assessments, and offender fines. While no one method is deemed more effective than another, there are strengths and weaknesses with any single method, and most states use a combination of methods (Parent, Auerbach, and Carlson, 1992).

Whether or not crime victim compensation programs actually accomplish any or all of their goals is questionable and has been subject to much research and scholarly debate (Carrow, 1980; Doerner and Lab, 1980; Elias, 1983a, 1983b, 1984, 1986, 1993; Kilpatrick et al., 1989; McShane and Williams, 1992). Questions of efficiency and effectiveness of the state compensation programs have also been put forth by victims' groups. Some research has characterized compensation programs as a "political placebo" because the number of individuals served and the amount each victim receives is relatively small compared with the number of victims and the extent of loss (physical, mental, and emotional) they suffer (Weed, 1995). While compensation awards from states total hundreds of millions of dollars, most of the money goes toward medical benefits and legal expenses, and crime victims may not see any actual dollars. Many crime victims have their claims rejected or fail to pursue their claims for various reasons (Jerin, 1988a). Further, the delay many crime victims experience between when a claim is filed and when it is paid can lead to their revictimization.

Some states have at times fallen over a year or more behind in paying claims, while other programs have run out of funds and had to seek more funds from the state general revenue to deal with pending claims. Other problems exist, such as the administrative cost of some programs that take up a large percentage of the funds available. A study done in the 1990s demonstrated the high costs of administering crime compensation programs. Administrative costs range from a low of approximately 5 percent to a high of over 25 percent (Parent, Auerbach, and Carlson, 1992). Crime victims can also be revictimized by the low benefit awards of some state programs and the restrictions placed upon those awards. Finally, many crime victims are not aware of their right to receive compensation because of the low visibility of many programs. An estimate of eligible crime victims served by state victim compensation programs was about 22 percent (Parent, Auerbach, and Carlson, 1992). Today it is unknown if there has been any improvement in the number of actual victims served.

ADDITIONAL VICTIM SERVICES

The next victim service to occur was the establishment of **victim/witness programs**. These programs were initially set up in prosecutors' offices to help guide crime victims through the court process to ensure better prosecutions (see Chapter 5). Beginning in 1974, 10 programs were started with LEAA funding. Today there are hundreds of programs running throughout the United States due to funding from the federal Crime Victims' Fund and local funding sources. All federal prosecutors' offices are required to have a victim/witness program staffed with advocates. Most states also have some type of victim/witness program staffed with professionals whose job it is to help crime victims negotiate the criminal justice system. No longer are they found only in the courts. Victim services programs are also located in local police and sheriffs' departments (see Chapter 4) (Wrobleski and Hess, 1993).

Crime victims' participation in the criminal justice system has changed dramatically over the last two decades. The perpetual role of crime victims in the criminal justice process has been to serve as witnesses for the state. The traditional responsibility of the state was to all citizens equally and not to any person individually. There was no reciprocal duty to provide victims of crime with anything not offered to the general public. However, the influence of crime victims' groups and supporters started changing the criminal justice system in the 1980s. One of the first changes was with the reinstitution of restitution. **Restitution** is an ancient form of punishment providing victims with some relief at the conclusion of criminal trials; however, most judges did not use it. An example of this is the state of Tennessee, which in 1932 had a law establishing restitution in felony cases. However, it was not until 1982 when the law was amended that enforcement of the statute took place. Today, most states require restitution as part of any sentencing for both felonies and misdemeanors.

Additional impact on the criminal justice system occurs with the changes in legal statutes and penalties put forth by victims' groups and their supporters. Many changes have occurred in the definition of what is a crime and what kind of punishment should be attached. The influence of **Mothers Against Drunk Driving (MADD)** on the seriousness of drunk driving and the sanctions imposed is most notable (see Chapter 13). For example, when MADD was founded in 1980, the average drinking age in the United States was 18; today it is 21 years old. The blood alcohol level necessary to convict someone of drunk driving has been lowered to .08 in most states. The penalties associated with drunk driving and vehicular homicide now include mandatory loss of license and mandatory jail terms.

Domestic violence was not considered a crime against society until very recently (see Chapter 8). Little more than a decade or two ago, most police failed to arrest violent husbands and most prosecutors refused to prosecute husbands for violence against wives or children. Even the public believed that this violence was only a family matter. Today, many states mandate an arrest in domestic violence situations; police, prosecutors, and judges receive training concerning domestic violence; and many police and prosecutors' offices have special domestic violence units (Buzawa and Buzawa, 1990).

Two other special interest groups that have influenced the criminal justice system are child victims' groups and the elderly. Child victims receive special services in court, including the use of video taping and programs to familiarize them with the operation of the criminal justice system. The elderly have specific laws that provide for increased penalties for any crimes committed against them (National Organization for Victim Assistance, 1990).

The influence of crime victims' groups can also be seen in the establishment of new laws dealing with stalking and hate crimes. The new "truth in sentencing" statutes and the "three-strikes-you're-out" statutes are all a result of the crime victims' movement over the last 40 years. Today, it is hard to recognize the crime victims' movement as the one that began some 40 years ago. Forty years from now it may be just as hard to recognize the crime victims' movement of today because of the continuing changes. In 1980, the first elocution of crime victims' rights was enacted by the state of Wisconsin. However, crime victims' rights are still not the law of the land. To achieve the goals of the crime victims' movement, additional principles and services must still be provided to all crime victims through legislation. For example, NOVA (2006) suggests these advancements for crime victims, witnesses, and communities:

1. Protections for victims, witnesses, and communities, such as:
   Rights to privacy.
   Effective enforcement of protection orders.
   Safety and security in criminal justice process.
   Establishment of safe havens and peace zones.
   Special protections for highly vulnerable populations.
   Violence prevention.
2. Information, notification, and consultation on case status, decision making, and implementation of decisions.
3. Participation through a voice "not a veto" by victims, witnesses, and communities.
4. Reparations to the injured.
5. Preservation of property and employment through innovative practices.
6. Due process for victims and communities.
7. Treatment of victims with dignity and compassion "throughout the nation and the world" by

   Training and education for justice professionals in all aspects of victim issues and victim rights.
   Adequately funded victim assistance programs in every jurisdiction so that victims are never more than a telephone call away from help.
   Increasing public understanding of the impact of victimization and appropriate responses through educational curricula, as well as mandatory continuing education courses for lawyers, public safety officers, health and mental health professionals, the clergy, and others who respond to victims. (National Organization for Victim Assistance, 3–5)

CONCLUSION

Victims' rights legislation addresses the "right" of all crime victims to be treated equally, feel safe in their homes, be protected and respected by the criminal justice system, and be made whole again if the government fails to protect them from harm. As noted in *New Directions,* "As a society we have made great progress in meeting victims' needs since the 1982 *Final Report* of the President's Task Force on Victims of Crime" (U.S. Department of Justice, 1997, 429). This progress continues today and into the foreseeable future. New programs for crime victims are being developed and new laws supporting crime victims are being passed. On the federal level, bills currently awaiting legislative action focus on rights for victims of hate crimes, stalking, gender violence, terrorism, identity theft, and children's rights, just to name a few. However, the Constitution of the United States still does not recognize the interests of the crime victim. The expansion of "rights" for crime victims will continue until such time as the public believe that they are getting a fair share from their government and the criminal justice system.

The true Golden Age of the crime victim may be closer at hand than at any other time in the history of mankind. However, with the amount of criminal victimization and the number of violations of human rights that take place throughout the United States and the world, it may be hard to believe. The crime victims' movement is here to stay and will play an increasingly important role in making governments accountable to their citizens. Cesare Beccaria (1764) once described the role of government as having a social contract with its people. People would give up a small portion of their individual rights to the state in exchange for peace and safety. Crime victims are asking that their state contract be enforced.

Study Questions

1. What does victimology mean? Trace the origin of the study of victims of crime from the early criminologists and victimologists, while focusing on the issues of victim blaming and the contribution of crime victims to their own victimization.
2. Explain the early beginnings of the crime victims' movement in the 1960s and 1970s. What social movements contributed to the advancement of the crime victims' movement, and what were some of the initial programs developed to assist crime victims?
3. What is meant by crime victims' "rights"? What are some of the significant pieces of legislation that directly affect crime victims' rights, and how does the criminal justice system currently respond to the needs of crime victims when compared to 40 years ago?
4. What are the problems the crime victims' movement has with the criminal justice system and how it currently operates? What additional legislation to improve the plight of the crime victim would you suggest, and why?

Key Terms

- Beniamin Mendelsohn   3
- biologically weak victims   4
- civil rights movement   9
- Babylonian Code of Hammurabi   6
- compensation programs   10
- crime victim   1
- crime victims' fund   15
- crime victims' movement   10
- criminal justice system   1
- critical victimology   9
- Dark Age   6
- Edwin Sutherland   7
- Ezzat Fattah   5
- felonies   5
- Golden Age   6
- Hans von Hentig   2
- law and order movement   10

- Law Enforcement Assistance Administration (LEAA)   10
- Margery Fry   16
- Megan's Law   12
- misdemeanors   5
- Mothers Against Drunk Driving (MADD)   19
- National Coalition Against Domestic Violence (NCADV)   11
- National Coalition Against Sexual Assault (NCASA)   11
- National Crime Survey (NCS)   8
- National Crime Victimization Survey (NCVS)   10

- National Organization for Victim Assistance (NOVA)   11
- Office for Victims of Crime (OVC)   12
- Parents of Murdered Children (POMC)   11
- political victims   4
- precipitative victim   5
- President's Commission on Law Enforcement and Administration of Justice   8
- **President's Task Force on Victims of Crime**   13
- provocative victim   4
- Reemergence of the Victim   7
- **Restitution**   19
- self-victimizing   5
- socially weak victims   4

Crime Victimization: Statistics, Theories, and Victimology

INTRODUCTION

How is crime and crime victimization measured? Criminologists traditionally have used several sources to estimate victimization: the Uniform Crime Reports (UCR), National Incident-Based Reporting System (NIBRS), the National Crime Victimization Survey (NCVS), and statewide crime polls or victimization surveys. The problem with these measures is that they only *estimate* crime or crime victimization. None of these sources can produce the actual amount of crime committed in a given area. Nevertheless, they represent the most established mechanisms for determining victimization rates.

When discussing victimization, some authors use the terms **prevalence** and **incidence**. These terms have their origins in epidemiology. Sometimes it is difficult to understand the logic of such terms in describing victimization; however, if explained correctly, these terms are useful. Incidence means the "number of new cases of a particular problem or condition that are identified or arise in a specified area during a specified period of time" (Rossi and Freeman, 1994, 56). Prevalence refers to "the number of existing cases in a particular area at a specified time" (Rossi and Freeman, 1994, 96). Although these definitions sound similar, they are indeed different, as the following example illustrates. The incidence of robberies during a particular month is defined as the number of *new* cases of robbery for that month. Robbery prevalence during the same month is the total number of robberies regardless of when the robberies occurred. Prevalence is a cumulative or additive summary of the total amount of existing cases of a certain phenomenon, while incidence reflects only the new cases in a given period.

Most often, prevalence is reported as a rate; that is, the number of existing cases is divided by the number of people in the defined population. The incidence number is a frequency or raw number without standardization. This means that anyone looking at the incidence of robbery would have great difficulty determining whether the number is high, low, or moderate. The number 30 in and of itself is neither large nor small. Without a comparative base, the number does little more than just provide a value. Usually, frequencies are compared to the overall population to determine a ratio that is divided by 100 to determine a rate. The rate then becomes something that is standardized and can be compared and contrasted with other rates to determine trends in data.

SOURCES OF VICTIMIZATION DATA

The **Uniform Crime Reports (UCR)**, the **National Incident-Based Reporting System (NIBRS)**, and the **National Crime Victimization Survey (NCVS)** are three sources of victimization data that will be explained in this section. "The Uniform Crime Reporting (UCR) program is a nationwide, cooperative statistical effort of more than 17,000 city, university and college, county, state, tribal, and federal law enforcement agencies voluntarily reporting data on crime brought to their attention" (U.S. Department of Justice, Federal Bureau of Investigation, 2007). The UCR, then, represent an official estimate of victimization rates as reported by police departments. These official statistics often underestimate victimization because a crime must be "known to the police" before it can be recorded (Siegel, 2006). Further, the accuracy of the UCR is dependent upon the police departments' ability and willingness to participate in the reporting system. In 1992, law enforcement agencies "active in the UCR program represented over 242 million United States inhabitants or 95 percent of the total population as established by the Bureau of the Census" (UCR, 1994, 1). In subsequent years, the FBI has been able to maintain similarly high percentages of participation by state law enforcement agencies. Currently 46 states and the District of Columbia submit their crime statistics to the FBI using state-level UCR programs; the remaining states submit directly to the FBI (U.S. Department of Justice, Federal Bureau of Investigation, 2007).

The UCR program was developed in the 1920s by the International Association of Chiefs of Police (IACP) to report uniform police statistics in an effort to gauge national crime statistics. Seven offenses were selected to serve as an index to establish fluctuations in the overall volume and rate of crime. The seven offenses included murder/non-negligent manslaughter, forcible rape, robbery, aggravated assault, burglary, larceny-theft, and motor vehicle theft. In 1979, Congress added arson to this list. Collectively, these offenses are known as the Crime Index.

To modernize the UCR program and improve the statistics collected, a major study and revision of the program was implemented in the 1980s. During the first phase of the evaluation, the UCR program was examined in terms of its historical evolution. In phase two, a conference was held to examine the future for the UCR and to conclude with specific recommendations of changes. At the same time, a law enforcement survey (phase three) was administered.

The final report, utilizing all the information collected from the three stages of the evaluation, was released in 1985. It specifically outlined the recommendations for the UCR program. Three recommendations were given, but the most powerful recommendation focused on the use of a new reporting system called the National Incident-Based Reporting System (NIBRS). NIBRS collects data on each single incident and arrest within 22 crime categories. In addition, incident, victim, property, and arrestee information, when known, is also collected for each offense known to police within these categories (U.S. Department of Justice, Federal Bureau of Investigation, 2007). Currently there are 31 state programs that are "certified for NIBRS participation," representing about 36 percent of the agencies reporting crime statistics to the FBI (U.S. Department of Justice, Federal Bureau of Investigation, 2007). The other programs are in various stages of certification, and in order for NIBRS to be a helpful crime prevention tool, all agencies participating in the UCR also need to participate in NIBRS.

Even with the NIBRS revision, law enforcement data can be collected only on crimes known to the police. Due to the limitations of the UCR program and NIBRS, researchers have been struggling to find ways to add to their knowledge about victimization. In 1965, the President's Commission on Law Enforcement and Administration of Justice initiated the first national survey on crime victimization ever conducted (Inciardi, 1993, 121). This survey demonstrated that the amount of crime known to the police was far less than the crimes actually committed. For example, during that year (1965), the survey revealed that forcible rapes occurred almost four times as often as reported in the UCR (Inciardi, 1993).

The Bureau of the Census continued with this self-report victimization survey, renaming it the National Crime Survey. Since 1972, the National Crime Survey has been administered annually to determine the unreported or "**dark figure**" of crime. The survey was renamed the National Crime Victimization Survey (NCVS) "to more clearly emphasize the measurements of those victimizations experienced by our citizens" (U.S. Department of Justice, Bureau of Justice Statistics, 1994, iii).

The NCVS collects data on personal and household victimizations through an ongoing national survey of residential addresses. Data are collected for both attempted and actual crime, including rape, robbery, assault, larceny, burglary, and motor vehicle theft. Murder is excluded. Whenever possible, information about the victim(s) is recorded as well. Thus, the NCVS is an estimate of the amount of actual crime, but it is a primary source of criminal victimization. According to the Bureau of Justice's website, ". . . NCVS provides the largest national forum for victims to describe the impact of crime and characteristics of violent offenders" (http://www.ojp.usdoj.gov/bjs/cvict.htm#Programs, retrieved January 5, 2008).

These three sources represent the data sources that most researchers, educators, students, practitioners, politicians, and news media rely on when reporting on criminal victimization. These sources are readily available and are consistently reported, meaning that each year statistics are released from each data set. Nevertheless, there are some criminal offenses that are not part of the index crimes and are not included in the National Criminal Victimization Survey that are indeed examples of victimization. Where does one find data on these crimes?

DATA SOURCES FOR SPECIFIC CRIMES

For crimes like family violence, statisticians have used multi-method approaches and multiple sources to gather data. The methods include official reports of criminal acts as well as surveys of the general public. One of the most recent and thorough reports on family violence examined several data sources (Durose et al., 2005). Included in their list of sources are the National Crime Victimization Survey, **Supplementary Homicide Reports** (an FBI database), National Incident-Based Reporting System, State Court Processing Statistics (a Bureau of Justice Statistics [BJS] data collection), Federal Justice Statistics Program (a BJS database), Survey of Inmates in State and Federal Correctional Facilities (a BJS survey), and Survey of Inmates in Local Jails (a BJS survey) (Durose et al., 2005). Relying on such a broad approach to collecting data on family violence provides very solid estimates of these incidents. These statistics are reported and discussed in Chapter 8.

As is demonstrated by listing all the sources that were consulted for the report on Family Violence Statistics (Durose et al., 2005), data collection and reporting on specific crimes is becoming more thorough and complete. Still, there are many conflicting reports about crime statistics if only one source is reviewed. Thus, caution should be paramount when reviewing crime statistics, especially when these statistics are self-reported and when surveys are employed. It is important to remember that survey results must be generalizable to the overall population for the results to have merit. Often the generalizability of the results is limited—maybe to a particular state, community, or to a geographical region within a state. Again, view these statistics with caution.

When examining child maltreatment, including child abuse and neglect (see Chapter 8), the best site for official statistics is the **Child Welfare Information Gateway**, formerly known as the National Clearinghouse on Child Abuse and Neglect (NCCAN) and the National Adoption Information Clearinghouse. Child Welfare Information Gateway is a service of the Children's Bureau, Administration of Children and Families, U.S. Department of Health and Human Services, and it provides access to information and resources to help protect children and strengthen families (http://www.childwelfare.gov/). Reports, databases, and other sources of statistics are available on the webpage for interested readers. The National Data Analysis System (NDAS) provides a searchable online database that includes data on child abuse and neglect and child abuse and neglect fatalities, among other information (http://www.childwelfare.gov/systemwide/statistics/).

Another excellent data source on juvenile victimization is the **Crimes Against Children Research Center** (http://www.unh.edu/ccrc). The Center provides data on criminal victimization of juveniles. This rich resource center provides easily assessable information on homicides, sexual assault, nonfamily abduction, assault, robbery, theft, child maltreatment, child abuse, child neglect, child physical abuse, child sexual abuse, family abduction, exposure to domestic violence, school assaults, and hate crimes.

Elderly abuse statistics, including data on elder abuse, neglect, and exploitation, can be found at the **National Center on Elder Abuse**. The NCEA "collects and analyzes national data on cases referred to and investigated by adult protective services and serves as a resource for investigators worldwide" (http://www.elderabusecenter.org/default.cfm?p=statistics.cfm). The NCEA provides funding for a Clearinghouse on Abuse and Neglect of the Elderly (CANE) that is housed at the University of Delaware. Included in the more than 3,000 journal articles, scholarly papers, and other data sources are several major research undertakings that the NCEA has led: (1) The National Elder Abuse Incidence Study (1996); (2) Elder Mistreatment: Abuse, Neglect, and Exploitation in an Aging America (2003); (3) National Research Council Panel to Review Risk and Prevalence of Elder Abuse and Neglect (2003); and (4) Violence in Families: Assessing Prevention and Treatment Programs (1998). These are all excellent sources of elderly victimization. Chapter 10 includes many of these references in the discussion of elderly victimization.

COMPARISON OF OFFICIAL VICTIMIZATION DATA SOURCES

The information reported above is often compared to indicate the strengths and weaknesses of each data source. These comparisons are often made focusing on methodological issues. However, Table 2.1 focuses on the criminal victimization itself and indicates what is learned by using each source. The UCR provides the least amount of

TABLE 2.1   Comparison of Data Sources

UCR   8 index crimes and 21 other offenses; however, only data on female rape is collected; attempted and completed victimizations are lumped together. No real additional information regarding the victim. UCR and NIBRS are the only major sources of data on child victimization, domestic and stranger homicide, and law enforcement homicides and injuries.

Hate crime statistics: These data are collected on victims of hate crime, which may be conceptualized as an individual, a business, an institution, or society as a whole. (See 2006 Hate Crime Statistics at http://www.fbi.gov/ucr/hc2006/index.html.)

Supplementary Homicide Report provides information regarding the age, sex, and race of the murder victim and the offender; the type of weapon used in the murder; the relationship of the victim to the offender; and the circumstance surrounding the incident (see http://www.fbi.gov/ucr/cius2006/documents/expandedhomicidemain.pdf).

NIBRS   8 index crimes and 32 other offenses; records rape of male victims by female offenders; attempted is separated from completed; restructured definition of assault. (See Rantala and Edwards, *Effects of NIBRS statistics on Crime Rates* available at: http://www.ojp. usdoj.gov/bjs/pub/pdf/enibrscs.pdf.)

NCVS   Estimates all crime victimizations including those not reported to the police, collecting data categorized as "personal" or "property." Personal crimes cover rape and sexual attack, robbery, aggravated and simple assault, and purse-snatching/pocket-picking, while property crimes cover burglary, theft, motor vehicle theft, and vandalism. Collects victimization data—including type of crime, month, time, and location of the crime; relationship between victim and offender; self-protective actions taken by the victim during the incident and results of those actions, consequences of the victimization; type of property lost; whether the crime was reported to the police and reasons for reporting or not reporting; and basic demographic information, such as age, race, gender, and income (see http://www.icpsr.umich.edu/NACJD/NCVS/).

information about victim characteristics and other variables regarding the victim but with the Hate Crime Statistics, Supplementary Homicide Report, and NIBRS more information regarding victims is collected and presented. The NCVS has the most thorough examination of the victim and victim characteristics because it was designed to gather additional information about criminal victimization. Taken together, all these sources, along with the others mentioned here begin to provide a thorough picture of the crime victim.

SCOPE OF VICTIMIZATION

Just how prevalent is victimization? The U.S. Census Bureau puts the current population of the United States at 304,206,721 (May 30, 2008,). This number constantly changes; as the website http://www.census.gov/population/www/popclockus.html reports, every 7 seconds a child is born and every 13 seconds a person dies. It is, however, important to understand how many people live in the United States related to the amount of crime known, either through official reports or through self-reports.

Another way to present FBI statistics about criminal victimization is with the **Crime Clock** (http://www.fbi.gov/ucr/cius2007/about/crime_clock.html). This clock is a pictorial representation of the relative frequency of the occurrence of Part I offenses. Below the Crime clock for 2007 has been reproduced. It's interesting to compare the Crime clock statistics with that of the Census Bureau population statistics. It is very dramatic to watch the numbers change in terms of the population as every 7 seconds a person is added and every 13 seconds someone is removed. The Crime Clock does not adjust the victimization numbers as such, but one can see from the clock that every 31.0 minutes a person is

Every 22.4 seconds   One Violent Crime

Every 31.0 minutes   One Murder
Every 5.8 minutes   One Forcible Rape
Every 1.2 minutes   One Robbery
Every 36.8 seconds   One Aggravated Assault

Every 3.2 seconds   One Property Crime

Every 14.5 seconds   One Burglary
Every 4.8 seconds   One Larceny-theft
Every 28.8 seconds   One Motor Vehicle Theft

The Crime Clock should be viewed with care. The most aggregate representation of UCR data, it conveys the annual reported crime experience by showing a relative frequency of occurrence of Part I offenses. It should not be taken to imply a regularity in the commission of crime. The Crime Clock represents the annual ratio of crime to fixed time intervals.
Crime in the United States, 2007
U.S. Department of Justice — Federal Bureau of Investigation
September 2008

murdered, every 6 minutes (5.8) someone is raped, every 1 minute (1.2) a person is
8 robbed, and every half hour (36.8) someone is the victim of aggravated assault.

These statistics represent the official UCR and NIBRS data. The question then
turns to what is known about victimization from the National Crime Victimization
Survey? A recent publication, *Criminal Victimization, 2005* (Catalano, 2006), reports
that data. Summarized below are some of the key findings:

- In 2005, U.S. residents age 12 or older experienced approximately 23 million crimes,
  according to findings from the National Crime Victimization Survey. Of this amount,
  - 77% (18.0 million) were property crimes,
  - 22% (5.2 million) were crimes of violence, and
  - 1% (227,000) were personal thefts.
- In 2005 for every 1,000 persons age 12 or older, there occurred
  - 1 rape or sexual assault,
  - 1 assault with injury, and
  - 3 robberies.
- Murders were the least frequent violent victimization with about 6 murder victims per
  100,000 persons in 2005. (Catalano, 2006)

VICTIMIZATION TRENDS

Overall, when comparing 2004 to 2005 data, violent crime rates remained stable or
unchanged, while property crime decreased slightly because of a decline in theft. There
were other interesting highlights that are presented below (Catalano, 2006):

- For most crimes, aggregated rates for the two-year period 2004–2005 were unchanged from
  the rates in 2002–2003, while minor declines were seen for some forms of robbery and
  simple assault without injury (1).
- From 1993 to 2005, the violent crime rate was down 58 percent, from 50 to 21 victims per
  1,000 persons age 12 or older (1).
- During 2005, 24 percent of all violent crime incidents were committed by an armed
  offender, including 9 percent by an offender with a firearm (1).
- The rate of firearm violence increased between 2004 and 2005, from 1.4 to 2.0 victimizations per 1,000 persons age 12 or older (1).
- Males were more vulnerable to violence by strangers (54% of the violence against males),
  while females were most often victimized by nonstrangers (64%) (1).
- Males, blacks, and persons age 24 or younger continued to be victimized at higher rates
  than females, whites, and persons age 25 or older in 2005 (1).
- During 2005, 47 percent of all violent victimizations and 40 percent of all property crimes
  were reported to the police (1).

The victim characteristics examined include gender, race, age, household income,
marital status, and region. As reported in the text of the bulletin (Catalano, 2006, 7–8):

- Males were victims of overall violent crime, robbery, total assault, simple assault, and
  aggravated assault at rates higher than those of females (8).
- Females were more likely than males to be victims of rape/sexual assault (8).
- Persons of two or more races were victims of overall violence at significantly higher rates
  than those for whites, blacks, and persons of other races (8).

- Blacks were victims of overall violence, robbery, and aggravated assault at higher rates than those for whites in 2005 (8).
- Blacks and whites were equally likely to experience simple assault in 2005 (8).
- Blacks were more likely than persons of other races to be victims of overall violence but not of simple assault (7).
- Hispanics were victims of overall violence at rates higher than those of non-Hispanics in 2005 (7).
- Hispanics and non-Hispanics were equally likely to experience rape/sexual assault and theft (7).
- During 2005, as in previous years, there was a general pattern of decreasing crime rates for persons of older age (8).
- During 2005, there was a general pattern of decreasing victimization rates for persons residing in households with higher incomes (8).
- During 2005, persons who were never married experienced somewhat higher rates of overall violence than did persons of other marital status (8).
- In 2005, residents in the South experienced the lowest rates of overall violent victimization (8).

As reported above, property crime victimization is much more prevalent than violent crime. Even though the information presented in this section can be found in subsequent chapters throughout the book, it is included here to emphasize that property crime victimization is often overlooked in terms of its impact on victims. Property crime according to official data collection sources includes the offenses of burglary, larceny-theft, motor vehicle theft, and arson. Also included would be a range of lesser offenses from vandalism, to fraud, to breaking and entering. As reported on York County (VA) website, "Any of these offenses can have tremendous impact on a victim's life: vandalism can include destructive hate messages; fraud can take an elderly victim's entire life savings, leaving them financially unable to care for themselves; burglary can destroy a business, or leave a family feeling shaken and vulnerable in their own home" (http://www.yorkcounty.gov/vw/property/property.htm, retrieved June 26, 2008) and those victimized by arson may suffer extreme property destruction losing their entire home, and they may be victimized again if they do not have insurance to cover the loss. The devastating effects of property victimization should not be overlooked, and it is important to remember that victims of property crime do have rights and services available to them. Most often victims are interested in getting their property returned to them or repaired if it is damaged. The return of property sometimes is a long process because of how the system works. First, an offender must be apprehended, and then the trial will most likely take some time to be scheduled and heard. Sometimes the hardest part for the victim is not knowing what is going on and not understanding why the property cannot be returned. Here victim advocates play a very important role, in that they can explain the process to the victim and help the victim complete the forms necessary to get restitution if applicable.

REPEAT VICTIMIZATION

The criminology literature indicates that a small number of offenders are responsible for a large amount of crime committed, but is the same true for victims? In other words, are a small number of victims repeatedly victimized? The answer oddly enough is *yes*. According to De Valve (2007, 241), "Just as a small proportion of all offenders represent a large amount of crime committed (Moffitt, 1997); so too do a small proportion of victims represent a surprisingly large (and therefore disproportionate) amount of victimization (Farrell, 1992; Farrell and Pease, 1993, 2001; Farrell and Bouloukos, 2001)." De Valve's work focused on crime-prevention strategies and how better to serve victims by targeting repeat victims instead of developing crime-prevention strategies that had more of a global application that might not serve as many as if the strategies were tailored to meet the needs of repeat victims.

There are some methodological problems with how **repeat victimization** has been captured, and hence refinements in the methods are needed. In particular, the time frame from one victimization to another must be clarified. However, what is important here is that repeat victimization is a concept that should be addressed when considering all aspects of victimology. Later in the book crime-prevention strategies and victims services are presented, and the reader should evaluate these strategies and services in relationship to repeat victimization.

As Ellingworth, Farrell, and Pease (1995) report, "For those people who are victimized, it is estimated that between 24% and 38% of crime is suffered by people who experience five or more such offenses . . . over a year" (362). Thus, as the same authors report, the majority of the public will not be victimized in their lifetimes, but a number of victims will experience repeat victimization. This repeat victimization must be considered when examining services and developing crime prevention strategies.

VICTIMIZATION THEORIES

Many theories attempt to explain why certain individuals become victims of crime. For the most part, these theories focus on behaviors that individuals engage in that put them in greater risk of being victimized.

Victim Precipitation Theory, Lifestyle Theory, Deviant Place Theory, Routine Activities Theory, Structural-Choice Model, and **Legal Cynicism Defense** perspective are some of the theories that explain victimization in a global sense. These theories look at victim behavior to gauge relative risk in terms of victimization. This perspective focuses on personal responsibility in terms of avoiding victimization. In other words, engaging in risky behaviors results in the greater likelihood that someone will be victimized in comparison to those who do not engage in such behaviors. For example, drinking at a bar late into the evening hours and then having to walk home because the person's ride left earlier than expected puts the person in a situation that is much more risky than if the person was at home, not drinking, and watching TV all night.

Victim Precipitation Theory

Victim precipitation theory focuses on individual actions that may lead to victimization. When examining this behavior, actions are described as "active precipitation" while other actions or behaviors as defined as "passive precipitation." Presenting these concepts, Siegel (2006) reminds the reader that Marvin Wolfgang discussed active precipitation as behaviors or actions where a person acts provocatively, uses threat or fighting words, or actually makes the first move in an attack. Wolfgang's student Menachem Amir expanded Wolfgang's active precipitation by focusing on female rape victims. Amir said that female victims who dress provocatively or pursue relationships with their rapists contribute to their own victimization. As you can imagine, this is a very controversial stance, and Amir has been under fire because of it (Siegel, 2006). However, if you have ever been to court for a rape trial, you know that there is a constant barrage of questions from defense attorneys trying to use this point of view as a defense. Many states have developed Rape Shield Laws that prohibit background history from coming into play during the trial; however, these laws do not preclude defense attorneys from questioning the degree of responsibility that a victim had in her victimization.

The other type of behavior associated with victim precipitation is passive precipitation. In this case, the victim "exhibits some personal characteristic that unknowingly either threatens or encourages the attacker" (Siegel, 2006, 77). Examples would include being in a position of authority, which someone resents, or competing for a position with someone who feels threatened by your ability to do a job, or getting the last parking space in an overcrowded parking lot. In each case, the person may not even be aware that he or she has provoked someone, which is why it is called passive precipitation. The victim–offender relationship in these situations may be conscious or unconscious. Obviously the relative risk associated with a conscious or active precipitation can be controlled or lessened. The unconscious or passive precipitation is much harder to avoid.

Lifestyle Theory

Hindelang, Gotffredson, and Garofalo (1978) are credited with developing what is called lifestyle theory to explain criminal victimization (Williams and McShane, 1994). Their theoretical model is the result of inquiry about why certain individuals are more likely to be victimized than others. They looked at patterns of activities, what they call lifestyles, to determine the relative risk of individual victimization.

They further explain that lifestyles and the relative risk associated with these lifestyles are influenced by three basic elements: social roles, position in the social structure, and a choice/decision component.

A social role signifies how a person is expected to act in a particular social situation. This expected behavior is often influenced by the age and gender, among other demographic variables, of an individual. Likelihood of victimization increases when social roles dictate behavior that is careless and unguarded, like going out late at night, drinking, using drugs, and hanging out with young males (Siegel, 2006, 77). Such behaviors are often attributed to college students or younger individuals. Thus the role of college student plays a part in potential victimization.

Position in the social structure refers to the status (e.g., honor or prestige attached to a social position) that one holds in the social structure. Social positions within society include occupation, profession, family, and hobby (Yorburg, 1982). Social position also affects the likelihood of victimization, with higher status positions being less vulnerable to crime.

The last component is decisions that must be made about what is desirable. Social role and social position greatly influence the choices and decisions that are made by an individual, and the decisions influence the risk of victimization. Decisions to engage in careless behaviors like those listed above are most likely to be different based on the social role and social position of the individual. A college student may engage in such behaviors, while a doctor probably will not. And such decisions affect the likelihood of victimization.

As Williams and McShane (1994, 224) summarize,

> When lifestyle variations are taken into account, victimization experiences and potential victimizations are relatively predictable. For those whose social and structural background creates greater interaction with offenders and places conducive to crime, there is indeed a greater risk of victimization. Similarly, individuals of higher social class engage in fewer routine activities (i.e., have a lifestyle) that involve crossing paths with fewer criminals (at least of the street criminal variety). Such risks can be decreased, or increased, beyond the levels normally expected for one's group by the conscious decisions individuals make to engage in certain lifestyles.

Deviant Place Theory

There are places, physical areas in a community, where more crime occurs. The term *social disorganization* has been used to label such communities. These places could also be labeled *deviant*. The characteristics of socially disorganized communities and deviant places are very similar: these locations are urban, poor, densely populated, heterogeneous, highly transient, and largely single-parent family units. Pockets or areas of a community where crime is concentrated are reminiscent of "hot-spot" analyses where concentrations of crime are identified by using geo-mapping software. It is thought that the place itself, with all the disorganization within it, explains the relative risk for individuals who frequent these places.

As summarized by Siegel (2006, 79),

> According to deviant place theory, victims do not encourage crime but are victim prone because they reside in socially disorganized high-crime areas where they have the greatest risk of coming into contact with criminal offenders, irrespective of their own behavior or lifestyle. The more often victims visit dangerous places, the more likely they will be exposed to crime and violence. Neighborhood crime levels, then, may be important for determining the chances of victimization than individual characteristics. Consequently, there may be little reason for residents in lower-class areas to alter their lifestyle or take safety precautions because personal behavior choices do not influence the likelihood of victimization.

Routine Activities Theory

Cohen and Felson (1979) examined crime victimization from a very practical perspective. Like the other theorists presented here, Cohen and Felson focused on behavior and suggested that crime is related to everyday activities that become routine, and just as you can predict your daily schedule of activities, so can criminals. Cohen and Felson said that three things needed to come together in proximity for a crime to occur: a motivated offender, a suitable target, and the absence of a capable guardian. When these three things are present at one time, a crime is likely to occur.

The concepts are pretty self-explanatory, if you think about them. A motivated offender is someone who wants to commit a crime. A suitable target is a person or thing that is considered "desirable" in terms of potential victimization. And the absence of a capable guardian means that there is no one or nothing watching over or protecting the target.

The popularity of Cohen and Felson's theory is based on the fact that, given their theory, there are definite ways to decrease the risk of victimization. Put quite simply, the first line of defense is to vary routines. Or, increase the capable guardians to protect against victimization.

By way of example, most college students go home during the Winter break, and while campus administrators, faculty, and staff see students leaving in droves to join family members or to vacation away from universities, so too do criminals. The end of the semester marks a change in student routine with classes ending, and it often also marks a time period when students may be away from apartments and dorms. Universities are astute about this, often making sure students take home all their personal belongings during breaks. Student apartment complexes, however, that also have other residents often do not tell residents what to do when they leave for an extended family visit or vacation.

STRUCTURAL-CHOICE MODEL

In 1990, Miethe and Meier proposed the Structural-Choice Model, which synthesized the key concepts of several popular theories of victimization. Their model stresses both macro- and micro-level processes that contribute to victimization. The macro-level processes focus on structure—the structural features in society that create opportunity for victimization—and the micro-level processes focus on choice—decisions made by the victim.

The structural features are proximity (closeness) to high-crime areas and exposure to offenders (deviant place theory). The literature has demonstrated that an important predictor of victimization is the proximity to higher-crime areas (Rodgers and Roberts, 1995). Proximity is measured in a variety of ways: place of residency, perceived safety in one's neighborhood, and living situations (e.g., homebound or homeless) (Wenzel, Koegel, and Gelberg, 2000).

Exposure to criminal opportunities is heightened by engaging in risky behaviors. The literature, for example, has demonstrated that problems with alcohol or illicit drugs increase exposure to criminality (Wenzel, Koegel, and Gelberg, 2000). Often to secure illicit drugs, a person has to go into a "tough" neighborhood to do so. Knowing that drugs are expensive, and knowing the areas where drug deals take place, a person is more vulnerable to robbery because of where the person has to purchase the illicit drugs, and the assumption that the person will have cash on them to purchase them.

There are several components of choice, including target attractiveness, physical guardianship, and social guardianship. These elements of choice are similar to the concepts in Routine Activities Theory (i.e., suitable target and lack of capable guardians). In the example above, the person buying drugs would be considered an attractive target because financially motivated crimes are perpetrated on targets that appear to have money. So a choice is made in terms of who to rob—and the model suggests that offenders will target those who are more attractive in terms of what they are trying to get. The physical and social guardianships factors have been "defined as whether persons over the age 16" who lives with another (maybe a spouse) and "whether one owns a dog, has a burglar alarm, or has a friend living in the neighborhood (Miethe and Meier, 1990)" (as cited in Wenzel, Koegel, and Gelberg, 2000, 370). These are personal crime prevention mechanisms (or capable guardians).

LEGAL CYNICISM DEFENSE PERSPECTIVE

Another theoretical perspective to consider is called Legal Cynicism Defense. This perspective examines the dynamic among victimization reporting, victim blaming, and police trust. In a recent presentation, Dr. Martin Schwartz, a prolific scholar who studies sexual victimization and policing, spoke about the concept of legal cynicism defense when asked specifically about victims of crime and police trust (Schwartz, 2006). He reminded the audience that only about 5 percent of the time do victims of sexual assault (or rape) report the crimes to the police. This is because the victims do not trust the police. He spoke about the second and third victimizations of a victim being the encounter with the police (second victimization) and the trial (third victimization). He also spoke about having to get sexual assault victims to tell their story about three times before the truth is really known. This may sound odd, but Schwartz was building his argument about "it takes three times to get to the truth" based on this observation: First, there is an inherent mistrust of the police. Second, a victim may have done something that she now feels makes her responsible for the victimization, perhaps something illegal. In fear of being blamed for the victimization, the victim will leave that part of the story out. So, the police are only getting half-truths. Schwartz says it takes about three iterations of the story to get to the absolute truth.

Schwartz provided this example: a woman has been told to stay off a certain street because it is not well lit and there have been a number of robberies on this street. Even with this knowledge, she walks down the street and gets mugged. Her wallet is stolen. When the victim talks to the police, she fudges where she was attacked. Instead of Laurel Street, it's now Franklin Street, but what the victim does not know is that there are cameras on Laurel, so the police know where she was. The next time they talk she changes the location from Franklin Street to Laurel Street. In this case, it took two iterations of the story to get the truth.

Schwartz was trying to explain that there is an interaction between police trust and legal cynicism that results in victims not wanting to be blamed or made to feel stupid for doing something that they were advised against doing in the first place. With this cynicism that the police will blame the victim and the lack of trust in the police in general, it becomes very difficult, especially in sexual assault cases, for victims to come forward and report crime.

ARGUMENTS AGAINST VICTIM BLAMING

Whether to blame victims for their victimization is a controversial issue in the field. Eigenberg (2003) addresses this controversy, attempting to debunk it. She states, "whether this is referred to as victim blaming, victim facilitation, or victim precipitation, the debate focuses on whether victims are responsible for their own victimization because of behaviors that they engage in that might be considered 'risky' behaviors" (15). Eigenberg outlines the controversy focusing on the historical tendency to place responsibility for the victimization on the victim. She explains von Hentig's typology, based on psychological, social, and biological factors, where he argued that there were "born victims" just like there were "born criminals." She further clarifies that according to von Hentig, "born victims were self-destructive individuals who solicited the action of their 'predators' (1941, 303) . . . [and] women, as a group, were born victims because they were weak and easy prey" (Eigenberg, 2003, 15). The conclusion from von Hentig's work is that victimization is a process of social interaction. There is reciprocal action between victims and offenders.

Others have expanded on this view of shared responsibility, developing typologies of their own. As Eigenberg points out, victim blaming often falls on a continuum with the model looking like this:

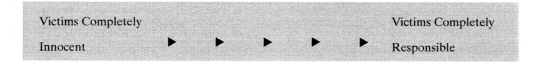

Eigenberg's arguments against using victim blaming as an explanation for victimization center on the inherent weakness of the conceptualization of the term. Her arguments focus on:

- Tautological or circular reasoning. Eigenberg points out that those who study the interaction of the process of victimization do so using victims. She concludes, "They rely upon samples of victims to determine common characteristics which contribute to victimization, although these studies fail to evaluate the degree to which non-victims in the general population exhibit similar behaviors" (19).
- Conceptual weaknesses in the concept of victim blaming. Eigenberg discusses the problematic nature of the "totally innocent victim" because this implies some degree of responsibility; however, the person does not know what could have been done to prevent a crime until *after* the crime has been committed. She concludes, "It also implies that victims know how to prevent their victimization and ignores that many people in our society face disproportionate risk of victimization" (19).
- Undue responsibility on victims. Eigenberg's argument here is that all risky behavior is not unavoidable. Thereby, it is unfair to place the blame on victims when the actual events of living put some people at more risk than others.
- Creates culturally legitimate victims. There must be something "wrong" with those people who are victimized, and in order to understand what is wrong, attempts are made to categorize what is different about victims and nonvictims. To avoid victimization, the differences found in individuals or groups that are victimized must be changed. Eigenberg argues that this perspective where the victim is seen as being deficient leads to creating culturally legitimate victims. She states that this process makes it more acceptable for some people to be victimized (e.g., homosexuals) and in turn society is less willing to use its resources to do anything about it.
- Excuses offender behavior and diminishes responsibility. Eigenberg argues that if there is any responsibility for the crime attributed to the victims, no matter how small, then the offenders escape the full responsibility of their acts. Offenders can use this to rationalize their behavior; "According to offenders, victims, then, ask for or deserved what they get; or at the extreme end of the continuum, they deny any harm whatsoever" (21).

The arguments presented above give pause to the automatic assumption that victims should be held responsible for their victimization. Nevertheless, there are instances when victim behavior must be examined in order not to assign blame but to solve a crime.

Law enforcement, especially the FBI's Behavioral Science Unit, routinely examines victim behavior, what they call **victimology**, in order to develop profiles about offenders in order to apprehend them. Information is collected about victims without applying any blame. The "victimology" in these cases helps investigators understand the crimes better. The victimology of a case would consist of examining what has happened in this particular situation, asking why it happened, and then exploring how the victim and the offender may have been related—or how they might have known each other prior to the victimization.

At a recent American Criminal Justice Association meeting, an FBI agent working in the Behavioral Sciences Unit who is now retired presented a case to the group (Jenkins, 2005). Agent Jenkins presented the victimology of the case to demonstrate how this information is used to solve a case. The analysis of the case is presented here because it shows another meaning or usage of the term *victimology*. Students should be aware that the study of victims often includes their actions and behaviors, as it is a tool used by law enforcement to solve cases.

During his presentation of the facts of the case, Agent Jenkins described a young woman who was single and living alone who was raped and killed in her apartment. When law enforcement arrived at the scene they noticed that a potted plant was knocked over by the window, and they found the victim in a pool of blood, having been stabbed multiple times. The crime scene looked like the victim was preparing her lunch for the next day prior to her death: police found lettuce on the counter that was being cut up for a salad. The apartment looked like a struggle between the victim and the perpetrator had ensued, and a bloody knife was found under a seat cushion of a chair. Through investigative techniques (questioning coworkers, family members, friends, and associates), law enforcement was able to determine that the victim had been employed full time, she did not seem to drink or utilize other substances, and she did not have a boyfriend or other male friends. She was very religious and very frugal with her money. This is considered the victimology of the case.

From this victimology and other evidence collected from the crime scene, the investigators made some assumptions concluding that this victim seemed to be at relatively low risk for being victimized. They also looked at other situational factors and considered these in terms of increasing or decreasing her risk of victimization. Two situational facts discovered at the crime scene: the victim lived on the first floor, and the management had put yellow lights outside the doors of female residents who lived alone in order for their security. Both of these situational factors increased the risk of victimization. One final situational factor was that the apartment building had several break-ins in the last six months.

Law enforcement was able to conclude, based on the information provided at the scene, including the victimology and situational factors, that the perpetrator was most likely a stranger to the victim who had committed similar crimes in the past and had most likely entered the victim's apartment through an open window. Using this knowledge, law enforcement began to rule out their first suspects. For example, since she was sexually assaulted and she did not have a boyfriend, yet she was very religious and very much a homebody, a rushed conclusion was that a family member had to be involved. However, the victimology and situational factors negated this assumption. The police were able to develop a profile of the offender using the victimology, crime scene clues, and interviews of neighbors and associates. Law enforcement began looking for suspects in the immediate neighborhood, and they used the media to inform residents about the profile of the offender. A very nervous and fearful sister of the offender called the police to turn in her brother, who matched the offender profile presented in the media. Law enforcement was able to solve this crime through the use of victimology, situational factors, the media, and of course, the help of a concerned citizen, the sister, who called the police about her brother.

CONCLUSION

How do we know how much criminal victimization is really occurring in the United States? This has been a question that researchers, public agencies, governmental organizations, politicians, and the general public have struggled with since we became interested in quantifying criminal activity. Many difficulties arise when attempting to measure criminal victimization, with the most prominent being that criminal acts must be made public before they can be counted. Thus, most of the data sources listed within this chapter report only an estimate of victimization, and estimates are often lower than what really occurs. Nevertheless, criminal victimization is a social problem that requires attention even as the official statistics balance from year to year, or in some cases decrease. The overall amount of victimization is just too high.

One clear message from the theoretical explanations of victimization presented here is that individuals must take more control over their own personal safety. It is important to emphasize that the theoretical explanations for victimization to varying degrees all have an underlying premise of victim responsibility. And, while it seems like victim blaming is something to be avoided, it also serves a vital purpose, especially when crime-prevention strategies are being developed. If victimization theory only focused on offenders, there would be little that could be done to protect victims. With the focus on victim responsibility, certain activities can be demonstrated to be riskier than others in putting people in harm's way. Therefore these behaviors can be avoided, reducing victimization.

Victimology is a term that has many meanings, the simplest being the study of victims. However, the term has a different connotation when used by law enforcement. Here too, the goal is to prevent victimization from occurring and to solve crimes. Thus, the information collected on a victim—his or her victimology—helps law enforcement to process crimes scenes, target suspect pools, and eventually solve crimes.

Study Questions

1. What is responsible for the downward trends in crime rates reported in the chapter?
2. Using any of the data sources listed in this chapter, look up the criminal statistics for your home state. How do they compare to what is presented in this chapter?

3. What are some of the methodological reasons that explain why different sources often have very different reported rates of crime?
4. Compare and contrast the major data sources where criminal justice researchers find data about crime. What do you see as the primary strengths and weaknesses of each source?

Key Terms

- "dark figure" of crime   25
- Child Welfare Information Gateway   26
- Crime Clock   28
- Crimes Against Children Research Center   26
- Deviant Place Theory   31
- incidence   23
- Legal Cynicism Defense   31
- Lifestyle Theory   31

- National Center on Elder Abuse   26
- National Crime Victimization Survey (NCVS)   24
- National Incident-Based Reporting System (NIBRS)   24
- prevalence   23
- repeat victimization   31

- Routine Activities Theory   31
- Structural-Choice Model   31
- Supplementary Homicide Reports   25
- Victim Precipitation Theory   31
- **victimology**   37

CHAPTER 3

Crime Prevention

INTRODUCTION

For the greatest part of its history, the criminal justice system has been reactive rather than proactive when trying to address the crime problem in this country. The vast majority of the time and resources of the criminal justice system are spent responding to crime after it occurs, not trying to stop crime. This reactive nature of the criminal justice system has allowed an extensive amount of victimization to occur, resulting in the creation of millions of crime victims. The simplest way to solve the problems faced by crime victims is to eliminate the criminal victimization of innocent people before it ever occurs. This is the goal of **crime prevention**, which has been defined as

> a pattern of attitudes and behaviors directed at both reducing the threat of crime and enhancing the sense of safety and security to positively influence the quality of life in our society and to develop environments where crime cannot flourish. (National Crime Prevention Council, 1994a)

In an effort to acquire a greater understanding of crime prevention, Congress required the Attorney General to provide a report on crime-prevention programs supported by the Justice Department's Office of Justice Programs and to assess their effectiveness (Sherman et al., 1997). The first task of this report was to provide a working definition of crime prevention. The report concluded that:

> Crime prevention is defined not by its intentions, but by its consequences. These consequences can be defined in at least two ways. One is by the number of criminal events; the other is by the number of criminal offenders (Hirschi and Gottfredson, 1987). Some would also define it by the amount of harm prevented (Reiss and Roth, 1993, 59–61) or by the number of victims harmed or harmed repeatedly (Farrell, 1995).

CRIME VICTIMS AND CRIME PREVENTION

Crime prevention is very important to crime victims. For every crime prevented, there is a reduction in the number of victims and the severity of victimization. Crime prevention can also give victims an opportunity to take back a sense of control over their lives. Additionally, avoiding further victimization and regaining a sense of safety are primary needs for crime victims (Waller, 1991). In many ways, crime prevention helps all crime victims by trying to eliminate the possibility of victimization happening again (Modglin and O'Neil, 1989). The beginning of current efforts to emphasize crime-prevention programs can be traced to 1965, when the federal role in local crime prevention moved into the Department of Justice (DOJ). The creation of the Office of Law Enforcement Assistance (OLEA) within the DOJ led to grants supporting new ideas, such as the Family Crisis Intervention Unit. Developed as a partnership between the City University of New York and the New York City Police Department under an OLEA grant, this project became the first clear example of federal guidance in the development of local crime-prevention programs (Sherman et al., 1997). By 1996, it was estimated that over $3 billion annually was being given by the DOJ in the form of grants to the states, local governments, and communities to help in preventing crime.

Crime prevention has come to the forefront of governmental policy in the twenty-first century as a result of the terrorist killings on September 11, 2001, and the extensive use of computers and the Internet. The victimization that occurred on September 11 has taught us what happens when we fail to prevent crime. The almost universal use of computers has brought numerous crimes right into our homes and lives with severe economic and personal victimizations. The pressing need for a greater amount of crime prevention has never been more apparent.

Crime-prevention measures focus on two different areas: reducing or eliminating opportunities for occasional offenders to commit crime and reducing or eliminating the social, economic, and environmental factors that generate habitual offenders (Waller, 1991). When one person suffers from victimization, the community as a whole suffers an increase in the fear of crime and a loss of security. The cost of crime to victims is estimated in the trillions annually in lost earnings, medical costs, public program costs for victim assistance, pain, suffering, and the reduced quality of life of those affected (Doerner and Lab, 2006). The ability of a society to reduce the amount and severity of crime victimization can substantially affect the health and well-being of society by redirecting funds that would otherwise be used to enhance the general welfare. This chapter examines society's attempts to define, carry out, and evaluate crime-prevention strategies and the impact these strategies have on crime victimization.

CRIME PREVENTION VERSUS CRIME CONTROL

The concept of crime prevention is central to all philosophies that seek to understand why criminal behavior occurs. If we can uncover why someone commits crime then we can influence those reasons and prevent future crime. The ideal that crime can be completely eliminated is unrealistic. At best, society tries to minimize the amount of crime and the seriousness of the criminal acts that occur. This is commonly known as crime control.

Crime control is an attempt to regulate and confine the amount of criminal behavior that occurs (Lab, 1992) and is part of a continuum of a crime-prevention model that ultimately seeks to eliminate the causes of crime. While crime prevention is the elimination of crime, crime control is the middle ground between complete prevention and the failure to act at all. Crime control rationalizes that it is impossible to stop everyone from committing a crime, but it makes the effort to minimize the amount of crime occurring and/or lessen the seriousness of criminal acts. The focus of both crime-prevention and crime-control techniques can be directed toward the two participants in the criminal act: the offender and the crime victim, and the environment in which the victimization may occur. For most, all crime to occur, three ingredients must be present: a motivated offender, the skills and tools needed to commit the crime, and opportunity or available target (National Crime Prevention Institute, 1986).

CRIME-PREVENTION THEORIES

Offender Crime-Prevention Theories

The **Classical School** of thought as put forth by Cesare Beccaria and Jeremy Bentham believes that crime prevention can be achieved through the use of deterrence. The Classical School focuses on the use of the criminal justice system to prevent crime by influencing the rational choice individuals make as to whether to commit a crime or not (See Table 3.1). Believing that men are rational beings, the Classical school incorporates the notion of "**hedonistic calculus**" as a method to prevent crime. According to the Classical School, people have free will; they choose to obey the law or not. People are also considered rational; they weigh the cost and the benefits of engaging in a certain action. Rational individuals choose what is in their best interest. If the punishment or pain of a sanction outweighs the pleasure gained from a criminal violation, then rational beings will not engage in those acts. In addition, if the laws are written so that everyone understands what is considered criminal and the consequences of violations, then no rational individual will commit any criminal acts against society (Siegel, 2008).

There are two types of deterrence according to the Classical doctrine: **specific deterrence** and **general deterrence** (Siegel, 2008). Specific deterrence occurs when the sanction applied to a certain deviant behavior is seen as less desirable than the possible benefit on an individual level. On the individual level, specific deterrence is used not to prevent an initial act but to keep the offender from committing any further criminal acts. General deterrence, however, is seen to benefit the masses and prevents crime from occurring in the first place. The punishment of an individual lawbreaker discourages others from engaging in similar criminal behaviors for fear of receiving the same punishment. Potential lawbreakers would recognize the lack of benefit of committing a crime and would choose to avoid crime and conform to socially accepted behaviors.

TABLE 3.1 Crime Prevention Strategies Based Upon Classical School Approach

Specific Deterrence Strategies
- Use of restitution, mandatory minimum sentences, selective incapacitation, three-strikes-your-out laws, habitual offender laws, community service, restorative justice programs.

General Deterrence Strategies
- Publication of the criminal law, mandatory sentences, public trials, public punishments (chain gangs), death penalty, DARE programs, greater police activities, shame and humiliation.

The central components of deterrence in the Classical doctrine are certainty, severity, and celerity. **Certainty** refers to the assurance of getting caught. As Beccaria believed, the certainty of being caught provided the greatest amount of deterrence. Why would rational beings engage in an action if they knew they would be caught after doing the crime? For Beccaria, the answer was, they wouldn't. The second component, severity, focuses upon the punishment for the crime. **Punishment** means applying a sanction to the perpetrator of the action that outweighs the benefit gained from the initial act. The more serious the act, the greater the punishment that is needed. The punishment should only be as severe as needed to prevent the reoccurrence of the act and/or to prevent others from deciding to break the law in the first place. The third component is celerity. **Celerity** means that if a criminal act does occur, the application of a sanction is guaranteed. This connection between the act and the sanction is important, because if individuals are unsure whether or not a sanction will be carried out, they might rationally decide to take a chance, because, even if they are caught, they might believe the sanction wouldn't apply (Siegel, 2008). Each and every component is necessary for deterrence to occur. Without certainty, rational individuals could justifiably choose to take a chance and violate the law, as we see with people who engage in speeding. When they see a police car, they go according to the speed limit because they believe there is a certainty of being caught. Without severity outweighing a crime, rational people could justifiably choose committing offenses and getting off with only a slap on the wrist. Without celerity, rational individuals could justifiably choose to engage in criminal behaviors believing they were above the law or that the criminal justice system did not apply to them.

The **Positivist School** as championed first by Cesare Lombroso, a medical doctor, and then by the sociologists in the Chicago School, believed that criminal behavior was a result of environmental (social), biological, and psychological influences. Positivist theorists focused on internal and external factors that were believed to cause crime. Positivist theories are broken down into various causal factors. Biological factors include biochemical, neurological, genetic, and evolutionary reasons. Psychological theories of crime prevention are based on treating psychodynamic problems, behavioral problems, and cognitive problems. Social structure theories look to eliminate criminal areas, poverty, and inequality, and improve the urban lifestyle. Social process theories look to strengthen the family and social institutions. They also reduce people's exposure to antisocial behavior and reinforce social rules and individuals' bonds to society. Social conflict theory seeks to prevent criminality through the elimination of class conflict. Through the reduction of inequality, greater reductions of crime can take place (Siegel, 2008).

Examples of specific factors that could cause crime were thought to be poverty, IQ, education, home life, abuse, peer group influences, psychopathology, social inequalities, and other factors beyond a person's control (Siegel, 2008). Once the specific influences or causes of criminal behavior were uncovered, they could then be controlled or the individual treated and crime would be prevented (see Table 3.2). The sociologists championed the idea of treating criminals and studying and eliminating environmental influences through the development of crime control and prevention programs (Williams and McShane, 1994).

TABLE 3.2 Crime Prevention Strategies Based Upon Positivist School Approach

Biological Theories
- Genetic testing for abnormalities, focus on biological reasons for violence, use of drugs to control behavior.

Psychological Theories
- Psychological profiling, counseling, group therapies, and family therapies.

Social Structure Theories
- Job training programs, after-school programs, community development programs, eliminating gangs.

Social Process Theories
- Parenting classes, school bullying programs, D.A.R.E. programs, mentoring programs.

Social Conflict Theories
- Poverty reduction programs, restorative justice programs, social justice programs.

VICTIM PREVENTION THEORIES

Potential victims can also play a role in preventing crime from happening to them. Theories that explain why certain individuals become crime victims (see Chapter 2) offer a template for a crime-prevention strategy that focuses on crime victims. One of the most important ways to prevent crime is by educating citizens about their potential victimization. If crime victims can reduce the likelihood of a crime happening to them, or their risk of victimization, then they have prevented the victimization. A central theory to understanding crime victimization risks is routine activities theory (Cohen and Felson, 1979).

As previously examined, routine activities theory hypothesizes that the likelihood of being a victim of a criminal act is directly related to three factors: presence of motivated offenders, absence of capable guardians, and availability of suitable targets. A central principle of routine activities theory is that the greater the opportunity to commit crime, the higher the crime and victimization rates (Felson, 1997). Consequently, if potential crime victims reduce the opportunity for offenders to commit crimes either by increasing guardianship or reducing target vulnerability, crime prevention is achieved. Prevention programs based upon criminological theory focus upon motivated offenders and try to control their actions. Prevention programs based upon victimization theory focus upon the absence of capable guardians and the availability of suitable targets.

SOCIETAL PREVENTION

Brantingham and Faust (1976) developed a model for understanding different crime-prevention methods and what they seek to accomplish by establishing three categories of programs or prevention strategies. Based upon a medical model for treating and preventing diseases, the three categories are primary prevention, secondary prevention, and tertiary prevention. **Primary prevention** is similar to immunization in the medical field. These programs or strategies seek to inoculate individuals, the way children are given vaccines against measles, polio, and smallpox. Likewise, the strategy is to prevent someone from ever committing crimes or becoming a crime victim.

According to a primary prevention strategy, if a person is not motivated to commit crime, never learns the skills necessary for the commission of a crime, or is not provided with the opportunity, then crime prevention is obtained

Secondary prevention focuses on identifying individuals with the capacity or inclination toward criminality and providing alternative options. If a person is genetically predisposed to heart disease, then doctors try to control the person's environment (such as diet, exercise, stress level, blood pressure, cholesterol) to reduce the chance of heart disease actually occurring. In the secondary crime-prevention model, trying to eliminate or control criminogenic factors (such as poverty, behavioral problems, and violence in the home) is central to crime prevention.

Tertiary prevention responds to those who already have offended and seeks to prevent or control criminals so it will not happen again. A medical example of this would be a program for persons who have communicable diseases and are isolated from the rest of the population and treated until they are no longer a threat to society. We will use the three crime-prevention approaches to examine policies and programs for eliminating criminal acts by offenders and the victimization of crime victims.

PRIMARY CRIME PREVENTION

Primary crime-prevention programs focus on making an environment crime-proof or instilling in children values that will keep them from wanting to engage in criminal behavior. The concept of the primary prevention of crime is twofold. First, professionals work with the general, physical, and societal factors that provide the opportunity for crime to occur, and they modify or eliminate them (Johnson, 1988). This is also known as **situational crime prevention.** The strategy is aimed at convincing potential criminals that a specific target is not available to them. Second, the system works with individuals before they even think about engaging in criminal acts to keep them from ever engaging in criminal behavior. Primary crime-prevention strategies for potential victims are also available. There are many ways to crime-proof communities, environments, and individuals.

In asking for the report on the effectiveness of crime-prevention efforts supported by the Justice Department's Office of Justice Programs (Sherman et al., 1997), the U.S. Congress has embraced the concept of primary crime prevention. It wanted to know about reduction of **risk factors** for crime (such as gang membership) and increases in **protective factors** (such as completing high school). Reducing risk factors and enhancing protective factors both seek to eliminate the likelihood of criminal violence from occurring, thus preventing victimization.

The use of the law is a method of primary prevention. Before 1990, the crime of stalking was not even recognized, and domestic violence was not treated as a crime. Neither had cybercrimes been heard of. Yet, many individuals were being victimized by these actions.

A widely accepted method of preventing crime from ever occurring works with the physical structures in society, Crime Prevention Through Environmental Design (CPTED) (Jeffery, 1977). CPTED tries to eliminate the incivility found within urban areas and some neighborhoods and to get individuals and neighbors concerned about what is happening outside their homes. One aspect of CPTED is the notion of "defensible space."

Defensible space is an area that by its physical expression of a social fabric suggests to both residents and potential offenders that it is not amenable to criminal activity (Newman, 1972). The idea of a social fabric is the establishment of ownership, either real or perceived, by legitimate users and the exclusion of illegitimate users.

Oscar Newman (1972) studied the physical environments where large amounts of criminal activity took place and concluded that one of the reasons crime occurs in particular locations is that some areas are perceived amenable to criminal activity. He identified four elements of his defensible space: (1) territoriality, (2) natural surveillance, (3) image, and (4) milieu or social setting. **Territoriality** is the ability of legitimate users to establish their rights to use an area to the exclusion of others. It incorporates the idea that people have to acquire a sense of ownership of an area if they are to defend it against others. **Natural surveillance** is the ability of legitimate users to observe the activities going on in the area. This allows legitimate users to feel comfortable in using the area, and it also allows legitimate users to recognize when others are violating their space. **Image** is the appearance of the area. If an area is well maintained, looks lived in, and is not accommodating to illegitimate users, crime will be less likely. Finally, **milieu** examines the social setting of an area, such as economic conditions, community cohesiveness, and cultural values. Areas in poor, urban settings are more likely to invite criminal activity than those in more wealthy, rural areas.

An example of territoriality is the saying "A man's home is his castle" (National Crime Prevention Institute, 1986). When people believe they can lay claim to an area, they will care for it and protect it from harmful intrusions. Similarly, if people perceive that an area is cared for and protected, they are less likely to violate the area because of the threat of being discovered and possibly caught. The way a private area is established is through the development of boundaries to promote a sense of separateness from the surrounding area (Newman, 1972). Once boundaries are established, a recognized area of control within the boundaries is assumed by the legitimate users to the exclusion of all others. Legitimate users can be homeowners or tenants or the small community who shares a common area. In Newman's study of the effectiveness of CPTED, he took a low-rise housing complex in New York City and redesigned the common areas outside the units, gave the buildings a facelift, put up fencing and gates around the complex, and engaged the residents of the complex to individualize their own areas. The results were unbelievable. The level of crime in the complex dropped nearly 90 percent, while crime in the surrounding communities continued to rise (Newman, 1972).

Natural surveillance refers to the ability of the community or individual to watch over a certain area. Natural surveillance is based on not letting crime have a place to hide. If areas are easily observable, the likelihood of someone trying to commit a crime is reduced. The use of lighting up areas, providing security cameras, and having windows facing common areas all contribute to natural surveillance. Additional methods are to cut down bushes, build buildings with rounded corners, have windows on all sides of the home, and encourage legitimate people to use certain areas so that illegitimate users will feel unwelcome. Newman set up outside video monitors at a high-rise complex and an intercom system so that parents could observe their children playing and could communicate with them. The changes also included extensive lighting of the area and round-the-clock surveillance. Not only did the tenants feel safer, but the rates of crime and criminal mischief were also reduced considerably (Newman, 1972).

Image is the perception that a home or community presents itself as being impervious to crime. The presence of "target-hardening" measures responds to this concern. **Target hardening** is the ability to restrict access to legitimate users and to prevent illegitimate users from taking control. If an individual or community can put forth an image that shows to the rest of the community that crime is not accepted within an area, crime can be prevented. Examples of this are gated communities and the use of security guards and entrance restrictions to certain communities. High-security buildings ward off criminal behavior just because of the image they portray. Additional target-hardening measures may be the installation of security systems or, for image, just the posting of a sign saying that various security measures are being used.

Target hardening has also become the method employed to secure air transportation systems. In an effort to prevent future airplane hijackings, the airlines have secured cockpits and armed pilots. Additionally, airports now have security and prevention as their first priority. As a direct result of the devastation of September 11, in 2002, the Homeland Security Act was passed, which created a new cabinet-level department—the Department of Homeland Security (Gaines and Miller, 2006). The Department brought together 22 existing agencies, revived the Federal Air Marshals program, which put undercover federal agents on commercial flights, and administers the Transportation Security Administration, which is responsible for providing security at all airports.

The last component of Newman's concept is the milieu or the setting. The placement of housing projects in areas having high crime rates invites greater criminality and urban blight. Newman (1972) believed that high-density population housing needed to be located in low-crime areas so that the design could incorporate the other three concepts of territoriality, natural surveillance, and image into the construction of the project. Building high-density population communities did not necessarily mean that crime would be a by-product if the use of environmental design techniques were employed. Other primary prevention target-hardening strategies include installation of street lights, locks, security doors, and windows, and installing antitheft devices. These crime-prevention measures are designed to reduce crime by increasing the risks of detention and limiting opportunities to commit crimes (Miethe and Meier, 1994).

Designing methods for blocking crime opportunities is the domain of situational crime prevention (Eck, 1997). Opportunity blocking at certain places may have a greater direct effect on offenders than other crime-prevention strategies. This is because place-focused tactics might influence offenders when they are deciding to commit a specific crime. Most offender-based strategies try to sway offenders weeks, months, or years before they confront a tempting criminal opportunity. If offenders pay more attention to the situation immediately before them than to the uncertain long-term risks of their behavior, then it is quite possible that prevention at places may have a greater impact on offending than increases in penalties or less tangible increases in risks (such as, decreases in police response time, increased police presence, or greater numbers of arrests and convictions). Because **hotspots** of crime are themselves clustered, if crime at these few places can be substantially reduced, communities can be made safer.

One widely used community crime-prevention program is the **neighborhood watch**. Neighborhood watch programs developed after an experiment done in Seattle, Washington, in the early 1970s (Waller, 1991). The program, called the Seattle Community Crime Prevention Program, focused on reducing residential burglaries. The neighborhoods that implemented the program focused upon two concepts: making their houses look lived in and looking after their neighbors' homes when they were out. The program resulted in a 50 percent reduction in the rates of residential burglaries for the test area in the first year. The initial reduction was maintained during the following 3 years of the study after implementation. Based on the success of this program, other neighborhood watch programs began to develop across the United States. Today, thousands of neighborhoods participate in watch programs.

Neighborhood crime prevention can take a variety of forms besides neighborhood watch (Lab, 1992). The key element is to engage the community so that it establishes cohesion and an identity as a place where crime is not tolerated. Other crime-prevention strategies that neighborhoods employ include citizen patrols, operation identification, and community policing. Citizen patrols involve the active participation of community members in providing surveillance of their neighborhoods. The patrols are connected to local police departments by means of walkie-talkies provided by the agencies. If the patrols spot an activity or situation they believe could be criminal, they do not take any action themselves but ask the police to respond. The citizens become extra sets of eyes and ears for the police and provide a deterrent force for would-be criminals. Operation identification is the labeling of personal property with identification numbers that cannot be removed to make them more difficult to dispose of. If offenders are unable to exchange items for cash, they are worthless to steal. Community policing (see Chapter 4) is another method of crime prevention. Citizens work with the police to learn how to better protect themselves and to become active participants with the police to combat crime.

A primary prevention strategy that incorporates the police and the community is the use of anticrime education programs, such as Drug Abuse Resistance Education (**D.A.R.E.**). Started in Los Angeles by the police department and the school district, this program has grown nationwide. The purpose of the D.A.R.E. program is to teach elementary school children to resist the temptation to use drugs. D.A.R.E. seeks to instill in youths knowledge of the dangers of drugs, how to build self-esteem, and how to resist peer pressure to try drugs (Wrobleski and Hess, 1990). Specially trained police officers go into classrooms over a period of time to talk with the students and answer their questions. The D.A.R.E officers also engage children outside the classroom with various sponsored activities that have antidrug themes. More than 15,000 officers have been trained in all 50 states and in several foreign countries.

According to Gottfredson (1997), D.A.R.E. program evaluations show that it is the most commonly implemented primary prevention program; however, D.A.R.E. programs do not reduce substance use to any significant degree. Lack of effectiveness of D.A.R.E. programs and governmental funding cuts led to a major reduction in the use of the program. Currently, a revised D.A.R.E. curriculum that employs follow-up sessions in later grades has been developed but has not been evaluated.

Another method of providing crime prevention is with private security. The underlying philosophy of the private security field is prevention. Private security companies have a long history of protecting businesses and individuals from crime victimization. Private security can employ many different methods to prevent crime. Examples of the services offered are individual protection for persons, homes, and communities; guard services at private colleges and business properties; security services for hospitals, shopping centers, and other large public facilities; and advice on internal and external security systems for homes, businesses, and factories. Over one million persons are employed in the private security field, and the number is growing at a faster pace than is the number of public police officers (Hess and Wrobleski, 1992).

One of the largest undertakings for a community crime-prevention approach began in Texas in 1991, called the Texas City Action Plan to Prevent Crime (T-CAP). T-CAP involved seven high-population cities in Texas that were committed to grass-roots-government, goal-oriented planning partnerships to tackle crime and its causes. They were also dedicated toward building a more nearly crime-free municipality. The program engaged representatives from municipal government and local business leaders, private entities, and citizens to be mutually responsible for planning and carrying out the crime-prevention plan. The project covered the full spectrum of crime prevention from target-hardening to social intervention initiatives (Gottfredson, 1997). The results were very positive and demonstrated the importance of local governments working with community agencies to prevent crime.

Last, focusing on how children are raised and the use of corporal punishment is another way to seek primary prevention (Straus, 2000b). **Corporal punishment** has been found to be a major risk factor for physical abuse. Corporal punishment is defined by Straus as "the use of physical force with the intention of causing a child to experience pain, but not injury, for the purpose of correction or control of the child's behavior. This includes spanking on the buttocks and slapping a child's hand for touching a forbidden or dangerous object" (p. 1109). In a comprehensive review of the research that examined the relationship between corporal punishment and child abuse, The Family Research Laboratory has concluded that corporal punishment is a risk factor for more severe attacks that are classified as physical abuse. Additionally, the research concludes that bringing up children with the use of corporal punishment puts children at a higher risk for the development of many social and psychological problems (Straus, 2000a).

In looking at the effect of primary prevention on potential offenders, researchers have produced some encouraging findings and offer suggestions for primary crime-prevention programs (see Reiss and Roth, 1993). Table 3.3 is a comprehensive listing of violence-prevention strategies based on Roth's (1994) review of research on understanding and preventing violence.

Initiating these strategies, along with altering or eliminating situations that present opportunities for violence to occur, such as underage and excessive alcohol consumption, presence and use of illegal drugs, and the accessibility to firearms, is predicted to achieve a significant reduction in criminal violence.

SECONDARY CRIME PREVENTION

The differences between primary and secondary crime prevention are based upon the targets of the programs involved. Primary crime prevention seeks to eliminate crime by educating all people and getting everyone in the community involved in attacking potential problems before victimization crime occurs. In secondary prevention, potential offenders or environmental factors known to contribute to criminality are targeted. However, both prevention strategies seek to eliminate criminal behavior before it occurs (Lab, 1992). The goal of secondary prevention programs is to identify those factors, either individual or environmental, that contribute to criminality and eliminate them.

TABLE 3.3   Violence Prevention Strategies

During Child Development
- Programs and materials to encourage and teach parents to be nonviolent role models, provide consistent discipline, and limit children's exposure to violent entertainment.
- Regular postpartum home visits by public health nurses to provide health information, teach parenting skills and give well-baby care, while taking the opportunity to detect signs of possible abuse.
- Programs such as Head Start preschool enrichment and early-grade tutoring to reduce the risk of early-grade school failure.
- Social learning programs for parents, teachers, and children to teach children social skills for avoiding violence, ways to view television critically, and nonviolent means to express anger and meet other needs.
- School-based anti-bullying programs.

Neurological and Genetic Processes
- Programs to reduce maternal substance abuse during pregnancy, children's exposure to lead in the environment, and head injuries.
- Intensive alcohol abuse treatment and counseling programs for those in their early adolescent years whose behavior patterns include both conduct disorder and alcohol abuse, especially if alcohol dependence runs in their families.
- Developing pharmacological therapies to reduce craving for nonopiate illegal drugs, such as methadone, reduces demand for heroin.
- Completing the development of medicines to reduce potentials for violent behavior during withdrawal from opiate addiction.

Social and Community-Level Interventions
- Housing policies to reverse the geographic concentration of low-income families.
- Programs to strengthen community organizations, social networks, and families that promote strong prosocial values.
- Economic revitalization in urban neighborhoods to restore opportunities for economic self-advancement through prosocial, nonviolent activities.
- Stronger community policing programs as a means of improving police responsiveness to community needs, stronger community-based violence prevention initiatives, reinforcement of prosocial values, and increased certainty of arrest and punishment for violent crimes.
- Strategies to reduce the violence-promoting effects of community transitions that occur in the course of new construction, gentrification, and other disruptions.
- Programs to reduce violence associated with prejudice and with the activities of some gangs.

Source: Based on Roth (1994, 7–9).

Programs that seek to prevent crime by attacking the social problems that foster crime fit under secondary prevention strategies when they focus on at-risk individuals. One of the first efforts was the development of Head Start projects during the 1960s. For example, the **Perry Preschool** program focused on children from ages 3–5 who were identified as at risk for future criminal behavior because of their home lives. Factors such as single-parent households, growing up in poverty, and lack of social controls are all believed to contribute to arrested development in some children. A special child-care program was provided to help teach special skills and prepare children to enter school and able to do the work. A subsequent evaluation of the program showed a substantial reduction in later arrests, dropping out of school, and use of welfare (Waller, 1991).

Another method for preventing crime, this time focusing upon at-risk middle-school children, involved two programs on violence prevention that were implemented in four New York City schools in 1995. The two programs were S.T.O.P. (Schools Teaching Options for Peace) and the Safe Harbor Program. Project S.T.O.P. is a traditional conflict-resolution program and Safe Harbor included a counseling component and a schoolwide antiviolence campaign. The programs were analyzed to study the following:

- Attitudes about the acceptability of violence.
- Knowledge of and skills in how to resolve conflict nonviolently.
- Aggressive behavior.
- Use of victim services.
- The number of disciplinary actions taken and cases of weapons possession. (National Institute of Justice, 1995).

The results showed that the effects of both Project S.T.O.P. and Safe Harbor on attitudes of more than 2,000 middle-school students were positive and strong. Students learned not to advocate retaliation when responding to conflict, became more knowledgeable of issues surrounding rape and sexual assault, and became more sympathetic toward their victims. Students also had a reduction in their feelings of helplessness in dealing with crime (National Institute of Justice, 1995).

The Job Corps is a program that focuses upon changing the social environment to prevent crime among teenagers. Job Corps provides training and career placements to disadvantaged youth. The idea is to reduce crime by breaking the cycle of unemployment and underemployment of disadvantaged youth that is related to higher criminality. Grants are provided to establish training programs that provide at-risk juveniles with the skills to get jobs, which reduce the likelihood of criminal behavior. The results of these programs are substantial, with evaluations showing a 30 percent reduction in arrests among those who participated in the program compared with those who did not (Waller, 1991).

Other programs that seek to prevent criminality are juvenile **diversion programs** (Davidson, Redner, and Amdur, 1990). Juveniles can get into trouble without violating the criminal law. Many juvenile offenses such as truancy, running away, incorrigibility, and curfew violations are considered status offenses for which juveniles can be arrested and prosecuted. While these violations are not serious, they are used to control juvenile behavior. The idea is that juveniles who commit status offenses may be headed toward more serious criminal activity if something is not done. Status offenses are used to identify juveniles who are not conforming and are at risk for criminal behavior. Once identified, juveniles are diverted to programs to prevent any future criminal behavior.

Juvenile diversion programs offer alternatives to the criminal justice system. The object is to eliminate the stigma of becoming involved with the criminal justice system and provide juveniles a second chance. In cases involving minor violations, the system recognizes the need to find out what is causing the antisocial behavior and rehabilitate the juvenile. The programs seek to prevent juveniles from being labeled criminals at an early age, a stigma that could follow them the rest of their lives. **Labeling theory** believes that once juveniles are labeled delinquent and treated as criminals they will be pushed toward future criminal behavior (see Schur, 1971).

Juvenile diversion programs can be housed in police departments or in the juvenile court system. Police-based programs involve an agreement between the police and the juveniles with whom they interact. Instead of arresting juveniles for status or other minor offenses, officers have the option of placing the juveniles in a program set up by the department. This program can include counseling, community service, or participation in treatment. Many programs involve the families of the juveniles as well. Once the juveniles complete the program, their arrest records are wiped clean and they are given a second chance. If juveniles fail to complete a program, they can then be subjected to the juvenile court system.

Diversion programs can work in two ways: (1) placing a juvenile in a program outside the criminal justice system or (2) suspending or terminating the juvenile justice process in favor of releasing or referring a juvenile to alternative services (Cox and Conrad, 1996). An example of a program outside the juvenile justice system is the use of wilderness programs. **Wilderness programs** are known by many different names, including Outward Bound, Vision Quest, and Ocean Quest. The concept of these programs is to involve juveniles in activities that encourage self-reliance skills, teamwork, and responsibility through physical labor, work projects, and living off the land. Juveniles are taken to the outdoors and are made to learn to provide for themselves to survive, giving them confidence in their own abilities. The goal of the program is for juveniles to take back this attitude with them to their communities and apply it to overcome problems and temptations to commit criminal activity they might face (Lab, 1992). While the success rates for these programs have varied, most subsequent research finds reductions in future criminal behavior (Quay and Love, 1977; Regoli, Wilderman, and Pogrebin, 1985).

Secondary prevention programs can also target victims of crime. One concern of prevention is to break the **cycle of violence** for children. It is known that children who observe violence within the family are more likely to engage in violence later in life. There is also evidence that men who are sexually abused as children are likely to engage in the same type of behavior (Siegel, 2006). In a study examining juveniles who were abused, neglected, or exposed to family violence compared with juveniles with no reported victimization, many of those who were victimized also reported committing violent acts before the age of 12 (Snyder and Sickmund, 1999).

Programs for juveniles who grow up in violent, abusive, or neglectful homes are located in every state. Most of these programs come under the title of child protective services (CPS). Such agencies are required under law to investigate reports of child abuse and neglect and to offer rehabilitative services if appropriate. The agencies are also charged with removing children from abusive homes for their own protection. However, it is difficult to prosecute abusive parents because children are often afraid to testify and lose their parents. Less than half of the investigations into possible child abuse or neglect are substantiated, and in only about 20 percent of substantiated cases is the child removed from the home (Snyder and Sickmund, 1999). The link between child victimization and future criminality is strong. Better prevention of child abuse can go a long way toward preventing future victimizations (see Chapter 9).

TERTIARY CRIME PREVENTION

Tertiary crime prevention focuses upon known offenders and seeks to eliminate the possibility of additional criminal behavior (Johnson, 1988). Tertiary prevention has been the main focus of the criminal justice system. Once offenders have been identified, there are many programs and sanctions that the criminal justice system can use to prevent them from committing future crime. Some of the methods used are specific deterrence, treatment programs, and incapacitation. Specific deterrence uses the threat of future sanctions, such as the three-strikes-you're-out law and mandatory imprisonment for repeat offenders, to prevent future criminality. Treatment programs can be focused on the crime, such as batterer's intervention programs, or on individual problems of the offenders, such as the treatment provided by Alcohol Anonymous and drug rehabilitation programs. Selective incapacitation programs seek to prevent any future criminal behavior and can range from the use of electronic monitoring or intensive probation to the death penalty.

Specific deterrence derives from the notion that if the punishment outweighs the crime, individuals will choose not to commit the crime. Specific deterrence focuses on individuals and seeks to establish sanctions that will convince offenders that it is not worth it to commit another crime. One such sanction is **three-strikes laws**. In 1994, California passed a law mandating that a person convicted of a third felony be given a prison term of 25 years to life. The judge could not give a lesser sentence unless the prosecutor agreed. Since then, 20 other states have passed similar laws. The object of these laws is to make offenders recognize that if they don't stop committing criminal acts, they will suffer severe consequences. The law also has an incapacitation focus, because removing repeat offenders from society will reduce future victimization. In 1995, the California Supreme Court ruled that not allowing judges' discretion in imposing the law violated the California Constitution, but the use of a 25-year to life sentence for a third felony is still legal (Pertman, 1996).

Another type of tertiary prevention is the use of treatment programs for offenders. All prisons in the United States offer some type of treatment program to their inmates. These programs include drug treatment, vocational training, anger management, and education. While there is little evidence to show that these programs are effective in preventing future criminality (the recidivism rate for inmates ranges from 40 to 70%) (Beck and Shipley, 1989; Siegel, 2008), the reasons may not have to do with the programs so much as the conditions within the prison systems themselves and the delivery of the services. Prisons today are extremely overcrowded (Siegel, 2006), and the ability of inmates to take advantage of treatment programs on the inside is very limited (Allen and Simonsen, 1995). Also, the treatment needs to be matched to the offender. The correctional literature shows that a one-size-fits-all model of treatment is not effective (see generally, Andrews and Bonta, 1994).

Many treatment programs are offered together with probation in an effort to keep offenders from engaging in further criminality. Drug testing of probationers and treatment programs are used extensively along with alcohol treatment programs. Historically, there are five major types of drug treatment programs available to criminal offenders: methadone maintenance, therapeutic communities, outpatient drug-free programs, detoxification programs, and correctional programs (McCarthy and McCarthy, 1991). Drug treatment programs try to eliminate the catalyst for criminal behavior of many offenders. Many offenders who are drug abusers cannot hold jobs and, therefore, must victimize innocent citizens to acquire money to feed their drug habits.

Batterers' intervention programs are also being developed to try and control the level of domestic violence. Batterers' programs work with small groups of men to try to find out why they abuse their wives and children, and also offer programs to prevent future violence. Many of the programs focus on anger management and eliminating traditional sex-based stereotyping. Other programs focus on teaching men to understand the consequences of their actions, especially if there are children involved, and to provide them with the opportunity to learn and practice new parenting skills. Research has shown that working with men whose children have witnessed their violence can benefit all family members (Barnett, Millar-Perrin, and Perrin, 2004).

Restitution programs (see Chapter 6) are also used as a method of tertiary prevention. The underlying principle of restitution is to have probationers learn that crime does not pay so they are deterred from engaging in further criminal behavior. If offenders pay their victims for the harm done, then they make no gain from the commission of the crime. This is one of the oldest forms of deterrence.

Electronic monitoring is the least intrusive form of incapacitation for nonviolent offenders. Electronic monitoring, also known as home arrest, requires offenders to have a monitor attached to their ankle or wrist. This monitor sends out a signal over the phone line which is monitored by a computer. If offenders move out of range of the monitor or if it is tampered with, the computer records the violation and the offender can be brought back into court. Programs can be set up so that offenders can go to work and treatment programs while being monitored. The idea is that while offenders are being monitored, they will be less likely to commit new crimes (McCarthy and McCarthy, 1991).

Incarceration as a means of incapacitating criminal offenders to prevent future victimizations has been used for over 200 years in the United States. This theory finds no hope for rehabilitating offenders and suggests that the only way to prevent future criminality is to isolate or remove them from society (Allen and Simonsen, 1995). This theory is popular today, and prison populations are at an all-time high. By the end of June, 2007, the Bureau of Justice Statistics estimated that there are almost 2.3 million individuals being held in our nation's prisons and jails. Most states also are providing longer sentences, especially for violent crimes. There is also a movement in this country to try juveniles in adult courts for violent offenses so that they will serve adult time.

Because of the expense of keeping inmates locked up for a long time, efforts are being made to better utilize prison space with **selective incapacitation** (Greenwood, 1983). Selective incapacitation seeks to identify those offenders most likely to commit future criminality and incapacitate them for longer periods of time. There is a tremendous amount of evidence that only a few career criminals are responsible for a majority of the crimes that are committed (U.S. Department of Justice, 1988).

A tertiary crime-prevention program that targets sexual predators is **community notification**. The use of community notification was first introduced in the state of Washington as a reaction to a brutal sexual assault on a 7-year-old boy near Tacoma by a recently released sexual offender. As a result of this violent crime, the state legislature passed a released sexual predator bill called the Community Protection Act in 1990 (Berliner, 1996). The Act required, among other things, that all convicted sexual predators must register with their local law enforcement agencies and that their information would be made available to the community. The purpose of notification is for people to be aware of potentially dangerous neighbors and to keep their children away from them. A few years later in Hamilton Township, New Jersey, a 7-year-old girl was lured into a neighbor's home and sexually assaulted and murdered. The victim was Megan Kanka and her neighbor was a recently released sexual predator. As a direct result of the national outrage over this crime, the New Jersey state legislature also passed a sexual-offender registry law, which came to be known as **Megan's Law**. Megan's Laws are now found in all 50 states.

Two final methods of tertiary crime prevention have gained in popularity over the last 10–15 years: three-strikes legislation, which provides for mandatory 25-year to life sentences, and the death penalty. The use of mandatory life sentences and the death penalty follows the ideal that rehabilitation does not work for certain offenders, and they must be incapacitated forever. Over 30 states and the federal government have authorized the use of the death penalty, and all states have mandatory life statutes. These sentences provide the ultimate protection against future criminal behavior. The rationale is that citizens must be protected from certain criminals and that these individuals should never be given the chance to commit any future crimes as they have been allowed to under previous sentencing guidelines.

An example of a habitual criminal is Richard Allen Davis. On October 1, 1993, 12-year-old Polly Klaas was last seen alive. Over the previous 20 years, Richard Allen Davis had been allowed to plea bargain and receive probation, early release, good time, and parole for an assortment of crimes, including robberies, burglaries, sexual assaults, kidnappings, and assaults with deadly weapons (Bidinotto, 1996). Had three-strikes legislation been in place, Polly Klaas would be alive today, and an unknown number of other crime victims would not have suffered because of Davis's sadistic violence.

Another example is the terrifying rampage of Leslie Allen Williams, which finally came to an end in 1992, when he was caught and confessed to four murders and eleven rapes. This serial murderer and rapist had been in and out of the criminal justice system for over 20 years. He had been paroled four separate times before his killing rampage (Bidinotto, 1996). The justice system had allowed him to serve less than half of his sentences, violate his paroles without punishment, plea bargain serious offenses down to minor ones, and continue to walk free in society, killing and raping innocent victims.

In November 1993, the federal three-strikes law was first approved in the Senate. The first person convicted under this statue, Tommy Farmer, had a 25-year criminal career that included assaults with dangerous weapons, aggravated batteries, robberies, and murders (Butterfield, 1996). Because of the federal statute, Tommy Farmer was sent to prison for life instead of walking free in a few years, thus preventing him from continuing to terrorize and kill innocent citizens.

Offenders and would-be third-time felons are now on notice that the public will no longer tolerate their criminal activities. Society has decided to get serious with the individuals who have been given multiple chances to change but have decided to continue their criminal way of life. Leading victimologists believe that the need to provide a criminal justice system that responds to the wishes of the law-abiding community is just starting to become a reality (Jerin, 2001).

EVALUATION OF CRIME-PREVENTION STRATEGIES

In a major examination of the effectiveness of crime-prevention programs, *Preventing Crime: What Works, What Doesn't, What's Promising*, Sherman and his colleagues (1997) concluded that substantial reductions in rates of serious crime can be achieved only by concentrating specific prevention programs in areas of substantial poverty. The report studied over 500 government-sponsored programs. The focus of the report was on seven institutions that contributed to crime prevention: communities, families, schools, labor markets, specific premises, the police, and corrections. The conclusions of this report established that when we examine crime-prevention efforts, communities are the central institution for crime prevention, the stage on which all other institutions perform. Families, schools, labor markets, retail establishments, police, and corrections must all confront the consequences of community life. Much of the success or failure of these other institutions is affected by the community context in which they operate. Our nation's ability to prevent serious violent crime may depend heavily on our ability to help reshape community life, at least in our most troubled communities. Our good fortune is that the number of those troubled communities is relatively small. Our challenge is that their problems are so profound (pp. 1–3).

Another federal effort to help states has been grant funding provisions of many new laws. The Violence Against Women Act provides grants (STOP Formula Grants) to try to prevent crimes against women. This program requires that states spend 25 percent of their STOP funds to prevent violence against women on each of the three priority areas: law enforcement, prosecution, and victim services (Sherman et al., 1997). The purpose of the money is not just to combat domestic violence but also to prevent stranger violence. Such community-based programs can focus on reducing rape, stalking, purse-snatchings, and car-jackings.

FAMILY-BASED PROGRAMS

Family risk factors have a major effect on crime (Sherman et al., 1997). Family-based crime prevention can directly address those risk factors with substantial success. The more risk factors these programs address, perhaps, the better. The earlier they start in life, it seems, the better. Programs for infants and young children may be more cost-effective in the long run, even if they are expensive in the short run. Combining home-visit parental support with preschool education reduces crime committed by children when they grow up. Rigorously evaluated pilot projects with tightly controlled prevention services are consistently effective. Family problems later in life are more difficult to address, especially family violence by adults. But it is still possible. The potential of early, adolescent, and adult family-based crime prevention is held back only by our failure to invest in more research and development. The need for testing programs that can work on a large scale is particularly great. An example of family-based crime prevention by ecological context is shown in Table 3.4.

TABLE 3.4   Family-Based Crime Prevention by Ecological Context

Ecological Context	Program	Prevention Agent
Home	Regular visits for emotional, informational, instrumental, and educational support for parents of preschool (or older) children	Nurses, teachers, para professionals, preschool teachers
	Foster care outplacement for the prevention of physical, sexual abuse, or neglect	Family services, social workers
	Family preservation of families at risk of outplacement of a child	Private families, preservation teams
	Personal alarm for victims of serious domestic violence	Police
	In-home proactive counseling for domestic violence	Police, social workers
Preschool	Involvement of mothers in parent groups, job training, parent training	Preschool teachers
School	Parent training	Psychologists, teachers
	Simultaneous parent and child training	Psychologists, child care workers, social workers
Clinics	Family therapy	Psychologists, psychiatrists, social workers
	Medication-psycho stimulants for treatment of hyper-activity and other child-hood conduct disorders	Psychiatrists, psychologists, pediatricians
Hospitals	Domestic violence counseling	Nurses, social workers
	"Low-birth weight baby" mothers' counseling and support	Nurses, social workers
Courts	Prosecution of batterers	Police, prosecutors
	Warrants for non-arrested batterers	Police, prosecutors
	Restraining orders or "stay-away" orders of protection	Police, prosecutors, judges, victim advocates
	Hotline notification of victim about release of incarcerated domestic batterer	Probation, victim advocates
Battered Women's Shelters	Safe refuge during high-risk 2–7 days, aftermath of domestic assault, counseling, hotlines	Volunteers, staff

Source: Based on Sherman et al. (1997).

SCHOOL-BASED PROGRAMS

Gottfredson (1997) has found that schools have great potential as a locus for crime prevention. Schools are the only dependable, consistent access to large numbers of the most crime-prone young children; they are staffed with individuals paid to help youth develop as healthy, happy, productive citizens; and the community usually supports schools' efforts to socialize youth. Many of the precursors of delinquent behavior are school related and, therefore, likely to be amenable to change through school-based intervention.

School environmental factors related to delinquency include availability of drugs, alcohol, and other criminogenic merchandise (such as weapons). Characteristics of the classroom and school social organization (such as strong academic mission, administrative leadership, and a climate of emotional support) provide environmental factors related to the prevention of delinquency (Gottfredson, 1997). School-related experiences and attitudes that often precede delinquency include poor school performance and attendance, low attachment to school, and low commitment to schooling. Peer-related experiences, many of which are school centered, include rejection by peers and association with delinquent peers. Individual factors include early problem behavior, impulsiveness or low levels of self-control, rebellious attitudes, beliefs favoring law violation, and low levels of social competency skills (such as identifying likely consequences of actions and alternative solutions to problems, taking the perspective of others, and correctly interpreting social cues).

POLICE-BASED CRIME PROGRAMS

There is a general belief that the more police we have, the less crime there will be. While citizens and public officials may espouse that view, social scientists often claim the opposite extreme: police make only minimal contributions to crime prevention in the context of far more powerful social institutions—the family and labor markets. According to the latest analysis of police-based prevention programs (Sherman et al., 1997), the truth appears to lie in between. Whether additional police prevent crime may depend on how well they are focused on specific objectives, tasks, places, times, and people. Most of all, it may depend upon putting police where serious crime is concentrated, at the times it is most likely to occur—policing focused on risk factors.

The connection of policing to risk factors is the most powerful conclusion reached from three decades of research. Hiring more police to provide rapid 911 responses, unfocused random patrol, and reactive arrests do not prevent serious crime. Community policing without a clear focus on crime risk factors generally shows no effect on crime. But directed patrols, proactive arrests, and problem solving at high-crime "hot spots" has shown substantial evidence of crime prevention (see Chapter 4). Police can prevent robbery, disorder, gun violence, drunk driving, and domestic violence, but only by using certain methods under certain conditions.

These conclusions are based largely on research supported by the National Institute of Justice, the research arm of the Office of Justice Programs in the U.S. Department of Justice. In recent years, increasing numbers of police executives have incorporated these findings into their crime-prevention strategies. University of Wisconsin law professor Herman Goldstein's (1979) paradigm of "problem-oriented policing" directed research

TABLE 3.5   Police Strategies for Crime Prevention

What's Promising:

- police traffic enforcement patrols against illegally carried handguns
- community policing with community participation in priority setting
- community policing focused on improving police legitimacy
- zero tolerance of disorder, if legitimacy issues can be addressed
- problem-oriented policing generally
- adding extra police to cities, regardless of assignments
- warrants for arrest of suspect absent when police respond to domestic violence

Source: Based on Sherman et al. (1997).

attention to the specific things police do and how they can focus their resources to attack the proximate causes of public safety problems (see Table 3.5). The Justice Department's adoption of this perspective has yielded an increasingly complex but useful body of knowledge about how policing affects crime.

One of the most striking recent findings is the extent to which the police themselves create a risk factor for crime simply by using bad manners. Modest but consistent scientific evidence supports the hypothesis that the less respectful police are toward suspects and citizens, generally, the less people will comply with the law. Changing police "style" may thus be as important as focusing police "substance." Making both the style and substance of police practices more "legitimate" in the eyes of the public, particularly high-risk juveniles, may be one of the most effective long-term police strategies for crime prevention.

What is notably absent from these findings, however, are many topics of great concern to police. Gang prevention, for example, is a matter about which we could not find a single impact evaluation of police practices. Police curfews and truancy programs lack rigorous tests. Police recreation activities with juveniles, such as police athletic leagues, also remain unevaluated. Automated identification systems, in-car computer terminals, and a host of other new technologies costing billions of dollars remain unevaluated for their impact on crime prevention. There is clearly a great deal of room for further testing of hypotheses not listed here due to the absence of available scientific evidence.

CONCLUSION

Crime prevention as a means to help crime victims is becoming more popular. Individual crime-prevention techniques are used by all citizens every day. Programs vary as to the target and the rationale, when they are offered in the life cycle of a criminal act (i.e., primary, secondary, or tertiary prevention), and whether they are directed at potential or current offenders, victims, or places.

The criminal justice system is still very reactive in its efforts to provide crime prevention. In part, ability of the criminal justice system is limited by its traditional role in preventing crime. Although new programs and sentencing policies are being implemented, the impact of these policies has yet to materialize. No one program can be expected to work in every situation, but crime-prevention programs provide hope for a reduction in the amount of victimization in the future.

Evaluations of numerous crime-prevention programs (Sherman et al., 1997) have shown us that some programs work, some don't, and many promising programs are out there. There is general agreement that much more needs to be done to truly achieve the goal of significant crime prevention.

There is also a growing recognition of the need for programs, especially for younger children, to prevent them from becoming victims of crime as well as to prevent them from growing up and engaging in criminal behavior. Bringing together various factions within communities seems to offer the best hope for crime prevention. The ability of a program to provide effective crime prevention depends on the planning that goes into the development of the program, the quality of the services delivered, and comprehensive evaluation and measurement of the results.

Study Questions

1. Explain the difference between crime prevention and crime control, and the effect of each on efforts to prevent crime victimization. Give examples for each.
2. What is needed for crime deterrence to take place using a primary crime-prevention strategy? Describe the various types of programs that come under the category of primary crime prevention.
3. Describe the concept of defensible space as put forth by Newman and Jeffery. How can the concept be used in an urban environment to prevent criminal acts from occurring?
4. What are some of the most promising crime-prevention programs for law enforcement? For schools? What problems arise in implementing these programs?

Key Terms

- celerity   43
- certainty   43
- classical school   42
- community notification   54
- corporal punishment   49
- crime control   41
- **crime prevention**   40
- cycle of violence   52
- D.A.R.E.   48
- defensible space   46
- diversion programs   51
- electronic monitoring   54
- general deterrence   42

- hedonistic calculus   42
- hotspots   47
- image   46
- Labeling theory   52
- Megan's Law   55
- milieu   46
- natural surveillance   46
- neighborhood watch   47
- Perry Preschool   50
- positivist school   43
- primary prevention   44
- protective factors   45
- punishment   43

- restitution programs   54
- risk factors   45
- secondary prevention   45
- selective incapacitation   54
- situational crime prevention   45
- specific deterrence   42
- target hardening   47
- territoriality   46
- tertiary prevention   45
- three-strikes laws   53
- wilderness programs   52

SECTION II

Crime Victims and the Criminal Justice System

CHAPTER

Crime Victims and Law Enforcement

INTRODUCTION

The motto "to protect and serve" defines the role of law enforcement for most citizens in the United States. We look to the police to prevent crime from happening to us; and if a crime does happen, we expect the police to catch the perpetrator, return what was taken, provide crisis assistance, and make us feel whole again. Crime victims expect that the police will believe them and do everything possible to **arrest** the perpetrators and bring them to justice. These expectations of the police by crime victims have rarely been fully met.

The way people cope as victims of crime depends largely on their experiences immediately following a crime. Law enforcement officers are usually the first officials to approach victims. They become the **first responders**. For this reason, they are in a unique position to help victims cope with the immediate trauma of the crime and to help restore their sense of security and control over their lives. The role law enforcement officers play vis-à-vis crime victims should not be underestimated. For most people, the actions of the police may determine how they will view the whole criminal justice process. From the way emergency 911 calls are answered, to the timeliness and attitude of the responding officers, to the actions of the detectives who follow up on their cases, all things matter to victims of crime. It is hoped that the police will treat crime victims with sensitivity and provide emergency assistance and essential information immediately (Office for Victims of Crime, 1998).

THE LAW ENFORCEMENT FUNCTION AND CRIME VICTIMS

Crime victims seek assistance from police officers to meet their immediate needs of dealing with the victimization and to reduce their fear. Law enforcement officers need as much accurate information as possible so they can affect arrests and clear cases. These dual expectations of law enforcement and victims have created many problems for both parties. Many times police won't respect a victim's needs because of a perception that the victim does not want to cooperate, the crime is not serious enough, or a crime may not really have occurred.

Due to the complexities of the law enforcement officers' role, many victims do not respect the role of law enforcement officers. Often victims do not cooperate with the police. Victims fail to report crimes, change their stories, or say they don't want to get involved in the investigation or prosecution because of how they have been treated by the criminal justice system. They have a general lack of faith that the criminal justice system will provide them with any justice.

The ability of the police to control crime is largely dependent upon reports by victims and witnesses of the crime and appropriate police responses. Studies (Kelly, 1990; Laub, 1997) have shown that the vast majority of reported crimes come to the attention of law enforcement agencies through victims' and witnesses' calls for assistance. This interdependence of crime victims and police is one of the most important relationships in the functioning of the criminal justice system. The cooperation of crime victims with the criminal justice system is essential for optimum law enforcement. Additionally, proper responses by law enforcement to crime victims' needs may go a long way toward providing recovery from the trauma of victimization.

This chapter examines the history of law enforcement and crime victims, the importance of crime victims to the law enforcement function, how different stages of the police–crime victim interaction can impact crime victims, the training of law enforcers in victims' issues, and programs for crime victims within law enforcement departments.

HISTORY OF POLICING AS IT RELATES TO CRIME VICTIMS

As noted in Chapter 1, in early societies, crime victims or their families were responsible for the capture, prosecution, and punishment of offenders. Each individual, family, clan, or village established its own rule of law based upon folkways, mores, and customs. In disputes between community members, aggrieved parties were responsible for bringing the accused before the community legal body for determination of guilt and the issuing of punishment. Victims usually had the right to say what type of justice should be handed down. This was the "Golden Age" as described by Schafer (1968), before the origination of police and prosecutors. The autonomy of crime victims to seek justice and decide how that justice needed to be carried out empowered victims as they have never been empowered since.

However, there were many problems with this system. **Blood feuds** between families erupted over the determination of who had been wronged and who was responsible. Revenge killings and fights continued for decades as families tried to achieve justice for the victims or their families. In most communities, a person's status in the community had more to do with his or her ability to obtain justice than the facts of the case. Most victims hadn't the time, resources, or ability to bring offenders to justice (Johnson, 1981).

With the institution of the county sheriff system in England, the role of victims as law enforcers and justice seekers declined. In an effort to reduce the violence associated with blood feuds and the seeking of revenge, to provide for greater protection of the new middle class, and to codify the rules of law, representatives of the king started to transform the justice system. These officials were given the role of making arrests and bringing the accused to justice. Crime victims now had to provide the complaints, pay for warrants to be issued, and testify in court against the offenders (Johnson, 1988).

While the role of law enforcer was being taken away from citizens in rural areas, the citizens' role as law enforcers in cities grew. In cities, new dangers arose because of the density of the population. A major problem facing communities was the threat of fire. In an attempt to protect the community and to enforce certain standards of behavior, communities started the watchman system. **Watchmen** were citizens in the community who were responsible for watching for fires during the night and guarding the city gates (Johnson, 1981).

Watchmen were also responsible for turning over any wrongdoers to the officers of the royal court, who were called constables. This hastened the process of discouraging victims from seeking justice by removing them from participation in the criminal justice system. Crime was viewed as victimization against the community or the king by the offender. For the most part, the system relied upon community members who often had little involvement, no skills, or no commitment to deal with crime. Even the recovery of payments of restitution to victims by offenders was superseded by the need of the king to obtain revenue to operate his court and recover expenses (Johnson, 1988). The payments that had gone for restitution to victims became fines paid to the state. Victims had to turn to the civil court, at their own expense, to seek monetary compensation.

Citizens in colonial America brought with them the English system and shared the duties of enforcing the law. The obligation of every capable male to participate in the law enforcement function was initially welcomed by members of each community (Johnson, 1981). As time went by, towns grew, and participating in the watchman system became more difficult as other obligations became more pressing. An informal system of paying individuals to cover the watch of well-to-do community members emerged. The job of law enforcement was soon passed to a paid watch.

In the mid-1800s, major cities turned to full-time paid police. Most of the original police were political appointees and served at the whim of the current political machine. By the early 1900s, with the arrival of civil service, a more professional police force took shape. The focus of the police was to provide citizens with a visible symbol of safety. How well they did their job depended greatly on how well they knew the community they patrolled and whether they could get the cooperation of citizens. The use of uniforms, assigned patrol beats, police call boxes, and local departments provided citizens with a viable crime-prevention organization (Johnson, 1981).

As police agencies evolved, they began losing touch with the citizens they served. With the advent of the motorized police patrol, officers no longer walked the beat, interacting with citizens, but were relegated to vehicles and had to be contacted by phone and dispatched to criminal events. As police became more detached from communities, they knew less about the people they served, but more people depended upon them to help solve crimes. The role of the victim became one of witness-informer of the criminal event. In most cases, victims talked to dispassionate strangers who were suspicious of their stories. Many crimes were viewed with disdain because they lacked a high-profile component. Because many officers did not understand the dynamics of the effects of victimization, they minimized the harm done and even blamed crime victims for their own victimization. This became a common occurrence in domestic violence, sexual assaults, and many other cases.

Since the mid-1980s, a renewal of policing strategy has sought to include citizens and victims. **Community policing** (Goldstein, 1990) requires more involvement of the police in the lives of citizens. No longer are the police just law enforcers; their role has become one of community resource people who can provide a sense of safety. By the 1990s, proactive policing procedure had taken hold. "Police officers spend 90 percent of their time providing a variety of services while protecting life, property, and personal liberty" (Wrobleski and Hess, 1993, 51). The focus of this policing policy was to establish community support and participation in the criminal justice process, to provide more services through a decentralized organization, and to become more involved with understanding and providing services to citizens and crime victims. In response to the final report of the President's Task Force on Victims of Crime (1982), police agencies started paying attention to the needs of crime victims. The report recommended the following:

- Police departments should develop and implement training programs to ensure that police officers are:
  - Sensitive to the needs of victims; and
  - Informed, knowledgeable, and supportive of the existing local services and programs for victims.
- Police departments should establish procedures for the prompt photographing and return of property to victims.
- Police departments should establish procedures to ensure that victims of violent crime are periodically informed of the status and closing of investigations.
- Police officers should give high priority to investigating witnesses' reports of threats or intimidation and should forward these reports to prosecutors (pp. 57–62).

POLICE INVESTIGATION OF CRIMES

While it may be unrealistic to suggest that the police should act as psychologists, social workers, or other acute care workers, they can learn basic crisis intervention practices and understand victims' needs to better serve crime victims during the investigative stage. During the initial interview, the actions of a police officer can profoundly affect the long-term effects of the victimization on a crime victim. The National Organization of Victim Assistance (NOVA) long ago established guidelines for victims' rights during the investigative process. The first stage after the emergency response is the interview process, which, if done with victims' needs as a priority, can provide for victim stabilization.

The report made 11 recommendations:

1. The officer should show a calm, objective manner.
2. The officer should have an air of authority—of knowing what to do.
3. The officer should express concern and understanding for what the victim is feeling.
4. The officer should encourage the victim to talk in his or her own way.
5. The officer should show a non-judgmental attitude.
6. The officer should explain the circumstances to the family member or friend if necessary.
7. The officer should explain what he or she and his colleagues are doing and what the victim can expect to happen in the future.
8. The officer should usually conduct the initial interview alone if possible.
9. The officer should make no promises he can't keep.
10. The officer should thank the victim for this trouble.
11. The officer should offer crime-prevention assistance in the future.

(National Organization for Victim Assistance, 1984, 25)

After the initial interview, the next important stage of police activity is to provide information concerning community services that will benefit the victim. Many victims have no idea of what programs are available to them or even the kind of help they may need. Referral needs of the victim at this point include follow-up counseling, assistance with financial claims, assistance with creditors and employers, legal aid, crime-prevention services (such as replacing locks and fixing windows), how to get property returned, and state-sponsored victim services. Many law enforcement agencies require that investigating officers provide victims with a list of victim service contacts or advocates either on a business card or in pamphlets or brochures (Cox, 1996). Having an investigating officer or a victims' advocate within the department responsible for immediate response to these needs is important to crime victims' recovery.

Victims also want to be informed of the progress of their cases. In many cases, police officers are the main contact between the criminal justice system and victims unless arrests are made and the decision to prosecute follows. While it may be unrealistic to expect that all offenders will be caught, keeping victims informed of the progress of their cases will help them recover from the effects of victimization and may increase their satisfaction with the police. It has been shown that when officers recontact victims in serious property crime cases, victim satisfaction improves (Brandi and Horvath, 1991; Siegel, 2006). The recontact can take two different routes. On the one hand, if the police recontact victims because they doubt the victims' stories or want more information, victims' well-being could be adversely affected. Having to relive the victimization repeatedly prevents crime victims from moving on with their lives. If, on the other hand, recontact provides valued information to the crime victims, such as the incarceration status of offenders, the return of stolen property, or other victim-interest information, there may be benefits for the criminal justice system as well as victims. The sensitivity of the police to these issues can pay off with greater participation by victims in the later prosecution or in future victimizations.

THE POLICE RESPONSE AND DOMESTIC VIOLENCE

The police response to victims of stranger violence has always received a great amount of attention. The media, movies, and television shows have always focused on crime victimization by strangers. Since most crime is not perpetrated by strangers, how law enforcement officials react in acquaintance victimization cases affects a majority of crime victims. No area of policing has received more attention over the last 25 years than how police respond to domestic violence victimizations.

The focus on the police response to domestic violence victims has been a major issue for crime victims. For many years, domestic violence was treated with general disregard, especially for the harm that it creates. Many police agencies treated domestic violence as a family matter, less serious than stranger assault, or they viewed it as a waste of time because victims often did not press charges. The inadequate response of police to victims of domestic violence came to the forefront in 1984 with the federal district court ruling in ***Thurman v. City of Torrington***. In this case, Tracey Thurman and her son brought a civil rights suit against the City of Torrington, Connecticut, and its police officers, alleging discriminatory treatment in violation of the Fourteenth Amendment's

Equal Protection Clause. The discriminatory treatment alleged in the complaint stated that police protection was fully provided to persons abused outside of a domestic relationship, but the police consistently afforded lesser protection when victims were abused or assaulted by spouses or boyfriends. During an 8-month period, Tracey Thurman repeatedly tried to have her husband arrested for threatening her life and her child. The complaint stated that the police ignored or rejected Tracey's many attempts to file complaints against her estranged husband. The inaction of the police resulted in her husband stabbing her repeatedly in the chest and neck and, in the presence of police officers, kicking her in the head. Although four police officers were at the scene of the initial attack, Charles Thurman was not arrested; instead, he continued to threaten his wife and was finally arrested when he tried to attack her again.

Tracey Thurman survived the attack by her estranged husband and sued the individual police officers who witnessed the attack or its results, the department, and the city for having an unwritten policy of treating domestic violence situations differently from other violence. The court ruled in favor of Tracey Thurman and found that the department had failed to perform its duty to protect women equally, no matter what their domestic relationship. In this case, liability was assessed against the police and the city in excess of $2 million (Jerin, 1988a).

Additionally, in 1984, a major study of the effects of arrest on subsequent domestic violence was published (Sherman and Berk, 1984). The Minneapolis Domestic Violence Experiment found that arresting batterers reduced by half the rate of subsequent offenses against the same victim within a 6-month follow-up period. The experiment focused upon various ways police could handle a domestic violence crime. The officers used a predetermined response of either mandatory arrest, having one party leave the scene of the violence, the use of onsite counseling by the officers, or a referral to a social service agency. Based upon the results of this study, the conclusions recommended a proarrest policy be implemented nationally (see Chapter 7 for more on police response to domestic violence). Even the Attorney General's Task Force on Family Violence endorsed the use of arrest as the preferred response in incidents of family violence (National Institute of Justice, 1995).

As a result of these two separate but related actions, many police departments changed their policies toward victims of domestic violence. Many departments now mandate arrest and train officers in their academies and in-service how to handle domestic violence cases in an effort to minimize the liability of officers and to provide additional crime victim services when responding. This is not to say every police department is responding in the same way. Often policies can be developed on the administrative level but fail to translate to the actual operation of the line officers. In 2003, the **International Association of Chiefs of Police (IACP)** recognized that institutional forces and training deficits remain that inhibit law enforcement agencies from effectively providing services to crime victims (International Association of Chiefs of Police, 2003).

MODERN-DAY POLICE RESPONSE

New efforts to better train police in victims' issues are occurring at all levels. Many state legislatures or governors' counsels have established minimum standards that must be followed during police academy training. The federal government has victims' rights training programs for all law enforcement recruits and in-service programs. Many police training programs now include, at a minimum, a day of instruction about victims' issues and the needs of crime victims. Victims' issues and rights training at some police academies are taught by former victims, victim advocates, or specially trained officers. Most departments also include in-service training programs in victims' issues and policies. Standards of training on various victims' issues are being carried out all across the country. Most new textbooks on law enforcement include a chapter on victims of crime and the effects of victimization. Many agencies work with local victim services, such as shelters for battered women, child protection agencies, and rape crisis hotlines, to provide protection and service to crime victims.

The International Association of Chiefs of Police (IACP) developed a policy back in the 1980s to encourage local departments to train their officers, establish procedures, and implement victims' rights. Victims were:

- To be free from intimidation.
- To be told of financial assistance and social services available and how to apply for them.
- To be provided a secure area during interviews and court proceedings and to be notified if presence in court is needed.
- To be provided a quick return of stolen or other personal property when no longer needed as evidence.
- To be interviewed by a female official in the case of rape and other sexual offenses (International Association of Chiefs of Police, 2003, 2).

A major reevaluation of the needs of crime victims and the role law enforcement must work toward accepting occurred with a publication of *New Directions From the Field* by the Office for Victims of Crime (1998). This publication was a follow-up to the ground-breaking President's Task Force Report on Victims of Crime in 1982. *New Directions* set forth 12 major recommendations for law enforcement agencies based upon the input of participants at numerous public hearings and the efforts of working groups. A summary of recommendations are:

- Agencies should adopt a community policing philosophy that is both victim and crime prevention oriented.
- Agencies should provide a basic level of support to crime victims through establishing victim assistance programs within their agencies and through community partnerships to ensure that victims have access to emergency services, counseling, financial assistance, information and referrals, and community programs.
- Agencies should establish policies for the provision of fundamental victims' rights and services and procedures for their implementation. These policies and procedures should be disseminated in writing throughout the agency.
- Compliance with victims' rights and procedures should be included as a standard in officers' performance appraisals.
- During their initial contact with law enforcement officers, victims of crime should receive verbal and written information about victims' rights and services. Law enforcement personnel should be required to follow up with victims because many individuals are unable to comprehend assistance and compensation information in the immediate aftermath of being severely traumatized.
- All agencies should adopt written policies and procedures and implement training programs for conducting sensitive and culturally appropriate death notification.

- State, federal, military, and tribal agencies must implement victims' rights laws and ensure that victims are regularly notified of the status of the investigation, including arrests, pretrial release of suspects, and case closings.
- Law enforcement should place a high priority on protecting victims and witnesses from intimidation and physical harm after they report a crime. Agencies that operate jails or any temporary custody facilities should, upon request of the victims, immediately notify victims of defendants' pretrial release.
- All personnel, from dispatchers through management, should receive initial and ongoing training about the impact of crime and how to respond sensitively and effectively to victims.
- Departments should develop specialized responses for family members of officers killed in the line of duty and protocols for responding to injured officers.
- Agencies should establish special protocols to ensure victim participation and confidence in the system when officers are accused of criminal offenses.
- Procedures for the swift return of property to victims and witnesses should be developed at the federal, state, and, local levels to serve as models for agencies nationwide. Emergency funds should be made available to victims to replace essential items (Office for Victims of Crime, 1998).

To accomplish these recommendations, the Office for Victims of Crime (OVC) put forward a list of comprehensive policies, protocols, and procedures for agencies and officers to follow to provide crime victims with the rights and services they deserved. OVC called on law enforcement to "take a leadership role" in protecting crime victims' rights and help develop a comprehensive community response. The envisioned law enforcement response proposed by the Office for Victims of Crime would include the following:

- Upon first contact with law enforcement, the responding officer should give victims verbal and written notification of their rights according to state or federal law, a so-called "Reverse Miranda."
- Law enforcement agencies should utilize community partnerships to ensure that victims have access to the following emergency services, financial assistance, information, and community programs.
- Law enforcement should provide protection from intimidation and harm.
- Law enforcement should inform the victim of the investigation process.
- If an arrest has been made, victims should be notified of all relevant dates in the criminal justice process.
- If the case has been submitted to a prosecution attorney's office, law enforcement should provide the victim with the prosecutor's information.
- Prompt property return.

(Office for Victims of Crime, 1998, 68–69)

The International Association of Chiefs of Police has also responded to the many calls for the improvement of the law enforcement response to crime victims. In 1999, IACP held a Summit on Victims of Crime that brought together law enforcement leaders, representatives from the criminal justice system, victim advocates, and victims themselves in order to improve police response to crime victims. The participants of the summit identified seven critical needs of crime victims from which the participants discerned seven criteria for effective crime victims' services.

1. **Access**—Helping crime victims feel comfortable contacting investigating officers to obtain or offer new information in their cases
2. **Continuity**—Coordination with local victim-service providers and prosecutors' offices.
3. **Information**—Availability of information in languages predominant in the community and in large print for the elderly.
4. **Justice**—Cooperation, communication, and support through the entire criminal justice process.
5. **Safety**—Understanding the crisis reaction of victims and protecting victims from future intimidation and harm.
6. **Support**—Helping victims feel comfortable to discuss the crimes and letting victims know that the police are concerned about their needs.
7. **Voice**—Allowing victims to express their needs and concerns. (International Association of Chiefs of Police, 2003).

Specifically, in 2003, IACP recognized the importance of line officers and detectives in providing crime victims with real improvement in services. Since the detectives and line officers are the law enforcement officers with whom victims have the most frequent interaction, they needed specific training. IACP recommended that officers receive improved education and training in the academy and in-service to improve their interpersonal skills to work better with crime victims (International Association of Chiefs of Police, 2003).

IMPORTANCE OF CRIME VICTIMS FOR LAW ENFORCEMENT

The police need to get crime victims to cooperate and provide them with information and evidence so that they can make arrests. However, about half of all crimes of violence are not reported to the police (National Crime Victim's Center, 2006). One reason for this is that many victims feel that the crimes were a private matter, and they do not want the police involved. Other reasons may include fear of revictimization, a view that the police can't solve the crime anyhow, a general distrust of the police, the feeling that the crimes were not serious enough, not wanting to get involved with the criminal justice system because of previous bad experiences, embarrassment, and belief that the victimizations were partly their own fault.

The advent of community policing has promoted the realization that crime victims are important contributors to the effectiveness of the police. Greater victim awareness may be one factor in reducing the amount of crime and victimization that occurs. Victimization rates have shown a steady decline for over a decade (National Crime Victim's Center, 2006). Crime rates have also been reduced in many major cities throughout the United States. Citizens have more positive impressions of the police, and satisfaction with police has been at an all-time high over the last couple of decades (Bohm and Haley, 2007).

Often the needs of officers to conduct investigations and to gather evidence conflict with crime victims' needs. Many rape victims find rape exams to be degrading and humiliating experiences, including the fact that their clothes are removed for evidence. Crimes in the home may require dusting for fingerprints and removal of objects that contain evidence, such as blood, hair, and tissue samples. In murders, the bodies of the victims become the property of the state, and various autopsies and examinations may be conducted upon it over periods of time without regard to the survivors' wishes. In one case, the body of a woman killed by Ted Bundy was held by the State of Florida until all of his appeals had been exhausted and he was put to death, more than 10 years later. When the woman's parents tried to recover the body so that they could give it a proper burial, they found that the body could no longer be located and was presumed to have been disposed of (Young, 1992). In too many cases, the police see crime victims as of no use after they have provided evidence. This perception is changing, however, and police are finding that how they treat victims during the investigative stage can greatly affect how well officers can do their jobs.

Police are trained to gather as much information as possible at the scene of the crime in order to affect an arrest. Many law enforcers believe that the need to obtain as much information as possible until the investigation is over outweighs victims' need for assistance. The preservation of evidence is of utmost importance to responding officers. Victims, usually still in a state of shock, are forced to cooperate with officers and to relive the terrifying events of their victimization. Law enforcement officers are trained to obtain as much information as possible from witnesses, no matter what their condition. The methods used to obtain this information "may prove to be a critical factor in the victim's recovery" (National Organization for Victim Assistance, 1984, 4).

Officers are also trained to be suspicious and to wonder if victims are lying or are telling the *whole* truth. Especially in nonstranger victimizations, police may not believe victims' accounts of the incidents. Many victims are only seeking help at this point and do not want to relive their victimization, or they may be fearful of additional victimization if they cooperate—so they may not want to cooperate. This puts law enforcement officials and victims at odds. Officers want to do their jobs and catch the offenders, but the lack of victim cooperation may be seen as an attempt by victims to prevent officers from completing this task. The emotional state of victims may also prevent them from cooperating even if they want to. However, this emotional state may be perceived by officers as an attempt to block the investigation. This interaction may also be dependent upon victims' attitude toward the officer. The police are usually not sensitive to the many problems victims are encountering (Bohm and Haley, 2007).

Meeting the needs of crime victims during the response and investigative stages increases the potential for cooperation with law enforcement. Not only could a positive response to the victims' needs by law enforcement help in current cases, but also it would most likely encourage greater assistance in future cases.

IMPORTANCE OF LAW ENFORCEMENT FOR CRIME VICTIMS

The dependence of crime victims on the police cannot be overestimated. The President's Task Force on Victims of Crime (1982) stated, "The police are often the first on the scene; it is to them, the first source of protection, that the victim first turns" (p. 57). Additionally, the follow-up report, *New Directions in the Field* (Office for Victims of Crime, 1998), stated, "Very often a victim's first view of the criminal justice system is the law enforcement officer who responds to the scene of the crime. It is critical that this officer be well-trained and informed about victims' rights and services. If this officer does not refer the victim to appropriate assistance and compensation programs, that victim may never receive the help needed to heal" (p. 47). Not only do police become the first to connect with crime victims, but also they may be the *only* criminal justice officials to respond (Rosenbaum, 1987). This uniquely important role of the police in crime victims' experiences with the criminal justice system has lasting effects on victims' perceptions of the system.

Over the last 30 years, many victims' rights have been written into state laws. However, there is a serious flaw in virtually all victims' rights laws that have been passed in the United States: when police, prosecutors, and other criminal justice officials violate crime victims' rights, even though these rights are clearly spelled out in the law, it is virtually impossible to hold the officials legally accountable. There are a number of reasons why this is so. Briefly, criminal justice officials in the United States are protected by strong legal immunities. The reason law enforcement officials have been granted immunity from civil redress is the belief that law enforcement officers do not have a duty to an individual person, but to the community at large. If crime victims were allowed to sue the police for failing to protect, then the system would grind to a halt with the lawsuits. There is an avenue to sue law enforcement officials if their actions are grossly negligent or they have established a "special relationship" with the crime victims (see Jerin, 1987). Nevertheless, the Supreme Court made suing governmental workers very difficult with their 1989 decision in the case of **DeShaney v. Winnebago County**. The U.S. Supreme Court ruled that law enforcement has no affirmative obligation to act to protect potential crime victims.

Because the courts refuse to recognize the rights of crime victims, victims are left without any practical legal remedy when law enforcement fails to act, fails to protect, or fails to abide by victims' rights. As a result, when officials violate victims' rights, victims must resort to other means to try to pressurize officials into abiding by the laws. Following each of the rights discussed next, we give some of the specific ways that have worked when officials violate victims' rights.

The police operations that affect crime victims are police response to calls for assistance, thoroughness of investigations, ability to make arrests, recovery of stolen property, protection from future harm, and keeping victims informed of the progress of their cases. As stated by the President's Task Force on Victims of Crime (1982) report, "The manner in which police officers treat a victim affects not only his or her immediate and long-term ability to deal with the event, but also his or her willingness to assist in the prosecution" (p. 57). Since most police operations are reactive (citizen initiated), citizen expectations of police action are very high and often unrealistic. Because most victims have very little contact with the criminal justice system until their victimizations, their expectations are governed by their perceptions of the police that could be based upon what they have seen on television or heard from someone else.

The first impression crime victims have of the police is based on how quickly they respond to calls for assistance. The development of 911 emergency response systems has greatly improved the police-response operation. The new enhanced 911 systems inform the operators of callers' addresses when calls are received. Even with these new systems, it is still up to victims or witnesses to contact the police. Delay in contacting the police has been shown to be responsible for a reduction in the probability of arrest (Bohm and Haley, 2007). However, because of the large number of calls to the emergency 911 number, police have to prioritize calls based upon seriousness of the crimes and threat to the victims.

Many problems still exist even with the more efficient 911 systems. Failure to train operators to recognize or deal with emergencies has created liability for municipalities. Sometimes police have responded to the wrong address, received incorrect information regarding a crime and its seriousness, and been given incomplete information so that a response was impossible (Jerin, 1987). The extensive use of 911 systems by the public has also created additional problems. Some people see the 911 system as a source of information, calling it to get directions or help with noncriminal problems. With the arrival of cellular phones, whenever there is an accident on a major highway, state police communications are swamped with calls, preventing other calls from coming in.

Call screening results in differing responses given the assumed seriousness of a call (Wallace, 1996). Victim–police encounters are governed mostly by the needs of officers, not victims. The police use experience, discretion, preconceptions, and biases to determine a course of action when called to a crime scene. Three factors seem to govern a police–citizen interaction (Cole, 1995). First are the characteristics of the crime, its seriousness, and whether there are any injuries. These factors seem to be the most important for police when deciding how to respond to the crime.

Second is the relationship between the victim and the alleged offender. This is a major determinant in the police perception of seriousness of an offense such as date rape versus stranger sexual assault, child abuse or abduction within a family versus a kidnapping by a stranger, and domestic violence versus stranger assault. Most victims of acquaintance crimes report that law enforcement officers fail to believe their stories or the police attach blame to the victims for their victimization. The relationship between the police and the victim can be strained if the police perceive that the victim is uncooperative or antagonistic toward the officer. If this is the case, it is less likely that the police will pursue a complete investigation. Sometimes the financial situation, race, age, or ethnic origin of a victim may have more to do with the quality of the police response than does the nature of crime itself (Wrobleski and Hess, 1993).

Finally, the policies of local departments in controlling officers' discretion also affect police–victim encounters. Many departments have detailed policy and procedures' manuals that explain what an officer is to do. Policies such as mandatory arrest in domestic violence cases have greatly affected the operations of police agencies and the processing of a criminal event (Sherman, 1984). Crime victims can complain to the administration of a local department if they feel that they are being discriminated against, and they can establish that there is a failure by local officers to follow departmental policies.

VICTIM ASSISTANCE PROGRAMS IN LAW ENFORCEMENT

One of the methods used by law enforcement agencies to improve police–victim interaction is to set up victims' assistance programs within local agencies. Law enforcement–based **victim assistance programs** began on the federal level after the enactment of the **Victim and Witness Protection Act of 1982** (Luthern, 1991). In Washington, DC, the first step toward providing service programs for crime victims was the development of the U.S. Capital Police *Victim-Witness Assistance Manual* (1990). The manual established for the first time the expectations the department has of its officers when interacting with witnesses. The officers now know that they are responsible for providing specific services to crime victims. This type of document is used by many law enforcement agencies throughout the federal system. It provides a standard point of reference for the law enforcer–crime victim interaction. Besides the manual, brochures explaining victims' rights and what is expected in terms of their cooperation are also made available to crime victims. To organize the victims' program, the agencies' specially trained officers represent all shifts and divisions and are available 24 hours a day, 7 days a week. The federal commitment to victims' rights and services in their law enforcement agencies set the stage for state, county, and local agencies to establish their own programs.

State police agencies have also set up victim service units that recognize the special needs and concerns of victims and witnesses of violent crimes and survivors of sudden deaths (New Jersey Department of Law and Public Safety, 1988). Special units administer to the specific needs of victims over the long term. One such unit has been in operation with the Delaware State Police for many years. The *Standard Operation Procedure Manual for Victim Services* establishes the role of the **victim service unit**. The manual states,

    A. The Victim Service Unit will respond to scenes, hospitals, etc. to provide emotional first aid to victims, witnesses, or survivors as requested by investigators.

    B. The Victim Service Unit will provide follow-up services to guarantee the well-being of victims, witnesses, or survivors.

    C. Victim Service Officers will provide referral information to victims, witnesses, or survivors of available resources.

    D. The Victim Service Unit will serve as a support unit to investigation officers.

    E. In the event of death or serious injury to a divisional employee, the Victim Services Unit will be notified to respond to assist with family, friends, and co-workers.

    F. The Unit will also work in cooperation with social service agencies and support groups throughout the state to ensure that the victim/witness/survivor is aware of all services available to help with the traumatic experience.

(Delaware State Police, 1993, 2–3)

These units may also be responsible for providing the training that takes place in police academies for new recruits and the in-service training that goes on for officers already in the field. Other state programs establish minimum numbers of contacts the officers must have to keep victims informed of the progress of their cases. The use of specially trained officers to provide early crisis response, the referral of victims to programs in the community that will help them, and follow-up of case information to victims should have a positive effect on victim cooperation and alleviation of many of the problems crime victims have with law enforcers (Finn and Lee, 1987).

The **National Sheriffs' Association (NSA)** in 1984 established the **Victim Assistance Program (NSAVAP)**. In collaboration with the U.S. Department of Justice Office for Victims of Crime, the NSA started a nationwide effort to bridge the gap between victims' needs and the justice system by assisting sheriffs and their associations to develop and expand victim and witness assistance programs. The NSA conducted many regional and national workshops for members from each state in an effort to expand existing programs and develop new ones. The NSA also developed a training program handbook as a source manual and guide for local departments (Miron et al., 1984). The efforts of the NSA have resulted in the establishment of hundreds of victim advocacy programs throughout the United States.

In 2001, the Office of Victims of Crime came out with a handbook for law enforcement officers providing them with guidelines on how to handle victims of crime in general, and how to handle certain specific victims of crime. This handbook offers law enforcement officers basic guidelines for approaching and interacting with six general categories of crime victims: elderly victims, sexual assault victims, child victims, domestic violence victims, victims of alcohol-related driving crashes, and survivors of homicide. Ideal for reminding officers of their earlier victim training and refreshing their perspective, awareness, and sensitivity toward victims, this handbook is very useful for retraining officers in the in-service setting, at roll calls, and in recertification programs. Also, located in the back of the handbook is a list of national victim resources that includes hotlines and other toll-free numbers to aid officers in helping victims find the resources they need to cope with and recover from their victimization. It has been suggested that placing a copy of this handbook with agency dispatchers would further serve victims of crime as they make telephone contact with law enforcement; the numbers and information would be valuable resources that law enforcement personnel could share with victims. Finally, if a law enforcement agency is without written directives or orders about the proper handling of victims, the handbook could be used as a working model for developing a victim policy for the department. This handbook is a reminder that every victim deserves to be treated with courtesy, respect, and fairness. When victims and law enforcement personnel work together and help each other, the effectiveness of the entire criminal justice system increases (Office for Victims of Crime, 2001).

Circumstances of crimes and crime scenes determine when and how the first responding officers are able to address victims and their needs. The book *First Response to Victims of Crime* recognizes that each crime and crime scene is different and requires officers to prioritize their performance of tasks in each situation (Office for Victims of Crime, 2001). The first recommendation provided by the book is to recognize that officers must attend to many tasks, including assessing medical needs, determining facts and circumstances, advising other personnel, and gathering and distributing suspect information. Apprehension of suspects is the primary duty of law enforcement, and accomplishing this task helps not only suspects' current victims but potential victims as well. Because of this, sometimes the first responders must delay their attendance to the victims if the situation requires. For example, if the crime is ongoing or if the collection of evidence or investigation of the crime is extremely time sensitive, first responders may not be able to direct their immediate attention to the victims. However, as soon as the most urgent and pressing tasks have been addressed, officers must focus their attention on the victims and their needs. At this point, how the officers respond to the victims, explain the competing law enforcement duties, and work with the victims is very important. By approaching victims appropriately, officers will gain their trust and cooperation. Victims may then be more willing to provide detailed information about crimes to officers and later to investigators and prosecutors, which, in turn, will lead to the conviction of more criminals. Remember that officers are there for the victims, and victims are not there for the officers.

Officers can help victims by understanding the three major needs they have after a crime has been committed: the need to feel safe, to express their emotions, and to know "what comes next" after their victimization (Office for Victims of Crime, 2001). The information in *First Response to Victims of Crime* is designed to show the officer how to meet these needs.

TIPS FOR RESPONDING TO VICTIMS' THREE MAJOR NEEDS

People often feel helpless, vulnerable, and frightened by the trauma of their victimization. First response officers can respond to victims' need to feel safe by following these guidelines, provided by the Office for Victims of Crime:

- Introduce yourself to victims by name and title.
- Reassure victims of their safety and your concern by paying close attention to your own words, posture, mannerisms, and tone of voice.
- Ask victims to tell you in just a sentence or two what happened. Ask if they have any physical injuries. Take care of their medical needs first.
- Offer to contact a family member, friend, or crisis counselor for victims.
- Ensure privacy during your interview.
- Ask simple questions that allow victims to make decisions, assert themselves, and regain control over their lives.
- Assure victims of the confidentiality of their comments whenever possible.
- Ask victims about any special concerns or needs they may have.
- Provide a "safety net" for victims before leaving them.
- Give victims—in writing—your name and information on how to reach you.

                                                            (Office for Victims of Crime, 2001, 3–4)

VICTIMS' NEEDS

Victims need to air their emotions and tell their stories after the trauma of a crime. They need to have their feelings accepted and have their stories heard by nonjudgmental listeners. In addition to fear, they may have feelings of self-blame, anger, shame, sadness, or denial. Their most common response is: "I don't believe this happened to me." Emotional distress may surface in seemingly peculiar ways, such as laughter. Sometimes victims feel rage at the sudden, unpredictable, and uncontrollable threat to their safety or lives. This rage can be directed even at the people who are trying to help them, perhaps even at law enforcement officers for not arriving at the scene of the crime sooner.

Victims often have concerns about their role in the investigation of a crime and in the legal proceedings. They may also be concerned about issues such as media attention or payment for healthcare or property damage. Officers can help relieve some of their anxiety by telling victims what to expect in the aftermath of a crime. This will also help prepare them for upcoming stressful events and changes in their lives. Officers can respond to victims' need to know about what comes next after their victimization by following these guidelines:

- Briefly explain law enforcement procedures for tasks such as the filing of your report, the investigation of the crime, and the arrest and arraignment of a suspect.
- Tell victims about subsequent law enforcement interviews or other kinds of interviews they can expect.
- Discuss the general nature of medical forensic examinations the victim will be asked to undergo and the importance of these examinations for law enforcement.

- Explain what specific information from the crime report will be available to news organizations.
- Counsel victims that lapses of concentration, memory losses, depression, and physical ailments are normal reactions for crime victims.

(Office for Victims of Crime, 2001)

STAND-ALONE VICTIM ASSISTANCE PROGRAMS

Local law enforcement departments have also developed stand-alone victim assistance programs. Smaller departments may have specially trained officers or make use of civilian victim advocates. Many larger departments have specific programs for victims of offenses such as spousal abuse, child abuse, and sexual assault.

An example of a police-based victim assistance program can be found in the Howard County (Maryland) Police Department. It recognizes that few events in someone's life are more traumatic than becoming a victim of crime. The Victim Assistance Section (VAS) of the department is staffed with trained personnel to provide crisis intervention, advocacy, and support services to crime victims. Having well-trained individuals providing direct assistance to crime victims at the scene or soon after is a major step forward. Assistance includes emotional support, referral to specific provider agencies for focused follow-up services, assistance with filing court papers and monetary claims, court accompaniment, guidance through the criminal justice process, and evaluation services for referral to trauma debriefing. VAS is staffed with two departmental employees and supplemented with several volunteers (Howard County Police Department, 2008).

State laws have also required the police to recognize the **trauma** that crime victims go through and to treat them with respect. Some examples of this can be found in California, such as:

California Penal Code Section 13730
> Police officers must write a police report on all domestic violence related calls.

California Family Code Section 6228
> Police must give domestic violence victims a free copy of the police report within 5 days of the victim's request.

California Penal Code Section 836 (c)(1)
> Police must arrest the perpetrator on domestic violence restraining order violations.

California Penal Code Section 679.04
> Sexual assault victims have the right to victim advocates and a support person during all police, district attorney, and defense attorney interviews.

Other innovative programs are being implemented on the local level to help crime victims. A Boston program provides cellphones that can only be used to dial 911 to battered women to give them a sense of security (Clinton urges amendment on victims rights, 1996). The only requirements are that they have **restraining orders** against their abusers and that they are willing to testify against them. Many local departments also have programs that provide locks and repair services to homeowners whose houses have been broken into. The establishment of local department-based victim service programs is helping crime victims get through the initial trauma of being victimized and on a road to recovery.

In Richmond, Virginia, an innovative program was established to assist the police, the medical community, and crime victims. The **Cops and Docs program** is a novel approach developed by the Richmond Police Department and local health-care providers to address the cycle of violence by combining the strengths and resources of the various and diverse professional groups affected directly by the problem. The program recognizes that violent crime is not just a law enforcement problem or just a healthcare problem, but a multidisciplinary problem that requires multidisciplinary solutions. In other words, the only meaningful, long-lasting solutions to the problem of violent crimes will come from the cooperation of, and collaboration between, all of the professions directly affected by the problem. Victim interviews, forensic evidence, and meaningful narcotics surveillance data, the common sources of conflict between law enforcement and healthcare providers, can become more readily available to investigators when partnerships are formed with healthcare providers. By working "handcuff-in-glove" to reduce violent crime, "cops" and "docs" can cross the traditional professional boundaries and work together to identify overlapping or even conflicting programming, while developing creative solutions to common problems. Ultimately, each group is able to do its own job better, while helping colleagues on the other side of the crime-scene tape achieve success, as well (McCue et al., 2008).

Cross-training is not only the most visible activity of the Cops and Docs program but perhaps the most valuable (McCue et al., 2008). **Cross-training** is where the health-care providers begin to get an understanding of the unique duties, obligations, and responsibilities associated with careers in law enforcement, and where law enforce-ment officers can gain an understanding of the role that healthcare providers play by "walking a mile in their scrubs." In many cross-training scenarios, however, it is difficult to determine who the teachers are and who the students are. Both groups have found that the opportunity to view their own jobs through the eyes of others can be both enlightening and invigorating.

CONCLUSION

The relationship between victims and the law enforcement function is changing. The victim–police encounter is of the utmost importance for law enforcement agencies and the successful operation of the criminal justice system as well as for crime victims' health and well-being. From the initial response to the closure of a case, how law enforcement meets the needs of crime victims has an enormous impact on survivors and victims, as well as an effect on the successful resolution of the case. Over the past decade, tremendous gains have been achieved by crime victims in how law enforcement agencies at the federal, state, county, and local levels respond to their needs for programs and information. This trend toward greater response by law enforcement agencies to crime victims' needs benefits all parties.

Many victims' service programs are currently in use or are being developed for law enforcement agencies with positive results. The implementation of victim assistance programs in local agencies is beneficial to both crime victims and law enforcement officers. Being able to provide crime victims with immediate services immediately after the victimization is discovered can go a long way toward helping crime victims recover.

Making police understand the importance of their role as first responders and providing them with the training and resources to be as effective as possible will benefit both law enforcement and crime victims.

Study Questions

1. Explain how the reaction of a law enforcement officer to a crime victim can affect the victim and influence the level of cooperation the officer will receive, both on the current case and in future ones.
2. Explain the importance of crime victims to law enforcement agencies when it comes to knowing how much crime occurs and the law enforcement agency's efforts to clear the crime.
3. Because law enforcement officers are usually the first people to interact with crime victims, what should they do to meet victims' needs when they arrive on the scene?
4. Describe some modern-day police-based victim assistance programs. How do these programs provide both short-term and long-term assistance for crime victims?

Key Terms

- arrest   61
- blood feuds   62
- community policing   63
- cops and docs program   77
- cross-training   77
- *DeShaney v. Winnebago County*   71
- Equal Protection Clause   66

- first responder   61
- International Association of Chiefs of Police (IACP)   66
- National Sheriffs' Association (NSA)   73
- Victim and Witness Protection Act of 1982   72
- restraining orders   76

- *Thurman v. City of Torrington*   65
- victim assistance programs   72
- victim service unit   73
- watchmen   63

CHAPTER

Crime Victims and the Courts

INTRODUCTION

The motto over the front entrance to the U.S. Supreme Court states, "Equal Protection Under Law." However, many victims believe that the court systems over the years have provided them with far less than equal protection. Ideally, in the criminal justice system, the courts are entrusted to administer justice for both offenders and crime victims. For many crime victims, this is not the case. Countless crime victims and witnesses have complained for years about how the courts have handled their cases (Neubauer, 1996). While there is a general expectation by the public that the courts will convict individuals of the offenses for which they are charged, in a public trial, rarely is this the case. An offender is more likely to be convicted of a lesser offense through a **plea bargain** or to be set free through a case dismissal than to be convicted of the original charges. A plea bargain is a preconviction deal-making process in which a defendant exchanges a plea of guilty for a reduction in the charges or a promise of sentencing leniency (Siegel, 2008).

Plea bargains have become a necessity for the courts. The only alternative to pleas would be to have all cases go to trial. The outcome of no plea bargaining could be a collapse of the criminal justice system as we know it. Neither option works in the crime victim's favor. As noted by the National District Attorneys Association, "Many citizens have lost faith in the criminal justice system. For years, victims have been treated as mere afterthoughts, expected to be there to testify when needed, but otherwise not informed, not consulted, and not made whole. Indeed, it seems that for many years the only right that a victim had was to be present at the scene of the crime" (U.S. Department of Justice, 1997, 2).

THE AMERICAN CRIMINAL COURT SYSTEM

Many victims feel excluded from decisions concerning the court process. The ability of crime victims to affect the decision making of the courts varies throughout the United States depending upon the various state laws, the training and attitudes of court personnel, the seriousness of the crime, the legal representation of the accused, and the resources of the court. A court is a passive body that relies on the public and police to provide cases. The court's main service to crime victims occurs when suspects have been caught by the police or when victims seek protection from offenders. While victims seek justice or protection from the court, the prosecution seeks cooperation and information from victims to make their cases. The court is also concerned with maintaining an efficient case flow to reduce delays and expenses. Sometimes the needs of courts and the needs of crime victims are in conflict. Victims may fail to cooperate, drop charges, or decide not to testify because of a need to get on with their lives or a belief that the courts are inconvenient and a waste of their time. The courts will seek plea bargains in order to get convictions they might not otherwise get or to reduce case backlog or save limited court resources. Often, the stronger a case is or the better the witnesses are, the easier it is to get offenders to agree to a plea bargain. Often, the more cooperative the crime victims are, the less they will be needed to secure a conviction.

HISTORY OF THE COURTS AND CRIME VICTIMS

In the past, crime victims' wishes provided the foundation for the sanctions that would be handed down by the court against offenders. The amount of punishment, restitution, or other sanction levied upon offenders was determined by the harm done to victims. Law and sanctions provided for restitution to crime victims by offenders or the state for injuries incurred. The decision to prosecute offenders was determined by victims or their survivors. During the American colonial period, the administration of justice was the responsibility of local magistrates who usually were appointed by the governor (Johnson, 1988). The magistrates had sole authority to decide the guilt or innocence of the accused and the sanction to be imposed. As the Revolutionary War was about to begin, concepts of criminal and civil law for the new colonies began to form. Following Blackstone's *Commentaries on the Laws of England* (1765–1769), the new colonies looked to written law to replace judicial opinion. The colonies also held a great respect for individual liberties that became embedded in the Constitution's Bill of Rights and protect individuals from the power of the state (Walker, 1980). During this time, crime victims started to lose their position as influential participants in the criminal justice process. Up until the 1800s, victims not only were responsible for catching offenders but also had to bring them to court and hire prosecutors. Judges were reluctant to imprison offenders, because their labor was needed by the community; however, they did design sanctions that would provide victims with compensation through convicted criminals' labor.

Bringing someone to justice was not easy. The courts met infrequently, so it could be many months before an offender was brought before a court. Many offenders were released on bail, because it was too troublesome for sheriffs to hold them or it cost too much money. Many communities turned to mob violence or vigilantism to seek justice within a reasonable time frame.

With the advent of public prosecutions, the role of victims in deciding who would be prosecuted, what the accused would be prosecuted for, and what sanction would be imposed all but disappeared. Crime victims' role in deciding what would happen to offenders no longer mattered. The needs of the criminal justice system and expediency were all-important.

The court system became a closed enterprise where only the principal players (**judges, prosecutors**, and **defense attorneys**) understood and had input into the operation of the system (Elias, 1986). Plea bargaining became the rule. In many cases, such as rape, victims were treated as defendants, and the concerns of victims and witnesses were ignored. Up until the 1970s, rape victims faced extreme scrutiny and were required to meet difficult standards not found in other laws. Epstein and Langenbahn (1994) found that most state statutes required the following after a rape:

- Prompt reporting, which barred victims' delayed criminal report.
- Cautionary instructions, which admonished jurors to evaluate complainants' testimony with special care because of the difficulty of determining its truth.
- Corroboration by other witnesses.
- Resistance, which required that victims physically resist their attackers.

This situation started to change in the early 1970s as a result of the women's movement and the law-and-order movement. The women's movement challenged the way rape victims and battered women were being treated by the criminal justice system and the courts in particular. Using newfound political power, women sought protection for rape victims by the passage of laws redefining rape and law recognizing marital rape, the elimination of witness corroboration, and the development of rape shield laws.

The law-and-order movement pushed for better law enforcement and prosecution of criminal offenders. Reacting to the offenders' rights movement of the 1960s, conservatives demanded that crime victims have more rights and more say in what happens in their cases. In an effort to increase victim participation in the court to secure more convictions, the establishment of victim-witness assistance offices began to take place in local district attorneys' offices. In the mid-1970s, eight district attorneys had established victim-witness-oriented programs within their offices (Dussich, 1986). During the 1970s, with funds provided by the Law Enforcement Assistance Administration (LEAA), many victim-witness assistance programs were established across the country.

Of great influence on the courts were the recommendations put forth in a report of the 1982 President's Task Force on Victims of Crime. Two sections were devoted to the interaction of crime victims with the courts—Recommendations for Prosecutors and Recommendations for the Judiciary. Prosecutors were encouraged to make crime victims their main focus and concern. The report stressed the need to keep crime victims informed about every step of the way during the court process. The report recommended the following:

- Prosecutors should assume ultimate responsibility for informing victims of the status of a case from the time of the initial charging decision to determinations of parole.
- Prosecutors have an obligation to bring to the attention of the court the views of victims of violent crime on bail decisions, continuances, plea bargains, dismissals, sentencing, and restitution.
- Prosecutors should charge and pursue to the fullest extent of the law defendants who harass, threaten, injure, or otherwise attempt to intimidate or retaliate against victims or witnesses.
- Prosecutors should strongly discourage case continuances.
- Prosecutors' offices should use a victim and witness on-call system.
- Prosecutors' offices should establish procedures to ensure the prompt return of victims' property, absent a need for the actual evidence in court.

- Prosecutors' offices should establish and maintain direct liaison with victim-witness units and other victim service agencies.
- Prosecutors must recognize the profound impact that crimes of sexual violence have on both child and adult victims and their families. (President's Task Force on Victims of Crime, 1982, 63–64)

The recommendations for the judiciary focus on the need for judges to recognize that crime victims have needs and interest at all proceedings of the court—from bail hearings to sentencing. The report establishes that judges need to understand what crime victims are going through. Recognizing that crime victims need to feel secure along with providing for restitution by offenders is also stressed. The report recommended the following:

- It should be mandatory that judges at both the trial and appellate levels participate in a training program addressing the needs and legal interests of crime victims.
- Judges should allow victims and witnesses to be on call for court proceedings.
- Judges or their court administrators should establish separate waiting rooms for prosecution and defense witnesses.
- When ruling on requests for continuances, judges should give the same weight to the interests of victims and witnesses as that given to the interests of defendants.
- Judges should bear their share of responsibility for reducing court congestion and ensuring that all participants fully and responsibly utilize court time.
- Judges should allow for, and give appropriate weight to, input at sentencing from victims of violent crime.
- Judges should order restitution to the victim in all cases in which the victim has suffered financial loss, unless they state compelling reasons for a contrary ruling on the record.
- Judges should allow the victim and a member of the victim's family to attend the trial, even if identified as witnesses, absent a compelling need to the contrary.
- Judges should give substantial weight to the victim's interest in speedy return of property before trial in ruling on the admissibility of photographs of that property.
- Judges should recognize the profound impact that sexual molestation of children has on victims and their families and treat it as a crime that should result in punishment, with treatment available when appropriate. (President's Task Force on Victims of Crime, 1982, 72–73)

CRIME VICTIMS' BILL OF RIGHTS

In 1982, the **Omnibus Victim and Witness Protection Act** (Public Law No. 97–291, 96 Stat. 1248) was passed by Congress and signed into law. This federal law laid the foundation for many states to provide greater protection and recognition of crime victims' needs. The act provided for criminal penalties for the intimidation of crime victims and witnesses by defendants or their associates in federal cases. The act also provided for a crime victims' bill of rights and victims' assistants in prosecutors offices on the federal level, which became a model for many states (Goldstein, 1984).

In the 1980s, crime victims gained rights in state courts. Many states passed **crime victims' bills of rights** that alleged to provide for humane treatment of crime victims by criminal justice personnel, especially in the courts. These legislative enactments directed specific personnel to keep crime victims informed, allow them certain amount of participation, and provide them with information of programs that could offer additional assistance. Most crime victims' bills of rights include

- The right to protection from harm and threats of harm arising from cooperation with peace officers or prosecutors.
- The right to have one's safety and that of one's family taken into consideration when bail is set.
- The right to be informed about court proceedings, including whether they have been canceled or rescheduled.
- The right to information about the progress of the criminal investigation.
- The right to information about procedures in the criminal justice system, including plea bargaining.
- The right to prepare a victim's impact statement.
- The right to be informed about the Crime Victims' Compensation Fund, the payment of certain medical expenses for victims of sexual assault, and the availability of social service agencies that may provide assistance.
- The right to be notified about parole proceedings.
- The right to include information in the defendant's file to be considered by the Board of Pardons and Paroles.
- The right to be present at all public court proceedings related to the offense, if the presiding judge approves.
- The right to a prompt return of property used as evidence.
- The right to notification of the general release of the offender.
- The right to reasonable restitution for the losses incurred (National Organization for Victim Assistance, 1990).

These "bills of rights" were without any teeth. There was initially no enforcement provisions provided to crime victims if these "rights" were not provided to them. It was up to each individual court, prosecutors' office or police department to decide if they were going to provide victims with the information and services requested by the legislatures. Even though crime victims' bills of rights were only guidelines for treatment, the groundwork had been laid for a greater inclusion of crime victims in the courtroom and better treatment by courtroom personnel. Keeping victims informed of the progress of their cases and the ability of crime victims to have their say during key steps in the criminal justice process form the foundation of the victims' bills of rights.

As with law enforcement (see Chapter 4), a major reevaluation of the needs of crime victims and the role the prosecution must engage in occurred with the publication by the Office for Victims of Crime of *New Directions From the Field* (1998). As previously stated, this publication was a follow-up to the groundbreaking President's Task Force Report on Victims of Crime in 1982. *New Directions* set forth 14 major recommendations for prosecutors, based upon the input of participants at numerous public hearings and the efforts of working groups. The recommendations contain policy, procedure, and program reforms that seek to implement better victims' rights and services by prosecutors. The recommendations are excerpted here:

1. Prosecutors' offices should notify victims in a timely manner of the date, time, and location of the following: charging of defendant, pretrial hearings, plea negotiations, the trial, all scheduled changes, and the sentencing hearing. Timely notification, orally or in writing, of advanced scheduling should be provided in relevant languages. Statutes should require

prosecutors to verify notifications with documentation in case files or through another mechanism.

2. Prosecutors should establish victim-witness assistance units to ensure that victims of crime receive at least a basic level of service, including information, notification, consultation, and participation. Prosecutors' offices should develop and incorporate into performance evaluations written definitions of the roles and responsibilities of prosecuting attorneys, victim-witness professionals, and other relevant staff and volunteers.

3. Prosecutors should use the full range of measures at their disposal to ensure that victims and witnesses are protected from intimidation and harassment. These measures include ensuring that victims are informed about safety precautions, advising the court of victims' fears and concerns about safety prior to any bail or bond proceedings, automatically requesting "no-contact" restraining orders and enforcing them if violated, and utilizing witness relocation programs and technology to help protect victims.

4. Prosecutors should address criminal and juvenile justice problems that afflict their communities by exploring the establishment of community prosecution programs as an adjunct to traditional prosecution. Prosecutors should recognize the important role that they can play in reducing crime and should use the authority of their office to support effective crime prevention strategies tailored to the cultures and language needs of their communities

5. Prosecutors should play a central role in establishing multidisciplinary efforts to respond to crime.

6. Prosecutors should advocate for the rights of victims to have their views heard by judges on bail decisions, continuances, plea bargains, dismissals, sentencing, and restitution. Policies and procedures should be put into place in all prosecutors' offices to ensure that victims are informed in a timely manner of these crucial rights in forms of communication they understand.

7. Prosecutors should make every effort, if the victim has provided a current address or telephone number, to consult with the victim on the terms of any negotiated plea, including the acceptance of a plea of guilty or nolo contendere.

8. In all cases, particularly those involving sexual assault, the prosecuting attorney should confer with the victim or survivors before deciding not to file charges or before deciding to seek dismissal of charges already filed.

9. Prosecutors should establish policies to "fast track" the prosecution of sexual assault, domestic violence, elderly and child abuse, and other particularly sensitive cases to shorten the length of time from arrest to disposition. Prosecutors should encourage judges to give top priority to these cases on the trial docket and should try to ensure that the case goes to trial when initially scheduled.

10. Prosecutors' offices should use technology to enhance the implementation of victims' rights.

11. Prosecutors should adopt vertical prosecution for domestic violence, sexual assault, and child abuse cases.

12. Prosecutors should work closely with victim service providers as well as victims of domestic violence to establish appropriate prosecution policies and support research to assess the effectiveness of proceeding without victim testimony in domestic violence cases.

13. Victims' rights and sensitivity education should be provided to all law students as part of their basic education in law school and to all prosecutors during their initial orientation and throughout their careers.

14. Prosecutors' offices should establish procedures to ensure the prompt return of victims' property, absent the need for it as actual evidence in court (1998, 73–93).

Today, courts are looking more at the needs of crime victims to try to improve the operation of the justice system. Most of the recommendations made by the

President's 1982 Task Force Report and the *New Directions From the Field* report have been incorporated into law or policy. Crime victims are becoming more involved in the decision stages of the court, and court officers are being trained to understand and meet the needs of crime victims (Young, 1996). Many programs have been established over the past two decades to meet the needs of crime victims and improve their satisfaction and cooperation with the criminal justice system. However, as of today, there are no national standards or programs for all crime victims, and there are great differences in the way crime victims are treated and included in the court process based upon state laws, court personnel training, and individual considerations.

The inclusion of crime victims in the court process provides many benefits for the criminal justice system. While the level of satisfaction and the benefits for crime victims due to victims' assistance programs are open to various interpretations (McShane and Williams, 1992; Elias, 1993; North Carolina Victim Assistance Network, 1994), they may have more to do with the type and quality of services provided than the program itself (Jerin and Moriarty, 1994).

COURT-BASED CRIME VICTIMS' PROGRAMS

Since an inauspicious beginning during the 1970s, the court-based victim-witness assistance programs have flourished. Starting as privately based programs or as a result of initial funding by the Law Enforcement Assistance Administration (LEAA), the court-based victims' assistance program has become institutionalized in the American court system (Dussich, 1986; Davis and Henley, 1990). In 1974, district attorneys' offices in Brooklyn, New York and Milwaukee, Wisconsin developed the first **victim-witness assistance programs** (National Organization for Victim Assistance, 1993). From this obscure beginning, hundreds of programs are now operational in all the states, employing thousands of people who work with crime victims.

On the federal level, every prosecutor's office houses a victim-witness assistance office and at least one full-time advocate. On the state level, statutes establish the position of **victim-witness assistance advocate** in district attorneys' offices (see National Organization for Victim Assistance, 1990). The different state victim-witness programs offer various services (Finn and Lee, 1987; Jerin and Moriarty, 1994), depending on state statute and personnel. However, most programs have similar goals: to reduce the level of secondary injury associated with the aftermath of crime and to aid in the prosecution of criminal cases by ensuring that crime victims and witnesses are provided with the entitlements and services mandated by victims' bills of rights.

Understanding how victim-witness programs affect the relationship between crime victims and the criminal justice system is important (Elias, 1986, 1993; Davis and Henley, 1990; Kelly, 1990; Luigio, Skogan, and Davis, 1990). Today, the growth of victim-witness assistance programs throughout the United States has resulted in a concerted effort to clearly define the goals, objectives, strategies, and personnel qualifications expected of victim-witness programs and advocates. Most state programs follow policies established by state statutes or state constitutional amendments (see National Organization for Victim Assistance, 1995a). Guidelines (Miron et al., 1984; Finn and Lee, 1987; Young, 1993) are also available to analyze current victim-witness programs.

Two types of programs have been identified: witness-oriented and victim-oriented programs (Finn and Lee, 1987). Witness-oriented programs emphasize the importance of victims as witnesses for prosecution of cases. This type of program focuses on providing the kinds of services necessary for crime victims to become reliable witnesses for the prosecution of offenders. These are the programs found in the prosecution attorneys' offices throughout the United States. Examples of services offered are providing a witness reception area, providing court orientation, providing transportation to and from court, use of a witness-alert program, and case status notification. The focus of these programs is to elicit complete cooperation from crime victims in the prosecution of offenders. Witness-oriented programs seek primarily to serve the needs of prosecutors' offices and the criminal justice system.

Victim-oriented programs seek to provide services to victims. This type of program engages in providing crisis intervention services or information to crime victims. These programs also serve crime victims whose offenders are not caught. Many of these programs are run by nonprofit crime victims organizations such as domestic violence centers or rape crisis centers. Examples of services offered by victim-oriented programs include crisis intervention, follow-up counseling, on-scene comfort, direct financial assistance, and assistance in applying for compensation. These programs put the needs of crime victims first. Young (1993, 137) maintains that "when program goals focus on recovery of the victim, the criminal justice performance is improved." Many programs combine aspects of each orientation depending upon program personnel and statutory mandates.

An example of a victim-orientated victim assistance programs is a legal advocacy program in Essex County, MA. This program provides paid staff and volunteers from the local domestic violence program to the courts to help victims of interpersonal violence obtain restraining orders. The advocates are able to provide confidential counseling, resource referrals, explain the court process and help the victim fill out the paperwork necessary to obtain a restraining order.

The personnel who administrate and run victim assistance programs help decide the direction their programs will take. In many states, when prosecution-based programs were first established, local district attorneys were able to use the new position of victim-witness advocate or victim-witness assistant as a political patronage position and moved legal secretaries and legal assistants into the new position as a reward for faithful service (Jerin, Moriarty, and Gibson, 1992). There were no standards or specific qualifications for the position, only a vague job description. Many programs are still run this way; however, a concerted effort was begun in the early 1990s to provide standards and training for victim-witness assistants (see Young, 1993), and training and educational programs for victim assistant providers are now found throughout the country. The federal Office for Victims of Crime has teamed up with various educational and nonprofit organizations to offer education and training to the professionals in the field. A number of colleges and universities have developed, or are currently developing, programs that allow students and professionals to receive college degrees or credit toward certifications in the crime victim services field. Even graduate programs in victim services are now being developed.

Many positions require candidates to have bachelor's degrees and experience in social services, criminal justice, or other related fields. Positions may also require fluency in a secondary language. What the positions lack are training and adequate salaries. Victim-witness advocates are not adequately compensated for the skills they need or the educational background required of them. A perfect example of this is the

TABLE 5.1   Differential Requirements and Benefits for Victim's Advocates and Correctional Officers

	Victim-Witness Advocate	Correctional Officer
Starting Salary	$25,000	$36,016–$46,325 (range provides for shift differentials, performance bonuses, educational incentives, uniform allowance, physical fitness incentive, and roll-call bonus.)
Education	Bachelor's Degree	Associate's Degree or 60 credits and/or 2 years of military experience
Experience	Experience needed in social services, criminal justice, or related field	None listed
Additional Requirements	Spanish and English fluency; excellent writing and communications skills	None listed
Training Provided	None listed	9-week academy
Job Protection	Serves at the pleasure of the district attorney	Union membership

recent posting of availability of two positions within the same county in Massachusetts for a victim-witness advocate at the local county district attorney's office and one for a correctional officer at the local county jail (see Table 5.1).

While the responsibilities of advocates vary from state to state or even program to program, an excellent example of the services typically carried out by victim-witness advocates is contained in the job description for a prosecution-based victim-witness advocate in Massachusetts:

DUTIES OF THE VICTIM-WITNESS ADVOCATE

The victim-witness advocate provides the following services to victims, witnesses, and their families:

- Information about entitlements and services in accordance with Massachusetts General Law c.258B
- Crisis intervention.
- Orientation to court process.
- Accompaniment to court.
- Referrals to support services.
- Caseload management.
- Data collection.
- Consultation in association with Assistant District Attorneys and other staff.

- Services to victims and witnesses in compliance with the Victim Bill of Rights. Examples are: provide notice of all court events and proceedings; assist with the preparation of a victim impact statement; assist with filing claims for compensation; and help expedite return of property.
- Direct services to victims and witnesses in addition to those enumerated in the Victims' Bill of Rights. Examples are: crisis intervention; referral for appropriate services; orientation to the court process; accompaniment to court; and supportive counseling.
- Case management. Examples are: complete intake and case screening; document case activity; consult with district attorneys on mutual cases; and consult with collateral service providers and criminal justice personnel.
- Public awareness and education. Examples are: provide information and training to criminal justice personnel; foster a cooperative working relationship with the district attorney's staff, courthouse staff, and police and community agencies; and provide and distribute written materials regarding victims' rights and services to victims, criminal justice personnel, and social service agencies (U.S. Department of Justice, Office of the United States Attorney General, 2006, 1–2).

The actual duties performed by advocates vary depending upon their position, program type, background, and the amount of control exerted over them by the prosecutor's office.

FEDERAL VICTIM-WITNESS ADVOCATES

The highest standards for government-based victims' advocates are found at the federal level in the offices of the various U.S. Attorneys. The U.S. Attorney's Office is very committed to protecting the rights of federal crime victims and witnesses. The Attorney General's (2006) *Guidelines for Victim and Witness Assistance* defines a victim as a person who has suffered direct physical, emotional, or pecuniary harm as a result of the commission of a federal crime. If the victim is a nongovernmental institution, such as a bank or corporation, this definition includes a representative of that institution. Government agencies are not considered victims for the purpose of victim services, but federal government employees who are harmed in the performance of their duties are. If the victim is deceased, less than 18 years of age, incompetent, or incapacitated, this definition includes one of the following persons (in order of preference):

- a spouse;
- a legal guardian;
- a parent;
- a child;
- a sibling;
- another family member; or
- another person designated by the court.

A person who is culpable for the crime being investigated or prosecuted is not considered a victim for purposes of victim rights and services.

The Attorney General's *Guidelines for Victim and Witness Assistance* defines *witness* as a person who has information or evidence concerning a crime and provides information regarding his or her knowledge to a law enforcement agency. Where the witness is a minor, the term "witness" includes an appropriate family member or legal guardian. The term does not include a person who is solely a defense witness. The U.S. Attorney's Office Victim and Witness Assistance Program can assist eligible federal crime victims and witnesses with the following:

- Provide information about the status of the case;
- Provide referrals for victims to crisis intervention, counseling, and other assistance services;
- Provide information on victim compensation to victims of violent crime;
- Provide notification, upon request, to the employer of the victim-witness if cooperation in the prosecution of the crime causes absence from work;
- Provide information about submitting written victim impact statements and seeking restitution, and for certain types of cases provide information about making verbal victim impact statements at the sentencing;
- Accompany victims to court for trial and sentencing;
- Register victims with the Federal Bureau of Prisons Victim-Witness Notification Program; and,
- Provide logistical information and assistance to witnesses with respect to directions, transportation, parking, witness fees, and travel reimbursement; assistance with airline and lodging arrangements is provided for out-of-state witnesses (adapted from U.S. Department of Justice, 1997).

STATE DEPARTMENT VICTIMS' PROGRAM FOR TRAVELERS TO OTHER COUNTRIES

The federal government also provides crime victim assistance to citizens victimized while visiting other countries. Specially trained victim advocates can be found in U.S. embassies, consulates, or consular agencies. The Bureau of Consular Affairs, Overseas Citizens Services, is committed to assisting American citizens who become victims of crime while traveling, working, or residing abroad. Government officials, known as consuls or consular officers, at embassies and consulates in nearly 250 cities throughout the world are responsible for assisting U.S. citizens who may be traveling, working, or residing abroad. In addition, in approximately 50 cities where a significant number of Americans reside or visit and there is no U.S. embassy or consulate, consular agents provide emergency assistance to U.S. citizens. Consuls, consular agents, and local employees work with their counterparts in the Bureau of Consular Affairs Overseas Citizens Services Office in Washington, DC to provide emergency and nonemergency services to Americans abroad.

Consular personnel provide various types of assistance to crime victims. When a U.S. citizen becomes the victim of a crime overseas, he or she may suffer physical, emotional, or financial injuries. Additionally, the emotional impact of the crime may be intensified because the victim is in unfamiliar surroundings. The victim may not be near sources of comfort and support, fluent in the local language, or knowledgeable about local laws and customs. Consuls, consular agents, and local employees at overseas posts are familiar with local government agencies and resources in the countries where they work. They can help American crime victims with issues such as

- Replacing a stolen passport;
- Contacting family, friends, or employers;

- Obtaining appropriate medical care;
- Addressing emergency needs that arise as a result of the crime;
- Obtaining general information about the local criminal justice process and information about a case;
- Obtaining information about local resources to assist victims, including foreign crime victim compensation programs;
- Obtaining information about crime victim assistance and compensation programs in the United States; and
- Obtaining a list of local attorneys who speak English (adapted from U.S. Department of State, 2006).

Consular officials cannot, however, investigate crimes, provide legal advice or represent victims in court, serve as official interpreters or translators, or pay legal, medical, or other fees.

EVALUATING VICTIM-WITNESS PROGRAMS

Evaluations of victim-witness assistance programs are rare. Even the evaluations made by state agencies usually examine only the number of clients served and a limited number of services (Tomz and McGillis, 1997). Research more often focuses on describing the organizational structure and functions of assistance programs, with evaluation components being secondary (Cromin and Borque, 1981; Finn and Lee, 1987; Davis and Henley, 1990; Roberts, 1990).

For example, Tomz and McGillis (1997) completed a comprehensive evaluation of crime-witness programs nationwide in terms of victim benefits and criminal justice benefits. Other studies have focused on funding concerns of victim and witness assistance programs (see Anderson and Woodard, 1985; Herrington, 1985; Curriden, 1990; Cullen, 1991). These authors did not conduct full-scale evaluation studies, but they maintained that funding was scarce and often threatened the very existence of the programs.

Finn and Lee (1987) conducted a national study to determine how best to serve crime victims and witnesses. Their research methodology consisted of reviewing the victim-witness program literature to identify the major issues in establishing and directing victim-witness programs. They conferred with a group of experts to determine what services (at a minimum) should be provided to victims and witnesses (see Finn and Lee, 1987, 19, Table 2). Finn and Lee then interviewed the directors of 25 victim-witness programs and conducted site visitations at six locations. They discovered many differences between various programs. In 1994, the 25 program directors were interviewed again (Tomz and McGillis, 1997), and program variation still existed.

Roberts (1990) conducted a national survey to establish the background, functions, and services of victim-witness assistance programs. He developed a list of services provided by the responding agencies in his research. He administered a self-evaluation on the strengths and weaknesses of each program. The major strengths of the responding programs can be grouped into five main categories: comprehensive services/specialized services; court support, advocacy, and/or court escort; referrals and interagency linkages; case information and status; and use of trained and dedicated staff and/or volunteers.

The three major weaknesses he found were insufficient funding, lack of space, and attrition of volunteers.

Other types of evaluations of programs have come from surveying victim satisfaction (North Carolina Victim Assistance Network, 1994). These studies pointed out the strengths and weaknesses of a program according to the crime victims who participated in the criminal justice system. Most victims expressed positive views of the programs but wished that more services were offered and that the court process could be shortened. Additional victims' services are being developed in courts. Many courts and victim-witness offices have established specialized units to handle specific crime victims. It is not unusual to find domestic violence units with their own victims' advocates housed in courthouses. Other specialized units or advocates also exist for victims of sexual violence and for children who become victims of criminal violence. The tremendous growth of victim-witness advocacy programs in courts continues, especially in the area of reducing the amount of secondary victimization inflicted upon crime victims by the criminal justice process.

CRIME VICTIMS AND THE JUDICIARY

The importance of the role judges play in assuring crime victims their rights cannot be underestimated. The President's Task Force on Victims of Crime (1982) recommended that the judiciary consider the plight of crime victims and ensure that victims' rights are considered alongside defendants' rights. The rights that victims seek do not try to reduce the rights of defendants. Instead, crime victims focus on how the criminal justice system can keep them better informed and more included in the criminal justice process. As noted, "Addressing these concerns requires a fundamental shift in viewpoint to allow judges and other court personnel to see the protection of victims' rights and services under law not as 'special,' but as appropriate and just" (Office for Victims of Crime, 1998, 97).

Based upon the President's Task Force Report, new efforts to train judges, prosecutors, and other court personnel did occur across the United States. The issues of judges taking an active role in assuring that victims receive equitable treatment was formalized in 1983 at the National Conference of the Judiciary on the Rights of Victims of Crime held at the National Judicial College. The conference was attended by judges from all 50 states; they were encouraged to take the lead in improving the treatment of crime victims by the criminal justice system. The conference concluded by stating: "Victims of crime should not be victims of the criminal justice system" (Nicholson, 1992, 817).

In Massachusetts, the Judicial Institute is charged with providing professional development and training for courtroom employees. In fiscal year 1995, the institute provided more than 23,000 hours of professional training and development to nearly 2,400 judges and other court employees. Included in these educational programs was the second phase of the Domestic Violence Education Project, which included the All Court Conference on Family Violence and workshops on holding trials without victims' testimony. Additional training programs to increase participants' sensitivity to the nature of domestic violence and its effects on victims and children were also conducted (State of Massachusetts, 1995). This effort has continued to grow.

However, the *New Directions* report still saw a need for a greater role of the **judiciary** to implement victims' rights laws and to assure fair treatment for crime victims. To this end, the report put forth the following 14 recommendations for the judiciary:

1. The voices and concerns of crime victims should be recognized and institutionalized within the justice system.

2. Judges and all court personnel at all levels of the court system must receive initial and continuing education on the law concerning victims' rights, the impact of crime on victims and their families, and how the judiciary can implement the spirit as well as the letter of these rights.

3. Judges should facilitate the rights of crime victims and their families to be present at court proceedings unless the defendant proves that their presence would interfere with the defendant's right to a fair trial.

4. Judges should consider victim and community safety in any prerelease or post-release decision.

5. Before imposing a sentence, judges should permit the victim, the victim's representative, or, when appropriate, representatives of the community, to present a victim impact statement.

6. Judges should facilitate the input of crime victims into plea agreements and resulting sentences, and they should request that prosecuting attorneys demonstrate that reasonable efforts were made to confer with the victim.

7. As leaders within the justice system, judges must ensure that victims' rights legislation is fully implemented.

8. Judges should play a leadership role in ensuring that police, prosecutors, defense counsel, judges and court administrators receive joint training so that all have a comprehensive picture of what happens to a victim as he or she navigates through the criminal justice system.

9. Judges have a responsibility to manage their cases and calendars to make victim involvement as feasible as possible.

10. Judges should order restitution from offenders to help compensate victims for the harm they have suffered.

11. Judges should play a leadership role in ensuring that separate and secure waiting areas are available in all courthouses for prosecution and defense witnesses to minimize the contact of victims with defendants, their relatives, and friends before, during and immediately after court proceedings.

12. Codes of Judicial Conduct should be amended to reflect the fact that crime victims play a pivotal role in the criminal justice system.

13. Judicial assignments to specialized courts or family law or juvenile courts should be based on experience and interest, not on lack of seniority or punishment.

14. Judges must take a leadership role in conceptualizing and advocating that the justice system encompasses not only traditional adjudication and punishment, but also holistic problem solving and treatment for victims as well as offenders. Principles of restorative community justice and therapeutic jurisprudence should be incorporated into court systems with due regard for differing cultures and ethnic groups (Office for Victims of Crime, 1998, 104–115).

VICTIM IMPACT STATEMENTS

In 1973, the first **victim impact statement (VIS)** was created by James Rowland, the chief probation officer in Fresno County, California. The goal was to provide the court with an objective listing of injuries suffered by crime victims before sentencing (National Organization for Victim Assistance, 1993; Alexander and Lord,

1994). The VIS can be delivered in different forms and can contain many different kinds of information. Generally, a VIS allows crime victims or their survivors to inform the court of the impact of the crime upon their lives. Impact can be financial, emotional, psychological, physical, or mental. The method of providing the court with this information varies depending on state statutes. The most common method is a written statement submitted to the court at sentencing or with the presentence investigation report. Many states also allow victims to present oral statements at sentencing.

Since 1973, states have by statute required that a VIS become part of the record at sentencing if the victim chooses to make one (see National Organization for Victim Assistance, 1990). An example of the statutory establishment can be found in South Carolina's victims' bill of rights:

> It is the responsibility of the solicitor's victim or witness assistance unit in each judicial circuit or a representative designated by the solicitor or law enforcement agency handling the case to advise all victims of their right to submit to the court, orally or in writing at the victim's option, a victim impact statement (S. C. Code Annotated 16-3-1550(b)).

In 1982, the President's Task Force report proposed that legislation be enacted that "requires victim impact statements at sentencing" (p. 18). The purpose of the VIS is to provide crime victims with a sense of participation in the system and to make sure that the courts have all the information necessary to determine the appropriate sentence. While many legal scholars question whether this information creates a bias against offenders, victims' advocates argue that no sentence should be determined unless the amount of harm done to the crime victim is known (Alicke and Davis, 1989; Erez, 1990; Polito, 1990; Field, 1991; Erez and Tontodonato, 1992; Sperry, 1992; Alexander and Lord, 1994). This recommendation has been enacted by all states and the federal government.

Questions concerning the constitutionality of the VIS or of providing information concerning the crime victim at the sentencing stage have been the subject of three separate U.S. Supreme Court cases. The Court first examined the issue of VIS in 1987 in *Booth v. Maryland.* An elderly couple was bound, gagged, and repeatedly stabbed during a robbery attempt at their home. A neighbor, John Booth, was arrested and convicted of first-degree murder. For the presentence investigation report, the couple's children and grandchild were interviewed, and they provided detailed information on how the crimes had affected their lives. As a result of the evidence presented during the sentencing hearing, the jury sentenced Booth to death. In a 5–4 decision, the Supreme Court ruled that the Maryland statute that required the presentence investigation report to include a VIS describing how the crime affected the victims and the victims' family violated the Eight Amendment. The majority opinion concluded that the VIS was irrelevant to an offender's culpability and that a VIS "creates the risk of arbitrary and capricious decisions to impose the death sentence and thus violates the Eight Amendment" (Sperry, 1992, 1284). The four dissenting justices argued that it should be left up to the states to decide and that disallowing VISs in sentencing silences victims.

The second case to rule on the admissibility of crime victim information during sentencing occurred in 1989 in *South Carolina v. Gathers.* In *Gathers,* the court examined not the question of the VIS but the introduction of evidence by the prosecutor relating to the crime victim's character and his value to the community.

This was another capital murder case where the defendant was convicted of first-degree murder "for beating, kicking, sexually assaulting, and stabbing to death, Richard Haynes" (Sperry, 1992, 1288–1289) and sentenced to death. Using *Booth* as the controlling opinion that the VIS may create an arbitrary sentence, the Court in a 5–4 decision ruled against the state of South Carolina and sent the case back to the trial court for a new sentencing hearing. The Court reasoned that there was no difference between a prosecutor presenting information concerning the victim, or it being provided by a VIS. While decisions in both *Booth* and *Gathers* concerned only capital punishment cases, the constitutionality of the VIS in all cases was very much in doubt.

The Supreme Court has seemed to eliminate any question as to the constitutionality of the VIS in all cases, even capital cases, with its decision in 1991 in *Payne v. Tennessee*. In a 7–2 decision, the U.S. Supreme Court overruled its previous decisions in *Booth* and *Gathers* and found that providing information concerning the victim by the prosecutor or through the use of a VIS does *not* violate the Eighth Amendment (Alexander and Lord, 1994). In this case, Pervis Payne was convicted of two counts of first-degree murder and one count of assault for the stabbing deaths of a mother and her 2-year-old daughter and the wounding of her 3-year-old son. During the sentencing hearing, the grandmother testified as to the effects the murders had upon her 3-year-old grandson. Additionally, the prosecutor included references to the pain and suffering the families of the victims incurred and the loss suffered by the young child (Field, 1991). The Court in so holding recognized that crime victims have a right to be heard during the sentencing phase. In its decision, the Court quoted from a 1934 case in which Justice Cardozo wrote: "Justice, though due to the accused, is due to the accuser also. The concept of fairness must not be strained till it is narrowed to a filament. We are to keep the balance true" (Sperry, 1992, 1296).

While the ideal of victim impact statements is to help in the restoration of crime victims, there can be many problems achieving this goal. The first problem lies with the timing of the impact statement. Of the amount of violent crime that occurs each year, less than 50 percent is reported to the police and of that amount only about 20 percent result in offenders being identified, arrested, or prosecuted (Bureau of Justice Statistics, 1996). Of those prosecuted, most agree to plea bargains that can include sentence recommendations, making victims' input minimal at best. This leaves the vast majority of crime victims without an outlet in the criminal justice process to express feelings concerning their victimization or the appropriate sanctions necessary for them to achieve restoration.

Even crime victims whose offenders are arrested, tried, and convicted fail to use the victim impact statement (Kelley, 1984; Erez and Tontodonato, 1992; National Organization for Victim Assistance, 1992; Alexander and Lord, 1994). There are many reasons why crime victims fail to use this right. In a study (Alexander and Lord, 1994) by Mothers Against Drunk Drivers (MADD), victim impact statements from over 20 states were reviewed in an effort to uncover whether there were problems with the forms themselves that contributed to their lack of use by crime victims. MADD identified multiple problems:

- *Indifferent Forms.* Crime victims are already overwhelmed with the number of forms generated as a result of crime including: police reports, medical forms, insurance claim forms, and crime victim compensation reimbursements.
- *Using the Victim Impact Statement Primarily as a Restitution Document.* Many victims are insulted that the criminal justice system would ask about the financial outlays first and ask about the victim's emotional loss last, as if it were merely an afterthought.

- *Limited Explanation and Instructions.* Many of the victim impact statement forms reviewed contained no explanation as to the purpose of the form, how it is used, confidentiality issues addressing who will have access to the form, and why the victim should even complete a victim impact statement.
- *Additional Concerns Identified.* The use of the form does not address the needs of the victim who does not read well or read at all, nor does it allow for the needs of a culturally diverse population (Alexander and Lord, 1994, 44).

Additional problems have also been identified. Some crime victims receive the forms in the mail only after indictments have been handed down in their cases. The time period from their victimization until they receive the forms can vary from a few days to many months after the crimes occur (Jerin, Moriarty, and Gibson, 1995). Another problem is that the use of victim impact statements in juvenile cases is minimal. With the increasing amount of juvenile violent crime, the exclusion of so many crime victims from participation in the process can only create a revictimization of the crime victims by the criminal justice system.

In an effort to eliminate these problems and increase the participation of crime victims in the criminal justice process, Alexander and Lord's national study on victim impact statements offered eight national recommendations:

1. The criminal justice system must adapt policies which allow crime victims to play an integral role in the American criminal justice process.
2. Legislation shall be enacted or amended at the federal, state, and local levels to provide crime victims with the right to submit victim impact statements by written, oral, video, audio or other electronic means at the time of sentencing and parole.
3. Legislation shall be drafted and enacted at the federal, state, and local levels that provides victims of juvenile crime with the right to submit victim impact information at the time of adjudication.
4. Legislation shall be enacted that delegates specific authority, roles, and responsibilities at the federal, state, and local levels for the distribution, collection, and dissemination of victim impact statements.
5. All criminal justice professionals who influence the victim impact statement procedure in any way must have a thorough understanding of their state's statutes and case law regarding the submission and use of victim impact statement.
6. All agencies that interact with crime victims should have victim impact statements, instruments, and supplementary guides that explain to victims the importance of victim impact statements, their right to submit one, and the criminal justice system's use of victim impact statement.
7. Statewide victim networks, coalitions, and criminal justice agencies shall join together to evaluate the effectiveness of their victim impact statement statute and, if it is inadequate, work together to amend it.
8. Training and continuing education on the traumatic effects of crime victimization must be made available to all criminal justice professionals who interact with crime victims (1994, 6–8).

Courts in recent years have shown a willingness to allow greater participation for crime victims, and the trend should continue. Victim impact statements, restitution, and victim participation are now well entrenched in the criminal justice system.

One area the courts will continue to evaluate is deciding what remedies will be available to crime victims if there is a failure to enforce their rights. The issue of liability of criminal justice personnel for failure to protect (see Jerin, 1988a) or to provide specifically requested services will come to the forefront in the near future. As more rights are granted to crime victims, remedies must be provided within the legal system to enforce those rights. Only two states (Connecticut and Alaska) have established Offices of the Victim Advocate, which have legal standing to go into court to demand that victims' rights be enforced. Other states use ombudsmen or committees and boards, but the ability to impose consequences on offending agencies or officials varies greatly from state to state. Crime victim litigation against the criminal justice system and its personnel may become more commonplace until the system adjusts to a new crime victim orientation instead of the self-serving orientation it still has.

CIVIL COURTS AND CRIME VICTIMS

The civil courts provide another avenue for crime victims to seek redress for the criminal violence against them. While the extent of crime victims' "rights" is still very fluid (see Chapter 1), there is one area of victims' rights that continues to be expanded upon—**tort liability**. A **tort** is any civil crime or wrongful act. Crime victims can seek the protection of the Court through the use of a civil process known as a **restraining order** or an **order of protection** (see Appendix C). In addition, any crime victim harmed by a criminal act has the right to sue the offender. Crime victims may also be able to sue third parties to recover financial compensation in addition to making offenders pay or in lieu of offenders being able to pay. In many cases, other parties may be partially responsible for the victimization either through an overt act or by failing to provide an adequate amount of protection.

RIGHT TO SUE

The right of crime victims to sue is based upon the civil law. Civil law focuses upon disputes between private parties or entities (Gaines and Miller, 2006). Regardless of the outcome of criminal prosecutions, or even if there was no prosecution, crime victims can file civil actions or lawsuits against offenders and other responsible parties. Unlike the criminal justice process, the civil justice system does not attempt to determine offenders' guilt or innocence. Offenders are also not put in prison. Rather, civil courts attempt to determine whether offenders or third parties are responsible or liable for the injuries or harm sustained and whether or not the victim needs to be protected or compensated for their harm.

THE CIVIL JUSTICE SYSTEM

There are many differences between the criminal and civil court systems (see Table 5.2). In civil cases, victims control all the essential decisions shaping a case. In civil cases, the **plaintiffs** are those who bring cases, who may be victims, survivors of the victims, or persons responsible for the victims. It is the plaintiffs who decide whether to sue, accept a settlement offer, or go to trial. For crime victims to win a judgment against accused parties, they must establish that there was harm done and that the accused parties had a

TABLE 5.2   Difference Between Civil Trial and Criminal Trial

	Civil Trial	*Criminal Trial*
Goal	Hold defendant accountable to the victim	Hold defendant accountable to the State
Who is in Control?	The victim controls the case and decides whom to sue and for how much	State controls the case and decides the charges and whether or not to prosecute
Role of the Victim	The victim is a party to the lawsuit and, as such, is entitled to all important information relating to the case	The victim is treated as a witness or piece of evidence if needed
Standing	Victim—plaintiff Offender—defendant	Victim—none or witness Offender—accused
Burden of Proof	On the plaintiff	On the State
Level of Proof	Preponderance of the evidence (51% sure)	Beyond a reasonable doubt (90–95% sure)
Jury Agreement	Usually a majority	Usually unanimous
Treatment of Offender	Seen as an equal party	Presumed innocent
Right to an Attorney	Must provide your own	Provided by the State if the defendant can't afford one
Who can be Tried?	Offenders and "third-party" defendants	Offenders and conspirators
Who must Testify?	Both parties must testify	Defendant can decide not to testify
If Defendant is Found Guilty	The defendant owes an obligation to the victim, such as money, or receives an injunction which prevents certain actions	The defendant is subject to punishment, such as fines, probation, or incarceration, and is held accountable to the State
Limitations of Prosecutions	The victim can sue the perpetrator in a civil court even if found not guilty in a criminal prosecution	If the defendant is found not guilty, the State cannot try the person again
Compensation	Compensation for out-of-pocket and non-economic damages as well as punitive damages	Restitution of out-of-pocket expenses if court orders

Source: Adapted from National Crime Victim Bar Association (2001). [Civil Justice for Victims of Crime. National Center for Victims of Crime.]

duty to not create the harm or prevent the harm, the duty was breached, the **defendants** caused the plaintiffs' harm, and the extent of the harm was enough to establish liability. The civil justice system often provides victims and their families with a sense of justice that criminal courts fail to provide. Rather than holding defendants accountable for their "crimes against the state," the civil justice system holds defendants who are found liable directly accountable to their victims (National Crime Victim Bar Association, 2001).

In the civil justice system, the **burden of proof** is very different than in the criminal justice system. In the civil justice system, liability must be proven by a **preponderance of the evidence**, which simply means that one side's evidence is more persuasive than the other's. In other words, plaintiffs must prove there is a 51 percent or greater chance that the defendants committed all the elements of the particular wrong. This standard is far lower than the proof "**beyond a reasonable doubt**" required for a conviction in the criminal justice system. For juries or judges to convict defendants in the criminal courts, they must be convinced to a point of 90–95 percent assuredness (Bohm and Haley, 2007). Therefore, sometimes defendants are found liable in civil cases even though verdicts of "not guilty" were rendered in the criminal cases. A civil case can also be successful even if the offender was never prosecuted.

If defendants are found civilly liable, courts may order them to pay monetary damages to victims. While money awarded in civil lawsuits can never fully compensate victims for the trauma of victimization or the loss of loved ones, it can be a valuable resource to help crime victims rebuild their lives. Moreover, the exposure to civil liability is a powerful incentive for landlords, businessmen, and other proprietors to enact the security measures necessary to prevent future victimizations.

A good example of the difference between the criminal and civil justice systems is the O. J. Simpson case (see Chapter 7 for more information). Simpson was prosecuted for the murder of his former wife, Nicole Brown, and her friend, Ron Goldman. In 1995, the jury in the criminal case found O. J. Simpson "not guilty" of the murders. O. J. Simpson was not required to testify during the year-long trial. Despite Simpson's acquittal, the families of Nicole Brown and Ron Goldman filed a civil wrongful death lawsuit against Simpson. A trial was held in 1997; O. J. Simpson was required to testify and was cross-examined by the Goldmans' attorney. Even though O. J. maintained his innocence, the jury did not believe him. In this case, Simpson was found liable for the deaths of Brown and Goldman. The jury in the civil case awarded the victims' families $33.5 million in **compensatory** and **punitive** damages. Compensatory damages are provided for actual, current, and future losses; and punitive damages are awarded to punish the defendant for their actions. While a criminal conviction may increase the chances of a perpetrator being held civilly liable, it is not a requirement for bringing a civil action (National Crime Victim Bar Association, 2001).

RESTRAINING ORDERS

Restraining Orders, also known as Abuse-Prevention Orders, Stay-Away Orders, or simply Prevention Orders, are **civil injunctions** or orders from a court which seeks to protect individuals from further physical harm or harassment. A victim can ask the court to require the offender to stay away from them and to stop harassing them. The Order enjoins or prohibits the defendant from harming or harassing the victim by establishing limitation on the defendant actions as they relate to the victim. Such limitations can include any further physical or sexual assault, threats, contacting the victims, leaving the home, contacting the victim through third parties, and even sending cards and flowers. While the order from the court is civil, any reported violation of the court's order is a criminal violation for which the offender will be held responsible in the criminal justice system. In most jurisdictions, the victim and offender must have an interpersonal relationship. This relationship can be from their spouse or intimate partner, ex-spouse or partner, child's biological parent, relative by blood or marriage or current or former roommate. The victims who ask the court for a restraining order must have also been physically injured, or are in fear of imminent harm from this person, or have been forced to engage in unwanted sexual relationships.

The courts issue two types of restraining orders, the emergency temporary order and the extended order. The emergency temporary order is granted by a municipal official based only upon the victim's testimony and can even be granted when the court is not in session. A victim can request an emergency restraining order from a magistrate at night and on weekends with the help of law enforcement which, if issued, prevents the defendant from coming near the victim. This order is only good until the next court session or for a limited time until both parties can be heard on the matter. The extended order is issued either when both parties come before a magistrate; the magistrate hears both sides and determines that a restraining order is necessary, or the victim comes before the magistrate and the defendant fails to show up even though the defendant has been given notice of the proceedings. The extended order is for a set period of time, usually for 6 months to a year, but in very serious cases the order can be made permanent.

CONCLUSION

Actively helping crime victims through the trauma of their victimization and reducing or eliminating the secondary victimization of innocent victims by the criminal justice system are the matters of importance in programs for crime victims in the courts. Over the past few decades since the first victim-witness assistance programs began, the movement has grown to include hundreds of programs in all 50 states, in the federal justice system, and even overseas. State crime victims' bills of rights provide the foundation for greater responsibility of criminal justice personnel for meeting the needs of crime victims.

A new participant, the victim-witness advocate, is now directly involved with helping crime victims recover from their victimization. While the position of victim advocate has been recognized as vitally important for assisting crime victims, the position is underfunded. The courts are also allowing crime victims greater participation and voice in the decision-making process that takes place in the courts. While there needs to be better continuity of services offered to assure that crime victims receive the treatment they require, continuation of educating the public and the personnel who work with crime victims and establishment of standards for service providers should alleviate much of the suffering crime victims have been subject to within the criminal justice system.

Last, crime victims have their own avenue to seek restoration for the victimization inflicted upon them: the civil justice system. In the civil justice system, crime victims are in control and are the decision makers. The civil justice system provides crime victims the opportunity to receive compensation for economic and noneconomic damages and to have defendants punished for their actions, even if the criminal justice system fails to do so.

Study Questions

1. How have crime victims been historically treated by the court system as compared to how they are treated today?
2. Explain the qualifications and the duties of a court-based victim-witness advocate and how the role of the victim-witness advocate helps crime victims recover from their victimization and prevents further victimization by the system.
3. Describe the importance of victim impact statements to the sentencing process and to the crime victim. What is the history of the victim impact statement?
4. Explain how the civil court process is different than the criminal court process for the crime victim. How can the crime victim seek justice in the civil courts?

Key Terms

- accused   79
- beyond a reasonable doubt   98
- burden of proof   98
- civil injunctions   98
- compensatory damages   98
- crime victims' bill of rights   82
- defendant   97
- defense attorneys   80

- judges   80
- judiciary   92
- Omnibus Victim and Witness Protection Act (1982)   82
- order of protection   96
- plaintiff   96
- plea bargain   79
- punitive damages   98
- preponderance of the evidence   98
- prosecutors   80

- restraining order   96
- tort   96
- tort liability   96
- victim impact statement (VIS)   92
- victim-witness assistant   86
- victim-witness programs or victim assistance programs   85
- witness-alert program   86

CHAPTER

Crime Victims, Corrections, and Restorative Justice

6

INTRODUCTION

Once a conviction is obtained, the correctional stage of the criminal justice process begins. The first step is to determine appropriate sanction for offenders convicted of crimes. Sentences given to those convicted of offenses serve many goals. The five goals used to justify contemporary sentencing policies are: (1) retribution, (2) incapacitation, (3) deterrence, (4) rehabilitation, and (5) **victim restoration** (Gaines and Miller, 2006). While differing goals are not mutually exclusive, this chapter focuses on both victim restoration and offender rehabilitation.

The concepts of victim restoration and offender rehabilitation are not mutually exclusive. They can coexist to benefit both parties. Crime victims seek restoration of the lives they had before the victimization occurred. If the offenders can be rehabilitated, future victimizations will not take place. These endeavors are complicated by physical and emotional scars, financial and psychological losses, and destruction of the sense of security resulting from criminal victimization. For offenders to become rehabilitated individual and social, changes need to take place. Crime victims becoming "whole again" also depends upon many factors. Two important factors are the beliefs that some level of justice has been achieved and that adequate compensation for losses suffered has been made.

JUSTICE AND RESTORATION

The ideal of **justice** is elusive, but its central components are: fairness, equality, and appropriate rewards or punishments (Pollock, 1994). The criminal justice system in the United States seeks to obtain justice during the sanctioning stage of this process. However, many question whether society's justice is also crime victims' justice (Hellerstein, 1989; Erez, 1990; Polito, 1990). Determination of appropriate sentencing for offenses committed is used to establish a sense of justice within society. However, if the crime victim is to achieve **restoration**, they should be reinstated to their original condition, that is, the condition before the victimization even occurred. Allowing crime victims a say in appropriate sentencing, based upon the amount of harm and loss incurred, is a way to achieve a level of justice for crime victims, but not restoration. Having offenders receive their "**just desserts**," or sanctions proportional to the amount of harm incurred, is necessary if society and crime victims are to believe justice has been done (Von Hirsch, 1976; Starkweather, 1992).

The method of financial remuneration for losses incurred is generally referred to as **compensation.** In the criminal justice system, there are two methods by which crime victims can receive financial remuneration: offender restitution and government-sponsored crime victims' compensation programs. **Restitution** is the payment of money or services by offenders to crime victims or the community to replace what was lost as a result of a criminal offense. Compensation, on the other hand, is the provision of monies by the government directly to crime victims or their survivors to lessen the financial impact of a crime upon them.

Justice for crime victims, or their surviving family members, is focused on returning victims to the positions they were in before the victimization occurred, or, in the case of a homicide, providing compensation for loss that has been incurred. The role the criminal justice system plays in providing justice for crime victims is multifaceted. This chapter focuses on the traditional role crime victims have in the correctional process, the development and use of victim impact statements (VIS), the use of restitution, and state-sponsored crime victim compensation programs.

HISTORY OF CRIME VICTIMS AND CORRECTIONS

Survivors of criminal offenses suffer many losses for which complete healing is impossible, but efforts by the criminal justice system, in trying to achieve restoration, have been the foundation for sanctions throughout history. Providing restoration for victims of crimes, as a matter of correctional policy or principle, enjoys an ancient history dating back to the Babylonian Code of Hammurabi about four thousand years ago (Ramker and Meagher, 1982). Other ancient cultures also recognized the need to provide restoration for injuries and loss of property. Early Germanic common law had a system of "composition"— payments by offenders to victims. In Greece, there was a death fine; in early Hebrew cultures, restitution; and the Bible and Islamic law both provided restitution for criminal acts against individuals (Schafer, 1970).

The early English system provided for paying **bots** to either injured victims or their families. Payment depended on a schedule of tariffs based on the amount of injury done. In addition to bots paid to crime victims, additional fines called *wites* were paid to the king, or his representative, for administering the settlement between offenders and crime victims (Schafer, 1977). Crime victims experienced a "decline" in influence during the twelfth and thirteenth centuries, when a greater share of the amount paid by offenders went to pay wites or fines, and crime victims were left to seek reparation through the civil courts (Schafer, 1977). The king replaced individual crime victims as the injured party, assumed responsibility for bringing offenders to justice, and decided the punishment. It is argued that while victims lost the right to compensation, they more than made up for that loss by gaining the advantage of being represented by the power of the state (Greenbery, 1984).

The early American system of corrections borrowed extensively from the English system. The concept of crimes against society and not against individuals became part of early American jurisprudence. The early American system used public humiliation, banishment, branding, mutilation, corporal punishment, and the death penalty. However, victims were included in the initial formation of the American justice system. Before the American Revolution, it was an accepted practice to sentence an offender to "serve his victim, in labor, for a period of time proportional to the magnitude of his crime" (Johnson, 1988, 149). Additionally, in 1785, the Virginia Assembly, in rewriting its criminal laws, provided for restitution in addition to prison sentences for property crimes.

As the American system moved toward imprisoning offenders, crime victims' need for restoration fell by the wayside. The development of long-term imprisonment as a sanction for criminal offenses began in 1790 when Philadelphia's Walnut Street Jail was converted into a penitentiary. The use and objectives of incarceration as a sanction became focused on offenders. First, the penitentiary system sought to rehabilitate offenders through solitary confinement. Next, the Auburn system came into effect in the early 1800s as an effort to provide more humane conditions at a lower cost to the government. By the latter part of the nineteenth century, correctional systems sought greater reform for inmates through the development of a reformatory system (Gaines and Miller, 2006). While new programs and policies such as indeterminate sentences, parole, education, and providing work-related skills to inmates were advanced, no efforts were directed at improving the conditions of offenders' victims. As Schafer noted, "History suggests that growing interest in the reformation of the criminal is matched by decreasing care for the victim" (1970, 12). Efforts at trying to reform, rehabilitate, punish, and reintegrate offenders through corrections continue to the present day, with crime victims becoming part of the process only in the last quarter century.

CORRECTIONAL VICTIMS' PROGRAMS

Historically, little attention has been given to the role of corrections in providing services and programs that benefit crime victims. The traditional role of corrections has been to provide programs and supervision of offenders; victims were not part of the equation. As in the rest of the criminal justice system during the 1980s, corrections started to take positive steps to provide needed assistance to crime victims. The initial steps taken by correctional agencies came as a result of leadership from the American Correctional Association (Office for Victims of Crime, 1998). In the mid-1980s the American Correctional Association published a landmark policy statement establishing that crime victims have the right to be treated with dignity and respect and the right to notification of their offenders' status. The Association went even further to publish recommendations to improve correctional-based victims' services (National Center for Victims of Crime, 1999).

During the 1990s, corrections took steps to train their personnel to improve victims' services and to develop programs directed at crime victims' needs. One of the first objectives was to provide training and technical assistance to the correctional systems to support the development of policies and procedures to initiate or enhance correctional-based crime victims' services. This effort was supported by the Office for Victims of Crime (OVC), which supplied resources to provide the necessary assistance to the federal and military correctional systems along with more than 40 states.

In 1998, the OVC published 15 recommendations for correctional agencies to use with their progress to provide a crime victim orientation to the correctional process:

1. Adult and juvenile correctional agencies should open channels of communication with the community and with crime victims.
2. Correctional agencies should designate staff to provide information, assistance, and referrals to victims of crime.

3. Mission statements guiding adult and juvenile correctional agencies and paroling authorities should recognize victims as an important constituency and address victims' rights and services.

4. Correctional agencies should notify victims, upon their request, of any change in the status of offenders, including clemency or pardon, which would allow them to have access to the community or to the victims themselves.

5. Correctional agencies should place a high priority on ensuring the protection of victims from inmate intimidation, threats, or physical or other harm from offenders under their supervision.

6. Correctional agencies should make information about offender status and victims' rights accessible to crime victims through multilingual, toll-free numbers and printed materials.

7. Correctional agencies should collect and distribute restitution payments consistent with the court's order to ensure that victims receive fair compensation from offenders who are incarcerated, released on probation or parole

8. Victims should have input into all decisions affecting the release of adult and juvenile offenders.

9. Special consideration should be given to the needs of victims who participate in parole proceedings.

10. Information regarding the rights and needs of crime victims should be incorporated into education for correctional staff at all levels, including administrative and line staff.

11. Each correctional agency should establish written policies and procedures for responding to correctional staff that are victimized on or off the job.

12. Correctional agencies should use victim impact panels and conduct courses about the effects of crime on people's lives to increase offender awareness of the consequences of their actions on victims' lives.

13. Victim–offender dialogue programs that ensure voluntary victim involvement, protect and support victims, and use highly trained facilitators and mediators should be available for victims upon their request.

14. Crime victims should be notified of any violation of the conditions of an offender's probation or parole.

15. When a sex offender is released, uniform community notification practices should be developed and implemented (Office for Victims of Crime, 1998, 132–142).

VICTIMS AND PAROLE

Victims' rights in the parole process have improved substantially in the last 25 years. All states that have parole as a correctional provision allow victims to give input at parole hearings. There are two types of **parole hearings**: (1) those where offenders seek to be released from institutions, and (2) revocation hearings that determine whether offenders on parole should be recommitted for violating their parole. The type of input asked of crime victims and witnesses can take on various forms. **Victim impact statements** (VIS) are the most common. The VIS provided to the paroling authority is very similar to those provided to crime victims during the sentencing process, described in Chapter 5. All states allow for a VIS at the time of parole considerations. Many states even allow crime victims to testify at inmates' parole hearings or to meet privately with the parole board. While parole has been to a certain extent abandoned at the federal level and in some states, in most states parole hearings provide a valuable opportunity for crime victims to make certain the sentences given by the courts are those offenders serve. As an example of the rights of victims and witnesses in parole hearings, the following are guidelines issued by the U.S. Parole Commission (2002):

- To be treated with dignity and respect throughout the process.
- To receive timely information about your participation in the process.
- To be informed of the charges against the alleged violator relating to your participation at the revocation hearing.
- To testify at a Parole Commission local revocation hearing.
- To an interpreter, if required.
- To be reimbursed for reasonable travel costs and paid the customary U.S. Government Witness Fee for your attendance pursuant to a subpoena at a Parole Commission revocation hearing.
- To bring a "support" person (for example, a relative or friend) to the hearing and have that person present during the hearing.
- To confidentiality of your address, telephone number, and any other locator information.
- To request a "no contact" order from the Parole Commission which will prohibit the offender from contacting you during any time the offender is under the jurisdiction of the Parole Commission.
- To be notified in a timely manner, upon request, of the outcome of the hearing.

Victims and witnesses will be notified, upon request, of the outcome of a hearing. Generally, the victim or witness will receive notification 3–4 weeks after the hearing. There are over 9,000 local, state, and national organizations that provide assistance and support to victims of crime. The U.S. Parole Commission Victim/Witness Coordinator has more information about referrals to counseling or other support services for victims. The Parole Commission has a Victim/Witness Coordinator to assist crime victims. The primary responsibilities of the Victim/Witness Coordinator are to arrange the scheduling for revocation hearings, to answer questions about the hearing process, and to provide timely information and referrals that can assist victims and witnesses before, during, and after the revocation hearing (U.S. Parole Commission, 2006).

Victims can also submit victim impact statements when inmates are considered for pardon or seeking work-release status (Alexander and Lord, 1994). Input during these stages provides for greater accountability of offenders and furthers the prospects for justice to the crime victims.

RESTORATIVE JUSTICE

Many crime victims seem dissatisfied with the operation of the criminal justice system and its punitive or rehabilitative model. When offenders are caught and convicted, many crime victims feel that very little healing takes place. In most cases, the offenses the offenders are convicted of are much different than the original crimes, and as 90 percent of convictions occur as a result of plea bargains, victims may have little input into the process. A new model of trying to provide for crime victims has been the establishment of restorative justice practices. **Restorative justice** is an alternative justice model being implemented throughout North America and the world. Historically, restorative justice principles were used in most local systems until the Norman invasion of Britain, when the preeminence of the king took hold (Van Ness and Strong, 1997). Most of the ancient legal codes, Hebrew, Germanic, Sumerian, and others, recognized the need of offenders to make amends to their victims and communities as the focus of the sanction, so that society could be restored to a sense of normalcy. Restorative approaches to victimizations are used in native cultures around the world. From the American Indian to the New Zealand Maori, to African tribes, to the Australian Aborigines, restorative justice has been a mainstay of their judicial systems.

Restorative justice views crimes as offenses against victims and communities and recognizes the need to repair the harm caused (Achilles and Zehr, 2001; Bazemore, Schiff, and Schiff, 2001; Zehr, 2002). The reparation of harm must include the victim, the offender, and the community as active participants working together seeking a resolution to the harm done as a result of a criminal event. The core principle behind restorative justice, when compared to the traditional criminal justice system, is the empowerment of victims. Restorative justice allows victims of crime to recover the sense of autonomy and control that they lost when they were victimized. In a restorative justice setting, victims become the central figures in the justice process (Bazemore, Schiff, and Schiff, 2001). Restorative justice can take on many forms, such as restitution, mediation, community service, family group conferences, sentencing circles, victim–offender reconciliation programs, and community courts. This section will distinguish the various programs as to their philosophies, assumptions, and applications in an effort to provide the reader with a comprehensive guide to the various programs and their applications.

HISTORY OF RESTORATIVE JUSTICE

The return of restorative justice in North America is a recent phenomenon, and yet it has a well-established history. In North America, principles of restorative justice were historically in place in Native American cultures and among American colonists and are recognized as being used since the establishment of social groups (Galaway and Hudson, 1996; Griffiths and Hamilton, 1996; Jerin and Moriarty, 1998). Modern restorative justice programs can trace their beginnings to a pilot project in 1975 in Ontario, Canada, which involved 61 offenders and 128 victims (Bazemore, Schiff, and Schiff, 2001). During the 1980s and 1990s, the implementation of restorative justice programs began to flourish across the North America. Championed by advocates from across a broad political spectrum, restorative justice programs are now found in some form or another across the continent (Bazemore, Schiff, and Schiff, 2001).

Over the centuries, since the settlement of Western Europeans in the new world, the restorative justice perspective has been replaced by a state-sponsored retributive justice system. Within the last three decades a revival of the restorative justice philosophy has begun to take hold throughout Canada and the United States. This effort has been lead by religious organizations, social activists, criminal justice system reformers, and Native Americans. Restorative justice focuses upon repairing the harm done to victims and the community through the use of programs such as restitution, mediation, victim empowerment, and victim–offender reconciliation. Restorative justice seeks to use a holistic approach to eliminating the effects of a criminal event as well as working toward eliminating the circumstances that created the crime to begin with (Zehr, 1990, 2002; Galaway and Hudson, 1996; Van Ness and Strong, 1997; Bazemore and Umbreit, 1998).

Galaway and Hudson (1996) describe the restorative justice philosophy as having three components:

First, crime is viewed primarily as a conflict between individuals that results in injuries to victims, communities, and the offenders themselves, and only secondarily as a violation against the state. Second, the aim of the criminal justice process should be to create peace in communities by reconciling the parties and repairing the injuries caused by the dispute. Third, the criminal justice process should facilitate active participation by victims, offenders, and their communities in order to find solutions to the conflict. (p. 2)

There are several core values implicit in the restorative justice process. One view is based upon the effort to provide complete justice and reconciliation to victims, offenders, and communities. The main value associated with this perspective includes participation of those most affected by the victimization, especially the victim. The victims, offenders, and community representatives need to be the primary decision-makers rather than trained professionals representing the state or offenders alone. A second value is respect for all participants involved. Mutual respect can establish trust and help with an adequate outcome. The third value of the restorative justice model is honesty. Honesty concerning the impact of offenses on victims as well as the experiences of offenders is important for the dialogue that must take place. The fourth value is humility. Restorative justice recognizes that all people are human and may have more in common than not and that empathy is important for understanding. The interconnectiveness of individuals to the community is the fifth value. This requires that society share in the responsibility of its members and help resolve the conflicts that occur. Accountability is a very important value of the restorative justice system. The acceptance of responsibility by offenders and efforts to seek forgiveness are at the core of the process. Empowerment of the affected members, especially victims, is also a core value. Encouraging active participation of crime victims to be part of the resolution allows victims to express what their needs are and how they should be met. Lastly, hope is the final value. The restorative justice process seeks to nurture the hope that victims will heal, that offenders will change, and that society will become more civil and peaceful (Zehr, 2002).

Virginia Mackey (1990) points out that there are six principles found in restorative justice programs: (1) the safety of all those involved should be a primary consideration; (2) the offenders need to be held responsible and accountable for their actions and any harm resulting from those actions; (3) victims, including the community, need to be restored; (4) any underlying conflicts that caused the harm should also be resolved, if possible; (5) treatment options and services must be available; and (6) both public and private resources must be made available to develop a coordinated and cooperative system to dispense this form of justice (as found in Van Ness and Strong, 1997). A comparison of the restorative justice model to the traditional justice model (see Table 6.1) shows the major differences between these two philosophies.

TABLE 6.1 Comparing the Current Justice Model to a Restorative Justice Model

	Traditional Criminal Justice Model	*Restorative Justice Model*
Who is harmed?	• Violation against the state.	• Harm done to individuals and/or communities.
Definition of crime?	• Crime is an individual act with individual responsibility.	• Crime has both individual and social dimensions and responsibilities.
Who decides what happens?	• Handled by members of the criminal justice system.	• Resolved by community members.
What is the sought-after outcome?	• To convict and punish offenders.	• Recovery of the victims.
How do the various parties approach finding an outcome?	• Adversary system.	• Negotiation and dialogue.
What is the crime victims' role?	• Little role for victims, they are peripheral.	• Victims are central figures.
What is the outcome?	• Punishment for offenders.	• Restitution for victims.
What is the offenders' role?	• Offenders held singularly responsible.	• Offenders must accept responsibility.
What is the central focus?	• Retribution.	• Rehabilitation and recovery for victims, offenders, and communities.

Source: Adapted from Zehr (1990).

RESTORATIVE JUSTICE VERSUS THE TRADITIONAL CRIMINAL JUSTICE MODEL

The traditional criminal justice model has been described as retributive (Zehr, 2002). It is very cold and unwelcoming to crime victims. It fails to consider the crime victims' needs, but considers only its own. Many observers of the traditional criminal justice system find victims to be the "forgotten party" (Wemmers and Canuto, 2002).

Restorative justice is a different way of thinking about crime, victimization, and society's response to crime. It focuses on harm caused by crime, the steps needed to repair harm done to victims, and how it can be prevented in the future. Offenders are required to take responsibility for their offenses and for the harm they have caused. Restorative justice seeks to make victims whole again, straighten out offenders, and allow both to reintegrate into the community. In all, restorative justice views criminal acts more comprehensively than do traditional justice systems and considers how the harm done by criminal acts affects victims, offenders, and communities. It recognizes the importance of victim and community involvement. As an end result, restorative justice seeks to strengthen victims, offenders, and communities as a way to achieve future crime prevention (Van Ness and Strong, 1997). There are many different types of restorative justice programs and each utilizes numerous methods to try to achieve restoration for crime victims. Central to these programs is the need to provide victims, and sometimes the community, with restitution.

RESTITUTION PROGRAMS

Restitution is one of the oldest sanctions imposed as a result of a criminal violation (Bazemore, Schiff, and Schiff, 2001). Forcing offenders to repay their victims for losses incurred has existed for centuries. However, the use of restitution as a criminal sanction had fallen out of use until recently. In the United States, the practice of requiring offenders to reimburse victims as part of criminal sanctions has only returned in the past few decades.

Historically, restitution or reparation for injuries or losses suffered by crime victims was "the chief and often the only element of punishment" offenders received (Schafer, 1970, 3). Even though many states had restitution laws, they were rarely enforced (Jerin, 1990). With the demise of restitution as part of the criminal sanction, crime victims were forced to seek restitution from offenders in the civil courts. The process of suing offenders is time-consuming and can be expensive. In many cases, the likelihood of receiving any money is quite small, considering offenders must first be identified and must have an ability to pay for any judgment crime victims receive.

The reinstitution of restitution as a criminal sanction occurred in the 1980s with the publication of the recommendation of the President's Task Force report and the passage of the Victim and Witness Protection Act of 1982 (Pub L. No. 97–291) (VWPA). The task force report recommended that state and federal legislatures pass laws that "require restitution in all cases, unless the court provides specific reasons for failing to require it" (President's Task Force on Victims of Crime, 1982, 18). The VWPA permitted sentencing judges in federal cases to add restitution to sentences of incarceration. Before passage of this act, a judge could require restitution only as part of probation, and that was rarely done. Many states followed the lead of the federal government and started to require restitution as part of all sentences whether incarceration was also required or not. An example of this is Tennessee, where a 1932 law authorized restitution in felony cases. It was not until 1982, when the law was amended, that enforcement of the statue took place (Jerin, 1987, 7).

In many types of federal criminal cases, defendants are required to pay restitution for offenses occurring after April 24, 1996. For most crimes committed prior to that date, sentencing judges have discretion in deciding whether or not to order restitution depending on the defendants' ability to pay. As a practical matter, however, defendants who do not have assets, or have little potential to make money, may be unlikely to make meaningful restitution to victims. The following provides an overview of restitution in the federal court system.

MANDATORY AND DISCRETIONARY RESTITUTION

The **Mandatory Victims Restitution Act of 1996** expanded the scope of mandatory restitution and consolidated procedures for the issuance of restitution orders. This act requires the court to order full restitution in certain cases if there is an identifiable victim or victims who have suffered a physical injury or pecuniary harm. It requires the court to enter a restitution order for each defendant, without regard to the defendant's ability to pay, who has been convicted or has pled guilty to charges of:

- a crime of violence.
- an offense against property, including offenses committed by fraud or deceit.

- telemarketing fraud.
- sexual abuse.
- sexual exploitation and other abuses of children, domestic violence, and tampering with consumer products.

The exception to mandatory restitution for the above categories is for an offense against property. If the court makes a finding that the number of identifiable victims is so large it would make restitution impracticable, or if complex issues would prolong the sentencing process to a degree that the need to provide restitution to any victim is outweighed by the burden on the sentencing process, discretionary restitution may take place.

In determining whether to award restitution in these cases, courts are required to consider the amount of the loss sustained by the victims as a result of the offenses, the financial resources of the defendants, the financial needs and earning ability of the defendants and their dependents, and such other factors as the court deems appropriate. To the extent the court determines that the complication and prolongation of the sentencing process involved in ordering restitution outweighs the need to provide restitution to any victims, the court may decline to do so (Office for Victims of Crime, 2006).

RESTITUTION PROCEDURES

Restitution can be ordered as a discretionary condition of probation or part of any confinement. There must be an identifiable victim who has suffered physical injury or pecuniary loss. Regardless of how restitution is imposed, as mandatory or discretionary, the procedures that must be followed are the same. Once a defendant pleads guilty or is found guilty at trial, the available information on each identified victim's loss, usually obtained by the case agent during the investigation of the case, is provided to the probation office of the court prosecuting the case. This victim loss information is incorporated into the **presentence investigation report** (PSI) by the probation office. It is during the time between the conviction or plea and the sentencing hearing that victim impact statements are solicited from the identified victims of the convicted offense. It is through the submission of a written victim impact statement that a victim has the opportunity to submit financial loss information, as well as emotional impact information, to the court. The findings of the presentence report are relied upon by the judge in determining the appropriate sentence and appropriate amount of restitution.

ALLOWABLE RESTITUTION COSTS

In most cases, pain and suffering, attorney fees, lost interest, opportunity costs, and tax penalties are not included in court-ordered restitution. In determining loss amounts for restitution, it is important to remember that the harm suffered must be as a result of the offense of conviction. The primary consideration is whether the harm was caused by the offense conduct. The court may, however, order restitution to persons other than victims of the convicted offense if agreed to in the plea agreement. Lost income and necessary child care, transportation, and other expenses related to participation in the investigation or prosecution of the offense, or attendance at court proceedings related to the offense, may be considered for restitution. Receipts and other supporting documentation should be provided to substantiate loss figures. The court may decline to order restitution if it finds that determining restitution is too complex.

Most victims are eager to know when they will receive their money. In most cases it takes a very long time, and often victims do not receive the full amount owed to them. Typically in fraud cases there are hundreds of victims and the amounts owed are quite substantial. Restitution payments to victims are dependent upon the defendants' ability to pay. In addition, while defendants are in prison, they may not make any payments, or may make only very small ones. Defendants' liability to pay restitution orders lasts 20 years or so, depending on jurisdiction, plus any period of incarceration, or until the death of the defendants. Orders of restitution are not dischargeable in bankruptcy.

Unless the court has ordered otherwise, restitution payments made by defendants are usually dispersed by probation offices to all victims named in the restitution orders in proportion to their loss. For example, if the total amount of a restitution order is $100,000 and victim A lost $25,000, while victim B lost $75,000, then victim A's loss would equal 25 percent of the total restitution order and victim B's loss would equal 75 percent of the total restitution order. Therefore, if the defendant makes a payment of $1,000, victim A would receive $250 and victim B would receive $750.

If defendants are placed on supervised release, assigned probation officers monitor the defendants' economic circumstances and ability to pay the restitution obligation during that time period. As noted above, restitution payments tend to be in small amounts, and it may take some time to accumulate enough money to send to victims. However, if victims have been receiving payment on a consistent basis and suddenly stop receiving it, and if the defendants are on supervised release, they must contact the probation office to determine the reason. If defendants are not on supervised release, the victims contact the prosecuting attorneys' office to see what avenues they have for redress. If victims have information concerning a material change in the defendants' economic condition that might affect their ability to make restitution payments, they should contact the probation office, which may have the means to ensure that restitution orders are enforced to the fullest extent possible.

Victims may also enforce restitution orders as if they are civil judgments. To pursue legal action on their own behalf, victims may register or record the verdicts in accordance with state law to obtain a lien against the defendants' property. Victims may wish to consult with private attorneys or legal services attorneys for guidance about proceeding individually against defendants to recover losses or damages sustained as a result of crimes. Usually prosecuting attorneys or probation officers cannot consult with victims or advise victims regarding their right to purse civil litigation against defendants (Office for Victims of Crime, 2006).

DOES RESTITUTION WORK?

This question has many answers. Historically, there have been many problems with restitution. For example, in Texas, almost $100 million was paid by probationers to crime victims over a 10-year period; however, much more restitution was never paid even though it was required (Jerin, 1988a). Restitution can be used with any sanction, and payment schedules can be set up. Even when offenders are not charged or convicted of offenses, as in the case of diversion, restitution as a condition of the program is available. The administration of restitution is usually the responsibility of the probation office, which works as the middleman between offenders and crime victims, but it can also be handled by correction agencies or private victims' organizations.

For the millions of crime victims whose offenders are never caught or are never convicted, restitution is an empty promise. Even if offenders are caught and ordered to pay restitution, little, if anything, will happen to those who decide not to pay. Because of jail and prison overcrowding problems, as well as the focus of the criminal justice system on more important offenders, offenders who do not pay restitution are rarely punished. Additionally, restitution is paid only for the crimes offenders are convicted of, rather than those they were charged with. In the case of *Hughey v. United States* (110 S. Ct. 1979), the Court held that the offender could be ordered to pay restitution only for the losses resulting from the offense of conviction (Adair, 1990). This means that in plea bargains and other cases, if offenders plead guilty to only one or two charges despite having committed many violations, they can be ordered to pay restitution only for the crimes of which they are convicted. The failure of restitution to provide for all crime victims and the questionable ability of the criminal justice system to collect funds due to crime victims has, in many cases, led to repeat victimization of crime victims by the criminal justice system. Unless offenders reoffended many times, the restitution orders may be rescinded because of their indigent status or cash flow problems caused from losing their jobs. Reinstitution can, at best, provide only part of the solution for the restoration of crime victims.

While most restitution is based upon monetary reimbursement, community service or service to the victims may also be considered restitution. In the United States, all states allow for the practice of restitution by offenders, with 11 states establishing it as a constitutional right (National Victims Center, 1997). Restitution amounts are set by judges and become part of offenders' probation requirements or can be sanctions on their own. There are, however, many problems with restitution programs in the United States (Bazemore, Schiff, and Schiff, 2001). While restitution may be part of a criminal sanction, this does not guarantee victims will receive the full amount ordered (Jerin, 1987). Judges and probation officers are reluctant to violate offenders if they fail to complete their restitution agreements; because of overcrowding in correctional facilities, they feel it is not worth the time and expense.

In many ways restitution is the cornerstone of the restorative justice philosophy. Victims need to be provided with restitution. It holds offenders accountable for the damages they inflicted and vindicates victims (Bazemore, Schiff, and Schiff, 2001). The process of healing injuries caused by offenders can begin only if the victims believe they are whole again or if they have been brought back to their original financial position that they were in before victimization. It has also been shown (Butts and Snyder, 1992) that restitution is associated with significant reductions in recidivism among juvenile offenders. Additionally, if restitution orders contain community service, the community becomes an added beneficiary.

One answer to the difficulty problem of crime victims' recovering restitution is the establishment of the Balanced and Restorative Justice (BARJ) Project (Bazemore and Umbreit, 1995; Freivalds, 1996). The BARJ Project is a program that seeks to structure restitution in such a way that traditional problems are eliminated and recidivism among offenders is reduced. The program "provides intensive training, technical assistance, and guideline materials" (Freivalds, 1996, 1). The program encourages community involvement, supervision of offenders, and accountability and competence of offenders in community improvement projects. The focus of these programs is to engage offenders to work on community-improvement projects as part of holding the offenders responsible. The project also provides competency development for offenders so they can pursue legitimate endeavors after they have completed their programs. Additionally, an added benefit to this training is that the staff can then involve the offenders and the crime victims in mediation programs as a means to fulfill the restorative justice philosophy (Freivalds, 1996).

MEDIATION

Mediation is the process of establishing a dialogue between a victim and an offender, with a third party present who orchestrates the dialogue between the parties. The role of the third party is to try to provide a forum for the offender and the victim in order to find a solution that meets the needs of both parties. Mediation may be thought of as "assisted negotiation." The negotiations that take place try to provide an avenue for an agreement between the two parties. Central to mediation is the concept of **informed consent**. The issue of informed consent centers on the understanding by all parties to the mediation, what the process is, and what outcomes might be anticipated. So long as participants understand the nature of a contemplated mediation process and effectively consent to participate in the described process, virtually any mediation process is possible and appropriate.

There are certain key components to mediation. First, it must be voluntary. All parties must attend the process of their own free will and know that they can also leave at any time for any reason. Second is the notion of collaboration. The parties must work together to solve the issues and to reach an agreement. Neither party can make a decision for the other; each has veto power over the other. It is important each party understand that nothing can be imposed on them. Third, it is important that the mediation be confidential, impartial, neutral, balanced, and safe. The mediator has an equal and balanced responsibility to assist each mediating party and cannot favor the interests of one party over another, nor should the mediator favor a particular result. The mediator is ethically obligated to acknowledge any bias on substantive issues in discussion. The mediator's role is to ensure that both parties reach agreements in a voluntarily and informed manner, and not as a result of coercion or intimidation (Melamed, 2008).

In a restorative justice model, victim–offender mediation is the most widely implemented technique (Bazemore, Schiff, and Schiff, 2001). Face-to-face meetings between offenders and victims provide an opportunity for the victims to have input into the process and also to receive sought-after information.

Mediation programs for crime victims go by many different names. **Victim–offender mediation (VOM)** and **victim–offender reconciliation programs (VORPs)** are some of the most popular. The procedures that usually take place in mediation follow the following model:

- Opening statement: Welcome, establishment of ground rules by mediators, explanation of procedure to be followed, and reminder to both parties that they have agreed to meet.
- Uninterrupted time: Each party has the opportunity to speak in turn without interruptions about the offense, what it has meant, and what it still means.

- Exchange: Responding to what has been said, asking questions, giving information, and beginning to identify what might put things right.
- Agreement: With both parties' permission, any agreement reached is written down and signed by those present.
- Closing statement: Mediators review what has been experienced and congratulate everyone for taking part (Wright, 1995).

In victim–offender mediation programs, no specific outcome is imposed by the mediators. The goals of victim–offender mediation are to empower the participants, promote dialogue between victims and offenders, and encourage mutual problem solving (Van Ness and Strong, 1997). The VOM or VORP seeks to use the mediation process to achieve reconciliation between victims and offenders. While this is not always possible, many participants benefit from just being allowed to engage in dialogue. Results from these programs have found many benefits for both victims and offenders (Bazemore, Schiff, and Schiff, 2001). The crime victims are able to confront the offenders, express their feelings, and ask questions, which is very empowering. Offenders are also given the opportunity to explain their actions, take responsibility, and make amends to their victims.

FAMILY GROUP CONFERENCES

Family group conferences, mainly used with juvenile offenders, may also be seen as part of a restorative justice program. Family group conferencing began in New Zealand in the late 1980s (Van Ness and Strong, 1997). Family group conferences are generally made up of young people who have committed offenses, members of their families and whomever the families invite, the victims or their representative, support people for the victims, representatives of the police, and the mediators or managers of the process. Sometimes social workers or lawyers are also present. The main goal of conferences is to formulate a plan regarding how best to deal with the offenses. There are three principal components to this process:

- Ascertaining whether or not the young people admit the offenses—conferences only proceed if they do so.
- Sharing information with all parties attending the conference about the nature of the offenses, the effects of the offenses on the victims, the reasons for the offending, and any prior offending by the young people.
- Deciding the outcome or recommendation.

Family group conferences occur in relatively informal settings. The rooms are usually arranged with comfortable chairs in a circle. When all are present, the meetings may open with prayers or blessings, depending on the customs of those involved. The coordinators or mediators then welcome the participants, introduce each of them, and describe the purposes of the meetings. What happens next can vary, but usually the police representatives then read out summaries of the offenses. The young people are asked if they agree about what happened, and any variation is noted. If they do not agree, the meetings progress no further and the police may consider referring the cases to court for hearings. Assuming the young people agree, the victims or spokespeople for the victims are then usually asked to describe what the events meant to them. Next, a general discussion of the offenses and the underlying circumstances occurs. At this interval, a lot of emotion may be expressed. This is also a point when the young people and their families may express remorse for what has happened and apologize to the victims—although this may not happen at all. Once everyone has discussed what the offending has meant and options for making good the damage, the professionals and the victims leave the families and the young people to meet privately to discuss what plans and recommendations they wish to make in order to repair the damage and to prevent any reoffending. The private family time can take as little as half an hour or much longer. When the families are ready, the others return and the meetings are reconvened; this is another point at which the young people and their families may apologize to the victims. Spokespeople for the families outline what they propose, and the proposal is discussed. Once there is agreement among all present, the details are formally recorded and the conferences conclude (Crawford and Clear, 2001).

Professionals are expected to play a low-key role in family group conferences. Youth justice coordinators ensure that everyone understands the tasks that need to be done, that all relevant issues are discussed, and that the venting of emotion is managed as constructively as possible. The role of the police is usually limited to describing the offenses and, possibly, their impact on the victims. The police may also voice their concerns if the proposals of the families seem inadequate or excessive. The main role of youth advocates is to advise on legal issues and to protect the young people's rights. They may also express opinions about the proposed penalties if they seem excessive. Social workers, if present, normally only provide background information on the young people and participate in supporting the plans of the families and the young people for the future. Practice can, however, vary considerably. Conferences are intended to be flexible and responsive to young people, families, and victims. The plans are meant to take into account the views of the victims, the need to make the young people accountable for their offending, and any measures that may prevent future reoffending by enhancing the well-being of the offenders or strengthening the families. The range of possible sanctions here is extensive and can include apologies, community work, reparations, or involvement in programs.

Family group conferences are mechanisms for making decisions on how best to deal with young people's criminal behavior. To the extent that they involve the young people, the victims, and their respective communities of interest in these decisions, they can be described as restorative. Outcomes may, and often do, include putting things right for victims. For example, the young people or their families may make restitution to the victims or may perform some community work either for the victims or for organizations nominated by the victims. To this extent outcomes may be restorative, but they may also involve counseling or some other program for the young people, while the victims' needs remain unmet. And, too often, promised outcomes are not delivered (usually as a result of some failure on the part of professionals rather than on the part of the young people or their families) (Maxwell and Morris, 2001). Moreover, it is not uncommon for victims to express satisfaction at the end of the family group conference or immediately afterwards, only to express dissatisfaction some time down the track. Such outcomes cannot be described as restorative. These need not, however, detract from the power and potential of the process as a restorative one.

Research (Maxwell and Morris, 1998) indicated that victims attended only about half of the family group conferences. The reasons for this were related primarily to poor practices—they were not invited, the time was unsuitable for them, or they were given inadequate notice. Good practice suggests victims should be consulted about the time and venue of conferences and informed of them in a timely manner. There will always be a minority of victims who choose not to participate in conferencing, but research (Maxwell and Morris, 1998) shows that only six percent of victims, when asked, said they did not wish to meet the offenders. This is a clear indicator of victims' willingness, indeed desire, to be involved in these processes. This research has also shown that, when victims were involved in conferencing, many found it a positive process. About 60 percent of victims interviewed described the family group conferences they attended as helpful, positive, and rewarding. Generally, they said they were effectively involved in the process and felt better as a result of participating. Victims also commented on two other specific benefits. First, it provided them with a voice in determining appropriate outcomes. Second, they were able to meet the offenders and their families face to face, so they could assess their attitudes, better understand why the offenses occurred, and assess the likelihood of their recurring.

COMMUNITY REPARATION BOARDS

One of the most powerful of the restorative justice processes falls under the category of community conferencing. The power comes from the emotions aroused, the likelihood of catharsis through the healing ritual, and the involvement of the whole community. Community reparation takes place at both the individual and societal levels.

Often referred to as the "Vermont model," community reparation, or reparative probation, this form of restorative conferencing can be implemented more quickly within existing structures and processes of the criminal justice system. Such is the case in Vermont. Vermont's radical restructuring of its corrections philosophy and practices stem from influences of the communitarian movement and to personalist philosophy generally (Thorvaldson, 1990). In 1991, Vermont decided to overhaul its system, setting up reparative boards statewide to focus on repairing the damage to victims and communities. Composed of volunteers, the reparative group is charged with ensuring that low-risk nonviolent offenders are made aware of the impact of their behavior on members of the community. Vermont, in fact, is the first state to implement such conferencing on a statewide basis and the first to institutionalize the restorative justice philosophy.

The goal is to have all offenders, even those in prison, pay back their victims (Karp and Walther, 2001). Treatment is provided not only to help victims but to meet offenders' needs as well. As with all restorative justice programs, the goal is to reduce the harm offenders have done to victims and the community and to reintegrate the offenders into the community.

This model involves a "reparative programs" track designed for offenders who commit nonviolent offenses and who are considered at low risk for reoffense. This track mandates that offenders make reparations to both the victims and to the community. A reparative probation program such as Vermont's directly engages the community in sentencing and monitoring offenders and depends heavily upon small-scale community-based committees to deal with minor crimes (Karp and Walther, 2001). Reparative agreements are made between perpetrators and these community representatives, while citizen volunteers furnish social support in order to facilitate victim and community reparation.

Here, members of the community are involved in meting out justice. Unlike other forms of restorative justice, the process is more formal, with "chairpeople" guiding participants through the questioning process. The victims' role has been minimal in the past, although it may be strengthened in the future. Preliminary studies from Vermont show that more than 80 percent of the 4,000-plus offenders who entered the mediation process have completed it successfully, and that they are less likely to reoffend than those who enter probation (Bazemore and Umbreit, 1995).

Similar to Vermont's community process in its focus on truth-telling and reconciliation of parties is some of the programming found in Hawaii. Social workers in Hawaii have been quietly incorporating Native Hawaiian cultural tradition into their human service interventions. The impetus for introducing culturally specific programming came in the 1970s when it was noted that Native children were not responding to standard forms of psychotherapy. Hurdle (2002) chronicles how social workers in collaboration with Hawaiian elders worked to revitalize the use of *ho'oponopono,* an ancient Hawaiian conflict-resolution process. This model is embedded in the traditional Hawaiian value of extended family, respect of elders, need for harmonious relationships, and restoration of good will or *aloha.* The process is ritualistic and follows a definite protocol. With the leader in tight control of communication, the opening prayer leads to an open discussion of the problem at hand. The resolution phase begins with a confession of wrongdoing and the seeking of forgiveness. Uniquely, as Hurdle relates, all parties to the conflict ask forgiveness of each other; this equalizes the status of participants. This process effectively promotes spiritual healing and can be used in many contexts. In drawing on guidance of the **Kupanas** (or wise elders) and a reliance on the family as a natural resource in relieving social problems, social workers are tapping in to the community's natural resources, a cardinal principle of the strengths perspective (Heffernan, Johnson, and Vakalahi, 2002).

VICTIM IMPACT PANELS

Victim impact panels (VIP) or **victim-offender panels** (VOP) can be attributed to the campaign against drunk driving. VIPs began after 1989. They were developed by Mothers Against Drunk Driving (MADD) as a means of giving convicted drunk drivers an appreciation of the human cost of drunk driving on victims and survivors, with the intention of decreasing the likelihood of repeat offenses (see Chapter 13 for more on MADD). It also offered victims and survivors a forum in which to express their experiences and thereby restore some sense of power. The panels are made up of groups of victims and groups of offenders who are unrelated by specific crimes but are related by the type of crime.

Bereaved victims make up the majority of panelists, but injured victims, police officers, emergency response personnel, and remorseful offenders also speak. Participation requirements for panelists include: (1) the criminal case must have been concluded, (2) a minimum time (usually 1 year) must have elapsed since the crash, and (3) victims must be emotionally ready, generally able to speak more from hurt than anger. Desirable characteristics of panel members (according to panel coordinators) include: willingness to speak, good speaking skills, ability to speak without hostility, good coping skills, availability, and having an experience with the potential to impact an offender audience. Audiences of 30–50 are most common. In about half the panels, law enforcement professionals regularly attend to assure order. Most panel coordinators ask for and receive written anonymous comments or evaluations from offenders who attend (Mercer, Lorden, and Lord, 1999).

Judges order offenders to attend VIPs as a condition of probation. Attendance is monitored, with sanctions assessed for failure to attend. The purpose of the panels is to provide a constructive atmosphere that allows victims to express their grief amongst others suffering from the effects of drunk driving. The victims may also receive some satisfaction from knowing they may help to save lives by changing offenders' attitudes about drunk driving. The process of telling their stories may be therapeutic in itself.

VIPs allow offenders to see firsthand the pain and suffering that drunk driving causes to other victims, acknowledge their own responsibilities instead of blaming "bad luck," and break through the denial of having drug or alcohol problems, with the hope that it will change their drunk driving behaviors (Lord, 1990).

MADD chapters choose three or four victims for whom it would be helpful to speak about the impact that drunk driving has had on their lives without attempting to blame or judge offenders in attendance A moderator is present to monitor the panel, and guidelines are issued to panelists. No victim ever speaks on a panel at which their own offender is present, and victims do not divulge personal information about their offenders. The panel does not serve as a forum for dialogue between victims and offenders, unless the victims agree to answer offenders' questions (Lord, 1990).

In a study conducted by Mercer, Lorden, and Lord (1999), 482 drunk-driving crash victims who participated on VIPs were compared to 903 victims who did not. In this study, 82 percent of the victims who speak or have spoken on VIPs said that telling their stories to offender audiences was very helpful. They said it helps because they believe they make a difference, even if it is to only one person in the audience. Ten percent felt it had been neither helpful nor hurtful, and eight percent said that telling their story felt more hurtful than helpful. Panel speakers reported the following significant reactions: an added sense of life purpose from their crashes, a belief that panels would save lives (bring some good from the crashes), a belief that they were changing people's attitudes and behaviors, and an opportunity to vent their feelings. The most common positive reaction noted was that participation on VIPs makes the trauma more bearable and gives them increased self-confidence. The research concluded that speaking on victim impact panels is a positive healing experience for most victims of drunken driving crashes. The majority of participants believed that speaking on panels has helped them heal. The research went on to suggest that VIP participation may also foster better adjustment by allowing victims to re-experience their trauma in a situation where there is a high degree of control, thus enhancing their sense of control over their lives. It may help them to build supportive relationships with other panelists, which enhances their self-confidence. Finally, panel participation may produce anger reduction by providing a positive method of coping with the traumatic event.

SENTENCING CIRCLES

Circle sentencing is an updated version of traditional sanctioning and healing practices of aboriginal peoples in Canada and American Indians in the United States (Stuart, 1996). These **Sentencing circles**—sometimes called peacemaking circles—were resurrected in 1991 by judges and community justice committees in the Yukon Territory and other northern Canadian communities. Its use spread to the United States in 1996, when a pilot project was initiated in Minnesota. Circle sentencing has been used for adult and juvenile offenders, for a variety of offenses, and in both rural and urban settings.

Sentencing circles are attempts to rediscover the traditional native method of dealing with members of the community who have broken the law. Circles are made up of the accused, the victims, their families, elders, and other interested members of the community. Judges, defense lawyers, prosecutors, or policemen may also sit in a circle. Once someone sits in a circle, he or she gives up any special powers or privileges. Everyone in a circle has the same power, as circles operate on the basis of consensus. Everyone in a circle must agree what to do about the people who have broken the law. After circles have reached consensus on sentencing the offenders, judges then step back into their judicial roles and may impose the sentences that the circles recommended.

Circle sentencing is a holistic reintegrative strategy designed not only to address the criminal and delinquent behavior of offenders but also to consider the needs of victims, families, and communities. Within the circle, crime victims, offenders, family and friends of both, justice and social service personnel, and interested community residents speak from the heart in a shared search for an understanding of the event. Together they identify the steps necessary to assist in healing all affected parties and prevent future crimes. The significance of the circle is more than symbolic as all circle members—police officers, lawyers, judges, victims, offenders, and community residents—participate in deliberations to arrive at a consensus for a sentencing plan that addresses the concerns of all interested parties.

Circle sentencing typically involves a multi-step procedure (Stuart, 2006) that includes (1) application by an offender to participate in the circle process, (2) a healing circle for the victim, (3) a healing circle for the offender, (4) a sentencing circle to develop consensus on the elements of a sentencing plan, and (5) follow up circles to monitor the progress of the offender. In addition to commitments by the offender, the sentencing plan may incorporate commitments by the justice system, community, and family members. Specifics of the circle process vary from community to community and are designed locally to fit community needs and culture.

Goals of circle sentencing include the following:

- Promoting healing for all affected parties.
- Providing an opportunity for the offender to make amends.
- Empowering victims, community members, families, and offenders by giving them a voice and a shared responsibility in finding constructive resolutions.
- Addressing the underlying causes of criminal behavior.
- Building a sense of community and its capacity for resolving conflict.
- Promoting and sharing community values (Stuart, 2006).

CONCLUSION

The traditional goal of corrections is to provide a secure environment for convicted offenders so they can serve their sanctions as provided by society. The role corrections plays for victims of crime is to make sure they are safe from their offenders and to provide notification if the offenders are to be released back into society. Changes have started to occur to traditional goals of corrections. Greater crime victim involvement in the sentences offenders receive and release decisions is beginning. Victims are being given some rights by the correctional community.

A major change in the treatment of crime victims has been the advent of restorative justice. The idea of restoration has a long history in the operation of historical criminal justice systems. The goal of restorative justice is to make victims, offenders, and communities whole again. The closer we come to achieving this goal, the more likely justice will be obtained. Restorative justice can take on many different forms. However, provision by federal and local governments of complete restoration to crime victims has not materialized. The growth of these programs and the improvement of services must continue if crime victims are to achieve restoration of their former lives. Additionally, victims would like to see offenders rehabilitated while under the control of correctional authorities so that neither they nor anyone else will ever be victimized by them again.

Study Questions

1. Explain the changes over the past 40 years in how victims have been treated by the correctional system. Explain the duties of a correctional system-based victim-witness advocate. What changes do you believe still need to occur?
2. Explain the differences in the roles crime victims and communities have in the criminal justice process as compared to their roles in a restorative justice process.
3. Define what is meant by mediation and describe the various types of mediation programs that exist. How does the use of mediation empower crime victims and offenders?
4. Explain the history of restorative justice systems. Describe how a restorative justice program can help victims, offenders, and communities heal.

Key Terms

- bot   102
- Code of Hammurabi   102
- community reparation   116
- compensation   102
- family group conferences   114
- informed consent   113
- just desserts   101
- justice   102
- Kupanas   117
- Mandatory Victims Restitution Act of 1996   109
- mediation   113
- parole   104
- parole hearings   104
- presentence investigative reports (PSI)   110
- probation   104
- reconciliation programs (VORP)   000
- restitution   102
- **restorative justice**   105
- retribution   102
- restoration   101
- revocation hearing   104
- sentencing circles   119
- victim impact panels (VIP)   104
- victim impact statements   104
- victim restoration   101
- victim–offender mediation (VOM)   113
- victim-offender panels   117

Interpersonal Victimization

CHAPTER 7

Sexual Victimization

INTRODUCTION

Rape and **sexual assault**—these terms are often used interchangeably. When a conservative definition of *rape* is applied, (e.g., carnal knowledge of a female forcibly and against her will by a male), then sexual assault encompasses all unwanted sexual behavior except sexual intercourse. When a more liberal definition is applied, then rape is part of sexual assault. The more liberal definition of rape is supported in this chapter, and therefore, the terms *sexual assault* and *rape* are used interchangeably throughout the chapter.

In 1975, Susan Brownmiller wrote the book *Against Our Will: Men, Women, and Rape.* Brownmiller combines historical information with her personal opinion to make the case that men have the power in society, from the beginning of time to the present day. Evidence of this power is illustrated throughout the book, with an emphasis on men's ability to rape women. She concludes, "When men discovered that they could rape, they proceeded to do it. . . . Rape is man's basic weapon of force against women, the principal agent of his will and her fear (p. 14)" (as cited in Horne, 1993).

Brownmiller's positions are controversial and often considered "extreme" (see Horne, 1993, 306) with perhaps the most controversial position being that rape is not a crime of lust but a crime of power and violence. Although this position might not be regarded as controversial by all (certainly not so from our perspective), there are still a number of people who think rape is a crime of passion or lust. Witness the recent publication of the book by two evolutionary biologists: Dr. Randy Thornhill and Dr. Craig Palmer, titled *A Natural History of Rape.* In this book, the authors theorize that rape has nothing to do with violence and domination and that it has everything to do with procreation and natural selection. In other words, rape and sex are interchangeable. Their controversial stance will not be delved into in this chapter; suffice it to say, however, that these authors would not argue the point that rape being an act of violence and control is a controversial perspective.

Brownmiller also attributes much of society's beliefs about rape to the traditional sex roles of men and women. Her book is considered revolutionary in feminist circles, and it has provided decades of discussion and argument about rape and the misconceptions about the crime, its victims, and offenders.

RAPE MYTHS

What is a rape myth? In layman's terms, a myth is a misconception. Specifically for rape, a rape myth is a belief or attitude about a rape victim or rapist that is generally false but which many in the public believe to be true (Burt, 1980, 1991; Lonsway and

Fitzgerald, 1994). Researchers have examined the acceptance of rape myths and have consistently found wide agreement with the myths—while the beliefs or attitudes are false, most people surveyed believed them to be true. Hence, controversy exists whenever rape myths are discussed. It is important to remember that both men and women hold these beliefs (Johnson and Sigler, 1997). Some of the reasons for these myths' persistence are "tradition, fear, ignorance, and disbelief" (Flowers, 1987, 32). Moreover, holding on to these beliefs places the blame for rape on females "by believing that some women deserve to be raped or ask to be raped by their dress or/and mannerism" (Johnson and Sigler, 1997, 68).

The literature, starting with the work of Brownmiller, provides many examples of rape myths. These myths can be categorized into several areas, including blaming, dress, language, mannerism, and prior sexual history, as presented in the work of Johnson and Sigler (1997). Others have included the myths as part of an overall presentation of crimes against women; including myths about incest, battering, and harassment with rape myths (see Weisheit and Mahan, 1988). Still others present the myths in no particular order or grouping and then provide context to dispel them (Flowers, 1987).

Stereotypes about race, gender, and class in relationship to victims, offenders, and violence sustain these rape myths. For example, "one stereotype is that of the black male rapist who attacks white women. This has little empirical basis in reality, for about 80 percent of sex offenders violate victims within their same racial group" (Schmidt, 2004b, 192).

Some of the myths listed in Table 7.1 deserve further consideration. For example, all of the myths that address *a woman wanted to be raped or deserved it or asked for it* negate that criminal activity has taken place. It is a crime to have forced intercourse, period. No one asks to be raped or likes to be raped, but acceptance of this myth actually "negates the harm of the crime and denies the legitimacy of the victim" (Weisheit and Mahan, 1988, 90). Other myths focus on victim precipitation (discussed in Chapter 2) and "puts the burden of proof on the victim to show, not only that the crime happened, but also that her own behavior was within the bounds of propriety" (Weisheit and Mahan, 1988, 90). Flowers (1987, 34) further observes that some studies have found victim-precipitated rape to occur when "the victim merely responded politely to a perpetrator's verbal overtures." The spectrum of precipitated behavior seems to run the full gamut. However, Flowers (1987) also points out that it is the offender's *interpretation* of the victim's actions, not her actual actions, that adds fuel to this misconception.

Most authors who study rape advocate for dispelling these popularly held beliefs. However, all it takes is one public example to reinforce the misconceptions.

DEFINITION OF SEXUAL VICTIMIZATION TERMS

The legal definition of **rape** is considered the conservative definition: "carnal knowledge of a female forcibly and against her will" (Koss and Harvey, 1991). *Carnal knowledge* means penile-vaginal penetration only. This definition excludes all other forms of penetration. This exclusion is why the definition is considered conservative. It also excludes male rape; when a male is raped by another male, he is most likely sodomized. Sodomy, or anal penetration, does not fit within the strict definition of rape, although most people would refer to this assault as rape.

TABLE 7.1   Myths or Misconceptions About Rape

If a woman resists, rape cannot occur (Flowers, 1987).

Women have a secret desire to be raped (Flowers, 1987); rape fantasies and the realization of these fantasies are common among women (Weisheit mad Mahan, 1988).

The majority of rapes are triggered by women being out alone at night (Flowers, 1987, 34).

Only young, attractive women are raped (Flowers, 1987, 34).

Women scream "rape" as a vengeful measure or to protect their reputations (Burt, 1980; Flowers, 1987; Johnson and Sigler, 1997); in other words, women lie.

It cannot happen to me (Flowers, 1987, 35).

Rape is motivated by the need for sexual gratification (Flowers, 1987, 35).

Most rapes are perpetrated by strangers (Flowers, 1987).

Rapists look the part (Flowers, 1987, 36).

Rape is an impulsive act (Flowers, 1987, 36).

Rape is a victim-precipitated crime (Flowers, 1987, 34), "she asked for it" . . . "yes means no" (Weisheit and Mahan, 1988, 90) or other variations on the same theme; she was in the wrong place at the wrong time (Weisheit and Mahan, 1988, 90); she asked for it by the way she dressed (Burt, 1980; Weisheit and Mahan, 1988, 90; Johnson and Sigler, 1997), or going out with that guy, or hitchhiking, or getting too drunk (Weisheit and Mahan, 1988, 90); she willingly went to the man's house or apartment on the first date, so she must be expecting and thus willing to have sex (Burt, 1980; Johnson and Sigler, 1997); saying yes to one man is saying yes to any man (Burt, 1980; Johnson and Sigler, 1997, 68).

Only promiscuous women or women with bad reputations are raped (Burt, 1980; Johnson and Sigler, 1997).

Men can't help themselves (Weisheit and Mahan, 1988, 91).

Rapists are insane sexual psychopaths (Weisheit and Mahan, 1988, 91).

Only a few careless women are raped (Weisheit and Mahan, 1988, 92).

As a result, a more liberal definition of rape has been espoused by researchers who have studied rape and rape victims extensively. Mary Koss is one such researcher. She and her coauthor, Mary Harvey, examined rape definitions and reported that most states have reformed their laws (Koss and Harvey, 1991). They note that most reforms of the definition of rape have expanded "penile-vaginal penetration to include other forms of intercourse, including oral and anal sodomy and penetration by fingers or objects other than the penis" (p. 4).

Sexual assault is any unwanted (not consented to) sexual activity. The spectrum includes fondling, oral, anal, and vaginal intercourse, and any other unwanted sexual activity (Wiehe and Richards, 1995). There is no mention of the gender of or relationship between the offender and victim. This means that the offender and victim can be the opposite or same gender, and the degree to which the victim knows the perpetrator is not an issue.

There are four types of rape based on the level of familiarity between the victim and offender—stranger, acquaintance, date, and marital rape. **Stranger rape** is the easiest to define and the best understood. Stranger rape occurs when a woman is raped by someone she does not know. There is no prior relationship between the two. According to the Rape, Abuse, and Incest National Network (2006), stranger rape has been conceptualized as having three distinct categories.

Major Categories:

1. ***Blitz Sexual Assault***—The perpetrator rapidly and brutally assaults the victim with no prior contact. Blitz assaults usually occur at night in a public place.
2. ***Contact Sexual Assault***—The suspect contacts the victim and tries to gain her or his trust and confidence before assaulting her or him. Contact perpetrators pick their victims in bars, lure them into their cars, or otherwise try to coerce the victim into a situation of sexual assault.
3. ***Home Invasion Sexual Assault***—When a stranger breaks into the victim's home to commit the assault.

Acquaintance rape is a term applied when a rape occurs between a victim and an offender who know each other. They can be casual acquaintances or more familiar, for example, friends, lovers, spouses, or someone just recently met. **Date rape** refers to a rape that occurs when two people are on a date. **Marital rape** is rape that occurs between married couples.

INCIDENCE AND PREVALENCE OF RAPE

Rape and sexual assault are crimes that are difficult to measure. Researchers have attempted to detect the scope of these crimes nationally, but such statistics are of dubious value (Kilpatrick, 1983). Koss and Harvey (1991, 200–203) summarized the empirical data on rape prevalence. These studies can be categorized by the unit of analysis—adolescent girls, college women, adult women, and special groups. Three of the 20 articles cited by Koss and Harvey examined statewide measures of rape and sexual assault. Those studies along with one from Virginia regarding sexual assault on campus are now presented.

Burt (1979) interviewed 328 Minnesota adult women regarding attitudes toward rape and subsequently estimated the prevalence of rape among these women to be 24 percent. Winfield and colleagues (1990) interviewed 1,157 North Carolina adult women and found that 13.5 percent had been sexually assaulted by the age of 15. Miller and Marshall (1987) interviewed 323 North Carolina college women and determined that 27 percent had been coerced or forced to have intercourse while at the university.

In 1993, there were 10.9 million violent crimes in the United States. A half million of these crimes were rapes and sexual assaults. There were two rapes per 1,000 persons aged 12 years or older in 1993. More than one-third of all rapes and 19 percent of sexual assaults were reported to law enforcement agencies (Bastian, 1995). Data for 2004 report that the average annual number of rape/sexual assault victimizations for 2003–2004 was 204,370—a rate of .9 per 1,000 households (Catalano, 2006, 3).

Table 7.2 summarizes the number of rapes per year by data source. In the UCR data, the number of rapes reported to the police reached an all-time high in 2003 and declined slightly over the next 3 years. The NCVS data shows a steady decline from 2000–2003, with an increase in 2004, a decline in 2005, and an increase again in 2006. Nevertheless, regardless of the source, nationally, rape has remained relatively stable.

The Task Force on Campus Sexual Assault (Senate Document No. 17, 1993) examined 60 Virginia institutions of higher education in 1992 to determine among other issues the number of sexual assault cases referred to the various campus psychological centers. The Task Force results indicated that in 1990–1991, 200 such

TABLE 7.2   UCR and NCVS Rape and Rape/Sexual Assault Statistics for 2000–2006

Source	2000	2001	2002	2003	2004	2005	2006
UCR Data	90,178	90,863	95,235	98,883	95,089	94,347	92,455
NCVS Data	260,950	248,250	247,730	198,850	209,880	191,670	272,350

cases were referred. In 1991–1992, a reported 317 such cases were referred, an increase of 117 reported sexual assaults since new awareness strategies were implemented at the various institutions.

The most recent and expansive college study of sexual assault was conducted by Bonnie Fisher and her colleagues. They conducted a telephone survey of a national sample of women attending 2- or 4-year colleges or universities. They surveyed 4,446 women. They found that "2.8 percent of the sample had experienced either a completed rape (1.7 percent) or an attempted rape incident (1.1 percent). The victimization rate (then) was 27.7 rapes per 1,000 female students" (Fisher, Cullen, and Turner, 2000, 10).

The **National Violence Against Women Survey** (NVAW) (Tjaden and Thoennes, 2000) reports lifetime victimization data. This survey found that "17.6 percent of surveyed women and 3.0 percent of surveyed men said they experienced a completed or attempted rape at some time in their life. Thus, 1 in 6 U.S. women and 1 of 33 U.S. men have been victims of a completed or attempted rape" (p. 13).

The authors also report general highlights about lifetime victimization focusing on the age, race, and gender of the victims. Their findings are reported below:

- Over their lifetimes, women who report being raped indicate that they were first raped at a young age. More than half of the women report being raped before they were 18 years old, with 22 percent indicating they were 12 or younger.
- Those who were raped before the age of 18 were found to be twice as likely to be adult victims of rape as those victims who were raped when they were older.
- Over their lifetimes, non-Hispanic women are more likely to be raped then Hispanic women.
- Women who were raped or physically assaulted by strangers were less likely to report being injured during their most recent rape or physical assault than were women who reported being raped by someone they knew.

RAPIST TYPOLOGY

Researchers have classified rapists into distinct categories focusing on their behavior. Groth, Burgess, and Holmstrom (1977) find rape to be about power. They agree with Brownmiller's statement that rape is a power issue, not a sexual crime. They developed a typology of rapists based on the accounts of 133 offenders and 92 victims of what occurs during a rape. These researchers concluded that "there were no rapes in which sex was the dominant issue; sexuality was always in the service of other, nonsexual needs" (Groth, Burgess, and Holmstrom, 1977, 1239).

Rapist typologies include the power-assertive rapist, the power-reassurance rapist, the anger-retaliation rapist, and the anger-excitation rapist. Each is explained by Groth, Burgess, and Holmstrom (1977, 1240–1242):

Power Assertive. Rapists in this category enjoy maintaining control and dominance over their victims. The rape itself becomes a manifestation of their supremacy; rape is viewed as an entitlement, a way to keep their women in line.

Power Reassurance. Rapists who doubt their sexual competence and capability. They often question their own masculinity. In order to increase their self-esteem and build their own sense of adequacy, the men rape helpless women as a way to ensure that the women cannot reject or refuse them.

Anger Retaliation. Rapists of this type commit rape out of rage or resentment towards women. The goal is to shame and humiliate.

Anger Excitation. Rapists in this category actually enjoy the suffering that rape victims endure. They are brutal, finding pleasure in the suffering. Their goal is to inflict pain, agony, and torment.

These typologies show that rape is an act of power and control. Offenders rape to control or dominate another, out of resentment, to see women suffer, or/and to build self-esteem. This typology focuses on power and has little to do with sexuality.

WHY IS REPORTING LOW?

Those interested in studying victims of crime often ask why rape victims do not report the crimes. There are many reasons why people do not report crimes: (1) they feel the police cannot do anything; (2) they feel responsible for the victimization; (3) they feel the victimization was minor; (4) they are afraid of retaliation from offenders; or (5) they have no confidence in the criminal justice system (see, for example, Siegel, 2006).

For rape victims, however, the reasons for not reporting offenses to the police might be very different. Male rape victims feel they will be ridiculed or not believed (Graham, 2006). There are few support groups for men, although more are being established (see http://www.aardvarc.org/rape/about/men.shtml); thus, it is very hard to admit to being the victims of rape by another male or a female. Cole (2006) finds that "women may decline to report rape for a variety of reasons, including shame, fear of social isolation from the assailant's friends, and self-reproach for drinking with the assailant before the rape" (abstract).

Although after being victimized many myths will be dispelled, some rape victims do not report the crime because they fear that their behavior will be on trial, and that they will to some extent be blamed. For example, suppose a woman had been drinking or out alone at night; this may be interpreted by some people as bad behavior that makes her somehow responsible for the crime. Many are fearful their names will be made public or that their past sexual history will be exposed.

No matter what data source is used, a clear finding emerges: Most women will not disclose being raped; it remains a hidden crime. Kilpatrick (1983) discusses five reasons for this nondisclosure: fear, negative expectations, issue not raised, rape is unacknowledged, and symptoms not connected to rape. Although this research is old, it does not refute the merit of what the researchers found in terms of why women do not report rapes; and although the research has not been replicated, the findings still seem to be true today. For our purposes, three of the five reasons need further clarification.

"Fear" refers to victims not reporting rape because of fear of the assailants, fear of stigma, or fear of being blamed for the attacks. "Negative expectations" refers to the reaction the disclosure may have already received from family members or close friends. For example, if a woman tells a friend she has been raped but the friend does not believe her, she may not further disclose the information.

"Unacknowledged" refers to the fact that women may not know they have been raped. Although under the legal definition the incidents would be considered rape, sometimes women do not think of it as such. This occurs most often when the assailants are husbands, lovers, friends, or acquaintances. More recent research conducted by Fisher and her colleagues confirms this finding. Fisher, Cullen, and Turner (2000) were interested in finding out if women in their survey perceived incidents that met the legal definition of rape as rape. This is interesting for this discussion because if women do not think that a crime has occurred, it makes sense that they would not report it to the police. In the Fisher, Cullen, and Turner (2000) study, the authors asked the respondents, "Do you consider this incident to be a rape?" Interesting findings were reported. Even though the researchers classified the assaults as rape, the women were split, with almost one-half stating that it was rape and about one-half stating that it was not. Thus, you can see that even today, as was the case in 1983, women have great difficulty accurately identifying this crime. This may be the reason that rape stays hidden, although fear of reprisal, as found by the Kilpatrick study, makes intuitive sense as well.

MALE RAPE

Students often ask if a man can be raped. The answer is yes. Sexual assaults are frequent in prisons, but men are raped or sexually assaulted outside of prison as well. Sexual assault statistics for men is detailed in a recent BJS report, "Rape and Sexual Assault: Reporting to Police and Medical Attention, 1992–2000" (Rennison, 2002). The full report focuses on females because of the small number of men who reported being raped or sexually assaulted; however, Table 7.3 gives the reader a good indication about the relative frequency of male rape over the 8-year period.

Sexual assault is not bound by gender. Males are raped and sexually assaulted, but not as often as females. A survey of 8,000 men and women found that almost 18 percent of the women and only 3 percent of the men reported being raped in their lifetimes (Tjaden and Thoennes, 2000). The "An Abuse, Rape, and Domestic Violence Aid and Resource Collection" website (AARDVARC.org) reports on male victims of sexual assault, including sexual abuse, rape, incest, and sex-based offenses (2007). It reports the following information:

- The majority of male victims are assaulted by other men. These assaults reflect offenders' need to commit violence and to wield power over their victims.
- The number of male victimizations is likely to be underestimated, as both males and females tend not to report such violence.
- An equal number of assailants are known to victims as are strangers. Males are raped by teachers, friends, coworkers, other acquaintances, and strangers.

TABLE 7.3   Number and Percentage of Rapes and Sexual Assaults, by Victims' Gender, 1992–2000

Gender of Victim	Average Annual, 1992–2000	
	Number	**Percent**
Completed Rape		
Total	140,990	100
Male	9,040	6
Female	131,950	94
Attempted Rape		
Total	109,230	100
Male	10,270	9
Female	98,970	91
Sexual Assault		
Total	150,680	100
Male	17,130	11
Female	135,550	89

Source: Based on Rennison (2002).

Although women can sexually assault men, they are usually thought of as victims rather than as offenders. Thus, it challenges perceptions about sexual assault when male rape is discussed, especially when the focus is on female offenders. Further, Mendel (1995) reports that females are often underrecognized as offenders because (1) the assumption that female perpetration is rare or nonexistent, (2) the denial of female sexuality and aggression, and (3) the assumption that females act under the initiation or coercion of male perpetrators (p. 22).

Laws and legal statutes vary by state; however, for the crime of rape the essential elements include "unlawful, carnal knowledge [sexual intercourse], by fear or force, without consent or against the will of the female" (Klotter, 2001, 126). Sodomy laws apply to female and male offenders in the sexual assault of males. The term *rape* is used, but the correct legal terminology would be *sodomy*. "Sodomy is defined as the carnal copulation by human beings with each other against nature, or with a beast" (Klotter, 2001, 145). This broad definition includes "bestiality, buggery [anal or oral copulation], cunnilingus, and fellatio" (p. 145).

The answer, then, to questions about whether a woman can "rape" a man is no. But, women can sexually assault men. Using the definitions listed above, women can sexually assault men in the same manner that men can sexually assault men: via anal or oral copulation. Anal copulation may occur with any type of object (e.g., broom stick, bottle, or penis) as long as there is penetration of the anus. Also, arousal does not constitute consent. Therefore, if a man has an erection, this does mean consent was granted.

Frazier (1993) conducted a study of male and female rape victims. These victims had been seen at a hospital-based rape crisis center and therefore self-defined the sexual assaults as rape. Frazier reports on the similarities and differences found among these victims. She first reports that male rape is more common than first thought, that it has devastating effects on some men, and that men victimized in this manner often do not report such violence. The males in her sample were primarily young (average age of 30), had a high rate of previous victimization (41% males had been raped previously; 27% were previously victims of incest), and a high percentage of the victimizations involved a weapon. Frazier concludes that male and female victims are similar in terms of age, race, and prior victimization, while the characteristics of the assaults differ somewhat. Both groups of victims were raped by single assailants who were known to the victims, but in cases of females being raped the victims were more likely to be harmed; however, a larger percentage of the males (82%) were afraid of being killed than were females (74%).

DATE RAPE

Mary Koss and Mary Harvey (1991) provide an example of **date rape**. It is modified here to illustrate the case:

> Diana, age 50, was vacationing alone in the Caribbean. She spent some of her time learning sailing and walking along the beach with a fellow guest nightly. At a hotel dance one evening, she accompanied this man to the dance. She danced with him and when he asked her to walk outside, she went. Once on the beach, this 6'4 man asked to have sex and forced her to cooperate by holding her down. Diana was too afraid to resist.

Diana was a victim of date rape. Date rape is sometimes also referred to as acquaintance rape, and either term has the elements of rape previously defined; however, the victims know their assailants (to some degree), and, as in the vignette above, have engaged in social activity with them. Schmidt (2004) defines date rape as a "subset of acquaintance rape . . . which refers to a rape scenario in which there is some romantic relationship between the two parties" (p. 54).

Sheer coercion is often used in date rape; however, more recently offenders have been using more nefarious methods to subdue victims. Offenders have drugged victims with so-called date rape drugs including ketamine, gamma-hydroxybutyric acid (GHB), and flunitrazepam (Rohypnol). These drugs render victims powerless against offenders, sometimes neutralizing resistance and oftentimes rendering the victim unconscious (U.S. Department of Health and Human Services, 2008).

College campuses have a particular problem with date rape (Schmidt, 2004a). The social interactions and age of typical female students make them especially vulnerable to date rape. Cole (2006) reports "that rape is the most common violent crime at U.S. universities. The incidence of rape is estimated to be 35 per 1,000 female college students per year in the United States, although less than 5% of these rapes are reported to police" (abstract). Fisher and her colleagues (2000) reported data on the national sample of women and their sexual assault victimization. They report the number of victims, along with the number of incidents or rate per 1,000 female students. The largest number of victims, 133, were victims of attempted sexual contact without force, with an incident rate of 66.4 per 1,000 female students. The other sexual assault behaviors measured included:

- Completed sexual coercion with 74 victims reporting this, and an incident rate of 24.1 per 1,000 female students reported,
- Attempted sexual coercion with 60 victims reporting this, and an incident rate of 25.6 per 1,000 female students reported,

- Completed sexual contact with force or threat of force with 85 victims reporting this, and an incident rate of 29.2 per 1,000 female students reported,
- Completed sexual contact without force with 80 victims reporting this, and an incident rate of 29.7 per 1,000 female students reported,
- Attempted sexual contact with force or threat of force with 89 victims reporting this, and an incident rate of 37.6 per 1,000 female students reported. (Fisher, Cullen, and Turner, 2000, 16)

CHARACTERISTICS OF ACQUAINTANCE RAPE OFFENDERS

Rape counselors have identified several factors or characteristics of acquaintance rape offenders. Women involved with men who exhibit some of these traits should be wary.

- Emotionally abusive: Men who show emotionally abusive traits, such as making offensive and disparaging comments about women, ignoring women's opinions, and getting upset or angry when women make decisions.
- Control extremists: Men who must be in control of even the most mundane decisions women make.
- Disregard for women: Men who have little regard for women and publicly talk negatively about them.
- Jealousy: Men who are resentful or distrustful of women for no apparent reason.
- Alcohol abuse: Men who abuse alcohol or drugs and who try to get women to engage in similar behavior.
- Physically violent: Men who abuse women by hitting, pushing, or shoving to get their way.
- Intimidation: Men who terrorize or frighten women by sitting too close, using their physical presence to block exits, or talking as if they know women better than they know themselves.
- Sexual and emotional frustration: Men who react inappropriately to sexual and emotional frustration. They may get angry and become physically aggressive as a way to address sexual frustration.
- Weapons: Men who are captivated by guns and other weaponry.
- Bully behavior: Men who are cruel to animals, small children, or anyone else who can be easily pushed around (Warshaw, 1994, 152).

Not all men who exhibit one or more of these characteristics will rape a woman, but the issues incorporated in the risk factors are important. The common themes are men with control issues and men who do not respect women. It is not too difficult to see the connection between men who exhibit these characteristics and the potential for violence.

Awareness is the key. Many college campuses sponsor rape awareness programs. These programs help everyone recognize the risk factors associated with violent behavior. Some universities use mock rape trials as a way to educate and inform. Whatever program is used, the experts agree that such programs are needed to increase people's awareness as well as help them be proactive instead of reactive when the crime is rape.

MARITAL RAPE

Marital violence, including sexual assault/marital rape, is a topic that is being studied more frequently by family violence researchers. Some of the more notable research on this topic has been conducted by Walker (1979), Gelles (1988), and Kilpatrick (1990).

These researchers collected some disturbing data regarding violence in the home. They noted high rates of violence, including sexual assaults of family members and of pregnant women.

Reporting on the incidence and prevalence of marital rape is difficult. Nonetheless, some researchers have attempted to measure marital rape; for example, Kilpatrick et al. (1988) studied a representative sample of 391 women and found marital rape to occur more frequently than stranger rape. Out of 101 rape cases, they found that 24 were marital rapes and 21 were stranger rapes.

Authors have found that anal intercourse occurs more frequently than vaginal intercourse in marital rapes (Barnett, Miller-Perrin, and Perrin, 1997, 2004). Battered women are also subjected to other forms of degradation, such as being raped with objects and being sexually abused in front of their children, and are often raped after returning home from the hospital after giving birth (Barnett, Miller-Perrin, and Perrin, 1997, 2004).

In a survey conducted by Wiehe and Richards (1995, 57), the results were slightly different than those found in the Kilpatrick et al. research. Forty women reported being victims of marital rape. This number represents 80 percent of the sample as compared to 82 percent that indicated they were raped by an acquaintance. Although the percentage is slightly higher for rape by an acquaintance, the percentages are just about equal.

In another more recent study conducted by Basile (2002), where she surveyed a nationally representative sample of women, she found that one-third of the women were victims of unwanted sex with a spouse or partner. And in the data presented previously by Durose et al., they found, "For all sex offenses including rape and sexual assault, almost 5 percent of the offenders were spouses" (2005, 1). Thus, marital violence occurs quite often; the difficulties for researchers, practitioners, and lawmakers lie in getting victims to report offenses and accurately classifying the behaviors.

Researchers agree that estimates of marital rape and violence are underestimates. Several reasons are provided for this: women are less likely to report rape when they know the perpetrators (Koss, 1983); women are less likely to define the acts as rape, even though such threats are associated with sexual behavior that would be objectively described as rape (Frieze, 1980); women are less likely to report rape if they do not consider the threats used to involve a high level of physical force (Koss, 1983); and women and men consider marital rape less serious than stranger or acquaintance rape (Gelles, 1977).

According to Bergen (1996, 1) it is false to think that marital rape is less serious than stranger rape. As she points out, "women who are raped by their husbands are likely to be raped many times. They experience not only vaginal rape, but also oral and anal rape" (as confirmed by Campbell above). Researchers generally categorize marital rape into three types:

- *Force-only rape:*   The man uses the level of power necessary to make the woman submit.
- *Battering rape:*   The man rapes and batters his wife. The assaults may take place at the same time or the battering may occur after the sexual assault.
- *Sadistic / obsessive rape:*   The man torments the woman into submission by using coercion or "perverse sexual acts." In this type of rape, pornography is often used.

Furthermore, Bergen goes on to explain just how invalid the assumption that marital rape is less serious than other types of sexual assault is. She finds the same trauma to be evident in this type of victimization regardless of offender, with both visible and hidden bodily injuries. Bergen notes: (Bergen 1996:1–2):

- Women suffer from broken bones, black eyes, bloody noses and knife wounds;
- Gynecological effects include vaginal stretching, miscarriages, stillbirths, bladder infections, sexually transmitted diseases, and infertility;
- Short-term psychological effects include PTSD, anxiety, shock, intense fear, depression and suicidal ideation; and
- Long-term psychological effects include disordered sleeping, disordered eating, depression, intimacy problems, negative self-images, and sexual dysfunction.

The laws regarding marital rape offer a clear picture of how society has viewed marital rape. In the early seventeenth century, Sir Matthew Hale, a British jurist, interpreted the English law to mean that it was not possible for husbands to "rape" their wives. Husbands were exempt from any rape laws. After all, the marriage contract stipulated that a wife willingly gave herself to her husband. As a result, she could not legally refuse her husband any sexual favor demanded. As a result, a husband could not rape his wife.

Another interpretation was that a woman was the property or chattel of her husband, and as such a husband could damage his property if he wanted. He could do whatever he wished with his property even if it meant defiling it. Thus, if the husband forced his wife to have sex, it was not rape according to the law, because she was *his* property. Yet another view stated that a man and a woman, upon marriage, became one legal body. This legal body could not be severed or destroyed by one of its parts. According to this line of reasoning then, rape did not occur because a man could not rape himself.

Today, however, thoughts regarding marital rape have changed. Women are no longer considered to be property or chattel belonging to their husbands, and marriages are considered to be more equal partnerships. The law, too, has reconsidered the marital rape exemption (Pagelow, 1992). This exemption would hold that husbands could not rape their wives because of some or all of the reasons listed above. However, as early as 1980, three states, New Jersey, Nebraska, and Oregon, had provisions written into statutes to repeal the marital rape exemption. Thus, in these three states husbands could be charged with marital rape. In most cases, husbands could be charged with rape only if the pair were separated and living apart. However, as of 1990, 48 states had laws stating that a husband could rape his wife while they were living together (Peacock, 1995, 60). Still, at that time, Peacock reports, North Carolina and Oklahoma were the only states where a man could not be charged with raping his wife unless he and his wife were separated or living apart.

Marital rape is now a crime in all 50 states, although there are still many states that have provisions written into statute that may exempt husbands from raping their wives. The majority of the states (33) have conditional exemptions while 19 states have no marital rape exemptions (Kirkwood and Cecil, 2001).

To summarize, in every state, marital rape is a crime (Bergen, 1996). Some states allow no exemptions to the law, while others have some kind of exemption. In the

33 states where there are exemptions to the marital rape laws, most exempt husbands when no force is used. Such cases involve women who are forced to have intercourse but are "mentally or physically impaired or unconscious" (Bergen, 1996, 150). These women legally cannot give consent; however, the state views the "no force" element as having more weight than the consent issue. In other words, force is a necessary element of wife rape in these states.

RAPE-PREVENTION PROGRAMS

Rape counselors have identified some strategies for women to consider when confronted with possible acquaintance rape. A word of caution—each crime is different. Critical variables such as the offender, the victim, the time of day, the area of the attack, and whether the offender has a weapon play a significant part in the attack. The purpose of this list is not to tell women to do all the things on the list but to demonstrate that women do have some degree of control. If at all possible, women should try one or all of these strategies. But, if women assess the situations and think none of these suggestions will help, then they should not feel compelled to do anything. After all, giving in and letting an attack occur is not the same as consent. Women must do what they feel is in their best interest. If fighting back escalates an attack into a killing, then what good did the fighting back do?

Following are some suggestions that seem logical and reasonable, and that can be easily remembered, to use when confronted with an acquaintance rape or date rape. These suggestions are provided by Warshaw (1994, 158) and are listed as they appear in her work:

- Stay calm. Be as assertive as you can.
- Appraise the situation and act accordingly.
- Try to get away.
- Yell for help.
- When necessary, attack forcefully.
- Buy time with talk.
- Destroy his idea of a "seduction."

Most of these strategies seem pretty self-explanatory. The last one—destroy his idea of a seduction—needs further clarification. Warshaw (1994) suggests that the woman should try to break the man's notion that this act is a seductive process. She maintains that the woman should tell the man anything that she thinks might turn him off. Her suggestions include telling the man that she has a sexually transmitted disease, she has her period, or she is pregnant (Warshaw, 1994, 159). She also suggests that the woman urinate on the floor, pick her nose, vomit, pass gas, belch—anything to break his perception of "seduction."

Many college campus resource centers have brochures and other information available for female students. An example from Virginia Commonwealth University's website lists victims' rights guaranteed by law to victims of rape:

Congress of the United States H.R. 2363

Victims Rights Guaranteed Under the Law!

You have the right to

- Have sexual assaults investigated by civil and criminal authorities.
- Be free from pressure to not report these crimes, or report them as lesser offenses.
- Have the same representation, and ability to have others present, in campus proceedings as campus authorities permit to the accused.
- Have cooperation in obtaining medical evidence.
- Be informed of any federal or state rights to test sexual assault suspects for communicable diseases.
- Have access to existing campus mental health and victim support services.
- Be provided housing which guarantees no unwanted contact with alleged sexual assault assailants.
- Live in campus housing free of sexual intimidating circumstances with the option to move out of such circumstances.

SOURCE: VCU Resource Center (2006).

STATUTORY RAPE

Statutory rape is non-forcible sexual intercourse with a person who is under the statutory age of consent (as defined in Chapter 7). It is a crime in every state, yet it is often not aggressively pursued by law enforcement or the judiciary because the behavior is consensual and involves teenagers, who make bad witnesses, and the public and criminal justice practitioners deem it better to focus on other crimes. But statutory rape laws are in place to protect victims, and must be enforced.

Statutory rape victims "share characteristics common among victims of childhood sexual abuse and domestic violence. This finding further indicates that these young people should be protected, not ignored" (Turman and Pover, 1998). These sexual relationships are illegal and must be stopped.

Statutory rape victimization "has potentially devastating consequences for teenagers, including pregnancy and parenthood, as well as sexually transmitted diseases, emotional abuse, and emotional scars for a lifetime (for both female and male victims)" (Turman and Pover, 1998). A recent example is Jamie Lynn Spears, the 16-year-old sister of Britney Spears, who was pregnant by her 18-year-old boyfriend. Although no one was charged with statutory rape, according to the definition listed above, it was a possibility that a charge could have been forthcoming, and it is well known that Spears is pregnant, demonstrating one of the devastating consequence of statutory rape as listed by Turman.

A recent research bulletin reports what is known about statutory rape. This bulletin proclaims that this is the "first large-scale look at the patterns and responses to statutory rape" (Troup-Leasure and Snyder, 2005, 1). Here's what the authors report:

- for every three forcible rapes, there is one statutory rape reported to law enforcement.
- In 95 percent of the cases, the victim is female.

- Almost 60 percent of all statutory rape victims are aged 14 or 15. In 18 percent of female statutory rape cases, the offender is less than 18 years of age.
- The offenders are the opposite sex of the victims in almost 100 percent of female cases, and about 94 percent of male cases.
- Thirty percent of statutory rape offenders are boyfriends or girlfriends, while in 60 percent of the cases, the offenders are acquaintances.
- The average age difference between offenders and victims for female statutory rape victims is 9 years. For male victims, it is 6 years.
- Seven out of 10 male statutory offenders are 21 years or older, while a little more than four out of 10 female statutory offenders are 21 years or older.

RAPE SHIELD LAWS

Rape shield laws are statutes or laws that limit the introduction of a victim's sexual history into the court process. In the past, information about a victim's sexual history was allowed in at trial because it was thought that this history played an important role in whether a woman had been raped. Also defense attorneys sought to have this information available at trial in an effort to put the blame for the attack on the victim away from the offender.

To some, the Kobe Bryant sexual assault case brought back renewed interest in the sexual backgrounds of victims. As you may recall, Kobe Bryant's victim alleged that Mr. Bryant forcibly raped her. The defense wanted to bring her past sexual history into their defense strategy. They wanted to introduce into evidence that the woman had had sex at least two other times, with perhaps two different men, earlier the same day that she was allegedly raped by Mr. Bryant. The defense hoped that the information that the victim had willingly participated in sex with two other men before being allegedly attacked by Mr. Bryant would negate her claim that she had been raped. In other words, the defense was making the claim that if a woman had sex with two other men before the Bryant "attack" then the "attack" must have been a consensual act. The Bryant case was settled before it ever went to court; thus, the public will never really know what happened between Mr. Bryant and the hotel employee. However, criminal justice pundits mercilessly held on to the victim's sexual history focusing on it extensively throughout the investigation of this case.

Rape shield laws are supposed to protect victims from public scrutiny by prohibiting the media from broadcasting or publishing their names and to protect them in court by prohibiting past sexual experiences from being introduced into evidence in order to negate the rapes. However, rape shield laws vary in terms of their effectiveness because challenges made to including rape victims' names in media outlets have not been supported by the courts, and in some cases past sexual history is slipped into testimony even though it should be challenged. Nevertheless, rape shield laws are found in nearly every jurisdiction in the United States. The assumption behind these laws is that consent in one sexual encounter does not imply consent in another, making previous experiences irrelevant. Just because a woman previously consented to sex does not mean she will lie in court, so why is it needed (Anderson, 2004, 1)?

According to Anderson (2004), Michigan was the first state to pass a rape shield law in 1974. She states that 48 other states and the District of Columbia also now have rape shield laws. The American Prosecutors Research Institute has compiled an excellent summary chart that provides a state-by-state analysis of what is generally admissible, what is exempted, and what are the circumstances for the exemption. (The chart is available at http://www.arte-sana.com/articles/rape_shield_laws_us.pdf). In general, any evidence that is related to past sexual behavior is excluded. However, exceptions are made, most notably when there is a past sexual history with the current defendant.

FALSE REPORTS

Do women lie about being raped? MacDonald (1995) addressed this issue. He examined the UCR data to determine the number of *unfounded* rapes. An unfounded crime is one that has not been substantiated by the police. MacDonald acknowledges that not all unfounded crimes are false reports. He claims that 8 percent of all the rapes reported in 1992 were unfounded.

False reports erode the credibility of women in general. It is true that most women do not lie, but it is also true that some will lie. False reporting does occur; however, the number of real rapes far exceeds the number of false reports.

SANE/SART PROGRAMS

Programs designed to help rape victims include sexual assault nurse examiner (SANE) programs and sexual assault response teams (SART). Each was developed to introduce nurses into the care of victims of sexual assault (Burgess et al., 2006). "SANE programs were created whereby specifically trained nurses provided 24-hour coverage as a first response to sexual assault victims in emergency rooms and nonhospital settings. . . . In addition, sexual assault response teams (SART) developed which included a coordinated community effort with law enforcement, detectives, victim advocates, and the SANE" (Burgess et al., 2006, 205–206). And while these programs have been shown to be successful, "little empirical evident is available on the efficacy of SANE/SART programs on the judicial process" (p. 206). Here we see community approaches and responses to victimization. It is similar to what is being done with intimate partner violence where the community rallies to offer services and support to the victims (see Chapter 8).

Burgess and her colleagues conducted a study that was sponsored by the American Prosecutors Research Institute and Boston College William F. Connell School of Nursing to test the efficacy of SANE/SART interventions and prosecutorial outcomes. There were 530 acute adult female sexual assault cases examined from three sites: New Jersey, Kansas, and Massachusetts. Three different responses were analyzed: (1) SANE-only cases, where sexual assault nurse examiners performed the evidentiary exams; (2) SANE/SART cases, which included SANE exams and SART responses; and (3) non-SANE/SART cases, where treatment was received from non-SANE personnel in medical facilities (Burgess et al., 2006, 206). Burgess and her colleagues analyzed the 530 cases and concluded: "The study findings are significant with regard to the efficacy of SANE/SART interventions in regards to prosecution. The two most defining elements of a SANE/SART intervention (on average, more evidence collected and significantly more biological evidence collected) are key factors with regard to SANE/SART intervention and the likelihood of charges being filed" (p. 206). Thus, SANE/SART interventions are supported especially when the end goal is to increase charges being filed against the offender.

SEXUAL HARASSMENT

Sexual harassment is a form of sexual violence that violates Title VII of the Civil Rights Act of 1964 (U.S. Equal Employment Opportunity Commission, 2007). The Code of Federal Regulations provides the following definition of sexual harassment:

> Unwelcome sexual advances, requests for sexual favors, and other verbal or physical conduct of a sexual nature constitute sexual harassment when (1) submission to such conduct is made either explicitly or implicitly a term or condition of an individual's employment, (2) submission to or rejection of such conduct by an individual is used as the basis for employment decisions affecting such individual, or (3) such conduct has the purpose or effect of unreasonably interfering with an individual's work performance or creating an intimidating, hostile, or offensive working environment. (29CFR1604.11)

From this regulation, two types of sexual harassment have been identified: *quid pro quo* cases and "working conditions" cases. In *quid pro quo* **cases**, harassment is a term or condition of employment. In **working condition cases**, harassment creates a "poisoned" or "hostile" working condition (College and University Personnel Association, 1986).

Quid pro quo cases occur when specific academic or employment benefits are withheld as a means of coercing sexual favors. This may happen between a supervisor and an employee or between a professor and student. The power differential must be clear in order for sexual harassment to be evident, for example, Professor Smith telling a student she can get an "A" in his class if she has sex with him.

In the typical working conditions case, a supervisor either creates or condones a work environment in which sexual harassment exists (*Bundy v. Jackson,* 1981). For example, sexually explicit and degrading cartoons are placed outside female graduate students' offices; the women complain to the dean, but the cartoons not only stay posted but increase in number. This is an example of a poisoned working condition: the women find it difficult to concentrate on their studies and feel unwelcome because of this behavior.

According to a report sponsored by the American Association of University Women (AAUW), there are misconceptions about sexual harassment that are found in both men and women. To clarify the issues, they ask via their website questions that should help victims know that they have been sexually harassed. For example, they indicate that verbal, nonverbal, and physical behavior is included in sexual harassment as are unwelcome and unwanted lewd jokes, gender-based slurs, and sexual contact. In particular, any behavior that creates a sexually hostile learning or teaching environment is considered sexual harassment. Additionally, sexual harassment can also occur between same-sex individuals. These behaviors are against the law and should not be tolerated. There is a tendency to think of sexual harassment in a more narrow way, that is, thinking only about physical contact as sexual harassment; however, as indicated in here, other behaviors including verbal and nonverbal behaviors, and unsolicited and unappreciated lewd jokes and gender-based slurs are examples of sexual harassment (Hill and Silva, 2005).

It is generally agreed that in order to establish sexual harassment, victims must report it to someone in authority and document its existence. Documentation is very important. In the Anita Hill/Clarence Thomas sexual harassment case, Anita Hill never formally alleged sexual harassment until Clarence Thomas was being considered for the U.S. Supreme Court. Although Anita Hill testified for days in an excruciating ordeal, Clarence Thomas was still appointed. Harassment must be reported to someone in authority immediately. If not, it will be almost impossible to prove in the future.

One study regarding sexual harassment and academe was conducted by Elizabeth Stanko (1992). The majority of the respondents were white, full-time university professors. Stanko found that 59 percent reported that they had received unwelcome comments or remarks about their sexuality during their professional and graduate training. Such comments usually had racist or homophobic overtones. The typical reactions of the victims were anger, shock, irritation, and disappointment. Seventeen percent indicated they felt sexually intimidated by someone in authority, usually a dissertation supervisor or a professor in the graduate program. The sample cited the following as examples or types of sexual intimidation (Stanko, 1992):

- financial and academic support for sex
- refusal to process data for one's dissertation because of refusal of sexual advances
- threats or promises related to grades
- recommendations or grant support for sex
- being given pornography as part of the "professional" reading materials (pp. 3–4).

The second part of Stanko's (1992) research addressed sexual comments and sexual intimidation during field work and on research projects. About one in three respondents reported encountering sexual harassment during this phase of their studies. Some of the women felt it was just part of their job to put up with this unwanted behavior.

Stanko (1992) recommends several strategies for addressing sexual harassment at the university level. She proposes: (1) increasing the awareness and recognition of the problem; (2) condemning sexual harassment and naming it as a discriminatory behavior; and (3) setting up special committees to investigate the issue. Many agree with Stanko's recommendations. The only way to stop sexual harassment is by making both men and women aware of the problem and condemning such behavior.

According to the U.S. Equal Opportunity Employment Commission (EEOC), "in Fiscal Year 2005, EEOC received 12,679 charges of sexual harassment. Males had filed 14.3% of those charges. EEOC resolved 12,859 sexual harassment charges in FY 2004 and recovered $47.9 million in monetary benefits for charging parties and other aggrieved individuals (not including monetary benefits obtained through litigation)" (U.S. Equal Employment Opportunity Commission, 2007).

According to the AAUW *Facts and Figure* page, the most recent available statistics for college student victimization regarding sexual harassment include:

- Both female (62%) and male (61%) college students have reported being sexually harassed at their university, with the percentage of reporting being about the same.
- A larger percentage personally know of someone who has been harassed. Almost two-thirds of the students report as such.
- Few students actually attempt to report these incidents. Ten percent or less indicated they attempt to report such victimization.
- A little more than one-third (35%) of those victimized do not tell anyone about the harassment.

- A large percent, 80 percent, report that the offender was a former or current student.
- Reported sexual harassment incidents occur most often in the dorms (39%).
- Over half of males (51%) report that they have sexually harassed someone in college, with almost one-quarter (22%) admitting to harassing someone often or occasionally.
- A large percentage, 31 percent, of females disclosed that they sexually harassed someone in college (Hill and Silva, 2005).

CONCLUSION

Many rape myths are still very prevalent today. Both men and women are victims of sexual assault. Rape is a crime of power; although this might be the hardest myth to debunk. The rapist typology created from information collected from victims and offenders reveals that rape is an act of power and control.

Women are particularly vulnerable to date rape on college campuses, although acquaintance rape is not exclusively a campus crime. Women need to be smart and use whatever means works in that particular situation.

Study Questions

1. Date rape is most prevalent on college campuses, what campus resources are available at your institution to address sexual assault? Do you think the campus provides enough resources to address this problem?
2. While examining all the rape myths presented in this chapter, which did you find to be the most difficult one or ones to accept? In other words, were you challenged by the myths in terms of your own beliefs? How did you reconcile this?
3. Male rape is a problem that does not occur only in prison, and yet we see that reporting of this kind is low. What are the reasons for this low reporting rate, and what are some ways to encourage rape survivors to report this victimization?
4. What are rape shield laws, and why do we need rape shield laws? How are these laws related to victim blaming discussed in Chapter 2?

Key Terms

- acquaintance rape   124
- anger excitation   126
- anger retaliation   126
- blitz sexual assault   124
- contact sexual assault   124
- date rape   124
- false reports   136
- home invasion sexual assault   124
- male rape   124
- marital rape   124
- marital violence   130
- National Violence Against Women Survey (NVAW)   125
- power assertive   126
- power reassurance   126
- *quid pro quo* cases   137
- rape   121
- rape myths   122
- rape shield laws   135
- SANE/SART programs   136
- sexual assault   121
- sexual harassment   137
- stranger rape   123
- working condition cases   137

CHAPTER

Intimate Partner Violence

8

INTRODUCTION

Violence against women where the offender is a spouse or cohabitant has been labeled **intimate partner violence (IPV), domestic violence (DV), spouse abuse**, or **wife battering**. These terms have similar meanings and are often used interchangeably when discussing the topic of violence against women. The difference in the definitions is the focus of the intimate relationship in terms of whether the couple is officially married or whether they have an intimate relationship like that of a married couple without being married. To be more inclusive of all types of victimization against women in a domestic setting, this chapter is entitled "Intimate Partner Violence," and while this remains its focus, also included are discussions of intimate partner violence where males are the victims and of stalking and cyberstalking, where females are more likely to be the victims, mostly at the hands of an intimate partner.

Traditionally, society has viewed intimate partner violence as a "private matter"—something not discussed in public but kept inside the home. Public discussions about intimate partner violence have created controversy in society, often challenging the belief that the home is a sanctuary where all are safe.

Examination of early American law reflects how women were treated in a less than admirable way: they were considered to have low status and were often abused without much thought given to their plight (Hampton and Coner-Edwards, 1993). Wives were considered property of their husbands, and as such, husbands were allowed to beat their wives in an attempt to change or correct inappropriate behavior.

These attitudes regarding women continued until the women's movement began to gain momentum and power. Officially, the women's movement began in 1973 (Hampton and Coner-Edwards, 1993), and it is credited with making society aware of spousal abuse. This movement forced the violence from the homes and into the public light; however, it took (and is taking) more time to have all types of intimate partner violence considered criminal offenses and to fully enforce the criminal code. There is still a great deal of reluctance to interfere with private family matters, even when the law prohibits such behavior. The exception to the unwillingness to interfere is the establishment of domestic violence shelters where women and their children can seek safe refuge from abusive partners. Nevertheless, domestic violence shelters, as will be discussed later, show mixed results in terms of usage among battered women.

As a result of the women's movement, social agents are more aware of intimate partner violence. For example, the medical community is now more aware of the issue and will question women about suspicious bruises, cuts, and lacerations.

Women, too, are more likely to be aware of the global rate of intimate partner violence and to report such abuse (although there still are many problems with reporting).

Nothing has brought intimate partner violence into the spotlight more than the O.J. Simpson case. In almost every intimate partner violence forum, this particular case is discussed because of the media attention that surrounded the trial. The media circus was sparked because the offender, O.J. Simpson, was a famous athlete, sports commentator, actor, and public spokesperson for a car rental agency. There was great interest in him—but for our purposes the O.J. Simpson case brought a great deal of attention or interest to spousal abuse.

In his case, Mr. Simpson was arrested and tried for the murder of his ex-wife, Nicole Brown Simpson. Although Mr. Simpson was found not guilty, the nation was forced to reconsider intimate partner violence as the stereotypical beliefs regarding intimate partner violence were challenged. Research has shown for a long period of time that intimate partner violence knows no demographic barriers—intimate partner violence is likely to occur at all income levels, and it crosses all educational lines, geographic boundaries, and racial and ethnic lines. The death of Nicole Brown Simpson made the nation take notice of these facts.

Spotlight or no spotlight, the majority of intimate partner violence remains hidden. No matter how many awareness programs are delivered where this information is presented—intimate partner violence knows no racial or class boundaries, women should report it, it is not acceptable behavior—it still remains true that a great deal of abuse stays hidden, for a variety of reasons. Thus, any attempt to quantify the instances of intimate partner violence that occurs in the United States or elsewhere becomes problematic, even more so than measuring other crimes. In these cases, there is the added difficulty that victims do not want to report it to the police nor in many cases do they want to report it on surveys. Much of the time, many women do nothing but suffer the abuse, until it gets to a point of no return.

DEFINING INTIMATE PARTNER VIOLENCE (IPV)

Some terms that have been used to describe intimate partner violence include spouse abuse, domestic partner violence, wife beating, **marital violence**, and wife assault (Harris and Dewdney, 1994). This section of the chapter will explore how the terms are similar and how they are often used interchangeably by researchers, practitioners, politicians, and the general public.

However it is labeled, **domestic partner violence** is the "abuse of a spouse (or intimate partner), *usually* a woman, to maintain control and power by the abuser, *usually* the man" (Dickstein, 1988; Gelles and Conte, 1990; Hampton and Coner-Edwards, 1993; emphasis added). In this intimate relationship, the person in power uses force to cause pain or injury to the person with less power (Pagelow, 1984). The intimate relationship dyad is the reason that "domestic partner violence" is viewed the same as spousal abuse or partner violence. The relationship between the two individuals may not be "official" in terms of being married, but the relationship is considered more intimate than, say, stranger violence.

Terms like *abuse, battering,* and *violence* have been used in definitions of spousal abuse and intimate partner violence. Others have used the term *aggression.* For the most part, *abuse* and *battering* have been used interchangeably. According to the Women's Rural Advocacy Program (http://www.letswrap.com/dvinfo/whatis.htm), there are four types of abuse:

1. ***Physical***—includes pushing, shoving, slapping, hitting with fist, kicking, choking, grabbing, pinching, pulling hair, or threatening with weapons.
2. ***Sexual***—includes forced sex with the threat of violence, sex after violence has occurred, or the use of objects or damaging acts without the woman's consent.
3. ***Psychological/Emotional***—includes brainwashing, control of the woman's freedom to come and go when she chooses.
4. ***Destruction*** of property or pets.

These types or categories of abuse may also be viewed as violent acts. The physical and sexual acts certainly are violent, although the level of violence can be categorized as mild to severe. Arguably, the destruction of property or pets and the psychological/emotional abuse can be viewed as violence too.

Kelley (1988) conceptualized all violence against women by men to have common characteristics. Those characteristics are displayed on a continuum and include "abuse, intimidation, coercion, intrusion, threat, and force." These characteristics are common in the acts men use to control women.

Other researchers also have attempted to categorize the intimate partner violence behaviors into types or typologies. Researchers have identified "three correlated but separate types of marital violence: verbal aggression, mild physical aggression, and severe physical aggression;" others have developed different alignments, proposing "four abuse dimensions: physical, sexual, psychological, and verbal;" and others have identified "four somewhat divergent clusters designated as emotional/controlling, physical, sexual/emotional, and miscellaneous" (Barnett, Miller-Perrin, and Perrin, 1997, 2004, 187).

As researchers define intimate partner violence and put certain behaviors into categories of violence, most often based on severity of the actions, they are attempting to help themselves to better measure the incidents. Still, it remains problematic if the research community cannot agree on the definitions of such violence. The literature tells us that the problem is not in the definitions themselves, as they are mostly based upon statutes or criminal codes. The problem lies in categorizing the behaviors, as was illustrated above, with several different ways to do so.

Decades of research has shown that measuring spousal abuse/domestic partner violence is difficult. However, some researchers have attempted to determine the prevalence of such violence. Most often, data on intimate partner violence comes from three sources—clinical samples, official report data, and social surveys (Gelles, 1993b). Clinical settings would include emergency rooms and domestic violence shelters, and while a great deal of information can be collected at these locations, the generalizability of the data is limited, because the data primarily represent case studies.

The Uniform Crime Reports include criminal family violence and family homicide, but, as mentioned previously, contain only incidents reported to the police. The National Family Violence Surveys conducted in 1975 and again in 1985 by Gelles and Straus (1988 Straus and Gelles 1986, 1990) measured family violence from a representative sample of 2,143 married and cohabitating couples in 1975 and 6,002 couples in 1985. Other researchers have conducted independent social surveys as well, but none have been as extensive as Gelles and Straus's; still, their data are old. Another source of family violence data is the National Crime Victimization Survey. With all these sources of data on intimate partner violence, the estimates of intimate partner violence varies greatly from source to source. And while Dwyer et al. (1996, 69) report that the range varies from "2.1 million to 8 million women abused," other researchers have concluded that "the true extent of intimate partner violence is an elusive research topic" (Dwyer et al., 1996, 69).

Recently, however, Durose and his colleagues (2005) examined multi-methods and multiple sources of family violence. Their overall conclusion is that family violence in the aggregate went down by more than one-half between 1993 and 2002. To date, their research findings are the most comprehensive statistics on family violence, and as such their findings on intimate partner violence will be reported. They conclude:

- Almost one-half of all violent crimes committed against family members are intimate partner violence offenses. The other half involves crimes against other family members (41%) and children attacking parents (11%).
- The majority (almost 75%) of the victims in intimate partner violence are female.
- The majority (almost 75%) of the offenders in intimate partner violence are male.
- Simple assault is the most frequently observed type of intimate partner violence; however, there are also reports of rape, sexual assault, and murder. Less than five percent of the time, however, these crimes are committed by spouses.
- The most prevalent offenses committed by spouses are simple assault (70%) and aggravated assault (about 16%).

Further, the results from the National Violence Against Women (NVAW) Survey (Tjaden and Thoennes, 2000) reveal lifetime estimates for intimate partner victimization. The survey methodology included surveying by telephone a nationally representative group of 8,000 U.S. women and men to determine their experience as victims of violence. The study included questions about violent victimization at the hands of an intimate partner. Their study results as they relate specifically to IPV are paraphrased below:

- When considering all types of rape (including attempted and completed forced vaginal, oral, and anal sex) by an intimate partner over the course of a lifetime, the survey found that about eight percent of women and less than one percent (0.3) of men were raped by either a former or current intimate partner.
- When examining physical assault to include the continuum of behaviors from slapping or pushing to using a weapon, over the course of a lifetime the survey found 22 percent of the women and about seven percent of the men had been physically assaulted by a former or current intimate partner.
- Most intimate partner violence is relatively minor, consisting of pushing, grabbing, shoving, slapping, and hitting, while others have been defined as simple assault.
- When considering intimate partner stalking, the NVAW results found that over a lifetime, stalking by an intimate partner that resulted in high levels of fear was reported by almost five percent of the women and less than one percent (0.6) of the men by former or current intimate partners.

Still, despite heroic efforts to measure intimate partner violence, there remains one significant problem—underreporting. Many women do not report their victimization to anyone because they are embarrassed, fear reprisal, or think that the act is too inconsequential (DeKeseredy and Hinch, 1991, 13). This has lead researchers to speculate or estimate from the known statistics to projected rates of undisclosed violence. This practice started in the 1970s and continues today despite the efforts to capture family violence regardless of whether or not it is reported.

For example, Walker (1979) estimated that over one-half of all wives would be assaulted sometime during their marriage. Since Walker made that estimation, other researchers have compiled data to determine the amount of intimate partner violence nationally. The National Family Violence Surveys (Gelles and Straus, 1988) report figures based on a nationally representative sample of married and cohabitating couples. Gelles and Straus (1988) found that in a one-year period, 16 out of 100 couples reported a violent incident. When this rate is applied to the "54 million couples living in the United States," the result is "an estimated 8.7 million couples who experienced at least one assault in 1985" (Hampton and Coner-Edwards, 1993, 117).

Most of the assaults reported above were minor. However, "63 of 1,000 couples reported serious assaults such as kicking, punching, biting, or choking" (Hampton and Coner-Edwards, 1993, 117). This rate, applied to couples in the United States, translates to 3.4 million instances of serious assault in 1985. The prevalence of intimate partner violence, that is, the percentage of couples who have experienced some violent event over their lifetime together, is approximately 30 percent (Hampton and Coner-Edwards, 1993, 117).

These data indicate that spousal/intimate partner abuse has a significant impact on its victims. The physical and psychological consequences include broken bones, miscarriages, broken families, and death (Busby and Inman, 1996). Some victims experience nightmares, anxiety, depression, social isolation, and loss of self-esteem. According to Busby and Inman, "each year over one million women seek medical care due to battering" (1996, 2).

Some researchers have attempted to explain the causes of wife assault. According to Harris and Dewdney (1994, 77), the rank order of the major causes of spousal abuse (determined by the number of respondents who indicated this particular risk factor was present in the abusive relationship) is as follows:

1. Man abuses alcohol.
2. Man grew up in a household where violence was present.
3. Money problems/issues.
4. Man has problems with self-confidence and sense of self-worth.
5. Psychological issues, including mental defect and instability.
6. Marriage is troubled and communication within the partnership is weak.
7. Man is suspicious and envious.
8. Control issues, especially in managing aggravation.
9. Stress.
10. Lack of respect for women.
11. Woman has problems with self-respect and her sense of self-worth.
12. Violence is seen as a viable solution to problems and issues.

EMOTIONAL AND PSYCHOLOGICAL ABUSE

Intimate partner violence also includes **emotional** and **psychological abuse**. These behaviors instill fear, increase dependency, and may lower or damage the self-esteem of victims (Murphy and Cascardi, 1993). Anderson, Boulette, and Schwartz (1991, 293)

TABLE 8.1 Emotional and Psychological Abuse Typology	
Isolation or **Restriction**	The victim is monitored, tracked, and controlled by the offender in all her activities and other social contacts.
Humiliation or **Degradation**	The victim is ridiculed, denigrated, or degraded (put down) by the offender.
Property Violence	The victim's personal property is deliberately destroyed.
Jealousy and **Possession**	The victim's commitment to the relationship is constantly challenged.
Economic Deprivation	The victim is deprived of money and resources in order to keep her dependent on the offender.
Male Privilege	Traditional sex roles that keep females subservient are employed.
Emotional Withholding	The victim is denied emotional support and contact.
Minimization and **Denial**	The victim is told that the abuse is not that bad and her feelings, perceptions, and sanity are questioned.

argue that psychological abuse or maltreatment "can quite reasonably be considered a common denominator in ongoing interpersonal relationships that are violent." All violent interpersonal relationships include psychological abuse in addition to other forms of abuse. Most researchers studying emotional or psychological abuse list some form of the following as measures of such abuse: isolation or restriction, humiliation or degradation, property violence, jealousy and **possessiveness**, economic deprivation, male privilege, emotional withholding, and minimization and denial (Murphy and Cascardi, 1993). Table 8.1 clarifies this emotional and psychological abuse typology, providing each term with a definition.

INTIMATE PARTNER VIOLENCE: MALES AS VICTIMS

The statistics reported above indicating that almost 75 percent of the victims of intimate personal violence are female, which means that 25 percent of the victims are males. Responding more recently to this debate about whether women victimize men, Joanne Belknap and Heather Melton (2005) found inconsistent findings in terms of the degree to which men are victims of intimate partner violence and the degree to which females are offenders. Their overall findings indicate that,

> IPA (**intimate partner abuse**) is gendered: Men and boys are more likely (than women and girls) to be the perpetrators, and women and girls are more likely (than men and boys) to be the victims of IPA. At the same time, it is necessary to recognize that *there are some women and girls who are abusive and violent to their intimate male partners*. This is estimated to be in five percent or fewer of the cases. Research (also) indicates that women's and girls' IPA needs to be

understood in the context of learning abuse/violence, the opportunity to use abuse/violence, and choosing to use abuse/violence (Emphasis in the original, Belknap and Melton, 2005, in brief).

Belknap and Melton indicate that there are important policy implications that stem from their findings. Included are better ways to collect useful data. They argue that intimate partner victims are often confused with intimate partner abusers, and to curtail this problem, they suggested designing instruments that avoid such confusion. Another methodological problem is sampling. They argue that a broad cross-section of individuals is necessary for samples to be representative and to be able to do anything with the categorical data. They argue for inclusion of ethnicities and races as well as immigrant status to name but a few demographics, in order to better understand intimate partner violence. Finally, they warn that "criminal processing personnel (e.g., police, prosecutors, judges) need to more carefully scrutinize whether a woman who is reported to be an intimate partner abuser is indeed abusive or instead, a victim of IPA, so as not to treat and process a victim as an offender" (Belknap and Melton, 2005, in brief).

Thus, while the current study is methodologically sound, it also is just one more piece of the puzzle, and caution should be invoked when reviewing it. Because Belknap and Melton found such a low rate of male victimization, it does not mean that women do not abuse men. And while the majority of the victims of intimate personal violence may be women, it does not mean that no focus or attention should be given to male victims of IPV.

DOMESTIC HOMICIDE

Saunders and Browne (1993, 379) refer to the murder of a spouse or other intimate partner as **domestic homicide** or **spousal homicide**. The perpetrator of the homicide is not a stranger but an intimate, usually a family member. Domestic homicide is a topic that has not been studied by many researchers because its occurrence is relatively rare as compared to nonlethal forms of intimate partner violence. As a result, our knowledge about domestic homicide is limited. But, as Saunders and Browne (1993) explain, we know that spousal homicide is far more prevalent than other types of domestic homicide. For example, spousal homicide occurs four times more often than child homicide, and women have a one-third greater chance than men of being murdered by their spouses (Plass and Straus, 1987). The National Crime Victimization Survey reports that female victims of homicide were significantly more likely to be killed by intimates than were male victims of homicide (Bachman and Saltzman, 1995).

Saunders and Browne (1993, 380) report that domestic homicides are rarely "out of the blue" occurrences. There usually are patterns of violence involving a series of assaults or threats that culminate in homicide. Also, they found that many "homicides are preceded by a series of attempts to gain intervention" (Saunders and Browne, 1993, 380).

One consistent finding in the research on domestic homicide is that African Americans are at greater risk (Saunders and Browne, 1993, 381). They point out that conditions like poverty and the stress of urban living create a high-risk environment where expressing violence is the norm (Hampton, 1987). Other factors associated with victimization such as employment status and low educational achievement disproportionately impact the black community. Taking together, these begin to explain why African Americans are at greater risk for domestic homicide and other forms of intimate partner violence.

Hawkins (1987) argues that American society devalues African American life. By way of example, he describes the reluctance of social agents to intervene with appropriate medical care on behalf of African Americans. Hawkins argues that the medical community and social agents are indifferent to African Americans, and this indifference results in the higher risks of death for African American women.

Peter Jaffe, Academic Director of the Centre for Research on Violence Against Women and Children (CRVAWC) at the University of Western Ontario, cautions that there are at least seven warning signs that proceed domestic homicides and suggests that family, friends, neighbors, coworkers, and abused women themselves should be familiar with them.

Jaffe lists the seven warning signs in order to help prevent such violence. The list is repeated here because awareness of it serves as a crime-prevention strategy. The warning signs include:

- The couple is not living together; may have temporarily or permanently separated.
- There is a history of domestic violence.
- There is a history of controlling or jealous behavior.
- The male partner is suicidal or has threatened to kill others.
- The male exhibits a sense of despair or hopelessness.
- The male has problems with drugs or alcohol.
- The male stalks or harasses his partner (Baker and Jaffe, 2006).

In 2005, the U.S. Bureau of Justice Statistics reported that 1,181 women and 329 men nationwide died at the hands of an intimate partner (Ress, 2008). Furthermore in Richmond, VA, dozens of women annually are victims of domestic homicides as reported by the Virginia Department of Health, Office of the Chief Medical Examiner (see Table 8.2). In 2008, 10 days into the new year, two women were victims of intimate partner violence. Unfortunately, one woman became a victim of domestic homicide. She was set on fire by her estranged boyfriend and the severity of the burns resulted in her gruesome death. The woman had previously lived with her boyfriend and four young children but had recently moved out of the dwelling they shared.

TABLE 8.2   Number of Women Killed in Domestic Homicides in Richmond, VA, 1999–2005

Year	Number of Women Killed
2005	45
2004	48
2003	42
2002	47
2001	55
2000	58
1999	52

Source: Based on Ress (2008, B1).

THEORIES OF INTIMATE PARTNER VIOLENCE

Intimate partner violence can be explained using any of a number of theories, paradigms, and perspectives regarding society. These theories and paradigms include psychological, sociological, and feminist perspectives. The psychological perspective focuses on violent individuals and proposes that personality traits and psychological disorders explain spousal abuse. The sociological perspective focuses on society and societal structures that affect behavior. In particular, age, sex, position in the socioeconomic structure, and race and/or ethnicity play important roles in spousal abuse. Examples of sociological theories that explain intimate partner violence are general systems theory, resource theory, exchange/social control theory, subculture of violence theory, and learned helplessness (which can fall into psychological or sociological).

General Systems Theory

General systems theory views violence as a "system product rather than the results of individual pathology" (Gelles, 1993b, 9). The family is a system; it has the same characteristics as other systems. These include input, process, output, and feedback loop. A system can "maintain, escalate, or reduce levels of violence" in a family. Using general systems theory, the interactions within families that are characterized by violence are explained. Straus (1973) maintains that a "general systems theory explaining family violence must include the following elements: alternative courses of action or causal flow; the feedback mechanisms that enable the system to make adjustments, and system goals" (Gelles, 1993b, 37). Straus explained how general systems theory applies to family violence using the following eight propositions:

1. Violence between family members has many causes and roots. Normative structures, personality traits, frustrations, and conflicts are only some.
2. More family violence occurs than is reported.
3. Most family violence is either denied or ignored.
4. Stereotyped family violence imagery is learned in childhood from parents, siblings, and other children.
5. The family violence stereotypes are continually reaffirmed for adults and children through ordinary social interactions and the mass media.
6. Violent acts by violent persons may generate positive feedback, that is, these acts may produce desired results.
7. Use of violence, when contrary to family norms, creates additional conflicts over ordinary violence.
8. Persons who are labeled violent may be encouraged to play out a violent role, either to live up to the expectations of others or to fulfill their own self-concept of being violent and dangerous (Gelles, 1993b, 37).

Further developing Straus's model to specifically address intimate partner violence (or as Giles-Sims called it, *wife battering*), temporal stages were added to the model to predict wife battering. Recalling the general systems approach, with its characteristics of input, process, output, and feedback, Giles-Sims indicated that the first stage is the development of the family system. We must conceptualize the family violence, or in this case the wife battering, as part of a system, and in this case as part of a family system. There is an incident of violence (Stage 2), and that violence is stabilized (Stage 3). Then, the family must make a choice about the violent relationship (Stage 4). The victim can either leave the family system and thus resolve the violence (Stage 5), or stay in the system, and the violence continues (Stage 3) (Gelles, 1993b).

Resource Theory

Resource theory assumes that all social systems rest to some degree on force or the threat of force (Gelles, 1993a, 1993b). Power or force is gained through resources. The more the resources, the more force. In the absence of personal, social, or economic resources, a person will use violence as a substitute for these resources to gain the force needed to control a situation. A husband with few resources will use violence as a way to dominate and maintain his control over his family.

Rodney K., a man who had recently lost his job of 25 years with a local telephone company where he was the section supervisor, a position that was considered to be very prestigious, came home to tell his wife of 10 years that he was unemployed. Much to Rodney's surprise, his wife had news of her own: She was taking the kids and leaving to go live with her parents. Rodney had never been one to physically abuse his wife, although later court testimony would show evidence of verbal abuse throughout their marriage. Upon hearing that his wife was leaving him, Rodney said he "just lost it" and severely beat up his wife. She was in the hospital for days with life-threatening injuries.

Using resource theory to help understand the dynamics of this case, one could argue that the physical abuse inflicted by Rodney on his wife resulted from Rodney's apparent loss of resources. Rodney experienced the devastating loss of his job (economic resources), his position in the company (personal resources), and his wife and family (social resources), all in the relatively short period of 24 hour. While resource theory does not justify or excuse Rodney's behavior, it does provide some understanding as to why Rodney reacted as he did. Unfortunately, however, it does not help in preventing the victimization.

Exchange/Social Control Theory

Exchange/social control theory espouses the belief that intimate partner violence is the result of costs and rewards (Gelles, 1983). When the rewards of violence are higher than the cost, violence will be used. When social control agents in society ignore abuse or refuse to intervene on behalf of a child or spouse, the cost of such violence to the perpetrator is reduced. The rewards outweigh the costs, and violence continues.

Peter L. was married for 40 years to his high-school sweetheart. They married young, right after graduation, because his wife was pregnant, despite opposition from both families. Mary had been warned that she was ruining her life by marrying Peter so young and that there were other options, like adoption, that could spare her from this huge mistake. Peter and Mary were determined to make their marriage work, but they soon experienced difficulties, especially after the baby was born with colic. The constant crying took its toll on both Peter and Mary. Peter started to be verbally and physically abusive towards his wife during this time. Peter would later say that verbally abusing Mary—blaming her for the colic, calling her a bad mother—made him feel better about the situation. Doing this made him feel not responsible in anyway for the baby's plight. Mary, for her part, never called the police or reported the incidents because she thought she caused the abuse because she bore a baby with colic. Within a year, the baby's colic subsided. Mary thought her marriage could now be saved and that the abuse would stop. Much to Mary's surprise, it did not. Peter just found other reasons to beat her. She called the local sheriff after one particularly bad beating. The sheriff suggested that Mary give Peter some space to cool off, and if he was still "misbehaving" in the morning to give him a call. Mary called her parents to see if she could stay with them; they refused. Mary soon learned that calling the local police or family members did not help her in anyway.

Using exchange/social control theory in this example and examining the cost and rewards of violence, it can be seen that Peter continued his violence because the cost of the violence did not outweigh the rewards of the violence. The social agents, in this case, the police and family, never intervened on behalf of Mary. Thus, the violence continued because the benefit of the violence outweighed the cost of it.

Subculture of Violence Theory

Subculture of violence theory (Wolfgang and Ferracuti, 1967, 1982) asserts that certain values and cultural rules of a subculture legitimate, even require, violence. The different levels of violence found in society are the result of different subculture values and cultural norms that condone and expect violence.

Maurice M. was raised in a household where family violence was prevalent. He witnessed his father routinely abusing his mother. He can remember with accuracy the words that were regularly exchanged between his mother and father after Friday night drinking bouts. Maurice also would later say that all his friends and other family members reported similar experiences. Thus, it was expected that family violence would be part of his upbringing. Nevertheless, Maurice promised himself that he would never treat the woman he would marry in such disregard. These good intentions, however, did not last. Maurice quit school before graduating from high school to get away from his abusive family situation. With little skills and no high-school diploma, Maurice soon fell into the trap of selling drugs to make a living. He always thought that being a drug runner would result in a substantial livelihood. However, he soon found out that others were making the money, not him. Through all this, Maurice had many girlfriends; and while he never married, he did have long-term relationships and children with some of the women. Maurice routinely abused his girlfriends by verbally, emotionally, and physically attacking them when he experienced frustration and difficulties.

The subculture of violence theory would most likely predict that Maurice was going to be abusive toward his female partners. He was raised in a household where violence was prevalent, and everyone he associated with described similar experiences in violent households. He was a low achiever, failing to complete high school, and he eventually entered into an illegal enterprise. It might be said that this situation supported violence—it was expected, as violence was prevalent in both the family and social situations.

Feminist Perspective

The **feminist perspective** maintains that the reason for spousal abuse is found in the structure of society. This perspective focuses on how this structure is formed to maintain the existing power structure. In society, there is a power differential between men and women: men have power while women do not. Further, "power is based on resources, and violence is the ultimate resource for ensuring compliance" (Yllo, 1993, 51). However, women have limited access to these resources. This perspective describes a husband's violence as a means to "maintain his dominance in a patriarchal marriage" (Yllo, 1993, 49).

William W. was raised in a family where his mother always did what his father said, and she never challenged his "authority." Their relationship would never be described as an equal partnership. The father ruled the family, and his mother obeyed. The family was very religious, and William's mother often cited the bible to justify her subservience to her husband.

All of William's friends, family, coworkers, and other associates had similar views of what made for a successful marriage. When William married, he unconsciously mirrored what he had experienced in his own family situation. He was the one who "provided" for his family, he made all the important decisions, and he controlled all the resources in the marriage. When his wife did not comply like his mother did, he would assert his authority by physically abusing his wife into submission. His wife was not allowed to work outside the home, nor was she allowed to be involved in any of the big or mundane household decisions.

The feminist perspective would argue that marriage is an equal partnership where both the husband and the wife are involved in the important and mundane decisions related to the household. Still, there are structures in society that guard against such a reality coming to fruition. For example, females are paid less than males in almost every employment position. Equal pay for equal work is a mantra of the feminist movement, but, in 2006 females still made about 70 cents for every one dollar that males made for the same job. Thus, William's abusive behavior towards his wife can be viewed as the result of living in and valuing a patriarchal society.

Learned Helplessness

Learned helplessness is a psychological theoretical explanation of helplessness. It is applied to various types of helplessness including human depression, anxiety, child development, sudden death (Knopf, 1991 as cited in Seligman, 1992) among others, and intimate partner violence. In general, "(l)earned helplessness refers to three interlocked things: first, an environment in which some important outcome is beyond control; second, the response is giving up; and third, the accompanying cognition: the expectation that no voluntary action can control the outcome" (Seligman, 1992). Lenore Walker is perhaps best known for applying learned helplessness to battered women. She coined the term *battered women syndrome* which has at its core learned helplessness. But she maintains that learned helplessness is not the same as being helpless, rather it means "having lost the ability to predict that what you do will make a particular outcome occur" (Walker, 2000, 116). In this case, stop the violence. Walker's research on learned helplessness and battered women focused on this hypothesis: "women's experiences of the noncontingent nature of their attempts to control the violence would, over time, produce learned helplessness and depression as the 'repeated batterings, like electrical shocks, diminish the woman's motivation to respond' (Walker, 1979)" (Walker, 2000, 118). This learned helplessness creates a barrier to the development of appropriate skills needed to escape the violence. This theoretical perspective begins to address why women stay in abusive relationships that might lead into battered women syndrome (BWS). According to Walker, BWS "is a collection of psychological symptoms, often considered a subset of Post Traumatic Stress Disorder, and can be measured by a trained mental health professional" (see Walker et al., 2008). At its core is the determination that normal reactions to behaviors are not observed in women experiencing BWS. Psychologists focus on the flight/fight reactions, where the average person responds appropriately to conditions that would result in either running away (flight) or fighting back. However, with BWS, victims do not react in a typical manner. For example, when confronted with danger, most people would get out of harm's way. They could either physically remove themselves from the danger or they could fight the danger. However, those experiencing BWS have different responses that might include experiencing panic disorders, denial, minimization, rationalization, or disassociation. Whatever the psychological symptom, the point is that the person with BWS does not run away or fight back. Further, women experiencing BWS often report negative impact on cognitive and memory areas such as not being able to remember important details or events (Walker et al., 2008).

CYCLE OF VIOLENCE

Lenore Walker is also credited with establishing the Walker Cycle Theory of Violence, which most often is just shortened to the Cycle of Violence (see Walker, 1979, 2000). "This is a tension-reduction theory that states that there are three distinct phases associated with a recurring battering cycle: (1) tension-building, (2) the acute battering incident, and (3) loving-contrition" (Walker, 2000, 126). Some authors and battered women advocates have adapted the phases of Walker's cycle renaming the phases as tension-building phase, crisis phase, and calmer phase; tension-building, explosion, false honeymoon; tension-building, making-up, calm; tension-building, acute-explosion, honeymoon. What the phases are labeled is not important. What is important is the pattern or the cycle of what occurs as part of the violent incident. In the first stage, tension building, the victim and the offender are experiencing behaviors that begin to build tension. Victims often describe feelings of "walking on eggshells." The offender starts to nitpick, perhaps yells, and withholds affection; the victim tries to remain calm, reason, and appease. The second stage is the acute battering incident. The offender may engage in any type of violent behavior, whether verbal, physical, or sexual. The victim may protect herself, reason with the offender, call or not call the police, or leave or not leave the premise. The third stage is the honeymoon stage where the offender apologizes, promises he will never do it again, tries to justify his behavior, tries to blame the behavior on something outside his control. The victim forgives the offender, may set up counseling appointments, drops the charges (if any were filed), becomes hopeful, relieved, and optimistic that life will get better. Unfortunately because this is a cycle or pattern of abuse, it is not too long until the tension-building phase starts up again. And soon after that another violent incident occurs.

LAW ENFORCEMENT AND JUDICIAL RESPONSES TO INTIMATE PARTNER VIOLENCE

In intimate partner violence situations, the response of the police in particular, and criminal justice in general, has not been favorable (see Chapter 4). Such crimes were considered private family matters different from other violent crimes. The police reaction to intimate partner violence was one of informal nonarrest policies focusing instead on intervention and counseling (Liebman and Schwartz, 1973).

However, as Roberts (1996) highlights, the range of responses from law enforcement has expanded and currently consists of specialized training, proarrest policies or mandates, and electronic monitoring. Specialized training focuses on teaching police officers how to control intimate partner violence. Arrest is one option the police have in intimate partner violence situations. Advocates argue that arresting offenders demonstrates to both offenders and victims the seriousness of the offenses, and proarrest policies or mandates are used by various police departments. However, research is inconclusive regarding the benefits of arrest.

Sherman and Berk (1984) were the first researchers to conduct a study to determine the impact of different police responses, including proarrest policies, had on intimate partner violence. In their study conducted in Minneapolis, the authors found that intimate partner violence decreased by 50 percent when the suspects were arrested. Although these findings are startling, attempts to replicate the work of Sherman and Berk have produced mixed results. Six replication studies were funded by the National Institute of Justice, but the results were inconsistent. Gardner, Fagan, and Maxwell (1995) stated the results as: (1) arrest produced no deterrent effect; (2) deterrence was found but only for certain types of offenders; or (3) the subsequent level of violence increased with arrest.

Proarrest policies are problematic in other ways as well. Roberts (1990, 92) maintains that proarrest policies do not protect unmarried cohabiting couples; there has been some evidence that offenders flee before the police arrive, and it is difficult to get officers to comply with the mandate. Some states are moving towards dual arrest policies, where both the victim and the offender are arrested. These policies take away police discretion and any doubt about who is initiating the violence. Dual arrest policies may save police time, get the offender and victim away from each other, and stop the immediate violence; but the vast majority of victim advocates do not support such a policy. The problem lies in whether females are the primary aggressors in the IPV event, and if they are not, should they really be arrested too? According to McCloskey (2005) "Three to five percent of all IPV arrests are of actual female primary perpetrators. One-half to three-quarters of female IPV arrests are erroneous."

Electronic monitoring devices are sometimes used by victims to keep in contact with the police. These devices include pendants, panic alarms, electronic monitors that operate when power lines are down, radios with satellite hook-ups (Roberts, 1996, 92–93), and cell phones.

The judicial response to intimate partner violence has included court orders to protect women from their abusive partners. Such orders are often labeled restraining orders, temporary restraining orders (TRO), or protective orders. With the help of police departments, these orders protect women by prohibiting the batterers from coming within a certain number of feet of the abused women.

Roberts (1996, 93) suggests probation as a judicial response to intimate partner violence because of the services provided to batterers and battered women via probation offices. Roberts notes that only two probation offices provide such services: San Francisco, California, and Ocean County, New Jersey (p. 93).

Some criminal justice professionals have advocated for intimate partner violence protocols to enhance a unified approach to deterring intimate partner violence.

Such protocols often include judges, district attorneys, victim advocates, sheriffs, chiefs, deputies, police officers, magistrates, probation officers, diversion officers, and so on. Each person involved in the protocol is theoretically wedded to the idea that proarrest policies deter intimate partner violence. As a result, the decisions made at each stage involving the various actors should support proarrest actions. There has been little empirical research conducted to test the effectiveness of such protocols; however, one study did examine the protocol in a Northern Virginia district (Volpone, 1995). Volpone questioned whether all the actors involved in the proarrest protocol were cooperative and supportive of such a protocol. Her methodology included a mail survey in which she asked each actor to rate the other actors associated with the protocol to determine who was the most supportive of and responsive to the protocol. She found the magistrate to be the least likely to be viewed as supportive by those participating in the protocol. Those viewed as the most supportive by those participating in the protocol were the domestic court judge, police officers, and the victim-witness coordinator. (See Chapters 4 and 5 for a more elaborate discussion about the policies and programs in law enforcement and the judiciary that address intimate partner violence.)

WHAT HAPPENS WHEN THE OFFENDERS ARE POLICE OFFICERS?

Law enforcement and intimate partner violence: it is quite a paradox when the protectors become the offenders. Law enforcement officers must protect themselves in domestic situations that become violent, because they can quite literally get caught in the middle of disputes and can get hurt badly. However, this is not the focus of this discussion. Here the concern is with law enforcement officers who commit intimate partner violence. How are families of police officers protected when the offenders are cops? How is intimate partner violence addressed within police ranks?

According to Andersen (2006, 1), "If intimate partner violence among the nation's 800,000 police officers occurs at the 10 percent rate estimated for the general population—some studies say the police rate is four times that—then 80,000 (conservatively) families are in trouble." As we know from the discussion above, intimate partner violence is not a private matter; however, many police officers still believe that it is, whether it happens within or outside their own families. Andersen suggests that this belief is what makes general law enforcement policies about criminal behavior ineffective in stopping intimate partner violence.

IPV is even more reprehensible when it is perpetrated by law enforcement officers who are supposed to uphold the law. Moreover, these victims are more vulnerable to abuse because law enforcement officers have legally issued weapons, they know where community resources are located (i.e., shelters), and they know how to shift the blame and avoid being considered offenders (Anderson, 2006). As such, victims are often apprehensive about calling the police. It is quite possible that an officer handling a case might know the victim and the offender, and thus might side with the offender, not investigate properly, or incorrectly document the crime (National Center for Women & Policing, 2006).

A new provision in the Violence Against Women Act of 1994, the Brame protocol, provides grant funds to law enforcement agencies to educate officers and supervisors about intimate partner violence and to provide trained advocates for victims of intimate partner violence. This provision is the first federal law addressing intimate partner violence within the ranks of law enforcement.

Federal law already prohibits police officers convicted of qualifying misdemeanor intimate partner violence crimes from possessing firearms. Further, two acts, the Violence Against Women Act of 1994 (VAWA) and the Omnibus Consolidated Appropriations Act of 1997, specifically address law enforcement, firearms, and intimate partner violence. It is a crime for anyone accused of domestic abuse where a protective order has been issued (VAWA, 1994) or convicted of a state or federal misdemeanor (Omnibus Consolidated Appropriations Act, 1997) to transport, receive, or possess firearms or ammunition. Law enforcement officers are not exempt from these acts (Women's Rural Advocacy Programs, 2006).

Many police organizations back this legislation, including the International Association of Chiefs of Police (IACP). This show of support by the largest national policing organization demonstrates the severity of IPV and law enforcement's lack of tolerance for this crime. IACP also has established a model intimate partner violence policy that includes prevention through the hiring process and training practices for police agencies. The policy is a direct response to the observation that law enforcement is not immune to such violence (International Association of Chiefs of Police, 2003).

To achieve their policy goals, IACP advocates for educational training on intimate partner violence to increase awareness of such behavior. Intervention strategies to be employed when supervisors become aware of such violence must be designed. Structured, uniform responses where a zero-tolerance perspective is advanced will provide law enforcement with the understanding and acknowledgement that such behavior is criminal, and that it will not be tolerated even among fellow officers. Continually updated training is necessary to appropriately reinforce the zero-tolerance policy.

Included in the IACP policy is a call for departments to develop plans or protocols for addressing victim safety. Throughout the protocols is an opportunity to reinforce that such behavior is criminal and that such behavior will not be tolerated. IACP advocates including everyone in the agency, from dispatchers to the chief, in the protocol. The message sent to law enforcement officers must be that IPV is not acceptable in civilians, and it will not be tolerated amongst law enforcement.

The IACP policy also provides specific directions about how to provide safety and protection to the victims. They specifically state:

- Departments shall work with community resources and advocacy agencies to connect victims and their children with appropriate services.
- The command staff designated as principal contact for the victim, shall inform the victim of the confidentiality of the police and their limitations, and ensure that confidentiality is maintained throughout the case.
- All officers shall be aware of possible victim/witness intimidation or coercion and the increased danger when the victim leaves an abusive partner. The designated principal contact shall assist the victim and children in safety planning and caution the victim to be alert to stalking activities.
- If an officer suspects intimidation or coercion of the victim/witness is occurring, the officer shall prepare a written report to be delivered immediately to the investigator in charge of the case through the chain of command. (International Association of Chiefs of Police, 2003, 6)

WHY DO WOMEN STAY IN ABUSIVE RELATIONSHIPS?

Students often ask an obvious question as they learn more about intimate partner violence: why do women stay in abusive relationships? It's an excellent question. IPV victims are acutely aware of their dependence on their abusers for financial resources and for emotional and psychological support; often they have normalized the violence, growing up with violence in their households and expecting such violence in their own homes; their own worth is undervalued, and their competence is frequently questioned. Abused women are fearful of the unknown, are often depressed, and have negative self-esteem. These factors can immobilize women, making them feel as if they have few choices or alternatives to their present situations. They are often isolated and have few connections outside the partner relationships, meaning that the women are dependent upon the abusers for emotional, psychological, financial, and social support. Those who have the courage to leave might not have anywhere else to go.

Abused women often have limited work histories, may have physical limitations due to abuse, do not have financial security, and don't see leaving as an option. These factors lead to the abusers having control and domination over the abused women, resulting in the women staying in the relationships even though to the outside world, leaving looks like an easy decision.

Older abused women have the added baggage of being raised with more traditional sex roles. Older women were expected to marry, raise children, and keep house. If women worked outside the house, the jobs were often menial and low paying. This all led to women feeling powerless, and as such, they were more likely to stay in abusive relationships.

Although leaving sounds like a simple, easy answer, the literature shows that women who do attempt to leave are often abused more severely than before. This reinforces to women that staying is the best option. They are fearful of what will happen if they leave. It's not as easy as just vacating the premises, removing the women from the place of abuse. Abusive relationships tend to continue even after leaving, and abused women know this; they have experienced it, and they often decide to stay in relationships rather than risking more severe bodily injury, or even death.

PREVENTION STRATEGIES

The American Bar Association (2006) reports five ways to eliminate intimate partner violence. These strategies, published on their website, are directed at victims of intimate partner violence.

Five Ways to Eliminate Intimate Partner Violence

1. ***What is meant by Intimate Partner Violence?***   Education is key. It is important that couples know what behaviors are acceptable and unacceptable in an intimate setting. The fact that someone is related to you, by blood or marriage, does not negate the fact that some behaviors are criminal acts. Physical violence, threats, emotional abuse, harassment, and stalking are all forms of intimate partner violence.

2. ***Develop a Safety Plan.***   Always be prepared. Women should develop escape routes and follow-up plans for how they will survive if they experience intimate partner violence. Places to go, people to stay with, resources, police contact information, important family documents, and locations of community domestic violence shelters should be ready in case of emergency.

3. ***Call 911.***   Most important, victims of intimate partner violence should call the police, without questioning anything about the incident. The main objective is to stop the violence, and in order to do so victims and offenders must be separated. The police can help find shelter, remove offenders from the premises, and provide other services available in the community.

4. ***Exercise Legal Rights.***   Victims of intimate partner violence can get court orders to stop the violence and to keep the perpetrator away from them, and there is help available to assist with completing the paperwork to get protective orders. Violence does not have to be accepted, there are legal options to curtail it.

5. ***Get Help; Stop the Violence.***   Many law enforcement agencies and courts employ victim advocates to help victims identify and locate services in the community to assist them. There are many such services available, such as counseling and legal services. Victims of intimate partner abuse should get the help available through the community in an effort to stop the violence. (American Bar Association Commission on Domestic Violence, 2006).

Likewise, intimate partner violence, in general, has been addressed using community resources. However, to be effective, community agencies must support the idea that family violence is unacceptable. But, as Barnett et al. report, "research on the availability, the attitudes, and the effectiveness of community professionals, however, indicates that progress in changing attitudes is slow" (Barnett, Miller-Perrin, and Perrin, 1997, 2004, 200). Thus, motivated and dedicated professionals have their work cut out for them, but that work is crucial in reducing and eliminating intimate partner violence, and should be encouraged and supported.

Specific community leaders and organizations must work together to provide resources for victims of intimate partner violence. These community organizations include churches (e.g., pastors and clergy), medical professionals (e.g., emergency room first responders, doctors, nurses, and insurance company claims adjusters), counseling professionals (e.g., psychologists and social workers), and victim advocacy professionals working at shelters and safe homes (Barnett, Miller-Perrin, and Perrin, 1997, 2004).

Victims of intimate partner violence have few resources and need a place to stay where they can be safe. Shelters and safe houses have been constructed to provide safe refuge for these women and their children. It seemed like a good idea; however, as reported below, shelters and safe houses have mixed results in terms of usage.

According to Barnett, Miller-Perrin, and Perrin (1997, 2004, 202) "less than half of the women who are battered seek emergency housing in shelters for battered women. Those who do are likely to have experienced the more serious battering and lack of family supports." Probably the most often cited reason why women do not seek refuge at shelters is that they are unaware of their existence. Shelters and safe houses must be hard for offenders to find, and thus a veil of secrecy surrounds them; but this seems to have the unintended consequence of shelters and safe houses not being known or made available to those who need them the most.

Shelters usually are not set up for long-term residency, but safe homes provide shelter to women and their children for a longer period of time. Networks of safe homes are created where women can relocate with host families who live close by the women's prior residences. These networks of safe houses also provide services for the victims, including help documenting abuse and completing and filing legal forms such as protective orders (Barnett, Miller-Perrin, and Perrin, 1997, 2004).

Turning to services for victims of marital rape, one form of intimate partner violence, we find a general lack of responsiveness to marital rape survivors on behalf of service providers. As Bergen reports, "A survey of battered women's shelters and rape crisis centers in the United States by Bergen in 1995 revealed several deficiencies in the services being provided. For example, less than half of battered women's shelter programs (42%) and 79% of rape crisis centers provide training on marital rape specifically to their staff members and volunteers" (Bergen, 1999a, 6).

A study conducted in Richmond, Virginia (Moriarty and Earl, 1999), found that there are resources for victims of marital rape; however, the resources are not different or distinguishable from other resources or sources available to female victims of intimate partner violence. As Bergen points out, and other authors agree, marital rape is a serious problem, especially when a woman is pregnant. Thus, there is a need to do more research on the topic and to develop better services for victims to encourage reporting as well as to provide the proper care needed to recover from this type of victimization.

STALKING

What is **stalking**? Stalking is defined as repeated conduct which places a person, or his or her family, in reasonable fear of death, sexual assault, or bodily injury (Code of Virginia §18.2–60.3). Stalking is also "the act or an instance of following another by stealth or the offense of following or loitering near another, often surreptitiously, with the purpose of annoying or harassing that person or committing a further crime such as assault or battery." (Black, 2001, 660).

The Honorable Diane M. Stuart, director of the U.S. Department of Justice Office on Violence Against Women, announced January as Stalking Awareness month (located at: http://www.usdoj.gov/ovw/). According to Stuart, more than one million people in the United States are stalked every year. Stalking is a crime that is widely misunderstood because of the variation in how the crime is committed. In an effort to help prevent stalking and keep people safe, Stuart is advocating for training of criminal justice professionals and advocacy workers.

The Office on Violence Against Women established a Stalking Resource Center in July, 2000. This resource center is a component of the National Center for Victims of Crime, and it has a dual mission: to raise awareness, on a national level, about stalking and to support and promote multidisciplinary programming to address stalking at all levels.

Funds have been provided through this endeavor to train hundreds of law enforcement officers, advocates, prosecutors, and judges every year. Training topics include stalking dynamics, legal remedies, multidisciplinary efforts, practitioner-specific practices, and cyberstalking. Thus, the awareness mission is moving forward.

In order to better quantify the amount of stalking as well as to develop training that can better assist victims of stalking, the Office of Violence Against Women, in conjunction with the Bureau of Justice Statistics, is funding a survey to measure stalking in the United States. The results of this national survey are expected to be very enlightening.

This is what we know about stalking in America as reported on the Stalking Resource Center website (National Center for Victims of Crime, 2008) restating the findings from the "Stalking in America" report by Tjaden and Thoenees (1998):

- 1,006,970 women and 370,990 men are stalked annually in the U.S.
- 1 in 12 women and 1 in 45 men will be stalked in their lifetime.
- 77 percent of female victims and 64 percent of male victims know their stalker.
- 87 percent of stalkers are men.
- 59 percent of female victims and 30 percent of male victims are stalked by an intimate partner.
- 81 percent of women stalked by a current or former intimate partner are also physically abused by that partner.
- 31 percent of women stalked by a current or former intimate partner are also sexually assaulted by that partner.
- 73 percent of intimate partner stalkers verbally threatened victims with physical violence, and almost 46 percent of victims experienced one or more violent incidents by the stalker.
- The average duration of stalking is 1.8 years.
- If stalking involves intimate partners, the average duration of stalking increases to 2.2 years.
- 28 percent of female victims and 10 percent of male victims obtained a protective order. 69 percent of female victims and 81 percent of male victims had the protection order violated (Tjaden and Thoennes, 2000, Stalking in America, NIJ).

Stalking has many negative effects on its victims. According to the *Fact Sheet,* which summarizes research conducted by Tjaden, Thoennes, Blauuw, and colleagues (National Center for Victims of Crime, 2005), many stalking victims report lost time from work, with a small percentage indicating that they had to quit their jobs. Some must seek psychological help. Some report anxiety, insomnia, social dysfunction, and severe depression at higher rates than the average person. Lastly, more than half of stalking victims took some kind of self-protective measure with some taking a very drastic step of relocating.

CYBERSTALKING

What is **cyberstalking**? In general, the definition of cyberstalking is similar to the definition of stalking with the added stipulation that the stalking be carried out over some electronic medium, usually the Internet, most typically through e-mail. *Black's Law Dictionary* defines cyberstalking as "the act of threatening, harassing or annoying someone through multiple e-mail messages, and through the Internet with the intent of placing the recipient in fear that an illegal act or injury will be inflicted on the recipient or a member of the recipient's family or household" (Black, 2001, 169). Bocij (2003) defines cyberstalking relying more on behaviors or examples of the concept. He starts by stating that cyberstalking "represents a new form of behavior where technology is used to harass one or more individuals" (2003, 2). He continues with a more detailed explanation:

> A group of behaviors in which an individual, group of individuals or organi-
> zation uses information and communications technology to harass another
> individual, group of individuals or organization. Such behaviors may
> include, but are not limited to, the transmission of threats and false accusa-
> tions, damage to data or equipment, identity theft, data theft, computer
> monitoring, the solicitation of minors for sexual purposes and any form of

aggression. Harassment is defined as a course of action that a reasonable person, in possession of the same information, would think causes another reasonable person to suffer emotional distress. (2003, 2).

Statistics on Cyberstalking

A nonprofit organization called Working to Halt Online Abuse (WHOA) provides some information about cyberstalking. Founded in 1997, WHOA is a volunteer organization where online harassment is fought. The site provides information about online harassment for victims, law enforcement, and the general public. The WHOA website (http://www.haltabuse.org) provides victimization statistics on cyberstalking.

The data in Table 8.3 are number of cases of cyberstalking that are self-reported to the WHOA site; therefore, these data only begin to scratch the surface regarding cyberstalking, and they should be viewed with caution as the data are not representative. As the table indicates, in 2005, there were 443 cases of cyberstalking. There is no explanation for this jump in reported cases from 2004 to 2005; however, one might assume that the increase is a function of the reporting site being more well known, as opposed to increase in victimization. Without further study, it is difficult to discern the reason for the increase.

When a person reports a cyberstalking incident to WHOA, he or she is asked to complete a survey about the victimization. Of those who reported an incident (443) in 2005, almost 92 percent (407) completed the survey. Of these cases of cyberstalking where a victim was identified, 67 percent of the victims were female. More than one-third (38%) were single and almost another third (32%) were married (WHOA, 2006).

Bocij (2003) has conducted a survey of Internet users to get a picture of cyberstalking. While his sample is not generalizable to the population of Internet users, he does provide some interesting information from a convenience sample of Internet users. Bocij recognizes that methodologically rigorous research needs to be conducted; however, for now, his research is a good place to start with to see the effects of cyberstalking on victims.

Bocij (2003) surveyed 169 respondents using an online questionnaire. He does not report raw numbers, just percentages, and the reader does not know the actual size of the sample because a set of data were discarded because "the questionnaire had obviously been completed with a view to contaminating the survey," but then he does not say how many were thrown out (Bocij, 2003, 5). Nevertheless, the data as presented in the manuscript will be discussed here.

TABLE 8.3   Number of Cyberstalking Cases Reported to WHOA Every Year

Year	Number of Cyberstalking Cases
2000	353
2001	256
2002	218
2003	198
2004	196
2005	443

A large percentage, 95 percent, owned their own computers, and 44 percent felt that their computer knowledge and expertise would be categorized as "intermediate." Seventy-two percent, regularly used chat rooms.

The author provided a set of behaviors that would be categorized as cyberstalking and asked the respondents to indicate if they had experienced any of them. The behaviors listed included:

- Receiving threats via email or instant message, or in chat rooms.
- Having false information about them posted in chat rooms.
- Being impersonated.
- Promoting harassment of them by others.
- Purchasing merchandise in their names or using their credit cards.
- Receiving destructive computer viruses.
- Monitoring their actions using tracking software.
- Accessing personal and confidential information.
- Other distressing behaviors not already listed.

The most common behaviors are "attempted to damage your computer by sending malicious programs to you, such as a computer virus" (40.48%), "sent you threatening or abusive e-mail messages" (39.88%), and "made threats or abusive comments via Instant Message software, such as MSN" (38.69%). The author then reports single and multiple victimizations with the largest percentage indicating having experienced six or more of the listed behaviors. Relatively uncommon behaviors include identity theft and making purchases without permission. Overall, Bocij found more than 80 percent of those responding to have been victims of cyberstalking in one form or another. (p. 9).

Respondents were also asked to rate the level of distress caused by the incidents described above. Almost one-quarter (22.8%) reported being distressed by the incidents to a level of 10 (highest). The mean for the sample was 7.16, indicating a fairly high level of distress resulting from the victimization. The harassers for the most part were unknown to the respondents: 42 percent indicated that the person did not know who was harassing him or her (Bocij, 2003). Moriarty and Freiberger (2006) reviewed 45 newspaper articles that reported incidents of cyberstalking. Using the Dziegielewski and Roberts (1995) typology, they coded data from the newspaper articles about victim–offender relationships, the gender of the victims and offenders, whether prior relationships existed between the victims and offenders, and the resolution of the stalking incidents (e.g., ended, ongoing, and reported to police). The Dziegielewski and Roberts typology consists of three stalker types: domestic violence stalker, erotomania/delusional stalker, and nuisance stalker. Each typology is described in Table 8.4.

Of the 45 cases reviewed, the majority, 60 percent were classified as domestic violence stalkers, followed by 18 percent as erotomania/delusional stalkers, and 22 percent as nuisance stalkers. Cyberstalking mirrored stalking, with the majority of the victims being female and 92 percent of the offenders being male. When comparing the patterns of victimization found in this research with that of other stalking research (see Tjaden and Thoennes, 1998), it was found:

- Most victims of both stalking and cyberstalking incidents are female
- The majority of stalking and cyberstalking incidents fall within the category and definition of domestic violence stalker

TABLE 8.4 Classification of Stalking Typology by Dziegielewski and Roberts

Domestic Violence Stalker	Motivated by the need to establish, continue, or reestablish a domestic relationship where he or she could have or maintain control over the victim.
Erotomania/Delusional Stalker	Motivated by the stalker's fixation with someone he or she cannot have (e.g., doctor, local FBI agent, local anchorwoman, or simply someone who represents the unobtainable ideal).
Nuisance Stalker	The victim is targeted and continually harassed by the stalker. Interaction attempts are often made over the telephone or by other means of contact, such as the Internet.

In most stalking and cyberstalking incidents, the victim will know or have had a previous relationship with the offender (Moriarty and Freiberger, 2006, 10).

CRIME-PREVENTION STRATEGIES

The crime-prevention strategies provided by WHOA to keep individuals safe from cyber-victimization are given in Figure 8.1. Most of these strategies are very easy to do and are based on common sense; however, sometimes the most obvious, commonsense approaches to prevention are the very strategies that are overlooked.

FIGURE 8.1 Online Safety Brochure From WHOA Website

Use Cyberspace Smarts
- Use a gender-neutral email address
- Use a free e-mail account such as Hotmail (www.hotmail.com) or YAHOO! (www.yahoo.com) for newsgroups/mailing lists, chat rooms, IMs, e-mails from strangers, message boards, filling out forms and other online activities
- Don't give your primary e-mail address to anyone you do not know or trust (see above)
- Instruct children to never give out their real name, age, address, or phone number over the Net without your permission
- Don't provide your credit card number or other information as proof of age to access or subscribe to a web site you're not familiar with
- Lurk on newsgroups, mailing lists, and chat rooms before "speaking" or posting messages
- When you do participate online, be careful—only type what you would say to someone's face
- Don't be so trusting online—don't reveal personal things about yourself until you really and truly know the other person
- Your first instinct may be to defend yourself—DON'T—this is how most online harassment situations begin
- Don't fall for phishing e-mails that claim your account has been suspended or needs to be updated—it's a scam!
- *If it looks too good to be true—it is.*

Source: http://whoa.femail.com/onlinesafety.PDF.

CONCLUSION

Intimate partner violence encompasses many types of violence with the common denominator being that the victim and offender have an intimate relationship. They don't have to be married or living together, but there is an intimate relationship between the two that goes beyond mere casual acquaintances. The violence includes physical, emotional, and verbal abuse. Not only are there problems with defining the term, but also victims are hesitant to report such violence.

A recent addition to interpersonal violence is the crime of stalking. Stalking has been recognized as being a potentially lethal type of victimization. Victims of stalking are even attacked in cyberspace, expanding the amount of victimization that occurs.

Study Questions

1. Define what is meant by interpersonal violence, and who are the ones most likely to be the victims of interpersonal violence. Describe the characteristics of the abusers.
2. What are the strengths and weaknesses of proarrest policies for intimate partner violence?
3. Intimate partner violence, in general, is still viewed by many as a private matter. What strategies can you propose to get it out in the public view?
4. Define stalking and explain how extensive the problem is today. How has the new electronic age added to the problem of stalking and what can be done about it?

Key Terms

- cyberstalking   159
- degradation   145
- domestic violence   140
- erotomania/delusional stalker   162
- domestic homicide   146
- domestic partner violence   141
- domestic violence stalker   162
- economic deprivation   145
- emotional abuse   144
- emotional withholding   145
- exchange/social control theory   149
- feminist perspective   150
- general systems theory   148
- humiliation   145
- intimate partner abuse   145
- **intimate partner violence (IPV)   140**
- isolation   145
- jealousy   145
- male privilege   145
- marital violence   141
- minimization and denial   145
- nuisance stalker   162
- possessiveness   145
- property violence   145
- psychological abuse   144
- resource theory   149
- restriction   145
- spousal homicide   146
- spouse abuse   140
- stalking   158
- subculture of violence theory   150
- wife battering   140

CHAPTER

Children as Victims

INTRODUCTION

Child abuse is not new. The legal definition for **child abuse** is the non-accidental physical and/or emotional harm to a child either through direct action or negligence. For centuries, parents and others have abused children. In many societies, children were viewed as chattel, or property of their parents, who were allowed to kill a child at birth, to sell a child, or to exploit his or her labor (Kadushin and Martin, 1988). A child had no rights, not even the right to live, until his or her father bestowed that right (Radbill, 1980). **Infanticide** was widely accepted in ancient cultures. Children were often left to die for many reasons—if they cried too much, were the wrong gender, were deformed or sickly, or were twins.

In the colonial era, fathers were encouraged to "beat the devil out" of unruly children. Child-rearing methods included mutilating, beating, and maltreating children, often using instruments such as rods, canes, and switches. A popular notion was "spare the rod, spoil the child," suggesting that a strong hand would prevent children from misbehaving or becoming obstinate.

Often, child disciplining or child-rearing has been taken to the extreme, with children of all ages being neglected, abandoned, abused, or summed up, victimized. It is particularly disheartening when this victimization comes at the hands of loved ones. Research shows that no family members are immune to offending: grandparents, parents, siblings, aunt/uncles, cousins—all have victimized children. The irony of the situation comes about when the "system" gets involved, because often when a child enters the child welfare system becoming a ward of the state, victimization continues, if not, worsens.

For some, the mere placement in foster care is a secondary victimization because children, regardless of how badly they have been treated, rarely want to leave their families. Foster care, where children are placed with other families, is a way to protect children from abuse/victimization at home. When foster care does not work, children can be placed in institutional care (e.g., group homes) and often the child is victimized by both the placement and the other individuals in the group home. Many times victims and offenders—whose common bond is age—are housed together. Thus, while it appears that institutional care protects children from the most extreme victimization by family members at home, it often only replaces the perpetrator from a family member to a stranger.

HISTORY OF CHILD VICTIMIZATION

The history of child abuse is well documented in various cultures; however, it is not always viewed as problematic. Likewise, concern for the welfare of children across the board has a more limited history. In the United States, child welfare agencies trace their origin to 1875 and the case of Mary Ellen Wilson. Mary Ellen was an illegitimate child born in New York City. She was cruelly beaten and neglected by the couple with whom she lived (not her parents). Mary Ellen had only two items of clothing, was always hungry, and was beaten daily by her guardian. There seemed to be no legal way to protect Mary Ellen from her primary caregivers' abuse. A social worker named Etta Wheeler pleaded with the president of the Society for the Prevention of Cruelty to Animals (SPCA), Henry Bergh, to advocate for Mary Ellen. Mr. Bergh, acting in his capacity as a private citizen, advocated on behalf of Mary Ellen. Based on court testimony, Mary Ellen was removed from her home and placed in the care of the judge. The judge decided to legally place Mary Ellen in a "home for grown children." Mrs. Wheeler, the social worker, pleaded with the judge to allow Mary Ellen to live with her. The judge agreed, and Mary Ellen lived happily with Mrs. Wheeler, eventually marrying at age 24 and bearing two children. Mary Ellen died in her late 80s.

The story of Mary Ellen Wilson is important to our understanding of the development of child welfare agencies. For years, many researchers have asserted that Mary Ellen had to be viewed as an "animal" in order to be rescued from her home environment. According to Watkins (1990), this is a myth. Watkins contends that the mistaken reference to Mary Ellen as an "animal" may have resulted because Mr. Bergh was the president of the SPCA. However, it was in his capacity as a private citizen that he interceded on behalf of Mary Ellen.

The Mary Ellen case is important because her plight led to the development of child welfare agencies. The New York Society for the Prevention of Cruelty to Children was created to protect children in similar situations (Robin, 1982; Nelson, 1984; Gelles, 1993b).

Similar societies developed in other cities: San Francisco, Boston, Rochester, Baltimore, Buffalo, and Philadelphia. Some of these were separate voluntary agencies, while others were subdivisions or parts of the SPCA. Over time, some of these agencies merged with other child welfare agencies, while others maintained their separate and distinct identities.

These societies and agencies focused on rescuing children from abusive situations—children who were being neglected, abused, or exploited. They focused on legal action to protect children from such behavior. Child abuse and neglect cases were investigated, and often legal measures were taken if parents or guardians were found to violate child protection laws.

This rapid development of child protective services peaked in the late 1800s and early 1900s and then declined between 1920 and 1960. During this period, there seemed to be little interest in child welfare as a public agenda item.

The issue of child abuse exploded onto the political scene in the 1960s and 1970s as a result of the medical profession identifying the "battered child syndrome" (Kempe et al., 1962). In a national survey, Dr. Kempe, a physician, and his colleagues reported 302 cases of child abuse. They studied children who were hospitalized, using technological advances (for the time period of the study) such as x-ray machines, and were able to detect broken bones and healed fractures that would otherwise have gone undetected. Medical professionals, including pediatric radiologists, pediatricians, and psychiatrists, are credited with the rediscovery of child abuse in the 1960s (Pfohl, 1977; Antler, 1978).

In 1974, the Child Abuse Prevention and Treatment Act was passed to provide direct assistance to states for developing child abuse and neglect programs. In order to qualify for assistance, a state had to agree to "protect all children under age eighteen; cover mental injury, physical injury, and sexual abuse; including neglect reports and abuse reports; guarantee confidentiality of records; guarantee legal immunity for reporters; and provide for a guardian *ad litem* for children whose cases come to court" (Kadushin and Martin, 1988, 223).

CHILD VICTIMIZATION AND MALTREATMENT

Child maltreatment includes **neglect, physical abuse, sexual abuse**, and **emotional abuse**. According to Kadushin and Martin (1988), a description of "maltreatment" is found in the Model Child Welfare Protective Services Act. Maltreatment occurs when a child's "physical or mental health or welfare is harmed or threatened with harm by the acts or omissions of his parents or other persons responsible for his welfare," including "emotional as well as physical harm, neglect as well as abuse, and potential damage as well as actual harm, and [the act] applies to institutional personnel as well as to biological parents and parent surrogates" (p. 227). Even though each of these is distinguished and defined below, together these behaviors are often categorized as child maltreatment.

It is important to remember that many of the people who deal directly with child maltreatment, such as social workers, lawyers, pediatricians, and police, have a difficult time agreeing on its definition. It is also difficult to accurately define terms such as *proper supervision, mental suffering,* and *serious harm.* The problems associated with defining child maltreatment are magnified when trying to determine when intervention is necessary.

The definition of *physical abuse* is less problematic. Physical abuse refers to "beating a child to the point at which the child sustains some physical damage" (Kadushin and Martin, 1988, 228). In a clinical setting, the scope of physical abuse may "range from relatively mild trauma causing bruising . . . to florid cases with organ and skeletal damage" (Oates, 1991, 115). Parents and guardians have been known to beat children with hairbrushes, fists, straps, electrical cords, ropes, TV antennas, rubber hoses, wooden spoons, paddles, bottles, and broom handles, to name but a few. Children have also been burned and had their bones broken or fractured.

Physical abuse is the most visible form of child abuse. The National Exchange Club Foundation's "Preventing Child Abuse . . . Serving America" website contains a comprehensive list of physical indicators of abuse (2007). This list, which is easy to comprehend and can be used as a tool to identify warning signs of physical child abuse, is reproduced in Table 9.1.

Practically any type of injury imaginable can be defined as abuse. The common factor is that a family member inflicted the injury. Most of what is listed above is well-known forms of abuse. However, there are two lesser known but just as severe forms of abuse: **Munchausen syndrome by proxy** and **shaken baby/shaken impact syndrome**.

TABLE 9.1   Physical Indicators of Abuse

Type of Abuse	Physical Indicators
Bruises	On body posterior, in unusual patterns, in clusters, in multiples, and in various stages of healing
Burns	Immersion burns, doughnut-shaped on the buttock, rope burns from confinement, dry burns, burns caused by irons
Lacerations and Abrasions	On lips, eyes, infant's face, on gum tissue, caused by force feeding, on external genitals
Skeletal Injuries	Fractures of long bones from twisting and pulling, separation of bone and shaft, detachment of tissue of bone and shaft, spiral fractures, stiff, swollen, enlarged joints
Head Injuries	Missing or loosened teeth, absence of hair, hemorrhaging beneath scalp from hair pulling, subdural/retinal hemorrhages from hitting or shaking
Internal Injuries	Intestinal injuries from hitting or kicking, rupture of heart-related blood vessels, inflammation of abdominal area.

Source: http://www.preventchildabuse.com/physical.htm.

Some parents (usually mothers) abuse children by subjecting them to repeated visits to doctors or hospitals because of imaginary illnesses. This is called *Munchausen syndrome by proxy,* or **MSBP** (Shnaps et al., 1982; Moore, 1995; Meadow, 1997). The disorder was first observed in the early twentieth century, but not named until 1951. A British psychiatrist coined the term, naming the disorder after Baron Karl F.H. von Munchausen. Munchausen was a German solider who concocted symptoms to gain medical attention and treatments. When individuals engage in such behavior focusing on themselves, it is called *Munchausen syndrome;* when parents or guardians do so moving the focus to another individual, most likely a child, it is called *Munchausen syndrome by proxy.* Some parents are thought to engage in Munchausen syndrome by proxy because they suggest or create medical symptoms in their children as a way for them to hold center stage while the children seek medical attention and treatments. It is often considered child abuse, because healthy children are subjected to the needless agony of painful tests and other treatments.

Parents, guardians, or caretakers may also abuse children by shaking them. Shaking a child, especially an infant whose neck is not strong, may result in brain damage. This is referred to as shaken baby/shaken impact syndrome (**SBS**) and it is defined as:

> . . . a form of inflicted head trauma. Head injury, as a form of child abuse, can be caused by direct blows to the head, dropping or throwing the child, or shaking the child. Head trauma is the leading cause of death in child abuse cases in the United States. Unlike other forms of inflicted head trauma, SBS results from injuries caused by someone vigorously shaking an infant. Because of the anatomy of infants, they're at particular risk for injury from this kind of action.

Therefore, the vast majority of incidents occur in infants who are younger than 1 year old. The average age of victims is between 3 and 8 months, although SBS is occasionally seen in children up to 4 years old. (The National Center on Shaken Baby Syndrome, 2008)

Just as the O.J. Simpson case brought intimate partner violence into the public eye, the death of 8-month-old Matthew Eappen in 1997 resulted in shaken baby/shaken impact syndrome being widely publicized. His young British au pair, Louise Woodward, was accused of shaking Matthew Eappen to death, and she was convicted and sentenced to life in prison. However, on appeal, the conviction was reduced to involuntary manslaughter, and her sentence was reduced to time served. Nevertheless, this case raised awareness about SBS like no other previous event had done.

NEGLECT

Children who are neglected are often left on their own to fend for themselves. As a result, they may be malnourished, dirty, and improperly dressed. The most severe form of neglect is child abandonment, when parents or guardians leave children with no intention of coming back. The two most common types of neglect are depriving a child of basic necessities (food, clothing, shelter, and love) and inadequate supervision.

Neglect can be divided into three categories: medical, educational, and emotional. Medical neglect refers to cases where parents or guardians make no effort to provide medical care when children need it. This may include preventive care, such as not taking children to the dentist or not getting children immunized.

Sometimes parents do not provide medical care for their children because of their religious beliefs. Is this lack of care considered neglect? Not typically, as Kadushin and Martin (1988, 233) assert: "Regulations formulated by the U.S. Department of Health and Human Resources indicate that failure to provide medical care is not neglect if such failure is in response to a person's religious beliefs." However, federal regulations also state that "nothing shall prohibit court intervention to protect the child."

Educational neglect includes not enrolling children in school and not caring when children are truant. **Emotional neglect** is depriving children of affection and support. Mulford et al. (1958, 21) also include "the deprivation suffered by children when their parents do not provide opportunities for normal experiences that produce feelings of being loved, wanted, secure, and worth which result in the ability to form healthy object relationships." **Emotional maltreatment** is often referred to as emotional neglect or emotional abuse. Some examples of emotional maltreatment are a mother telling her child she wishes she had never been born, a father telling his son he hates him, and a mother consistently ignoring her son until he feels like he does not exist.

SEXUAL ABUSE

Child sexual abuse involves adults using children for sexual relations and sexual gratification. The perpetrator may or may not be a family member. Sexual abuse includes intercourse, masturbation, hand-genital or oral-genital contact, sexual fondling, exhibitionism, pornography, voyeurism, or sexual propositioning (Peters, Wyatt, and Finkelhor, 1986; Bass and Davis, 1988; Hayes and Emshoff, 1993).

There is an apparent association between childhood victimization and adult victimization. Those who have been abused either physically or sexually are more likely to be abused physically and sexually as adults; the experience of violent victimization often carries over to adulthood. This relationship is common in homeless women who are victimized in both childhood and adulthood (Wenzel, Koegel, and Gelberg, 2000).

RECOGNIZING CHILD ABUSE

Aside from physical indicators, it is important to know the behavioral signs of child abuse. The Child Welfare Information Gateway maintains an excellent website that contains a wealth of information. One of the most valuable items in this chapter is a list of signs that may signal the presence of child abuse or neglect focusing on the child, the parent, and the interaction between the child and the parent. The following signs may signal the presence of child abuse or neglect.

The Child

There are sudden changes in the child's behavior or school performance.

The child does not receive proper help/treatment for physical and medical problems.

The child has difficulty concentrating.

The child is pessimistic; always expecting bad things to happen.

The child is overly obedient, yields quickly, is submissive, or reserved.

The child attends activities; however, he often is early, stays late, or does not want to leave when the event is over.

The Parent

The parent worries little about the child.

The parent negates problems identified at school or blames the child for these problems.

The parent allows others to enforce rules with harsh punishment as an option for reinforcement.

The parent views the child as troublesome, taxing, or insignificant.

The parent stresses an unreasonable physical or academic performance level from the child.

The parent relies on the child for comfort, care, and attention.

The Parent and Child

The parent and child are not demonstrative; rarely do they touch or look at each other.

The parent and child feel the relationship is negative, and neither considers the relationship to be positive.

The parent and child do not like each other (Child Welfare Information Gateway, 2008).

STATISTICS ON THE EXTENT OF CHILD ABUSE

Kilpatrick and Saunders (1997) conducted a comprehensive study on the prevalence of child victimization using a sample of 4,023 adolescents and their parents. They found that "approximately 1.8 million [adolescents] have been victims of serious sexual assault [and] 3.9 million . . . victims of a serious physical assault" (p. 1). Trend data reported by the Child Welfare Information Gateway finds, "During the past 3 years, the rate of victimization and the number of victims have been decreasing. An estimated 872,000 children were determined to be victims of child abuse or neglect for 2004. The rate of victimization per 1,000 children in the national population has dropped from 12.5 children in 2001 to 11.9 children in 2004" (Administration for Children and Families, 2005).

When examining the most recent statistics, the Child Welfare Information Gateway reports "Based on a rate of 47.8 per 1,000 children, an estimated 3,503,000 children received an investigation by Children Protection Service agencies in 2004. Based on a victim rate of 11.9 per 1,000 children, an estimated 872,000 children were found to be victims" (Administration for Children and Families, 2005). Based on data provided from 39 states, it was found that almost 75 percent of the children victimized were first-time victims. Of the maltreatment types, neglect has the highest rate per 1,000 child victims per year. As reported, "During 2004, 62.4 percent of victims experienced neglect, 17.5 percent were physically abused, 9.7 percent were sexually abused, 7.0 percent were psychologically maltreated, and 2.1 percent were medically neglected. In addition, 14.5 percent of victims experienced such 'other' types of maltreatment as 'abandonment,' 'threats of harm to the child,' or 'congenital drug addiction.' "

A recent Office of Juvenile Justice and Delinquency Prevention (OJJDP) report details the victimization of juveniles including trends in child maltreatment (Snyder and Sickmund, 2006). The most significant findings from this report are listed below:

- Most abuse and neglect cases enter the child welfare system through child protective services agencies (p. 47).
- Child protective services agencies receive 50,000 maltreatment referrals weekly—18 percent are substantiated (p. 51).
- Rates of child maltreatment victimization vary across demographic groups (p. 54).
- The overwhelming majority of child maltreatment perpetrators are parents of the victims (p. 55).
- Reported child maltreatment fatalities typically involve infants and toddlers and result from neglect (p. 56).
- Increases in children exiting foster care led to a drop in the foster care rolls between 1998 and 2003 (p. 57).
- The number of children adopted from public foster care increased 40 percent from 1998 to 2003 (p. 58).

THEORETICAL EXPLANATIONS FOR PHYSICAL ABUSE

Milner and Crouch (1993) provide an excellent overview of theoretical explanations for physical abuse of children. Just as criminological theory has evolved from several perspectives, so has child physical abuse theory. At first, abusers were characterized as people with mental illnesses. The psychiatric model explained abuse as resulting from psychological abnormality. Kempe et al. (1962) were the first researchers to list the psychiatric characteristics common among perpetrators of child abuse.

Later, the emphasis shifted from the psychiatric model to a sociological model or explanation. In 1970, Gil focused on the sociological conditions that resulted in child abuse. He explained physical child abuse as a result of economic conditions, societal values, and social systems found in society.

Both of these models are problematic, however. First, neither addresses the interaction between victims and offenders. Second, both focus on a single domain—either the individual or the society. Recognizing these limitations, researchers began to develop "**multi-domain, multi-factor interactional models**" (Milner and Crouch, 1993, 26). These interactional models are organizational models. The researchers focused on the factors related to child abuse. One example of such a model is the ecological model devised by Belsky (1980). In this model, there are four categories of factors related to child abuse: individual factors, family factors, community factors, and cultural factors.

Two of the more recent explanations of physical child abuse are the transitional model and the cognitive-behavioral model. The transitional model focuses on stress and the lack of stress-management skills among individuals who abuse children. The cognitive-behavioral model focuses on parents' unrealistic expectations of their children. Four stages occur before abuse develops. First, the parent develops unrealistic expectations of the child. Second, the child behaves in a manner that is inconsistent with the parent's expectations. Third, the parent misinterprets the child's behavior as having a negative intent (the reason the child is misbehaving is to annoy the parent). Fourth, the parent overreacts to the conditions described in the first three stages and engages in "excessive and severe punishment" (Milner and Crouch, 1993, 30).

We now turn to a recent report, that provides many current statistics on juvenile victimization including, but not limited to, child abuse and neglect. Other victimizations are included as well and are discussed below.

JUVENILES AS VICTIMS

The recent OJJDP (Office of Juvenile Justice and Delinquency Prevention) report referenced above details the victimization of juveniles, including how often juveniles are the victims of crime (Snyder and Sickmund, 2006). The publication reports findings from the National Center for Injury Prevention and Control, which is located within the CDC, along with FBI and NIBRS data. Below are the major findings from this publication as they relate to juvenile victimization. The commentary below each entry is summarized from the overall report.

> On average, between 1980 and 2002 about 2,000 juveniles were murdered annually in the United States (p. 20).

The top three causes of juvenile deaths in 2004 were unintentional injury, suicide, and juvenile homicide. Other demographic information beyond age of the victim is collected in the Supplementary Homicide Reports (SHR). Such information includes victim demographics, circumstances surrounding the deaths, and relationships between the victims and offenders. As reported in SHR, the offenders are known to the police in almost two-thirds (64%) of murders. Thus, there are many cases of juvenile murder where the offenders are not known to the police. The overall likelihood of being murdered appears to be relatively stable, with similar risks reported in 1996 and 2002.

Between 1980 and 2002, at least three of every four murder victims aged 15–17 were killed with a firearm (p. 23).

The same trend holds true when looking at 2002 alone: most victims were killed by firearms. Other types of weapons used to kill juveniles included hands, feet, knives, and blunt objects. The report also indicates that younger children are more likely to be killed by family members, while older juveniles are more likely to be killed by acquaintances. It also indicates that 84 percent of the victims of juvenile murder were males.

Persons aged 7–17 are about as likely to be victims of suicide as they are to be victims of homicide (p. 25).

Data gathered from death certificates reveal that the most common causes of death in juveniles aged 7–17 are unintentional injury, homicide, cancer, and suicide, in rank order, and the risk of homicide and suicide is just about the same. When examining suicide specifically, it was found that Native Americans have the highest juvenile suicide rate. The Native American juvenile suicide rate is nearly double the white non-Hispanic rate.

The nonfatal violent victimization rate of youth aged 12–17 in 2003 was half the rate in 1993 (p. 27).

Nonfatal violent victimization, while it decreased in 2003, was still evident. Juvenile males were about 50 percent more likely to be victims of nonfatal violent victimization than were female juveniles. Urban youth were more likely to be victims of nonfatal violence than were rural and suburban youth. Even though the violence was not fatal, 23 percent of the time a weapon was used in a violent attack. The most common setting for these nonfatal violent victimizations was schools.

Students were found to be safer in school and on their way to and from school in 2001 than they were in 1992 (p. 29).

Compared to 1992, juveniles are safer going to and returning from school. There was a 50 percent decline in theft over the study period; however, about 60 percent of the thefts occurred at school. White students experienced more theft at school than either blacks or Hispanics, and black and urban students experienced more theft outside of school.

A youth's risk of being a violent crime victim is tied to family and community characteristics, not race (p. 30).

This is an interesting finding, as many people think that race is a good predictor of risk for violent victimization. However, in this research, community and family variables were better predictors. Juveniles living in areas where there are high concentrations of single-parent families and young children, as well as juveniles living with families who recently moved to the community, tend to be more at risk for violent victimization than their counterparts. What is more interesting is that when these variables, community characteristics and family movement, were controlled, there was no difference in the relative risk of violent victimization by race or ethnicity.

> One in four violent crime victims known to law enforcement is a juvenile, and most juvenile victims are female (p. 31).

Since most victims are female, the type of crime committed against them is easy to guess: sexual assault. As reported, "sexual assault accounted for just over half of the juvenile victims of violent crime known to the police" (p. 31).

> As juveniles age, offenders who violently victimize them are less likely to be family members (p. 33).

Younger juvenile victims (under 6) are more likely to be victimized by family members, while older juveniles (6–17) are more likely to be victimized by acquaintances and strangers, although the number of stranger victimizations is low in relationship to victimization by an acquaintance. The type of crime where strangers are most likely to be the offenders is robbery, although robbery is uncommon.

> Some violent crimes with juvenile victims are most common after school, others around 9 p.m. (p. 34).

This might sound like a strange finding, but the authors examined the time of the day when juveniles are most likely to be victimized. They found results that are consistent with previous research, that is, the timing of violent crime victimization differs for juveniles and adults. "In general, the number of violent crimes with adult victims increased hourly from morning through the evening hours, peaking between 9 p.m. to midnight. In contrast, violent crimes with juvenile victims peaked between 3 and 4 p.m., fell to a lower level in the early evening hours, and declined substantially after 9 p.m." (p. 34).

> About two-thirds of violent crimes with juvenile victims occur in a residence (p. 36).

The authors examined the data to determine the location of the victimization. They found differences in location by type of crime. For instance, sexual assault occurs more frequently inside a residence than does robbery and aggravated assault. Also, the age of the victim affects where the victimization occurs: younger victims of violence, under 6 years of age, are most often (88% of the time) victimized in a residence.

> Few statutory rapes reported to law enforcement involve both juvenile victims and juvenile offenders (p. 37).

Although statutory rape is a difficult concept for some understanding, it nevertheless is illegal to engage in sexual relations with someone who is too young or otherwise unable to legally consent to the behavior. The authors point out that "the victims of statutory rape are primarily juveniles, and the crime has some attributes of child abuse." Using the definition of "non-forcible sexual intercourse with a person who is under the statutory age of consent," the authors found "1 statutory rape for every 3 forcible rapes" (p. 37). Statutory rape is discussed in more detail later in this chapter when focusing on teacher/student misconduct and also in Chapter 7.

JUVENILE KIDNAPPING

What is known about **juvenile kidnapping**? According to the OJJPD report, kidnapping is defined as "the unlawful seizure, transportation, and/or detention of a person against his or her will. For minors (who are legally too young to provide consent), kidnapping includes situations in which a minor is transported without consent of the custodial parent(s) or legal guardians" (p. 40). Here are some of the pertinent findings as reported by Snyder and Sickmund (2006):

- One-third of all kidnap victims known to law enforcement are under age 18 (p. 40).
- Only a small fraction of missing children are abducted—most by family members (p. 42).
- An estimated 1.7 million youth had a runaway or throwaway episode; fewer than 4 in 10 were missing (p. 45).

As the authors point out, data examined from 1988 to 1999 of family abductions, runaways, and lost, injured, or otherwise missing children indicated that the incidence rates for these "missing" children declined over the time period examined.

Another source of data focusing on missing children is NISMART: National Incident Studies of Missing, Abducted, Runaway, and Thrown-away Children. According to the *NISMART Bulletin* (Hammer, Finkelhor, and Sedlak, 2002), missing children are often distinguished from abducted or kidnapped as lost children. These lost children are runaways (children who voluntarily leave their homes) and thrown-aways (children who are not allowed back into their homes). In either case, these missing children are vulnerable to further victimization while being out on the street. According to the NISMART publication, "of the total runaway/thrownaway youth, an estimated 1,190,900 (71%) could have been endangered during their runaway/thrownaway episode by virtue of factors such as substance dependency, use of hard drugs, sexual or physical abuse, presence in a place where criminal activity was occurring, or extremely young age (13 years or younger)" (Hammer, Finkelhor, and Sedlak, 2002).

SIBLING VIOLENCE

Sibling violence is the most common form of abuse in families (Caffaro and Conn-Caffaro, 1998; Gelles and Straus, 1988). Similar to bullying, the immediate thought is often that fighting amongst siblings is not serious violence. Weihe reminds us that often such behavior is also considered "normal," just part of the growing-up process. Some familiar adages that are frequently heard to dismiss such behavior include: "Kids will be kids," "All kids call each other names," "Didn't you play doctor when you were a child?" or "It's just normal sibling rivalry" (Weihe, 1997, 4). However, sibling violence is a serious form of abuse. According to Sibling Abuse, a website sponsored by the University of Michigan Health System (2007), while all siblings squabble and call each other names, the difference between typical sibling behavior and abuse occurs when one sibling is always the aggressor and the other is always the victim.

Sibling violence takes place in a large percentage (63–73%) of American homes (Lystad, 1986). Researchers have found that the most frequent way conflicts between siblings are settled is by kicking, pushing, or throwing things (Roscoe, Goodwin, and Kennedy, 1987). A survey conducted using college students as subjects found that 28 percent reported high levels of conflict or violence with a sibling (Graham-Bermann et al., 1994). Female students and those who were younger siblings experienced more conflict or violence compared to male students who were older siblings.

Sibling violence also includes such mild forms of violence as biting, slapping, pinching, and hair pulling (Weihe, 1997). It also includes behaviors that fall into the categories of sexual, physical, and emotional abuse. Given the gamut of behaviors included in sibling violence, it is easy to see why it is the most common type of family violence.

The University of Michigan website provides possible signs that may indicate sibling abuse.

Some possible signs of sibling abuse:

- One child regularly stays away from another child.
- A child has changes in behavior, sleep patterns, eating habits, or has nightmares.
- A child acts out abuse in play.
- A child acts out sexually in inappropriate ways (University of Michigan Health System, 2007).

As bizarre as it might sound, siblings also kill each other. The killing of one sibling by another is called ***siblicide.*** Although this topic has not been widely researched, some literature does speak of the relationship between this type of violence and the age, gender, and race of offenders. Erika Gebo (2002) examined the Uniform Crime Reports and the Supplementary Homicide Reports (SHS) for the years 1976–1994, looking specifically at siblicide and its relationship to age, gender, and race. She found that although it is a common perception that those who kill are relatively close in age to their victims, this finding did not hold steady for siblicide. Gebo's work found that in more than half of the incidents (65%), younger siblings were killed by older siblings. She also found that male-on-male violence was most prevalent, with sisters killing sisters being the least likely type of siblicide. In previous research, African Americans have been found to have higher rates of victimization in the sibling relationship; however, in Gebo's work, she found a disproportionate number of siblicides among Native Americans (p. 162).

The overall conclusion of her research is that siblicides make up less than two percent of all homicides. For adults, most of the offenders were younger than their victims, and most were male. For juveniles, older siblings were more likely to murder younger siblings than vice versa.

Ritualistic Child Abuse

A chapter focusing on children as victims would not be complete without a discussion of ritualistic child abuse. However, as Lanning (1992) points out, the term is hard to define, often has multiple meanings, and other forms of child abuse often involve some type of ritual practice, which causes confusion when discussing ritualistic child abuse (RCA). In this discussion, RCA focuses on child abuse, physical, emotional, or sexual, that takes place in a context linked to religious symbols, traditions, or ceremonies (Pazder, 1980). The religious nature of the abuse is often associated with Satanism or the occult, but not always. As Lanning states, "Not all ritualistic activity is spiritually motivated. Not all spiritually motivated ritualistic activity is Satanic" (1991, 171).

Researchers have described three distinct types of Satanic groups (Kahaner, 1988). The Church of Satan and Temple of Set are two examples of one type of well-known satanic group. Members of these groups deny being involved in illegal activities and maintain that their religious practices are within the boundaries of the law. The second type is composed of "self-styled Satanists." These individuals, often adolescents, explore the occult and tend to be greatly influenced by heavy metal music and role-playing games such as *Dungeons and Dragons*. The third type of Satanic group is more organized, has a hierarchical structure, and is more secretive than the other two types. This type of group is more likely to be involved in ritualistic abuse. Members celebrate "holy" days that correspond closely to Christian holidays. Instead of prayer and communion, Satanic cults conduct blood sacrifices and blood and flesh ingestion, supposedly to please Satan.

Because of the lack of corroborating evidence supporting victim allegations, ritualistic child abuse remains a controversial topic. The controversial nature is further exasperated by low levels of reporting (maybe because it does not occur as frequently as once believed, or maybe because victims are fearful of retaliation if they do report). The literature on the topic is inconclusive in this regard. However, when victims do report, and these reports are studied by psychologists and clinicians, remarkably similar characteristics of abuse have been found (Jones, 1991; Young et al., 1991). For example, Young and colleagues found that almost all of the patients reporting incidents of RCA ($n = 37$) reported the following: "forced drug usage, sexual abuse, witnessing and receiving physical abuse/torture, witnessing animal mutilation and killing, being buried alive in coffins or graves, death threats, witnessing and forced participation in infant 'sacrifice' and adult murder, 'marriage' to Satan, forced impregnation and sacrifice of own child, and force cannibalism" (Young et al., 1991, 183). Also, clinicians question how young children can make up such horrible and graphic detail about something that did not actually happen (Jones, 1991). Still, there is little scholarly research on the topic, with much of what we know about RCA coming from workshops or seminars that report knowledge or information gathered from small case samples.

There do seem, however, to be more reports of RCA in patients diagnosed with dissociative disorder (although again, these claims cannot be substantiated beyond self-report and clinicians' belief in the subjects' veracity). The therapists then treat the primary condition, in this case the dissociative disorder, and it becomes difficult to separate those traits and symptoms associated with ritualistic child abuse and those attributed to the psychological disorder. For example, sleep disturbances, anger, anxiety, acting out etc are traits associated with both dissociative disorder and RCA (Putnam, 1991). Therefore, it might be suggested that the same types of treatment used to address dissociative disorder be used to address RCA. Such treatment options might include counseling.

VIOLENCE IN SCHOOLS

Once regarded as a problem associated only with inner-city schools, school violence is increasing across all sectors. As O'Donoghue (1995, 101) reports, after reviewing national media reports of school violence, the number of serious injuries or deaths of students and teachers are "dramatically increasing in the 1990s, and . . . acts of school violence are now distributed across the entire spectrum of U.S. American schools."

Along with the increase in school violence, and perhaps in response to it, more students are arming themselves with weapons. A study found that one in five American high school students and almost "one in three American boys now routinely carries a gun, knife, or some other weapon, and this pattern of weapon carrying by students has become a national phenomenon applicable to schools in all regions" (National Center for Disease Control, 1992, as cited in O'Donoghue, 1995, 101). Others have found even more staggering numbers, with Nansel and colleagues (2001) reporting that 2.7 million students had carried a weapon in the last 30 days, and 1.8 million had actually carried a weapon to school.

Schools have responded by installing metal detectors and conducting mandatory searches to detect students with weapons. Unfortunately, these prevention devices are not very effective. In response, some school districts have employed armed security personnel. Regardless of the strategies used to alleviate or diminish school violence, these methods have had only a small effect on reducing school violence (Cohn and Thomas, 1989; Kopetman, 1989).

What can be done to help students deal with such violence? Some schools have developed programs designed to offer counterviolence measures, which have been shown to reduce violent acts (Greenbaum, 1987). Preventive strategies include empathy, impulsive control, and anger management (Beland, 1996). McEvoy (1990) found that rehearsing an unexpected burst of anger or violent behavior, where both students and faculty play out their expected roles in the drama, has a positive impact on school children's reaction to violence.

Violence at schools extends to college campuses. Federal legislation has made it mandatory for colleges and universities to report crime rates to students currently enrolled in the institution and people considering attending the institution. This act, called the Student Right to Know and Campus Security Act, requires all state institutions receiving federal funds to collect statistics on campus crimes and disseminate them to students (Student Right to Know and Campus Security Act, 1990). Most of the research conducted on college campuses focuses on sexual assault and rape. Campus victimization of this type is discussed in this chapter, and a much more detailed presentation on school violence, with a particular emphasis on school shootings, is included in Chapter 13.

Teacher–Student Sexual Misconduct

Statutory rape is discussed in detail in Chapter 7, but there needs to be a discussion about statutory rape charges that occur with students and teachers. The nation sat up and took notice when Pamela Smart was convicted of conspiring to kill her husband. While this violent act was appalling in and of itself, what engrossed the nation more was the statutory rape claims alleged against Pamela Smart for having sexual relations with one of her students. Since that infamous case, there have been many teachers who have been accused and convicted of statutory rape charges. The percentage of students victimized by educators is provided in Table 9.2.

The U.S. Department of Education has conducted research to examine educator sexual misconduct (Shakeshaft, 2004). The author provided a thorough and exhaustive synthesis of the scant literature on the topic. Early in the report a distinction is made between incidence studies and prevalence studies. Incidence studies examine official records to determine the amount of educator sexual misconduct. Prevalence studies are self-report data where children and adults are asked if they "have ever been sexually abused as a child by an adult" (p. 16).

Shakeshaft (2004, 16) identified seven studies that examined educator sexual misconduct, however, none of these studied educator sexual abuse as the *primary* purpose of the research. She reports on data that were reanalyzed, examining one question in particular. Students were asked to respond to this question:

> During your whole school life, how often, if at all, has anyone (this includes students, teachers, other school employees, or anyone else) done the following things to you when you did not want them to?
>
> Made sexual comments, jokes, gestures or looks?
> Showed, gave or left you sexual pictures, photographs, illustrations, messages or notes?
> Wrote sexual messages/graffiti about you on the bathroom walls, in locker rooms, etc.?
> Spread sexual rumors about you?
> Said you were gay or a lesbian?
> Spied on you as you dressed or showered at school?
> Flashed or "mooned" you?

TABLE 9.2   Student Victimization by Educators

Incident	Percentage
Unwanted contact and/or noncontact educator sexual misconduct	Almost 10%
Only noncontact sexual misconduct	Almost 9%
Only contact sexual misconduct	Almost 7%
Of those who experienced any kind of sexual misconduct: Any kind of sexual misconduct by student	79%
Of those who experienced any kind of sexual misconduct: Any kind of sexualmisconduct by educator	21%

Touched, grabbed, or pinched you in a sexual way?
Intentionally brushed up against you in a sexual way?
Pulled at your clothing in a sexual way?
Pulled off or down your clothing?
Blocked your way or cornered you in a sexual way?
Forced you to kiss him/her?
Forced you to do something sexual, other than kissing? (p. 16)

For each stem question, respondents were asked to indicate who the offender was, where it happened, and when it occurred. The sample was a representative sample of public school students in grades 8 through 11. "The findings can be generalized to all public school students in 8th to 11th grades at a 95 percent confidence level with a margin of error of plus or minus 4 percentage points" (Shakeshaft, 2004, 17).

"To get a sense of the extent of the number of students who have been targets of educator sexual misconduct . . . [Shakeshaft] applied the percent of students who report experiencing educator sexual misconduct to the population of K–12 students. Based on the assumption that the . . . surveys accurately represent the experiences of all K–12 students, more than 4.5 million students are subject to sexual misconduct by an employee of a school sometime between kindergarten and 12th grade" (Shakeshaft, 2004, 18). This conclusion is mind boggling. This problem needs to be addressed and active ways to protect our children are paramount.

CATHOLIC CHURCH ABUSE

John Jay College (New York) was commissioned to do a full investigation of the sexual abuses in the Catholic Church. Principal investigator Karen Terry and her research team surveyed 202 dioceses to provide information about the nature and scope of the crisis. The researchers' response rate was extraordinarily high, with 195 of the 202 dioceses completing the survey. The report listed common attributes of these incidents (Bono, 2006):

- Over 80 percent of the victims were males. The age when abuse occurred most frequently was between 11 and 14. Findings of males victimizing boys in the Catholic Church setting go against what is observed in the general population, where men are more likely to abuse girls.
- The victims were often postpubescent; however, a small percentage of the victims had not reached puberty. A variety of sex acts were committed against the victims, and many serious offenses were reported.
- Priests often abused their victims at social events, and many had social relationships with the families of their victims.
- The rectory was the most common site of abuse.

In early 2006, a U.S. Catholic bishop reported that he had been a victim of sexual abuse by a priest (Ghose, 2006). Bishop Thomas Gumbleton indicated that when he was a teenager he was inappropriately touched by a priest. Gumbleton's admission was made to show support for a bill in Ohio that would extend the time limits for individuals who are sexually abused by the clergy to sue the church. Gumbleton wanted others to know he understood the complex and difficult decision that must be made before a person comes forward to reveal abuse. After all, Gumbleton, who is 75, only now made his first public announcement of the abuse that occurred when he was a teen. Gumbleton said, "I understand why victims of sexual abuse need this new window of opportunity. For many of them, probably almost all of them, it would be very difficult to come forward and speak" (Ghose, 2006, 1).

Bishop Gumbleton, who is retired, said he is embarrassed today to talk about the abuse and believes that others probably feel the same way he does. He also thinks that the church's response to have time limits on civil suits, to handle abuse by counseling, and to develop church-created registries of both perpetrators and those who have participated in cover-ups are not adequate reforms for addressing the abuse scandal and for helping victims.

INTERNET VICTIMIZATION

Christina Bryce-Rosen (2005) presented information about the hidden dangers of the Internet to a group of concerned citizens. Her presentation began with an examination of how computers can be used to advance victimization. She discussed how individuals use computers to hack into bank accounts and other confidential data sets, to send destructive Internet viruses, and to carry out "traditional" crimes over the Internet (e.g., counterfeiting and trafficking).

She explained how computers facilitate criminal activity in that they provide a relatively secure way for criminals to interact, offer access to all kinds of personal information that can identify possible victims, contain inventory records that can be hacked, and allow criminals to find accomplices. She warned that children who use computers are victimized by criminals, in particular pedophiles, who use the Internet to find others with the same fantasies and to share erotic pictures and videos of children and written stories about children being abused.

Bryce-Rosen also indicated that there are warning signs that parents, teachers, friends, and other concerned citizens should be aware of to help determine if children are being stalked by online perpetrators: spending many hours on the computer, especially at night and away from parental observation; abruptly covering up the computer screen or turning off the computer when parents are present; and changes in children's behavior, perhaps becoming unsocial with family members or being unwilling to talk about computer activities with family members. As a measure of precaution, if a child receives a child pornography offer on the Internet, parents should notify the local police. If a child has been victimized by a computer sex offender, local and federal law enforcement agencies should be contacted. Bryce-Rosen assured parents that the best crime-prevention method to avoid Internet victimization is for parents to be involved and take an active role in the Internet usage and activities of their children.

Internet victimization is a relatively new term and most often the predators are older men and the victims are teenagers or children. It is not a crime that is exclusive to male predators, but the majority of predators are male. The Office for Victims of Crimes says, "Predators will contact victims over the Internet and will victimize them by:"

- Enticing children/teenagers through online contact for the purpose of engaging them in sexual acts.
- Using the internet for the production, manufacture, and distribution of child pornography.

- Using the internet to expose youth to child pornography and encourage them to exchange pornography.
- Enticing and exploiting children for the purpose of sexual tourism (travel with the intent to engage in sexual behavior) for commercial gain and/or personal gratification (2001, 2).

HOW PREVALENT IS INTERNET VICTIMIZATION?

David Finkelhor, Kimberly Mitchell, and Janis Wolak (2001) conducted a national survey entitled the Youth Internet Safety Survey, where they gathered information about "incidents of possible online victimization" (p. 1). They conducted telephone interviews with 1,501 youth aged 10 through 17. The survey addressed three areas: "sexual solicitations and approaches, unwanted exposure to sexual material, and harassment" (p. 2).

The results of their study are recounted below:

- About 20 percent of the youth surveyed reported that they had experienced unwanted sexual solicitations over the Internet within the last year. Further, 5 percent had described the unwanted sexual solicitations as "distressing," meaning that it made them feel very upset or afraid.
- Three percent reported that they received aggressive solicitations that involved offline contacts or attempts to engage in offline contacts.
- As reported, no solicitation actually led to sexual contact or assault.
- Almost one-quarter of those responding reported exposure to unwanted sexual material, with 6 percent describing this exposure as distressing.
- Six percent of the youth reported harassment had occurred over the past year, with 2 percent indicating that the harassment was distressing.

The survey also found that only a small number of these incidents were reported to law enforcement (e.g., police or hotlines) or anyone else in authority, like teachers or Internet service providers. Only about 18 percent of serious offenses were reported, and these were reported to the Internet service providers rather than law enforcement.

In a follow-up article to the national survey report, Mitchell, Finkelhor, and Wolak (2003, 26–29) list their key conclusions:

- A large percentage of youth seem to be experiencing offensive interaction on the Internet.
- Diversity among the types of offenses and types of offenders on the Internet is increasing.
- Although most fail, the number of sexual solicitations is alarming.
- Teenagers are especially vulnerable to such solicitations.
- The sexually explicit material found on the Internet is pervasive and insidious.
- There are a number of youth who are distressed by such behavior; however, most youth are unfazed by it.
- Many youth remain silent about their encounters.
- Often, youth and parents do not know where to report such behavior.

Based on these key conclusions, the authors also provide recommendations on how to address Internet victimization. Their ideas are largely common sense, but need to be reported here because of their major finding that youth and parents rarely report these experiences because they often do not know where to do so.

- In order to prevent Internet sexual exploitation, there need to be frank discussions about the problem and warnings about threats from young and female offenders.
- Law enforcement needs to be involved in the discussion.
- Resources that include how and where to report such offenses must be made available to those using the Internet. The process for reporting should be streamlined to make reporting easier.
- Age-appropriate prevention and intervention strategies must be developed.
- Youth should be made aware of their role in helping to prevent such behavior.
- Adults who work with youth, including mental health workers, teachers, and counselors, must be made aware of the hazards of the Internet and how distressing such incidents can be.
- The impact on children's development when they have been exposed to unwanted pornographic images should be researched.
- Filtering devices and blocking mechanisms are available to protect youth; however, we don't know how families feel about these devices, or if they use them.
- If a behavior is illegal offline it should be illegal in cyberspace, and laws need to be written to support this position.
- Although youth Internet victimization is important, it should not overshadow prevention and intervention efforts to reduce other more conventional forms of youth victimization (Mitchell, Finkelhor, and Wolak, 2003).

Some other commonsense advice to parents and kids about Internet safety is found on a website sponsored by EarthLink and the FBI. The site provides several recommendations from the FBI directed to parents and kids. These recommended online safety tips include:

Online Safety Tips for *Parents:*

1. Communication is key. Make sure parents talk to children about the Internet and computer safety issues.
2. Remain in Sight. Do not put a computer into a child's room where the parent cannot see it. Move it to a center location and make an effort to check to see what the child is doing on the computer.
3. Parental Controls Should Be Invoked. Use the parental controls that are available to prohibit children from getting to information and sites that are questionable.
4. Chat rooms and Email Communication Should Be Monitored. Make sure your child knows that you will regularly check these forums.
5. Internet Users Should Be Responsible. Teach children to be responsible and to be careful when using computer and when surfing the internet.

Online Safety Tips for *Kids:*

1. Keep personal information private. Don't share any information that is personal with anyone over the internet.
2. Don't meet anyone who you only know via the Internet. Don't make plans to meet with anyone you only know from Internet contacts. If a meeting is arranged, because a parent says it will be okay, make sure you bring someone with you, and that your parents know where you are going.
3. Don't send pictures.
4. Don't answer emails that are mean. Just delete them. (Earthlink, 2003).

CHILD VICTIMIZATION: PROGRAMS TO ASSIST VICTIMS

Many programs have been designed to help children who are victimized. One such program is the **Guardian *ad Litem*** or **Court Appointed Special Advocates (CASA)** program. Regardless of which name is used (it varies by state), both are designed to help the courts understand children. The advocates become the "eyes and ears" of the court—often appearing in court on behalf of children.

When a complaint alleging child maltreatment is filed in a juvenile court, the state is represented by an attorney. The parents or guardians also usually have an attorney. But who represents the child? Who looks out for his or her welfare? Typically a guardian *ad litem* (GAL) and court-appointed special advocate are both appointed by the judge, and they act as advocates for the juvenile during judicial proceedings. The difference in the label results from the model of child representation the state follows. For example, in North Carolina, the guardian *ad litem* can be a lay volunteer. In Virginia, the guardian *ad litem* must be an attorney (Kenworthy, 1997, 3). Court-appointed special advocates may be assigned to the guardian *ad litem* attorney to assist with the case, or the GAL attorney may do the investigation as well. In no state does a layperson speak solely without an attorney for the child in court. In North Carolina, the lay volunteer investigates the case for the attorney. In Virginia, the attorney may use the services of the court-appointed special advocate, may investigate the case himself or herself, or may do both. CASAs are extensively trained in child maltreatment and know how to recognize such incidents. They are also trained investigators. Their job is to uncover as much information as possible in order to assess the petition. They may find information that substantiates the petition, or they may find that the petition is unfounded. Either way, the main goal of the Guardian *ad litem* and CASA programs is to protect children. The GAL or CASA visits with the child and consults with him or her to make a recommendation to the court as to what is best for the child. Sometimes the GAL recommends removal of the child from the home; other times the GAL or CASA sees that the child needs to be with their birth parents and recommends temporary placement until the parents can have counseling or take parenting skills classes. The advocate is interested in the welfare of the child. These programs allow the child to have a voice in what happens to him or her. (For a more thorough and detailed examination of Guardian *ad litem* programs, see Whitcombe, 1988).

Safe Haven Laws

Many states have enacted **safe haven legislation** that allows a parent or guardian to abandon an infant without fear of criminal charges, or with reduced criminal charges. The intent of the legislation is to protect children who otherwise would be abandoned and literally left for dead. You may remember hearing about teenagers in New Jersey who delivered a child and left him to die without food or other care and went back to the high school dance they were attending. Public outcry about such situations led many states to consider enacting safe haven legislation (AMT Children of Hope Foundation, 2007). There are subtle differences between the laws that have been enacted.

Texas was the first state to develop and enact safe haven legislation. In most states, a safe haven is considered any type of medical facility usually listed as an emergency room, hospital, or clinic. Other safe havens include fire departments, police departments, or churches. In 27 of the states that have safe haven legislation, parents or guardians are immune from prosecution.

Are These Laws Making a Difference?

It remains to be seen if these laws can be effective. According to the National Conference of State Legislatures, results are mixed. Only 10 states are represented when considering where babies where abandoned in 2001. The numbers are about 33 babies safely abandoned in the states of Texas (5), Michigan (5), Alabama (5), New Jersey (6), California (4), Connecticut (2), Minnesota (2), Ohio (2), Kansas (1), and South Carolina (1). Some of the problems with low reporting numbers are that many states do not track abandonment or do not have reporting mechanisms to tally the information. Some states rely on media reports to gauge the amount of abandonment. In 2002, the number of babies safely abandoned increased as laws were enacted: California increased by 16 and New Jersey increased by four. Illinois reported two babies safely abandoned, up from zero in 2001. Nevertheless, unlawful abandonment remains a problem Williams-Mbengue (2001).

Illegal infant abandonment is reported by Texas, Louisiana, California, Michigan, Connecticut, and Illinois. In some cases the infants died and the parents were prosecuted, but not always. Thus, the overall effectiveness of the legislation is minor at best. There is safe infant abandonment; however, it seems to be concentrated in certain states. And illegal abandonment still occurs, sometimes leading to infants' deaths.

Self-Defense Programs for Children

As with all types of criminal victimization, the best defense is a good offense. We must practice good crime prevention (i.e., personal safety) in order to safeguard our children. Paul Stanley developed a website (http://www.kidsfightingchance.com/) with a childhood friend after his son walked away with a stranger during a safety seminar. The purpose of the website is to promote children safety. A video called *Kids Fighting Chance* "*teaches, empowers and prepares* any school aged child—any size, any gender, any age—to avoid dangerous situations, ward off attack and escape abduction" (Kids Fighting Chance, 2007, emphasis in original).

The video teaches children, no matter how young, commonsense approaches to personal safety. On the video, two experienced self-defense experts teach children how to protect themselves and how to avoid trouble (i.e., recognize and avoid dangerous situations). The video demonstrates "strikes, kicks, bits, foot stomps, pushes and other techniques that can enable a child to stun an attacker temporarily and escape" (Brody, 2003).

Brody (2003) provides some specific tactics discussed on the video that will be reiterated here. These examples are very straightforward and useful. For example, a young child, age 5 or under, can get away from an attacker who may be a full-grown man by "using her fingertips to strike a man in his eyes and follow that with kicks to the groin" (Brody, 2003, 6). Other strategies include:

- Biting hard on fingers if a mouth is being held shut.
- Head butts followed by hand strikes to the groin or stomping on feet can provide release from a rear bear hug.
- Once a child is free, he or she can run away from an attacker possibly hiding under a car so the attacker cannot get the child (Brody, 2003, 6).

The overall message is to never stop fighting—to get away by whatever means available. The video also clearly advocates this message for individuals of all ages—these strategies and the mantra of "don't give up" clearly work for adults as well. These same self-defense techniques can be used against carjackers, muggers, and other criminals.

CONCLUSION

Children are the future and it is society's responsibility to take care of them and to help them grow into productive, happy, fulfilled adults. Children were not always viewed with such high regard. They were at the mercy of their fathers in terms of their overall welfare and possible contribution to the family, community, and society as a whole. With the advent of the child welfare system, things have changed, and children are being seen as valuable members of families, communities, and society. Agencies, policies, and laws have been created to protect children.

Still, children are victims of violence at the hands of loved ones and strangers. All the child welfare legislation that has been created has not prevented children from being victimized. They are mistreated, abused, neglected, physically and sexually assaulted by family members, strangers, acquaintances, and peers. Juveniles are victims of many types of violent crimes, with many incidents of these victimizations occurring in the home, at church, as well as at school.

Study Questions

1. How do you think we can protect our most vulnerable populations (young children and pre-teens) from being victims of Internet crimes?
2. Describe what is meant by shaken baby syndrome. What steps can parents take to ensure that their children are safe when they are in someone else's care?
3. Sibling violence is reported to be the most common type of family violence. Given its magnitude, what can be done to curtail this violence? How do we make parents aware of this violence and subsequently prevent it?
4. How does safe haven legislation work? Why do you think that this legislation has had mixed results in terms of its effectiveness?

Key Terms

- Court Appointed Special Advocate (CASA)   183
- emotional abuse   166
- emotional maltreatment   168
- emotional neglect   168
- Guardian *ad Litem*   183
- juvenile kidnapping   174
- Munchausen syndrome by proxy (MSBP)   167
- neglect   166
- physical abuse   166
- ritualistic child abuse   176
- safe haven legislation   183
- sexual abuse   166
- shaken baby/shaken impact syndrome (SBS)   167
- siblicide   175
- sibling violence   175
- statutory rape   178

C H A P T E R

10
Victimization of the Elderly

INTRODUCTION

The elderly are the "fastest growing age group in the United States, and their protection and well-being are viewed as a paramount concern" (Dillingham, 1992, 1); however, according to Payne and Gainey (2006), up to 2 million older adults are thought to be mistreated each year. These numbers should cause great concern. As the population continues to age, with individual life expectancies being longer than any period in history, it is our collective responsibility to care for elders.

Elderly victimization encompasses abuse, neglect, and criminal victimization. However, not every discipline conceptualizes elderly victimization this way. Some view elderly victimization as two mutually exclusive categories of behavior including abuse and neglect (see Table 10.1 for different types of each) and criminal victimization (index crime victimization). Distinguishing elderly victimization in this way explains why disciplines have a different focus when explaining elderly victimization. For example, social workers and the social work literature will focus on elderly abuse—neglect, abandonment, and so on—behaviors that are problematic but not criminal, while criminal justice professionals and the criminal justice literature focuses on criminal victimization: behavior that is illegal in criminal courts. The two perspectives start to blur when abuse and neglect occur at the hands of professionals who are supposed to ensure the safety and protection of the elderly.

DEFINING ELDER ABUSE AND NEGLECT

It is somewhat difficult to define elder abuse and neglect as consistency across agencies dealing with the elderly is hard to find. As researchers and practitioners grappled with terminology, some authors have developed abuse and neglect typologies, lists of characteristics common to each type of abuse, to better define them. Other researchers have attempted to conceptualize elder abuse and neglect and to provide working definitions, much like those found in a dictionary. Table 10.1 presents the definitions and typologies extracted from the literature, relying primarily on the work of Glendenning (1993) and Payne and Gainey (2005).

The National Center on Elder Abuse provides a list of all the major types of elder abuse (2006). The warning signs and symptoms for each type of abuse is given in Table 10.2.

Even with all these definitions, clarifications, and examples, a clear definition of elder abuse is not forthcoming. And it is still not clear as to whether criminal victimization and

TABLE 10.1 Type of Abuse	
Physical Abuse	Involves being hit, beaten, slapped, bruised, cut, sexually assaulted, burned, physically restrained, or drugged by a care-taker (Hickey and Douglass, 1981; Breckman and Adelman, 1988). It can also include "cases in which elderly persons are over-medicated, under-medicated, or restrained" (Payne and Gainey, 2005, 3).
Psychological Abuse/ Mistreatment	Involves the abused person being ridiculed, manipulated, insulted, frightened, shamed, called names, humiliated, or treated like a child (Hickey and Douglass, 1981; Breckman and Adelman, 1988). Further, verbal abuse is also considered a form of psychological mistreatment (Payne and Gainey, 2005).
Medical Abuse	Involves the withholding of, or careless administration of, drugs (Block and Sinnott, 1979). It may also include what Payne and Gainey (2005) put in the category of physical abuse, that is, the overmedicating or undermedicating of the elderly.
Financial Abuse/ Material Abuse	Involves the inappropriate and illegal exploitation of an elderly person's resources (Breckman and Adelman, 1988; Krummel, 1996) including the misuse of property or money, theft, forced entry into a nursing home, financial dependence, and exploitation (Rathbone-McCuan and Voyles, 1982).
Social and Environmental Abuse	Includes the deprivation of human services, involuntary isolation, and financial abuse (Chen et al., 1981). Such abuse would include denying an elderly person access to his or her social security check, keeping a person house-bound because all access to transportation is cut off, or living in hazardous living conditions.

Type of Neglect

Passive Neglect	Refers to an elderly person being left alone, isolated, or forgotten (Hickey and Douglass, 1981). It also refers to the harm inflicted on the elderly because of inadequate knowledge of the changing needs of aging adults (Krummel, 1996).
Active Neglect	Involves withholding items that are necessary for daily living (food, medicine, companionship, bathing), withholding life resources, and not providing care for a physically dependent person (Rathbone-McCuan and Voyles, 1982).
Self-Neglect	Involves an elderly person not taking care of him- or herself. As Payne and Gainey (2006, 5) explain, . . . "Self-neglect is characterized as the behavior of an elderly person that threatens his/her own safety. . . . (it) manifests itself in an older person as a refusal or failure to provide himself/herself with adequate food, water, clothing, shelter, personal hygiene, medication (when needed), and safety precautions."

TABLE 10.2 Signs and Symptoms of the Major Types of Elder Abuse

Physical Abuse

The elderly may show signs of injury such as:

- Contusions, discoloration, bumps, swelling.
- Bone damage—breaks, fractures, splintering, sprains, or dislocations.
- Sores, cuts, or lesions that remain untreated.
- Internal damage or organ bleeding.

There may also be additional symptoms of physical abuse such as:

- Wearing broken eyeglasses, exhibiting any of the visible signs of injury listed above, or showing indications of being restrained (i.e., wrist marks or ankle marks).
- Prescription medicines found to be either over- or underutilized.
- Elderly self-reporting that she or he has been mistreated.
- A sudden change in the elderly person's behavior.
- Refusal of the caregiver to let anyone see the elderly person.

Sexual Abuse

The elderly may show signs of injury that include:

- Discoloration or bruises around the breasts for women and around the genitals for both women and men.
- Unexplained bleeding in the vagina or anus.

There may also be additional symptoms of sexual abuse such as:

- Sudden and unexplained sexual diseases such as venereal disease or genital infection.
- Undergarments that are ripped, discolored, or bloody.
- Elderly self-reporting that she or he has been sexually assaulted or raped.

Emotional/Psychological Abuse

The elderly may show signs of emotional/psychological abuse that include:

- Elderly person is nervous, distressed, disturbed, or troubled.
- Elderly person is quiet, reserved, does not talk often, and does not respond to direct questions.
- Elderly person begins to exhibit behaviors associated with dementia such as sucking, biting, or rocking.
- Elderly person self-reports being verbally or emotionally abused.

Neglect

The elderly may show signs of neglect that include:

- Lack of care—elderly person may not be fed properly, may be dehydrated, might have injuries that have been left untreated, and may have poor hygiene.
- Health problems, even minor ones, may be ignored and left untreated.
- Living arrangements may be unsafe and dangerous, with inadequate resources such as lack of running water or heat.
- Living arrangements may be unhygienic, dirty, and possibly contaminated with rodents, bedbugs, or parasites. Bedding in particular may be filthy.
- Elderly self-reports being neglected.

Abandonment

The elderly may show signs of abandonment that include:

- Leaving the person, and never visiting, at a nursing home or hospital.
- Deserting the person in public with no intention of returning to pick him or her up.
- Elderly self-reports being deserted.

(*Continued*)

TABLE 10.2   *(Continued)*

Financial or Material Exploitation

The elderly may show signs of financial or material exploitation that include:
- Banking behaviors that suddenly change—taking large amounts of money from savings or investment accounts.
- Adding names to savings and checking accounts.
- Automatic Teller Machine withdrawals from the elder's account without permission by the elder to do so. Forged financial transactions.
- Hasty changes to financial documents including wills, names of bank accounts, and property deeds.
- Valuable possessions mysteriously disappear.
- Poor care of the elderly even though there are adequate financial resources. Bills unpaid despite adequate financial resources.
- Large sums of money being transferred to another person's account.
- Uninvolved relatives suddenly becoming involved in the elderly person's financial affairs.
- Elderly self-reports financial exploitation.

Self-Neglect

The elderly may show signs of self-neglect that include:
- Lack of care—elderly person may not be fed properly, may be dehydrated, might have injuries that have been left untreated, and may have poor hygiene.
- Unsafe and unhealthy living conditions—Living arrangements may be unsafe and dangerous with inadequate resources such a running water and heat, may be unhygienic, dirty and possibly contaminated with rodents, bedbugs, or parasites. Bedding in particular may be filthy.
- Inadequate clothing and medical devices—elderly may have inappropriate or inadequate clothing for the season and they may not have eyeglasses, hearing aids, or dentures.
- Inadequate living space—elderly may be grossly underhoused or homeless. Adapted from the National Center on Elder Abuse (2006).

elderly abuse should be considered part of one larger phenomenon, for example, elderly victimization, or whether the two should be separate and distinct.

One researcher attempts to address this concern. Professor Brian Payne (2002), a noted scholar who studies elderly victimization, has proposed looking at elderly abuse from an integrated perspective. He finds that examining or studying elderly abuse from an interdisciplinary perspective, utilizing the disciplines of gerontology, sociology, criminology and criminal justice, social work, victimology, medicine, and psychology does not help us understand the phenomenon. Further, he suggests that each discipline has only a fragmented understanding of the issues, and that there is no real understanding of elderly victimization until an intradisciplinary approach is invoked.

An intradisciplinary approach, or integrated approach, would involve "promoting six related areas: (1) an integrated definition of elder abuse, (2) an integrated approach to determine the extent of elder abuse, (3) an integrated explanation of crime and elder abuse, (4) a broad understanding of the consequences of elder abuse, (5) a coordinated multi-practitioner response to allegations of abuse, and (6) broad prevention measures empowering seniors to be involved in preventing offenses" (Payne, 2002, 538). As Payne points out, when you pull together all these disciplines to define elder abuse, some disciplines want to include certain behaviors as "criminal," while others do not see the behaviors as such. It becomes a problem if the "criminal" aspect—or lack thereof—cannot be reconciled among the group.

Nevertheless, Payne and his colleagues attempted to derive a definition of elder abuse from an integrated perspective by surveying police chiefs, nursing home professionals, and sociology and social work students. In conclusion, they recommended this definition after analyzing their findings: "Based on the input from these groups, the researchers suggested the following definition of elder abuse: 'any criminal, physical, or emotional harm or unethical taking advantage that negatively affects the physical, financial, or general well being of an elderly person' (Payne, Berg, and Byars, 1999, 81)," as cited in Payne (2002, 539).

MEASURING ELDER ABUSE

Elder abuse is similar to other forms of family violence in that the abuse often stays hidden (Barnett et al., 1997, 2004). Couple this with the lack of a clear and precise definition of elder abuse, and you can see why it is hard to estimate the prevalence of the problem. Nevertheless, there are estimates of elder abuse discussed below.

One of the earliest studies of elderly abuse was conducted by Pillemer and Finklehor (1988) in Boston. The study involved more than 2000 people over the age of 65. The prevalence of elder abuse in the study was 32 per 1000 people. The researchers extrapolated the overall prevalence of elder abuse to be between 701,000 and 1,093,560 victims in the United States (Pillemer and Finklehor, 1988, 54). Almost 10 years later, Payne and Cikovic (1995) reported on the amount of elderly victimization based on official reports. Approximately 1 to 2 million victimizations are reported yearly, and such abuse occurs in all types of settings (Payne and Cikovic, 1995, 61).

The **National Center on Elder Abuse (NCEA)** is a national clearinghouse that provides statistics about elderly abuse. They frequently publish surveys of **Adult Protective Services (APS)** employees to get a sense of how prevalent elder abuse is. According to the webpage, "The National Center on Elder Abuse (NCEA) serves as a national resource for elder rights advocates, law enforcement and legal professionals, public policy leaders, researchers, and citizens. It is the mission of the NCEA to promote understanding, knowledge-sharing, and action on elder abuse, neglect, and exploitation" (Wood, 2006).

The NCEA recently reported survey results of adult protective services providers on the extent of abuse of adults 60 years or older (Teaser et al., 2006, 5–6). Some important results are provided in Table 10.3.

Several recommendations are listed in the report focusing on how to improve the quality of the data collected on elderly abuse and neglect. Those recommendations are summarized below.

- In order to increase the reliability and validity of the data reported in the summary report, definitions and measures of abuse and neglect must be uniform throughout the states. To know more about the patterns and trends in elderly abuse cases, there must be a concerted effort to regularly and systematically collect such information.
- Demographic information about victims and alleged offenders should be collected—at a minimum, age, race, gender, and ethnicity.
- Since reports of abuse and neglect are made by various groups of individuals, including municipal agents and hospital workers, it is prudent to expand the training opportunities for identifying such abuse and neglect to those individuals who may not readily know the signs.

- Outcome data—how the report was resolved—must be collected by all states. Additional information about what happened to the offender should also be sought.
- To keep current with the incidence and prevalence of elder abuse, national survey should be conducted at least every four years (Teaser et al., 2006, 5–6).

TABLE 10.3   Summary of the NCEA Report

Numbers of Elder Abuse Reports Received by Adult Protective Service (APS)

In a one-year period (2004), there were over a half million reported incidents of elder abuse. There are 2.7 reports of abuse for every 1000 persons living in the United States. Individual state reports find South Dakota to have the lowest average of elder abuse reports and Oklahoma to have the highest. Changes in the number of reports from 2000 to 2004 indicate an increase of about 20 percent.

National Trends—Abuse of Vulnerable Adults of All Ages

- The number of reported cases of elder abuse is steadily increasing, and therefore protective services investigate more abuse cases. There was a 16 percent increase in the number of cases investigated from 2000 to 2004.
- With the number of cases investigated increasing, there are also more cases being substantiated. There was a 16 percent increase in the number of cases substantiated from 2000 to 2004.
- As the workload increases the budget is increasing as well. The national average annual budget for state APS is $8.5 million.

Statewide Reporting Numbers

- When focusing on abuse reports of individuals aged 60 or above, over 2.5 million reports were made. However, not all of these reports were investigated or substantiated by Adult Protective Services. About 193,000 were investigated, with about 88,000 being substantiated.
- When focusing on self-neglect reports for the same age group, there were about 84,000 such reports. Slightly less than all these reports were investigated, and only slightly more than one-half were found to be substantiated.
- The reports of elderly abuse and neglect to Adult Protective Services were made by family members, social workers, and neighbors.

Categories of Elder Abuse, Victims Aged 60+

- Elderly report being victims of self-neglect, caregiver neglect, and financial exploitation. These are the categories of abuse that are reported, investigated, and substantiated most often.

Substantiated Reports, Victims Aged 60+

- Of all the abuse reports that were substantiated, in two of three cases the victims are females, about 43 percent are 80 years or older, and 77 percent are Caucasian. Abuse occurs most often in a domestic setting.

Substantiated Reports, Alleged Perpetrators of Victims Aged 60+

- In more than half of substantiated abuse reports, the offenders were female, and 75 percent were under the age of 60. Most often adult children or other family members were the offenders.
- More than one-half of the states do not maintain an offender registry where offender characteristics are kept.

Interventions and Outcomes, Victims Aged 60+

- Many of the substantiated cases were closed; however, none was closed due to the abuse being terminated. Some of the reasons for closing cases included the patients dying, entering long-term facility, refusing services, moving out of service area, being unable to locate, or being referred to law enforcement.

MEASURING CRIMINAL VICTIMIZATION AGAINST THE ELDERLY

Criminal victimization includes crimes against the elderly that fall into the eight index crimes. (These crimes include murder, forcible rape, robbery, aggravated assault, burglary, larceny-theft, motor vehicle theft, and arson.) Such criminal victimization has been collected in the UCR, NIBRS, and NCVS sources. These data sources focus on criminal behavior, not abuse. It is important to report such statistics because, as we will see later on, the elderly are very fearful of criminal victimization even though their relative risk of victimization is very low.

What do we know about elderly criminal victimization? Catalano (2006) reports the crime statistics for all ages for the year 2004. Focusing on older victims, the report finds: "During 2004, as in previous years, there was a general pattern of decreasing crime rates for persons of older age categories" (p. 8). Additionally, in a special report entitled, "Crime against Persons Age 65 or Older, 1993–2002," Klaus (2005) provides the most recent trend data for criminal victimization against the elderly. The trend data indicate that the elderly are victimized at a much lower rate than their younger counterparts (p. 1). Other trend highlights for this age group from the report include:

- Nonfatal violent crime victimization among the elderly is very low. For every 1000 elderly persons, only four are victimized in such a manner. Additionally, the elderly had the lowest rate of nonfatal violent crime over the study period (1993–2000).
- Elderly people are victimized less often than younger adults when focusing on property crime. However, property victimization including burglary, auto theft, and theft is one area where the elderly are vulnerable. They are disproportionately victims of theft. Nevertheless, property crime victimization of the elderly declined over the study period.
- Murder rates of the elderly declined over the study period. The elderly had the lowest murder rate of any age category.

Thus, overall, the criminal victimization of the elderly as a group is relatively low in comparison to other age groups. Criminal victimization in relation to elderly abuse, neglect, and abandonment is also relatively low. These findings are interesting as much research has focused on the elderly's fear of crime—fear of criminal victimization—when that fear may be unwarranted. However, little research has focused on fear of elderly abuse, neglect, and abandonment, and perhaps since this fear is warranted, it should be studied in order to promote ways to prevent such abuse.

FEAR OF CRIME

The NCVS data has indicated consistently that the elderly are the least likely to be victims of all crimes (Bachman, 1992; Pain, 1995). Nevertheless, the elderly as a group are the most fearful of crime—especially elderly women (LaGrange and Ferraro, 1989; Smith and Hill, 1991; Pain, 1995; Hannah, 2003). Numerous research studies have reported the paradoxical relationship between age and **fear of crime**—that is, despite experiencing lower rates of victimization, the elderly, especially elderly women, are more fearful of crime than are younger males. Thus, this relationship raises the question about whether such fear of crime is rational.

When addressing the rationality question, some researchers have theorized that perhaps the fear is rational, because the elderly are more vulnerable to the ramifications of crime. For example, they are not as financially independent or physically able to rebound as are younger people: they live on fixed incomes and cannot recover as quickly when resources are depleted, and their physical strength and ability to maneuver quickly are somewhat limited. Given these considerations, then, it might be rational to have a higher level of fear of crime even when the relative risk of crime victimization is low, because the ramifications of elderly crime victimization are arguably much more devastating.

Fear of crime research, in general, has been plagued with methodological issues, in particular, the measurement of the concept itself. Different measurements produce different relationships between fear of crime and age. For example, some researchers using a single-item indicator to measure fear of crime have found a direct relationship between fear of crime and age (Conklin, 1975; Clemente and Kleinman, 1977; Ollenburger, 1981; Skogan and Maxfield, 1981; Stafford and Galle, 1984; Warr, 1984; Hill, Howell, and Driver, 1985; Ortega and Myles, 1987; Smith and Hill, 1991). The single-item measure most typically addresses relative "safeness" in a geographical area. The question, "Is there any area right around here—that is, within one mile—where you would be afraid to walk alone at night?" is a typical one-item measure of fear of crime often used (Skogan and Maxfield, 1981, 57).

Others have conceptualized fear of crime differently (see Taylor and Hale, 1986). For example, LaGrange and Ferraro (1989) have argued that fear of crime should be measured by asking respondents how fearful they are of being victims of certain crimes. When fear of crime is measured this way, LaGrange and Ferraro found older people (65 years and older) had a lower fear of crime level than younger people (18–28 years of age.)

In recent research conducted using the General Social Surveys, Sacco and Nakhaie (2001) explored whether the elderly were more fearful of crime than the nonelderly. They specifically explored crime-prevention measures taken by both groups and then compared these behaviors. They found interesting, contradictory findings to those found in early research on the topic: "older respondents do not, in general, engage in more fear-related precautions than younger respondents. In fact, they tend to take fewer precautions. Overall, this finding is contrary to the traditional stereotypes of the elderly as fearful. Notably, though, older respondents are more likely than the young to report that they stay home because of fear: This observation is consistent with the traditional model" (Sacco and Nakhaie, 2001, 321).

One final consideration: perhaps socially desirable responding to fear of crime questions, no matter how they are posed, needs to be examined. One study conducted by Sutton and Farrall (2005) did exactly this. Socially desirable responding in this case is the reluctance or willingness of an individual to accurately report when asked about fear of crime. The authors studied the different responses given by men and women on fear of crime surveys. They assert that men who do not report fear of crime because of social pressures to remain unafraid and who report high concern about giving socially desirable answers will not tell the truth, thus scoring high on the lie scales, and also will report low levels of fear. The authors found interesting results.

There was an inverse relationship between fear of crime levels and so-called lie scales, leading the authors to conclude that men are led by social pressure to report lower fear of crime. They find this pattern to hold true regardless of age. And they question whether the amount of fear of crime in males would increase beyond that fear level in women if the socially desirable element could be removed. In other words, if men did not feel compelled to give answers that were socially acceptable (in this case, low fear levels), would an honest answer, one not dictated by peer pressure, indicate higher levels of fear? This is something that should be explored further. This is very thought-provoking research and it takes into account another perspective that should be included when studying fear of crime: Do people lie about their fear levels?

THE VICTIM AND OFFENDER RELATIONSHIP

Information from the National Crime Victimization Survey looks at the offenders of violent crime victimization by the age of the victim. Below is a table reproduced from that report:

As Table 10.4 indicates, when comparing elderly victims (65 or older) to younger victims (12–24), the elderly were more likely to be victimized by strangers who were young (under age 30). Both age groups were just as likely to be victimized by male offenders.

ELDER SEXUAL ABUSE

A recent study conducted by Ann Burgess (2006) focused on **elder sexual abuse**. It is included in this chapter because Burgess's research included both male and female victims. The study sample consisted of cases of persons 60 years and older where sexual

TABLE 10.4   Characteristics of Violent Offenders by Age of Victims

Characteristics of Violent Offender	Age of Victim	
	12–64	**65 and older**
Known to Victim	31.7	23.6
Spouse/ex-spouse	5.1	2.4
Boyfriend/girlfriend	5.9	0.6[a]
Own child	0.9	2.6
Other relatives	4.0	4.1
Well-known person	15.8	13.9
Casual Acquaintance	18.2	15.7
Stranger	46.3	52.5
Don't-know relationships	3.7	8.2
Age 30 or older	30.2	48.3
Male	78.8	75.6

Source: Based on Klaus (2005, 3).
[a]Based on 10 or fewer cases.

abuse was reported to the Criminal Justice System or Adult Protective Services; the incidents were predatory criminal acts and nonconsenting sexual acts; and the abuse was done by persons in position of trust or authority as well as strangers (Burgess, 2006, slide 2). Using these criteria, Burgess identified 284 cases to be reviewed. The research questions posted by Burgess (2006, slide 7) included:

1. What are the characteristics of elder sexual abuse victims?
2. What are markers of elder sexual abuse?
3. Who are the perpetrators of elder sexual abuse?
4. What is the nature of elder sexual abuse?
5. What are the similarities and differences by route of report and disability?

The results found 93.6 percent of the victims to be female, with 19 cases of male sexual abuse. A large percentage, 73 percent, reported that the abuse took place in the victims' homes. Most often the abuse was disclosed by the victims (33.2%), followed by healthcare professionals (20.8%), social or mental health professionals (12.1%), someone else (21.8%), or family members (12.1%) (slide 9). The behavior markers that indicated that abuse had occurred included: shame or guilt (21.1%); fear toward suspect (44.5%), upset receiving personal care (25.5%), inappropriate boundaries (17%), and suspect made sexual remarks (29.7%) (Burgess, 2006, slide 10).

Importantly, Burgess gathered information on the offenders as well. She found that 210 offenders were male and 20 were female. The age range for the offenders was 13–90 years old. The relationship of the offender to the victim was (slide 11):

Stranger	26.1%
Incest	23.2%
Partner	15.5%
Unrelated caregiver	10.9%
Resident	6.0%
Known but no specific relationship	7.4%

Some very interesting findings are reported by Burgess. First, not all victims are females, and not all offenders are male. This is perhaps unexpected but it sheds light on the crime of elderly sexual abuse. Second, it might be surprising to find so many cases of elderly sexual assault. As Burgess concludes, "age is no defense against sexual assault" (slide 15). Third, the offenders' wide range in age, from 13 to 90, means that offenders truly can be any age.

MYTHS ABOUT CRIME AND ELDER ABUSE

Brian Payne (2002) has debunked some well-established myths about crime and elder abuse.

MYTH:	Most crimes committed against older persons are violent street crimes.
FACT:	Older persons are more likely to be victims of financial crimes, neglect, and white-collar offenses.
MYTH:	The consequences of victimization are the same for older and younger victims.
FACT:	In some instances, older victims suffer more severe consequences than younger victims do.
MYTH:	The best way to deal with older abuse is to pass laws that will protect the elderly.
FACT:	Many elder abuse laws have been passed with virtually no attention given to the need for laws, their implementation, or their cost.
MYTH:	Elder abuse is similar to child abuse.
FACT:	Elder abuse is more similar to spouse abuse than child abuse.
MYTH:	Adult offspring who abuse their parents do so because their parent[s are] dependent upon them.
FACT:	In many instances, particularly financial abuse cases, the abuser[s are] dependent on the older person[s].
MYTH:	Adult offspring who abuse their parents do so because they were beaten as children.
FACT:	Child abuse victims are more likely to become child abusers than elder abusers.
MYTH:	Many older victims are victims because they are in the wrong place at the wrong time.
FACT:	Most older victims are victimized in or near their homes.
MYTH:	Crimes against the elderly persons are not a big problem in our society.
FACT:	Statistics do not paint a true picture of crime in the lives of older persons.
MYTH:	In order to best prevent elder abuse, criminal justice agencies must declare a war on elder abuse.
FACT:	An integrated approach is the best response to elder abuse.

SOURCE: Payne (2002, 536).

THEORETICAL EXPLANATIONS OF ELDER ABUSE

Nadien (1995) explains the risk factors that emanate from these theoretical perspectives in an effort to explain what causes or contributes to the abuse. Included in the theoretical perspectives are psychoanalysis, social learning theory, social exchange theory, conflict theory, symbolic interactionism, role theory, situational theory, and functionalism (Nadien, 1995).

Psychoanalysis is a perspective stemming from psychology. Here abuse is attributed to some personality/mental disorder in either the victim or the perpetrator. The 10 most recognized personality disorders include Paranoid, Schizoid, Schizotypal, Antisocial, Borderline, Histrionic, Narcissistic, Avoidant, Dependent, and Obsessive-Compulsive (Comer, 1999). The psychoanalysis perspective says that illness causes the abuse.

An illustration: Becky is 31 years old, married, with two children, and was recently diagnosed with clinical depression. She has become hopeless and despondent, but she is getting medical treatment for her illness. Becky's father is a 69-year-old man who lives with his wife in another state. Becky and her family routinely see her parents on holidays and for two-week visits in the summer and fall. Of late, when Becky's parents visit at her house, Becky verbally abuses them. She is very mean to them, often calling them names, and she often treats them as though they are children. She says she does this because they are old and they need to be directed. Becky's husband realizes that when they were first married Becky never treated her parents like this. Becky and her family believe that Becky should seek further help from mental health professionals who can help her understand what might be causing her to treat her parents this way. After hours of treatment, it is determined that Becky's treatment of her parents is a result of her clinical depression. Becky is put on different medication for her clinical depression, and her treatment of her parents improves.

In this case, the verbal abuse of Becky's parents was the result of her personality disorder—clinical depression. The scenario is basic and easily understood, but, most cases are not so easily diagnosed or resolved.

Social learning theory proposes that abusive behavior is learned. Transgenerational violence, that is, violence that has been passed along from generation to generation, is learned by observing adult behavior. Those who abuse the elderly may have been abused themselves. They have learned that the appropriate response to unwanted behavior or stressful situations is to be abusive (Nadien, 1995).

An illustration: Skip was raised in a household where his father routinely beat his mother. The abuse continued from when Skip was very young, until he finally left the house when he entered the Army. Skip completed his tour of duty and married a woman he met in the Army. Both Skip and his wife were commissioned officers who served in the Vietnam conflict. Skip had a family with seven children: three boys and four girls. When it came time to "discipline" his children, Skip believed in the old adage, "Spare the rod, spoil the child." Therefore, his children were accustomed to being slapped, hit, or smacked as a way to discipline or punish misbehavior. Several years ago, Skip and his wife took in his wife's mother when she became too old and sickly to live independently. Soon thereafter Skip's oldest child started to abuse his grandmother. He would routinely withhold her medication, cash her Social Security checks and keep the money, steal from her, and give her very little food. This behavior is considered abusive, and it may indeed have been learned. The transgenerational abuse in this family spans from Skip's father beating the mother, to Skip abusing his children, to Skip's son abusing his grandmother.

Social exchange theory examines dependency in the relationship between the caregiver and the elderly person. Both are viewed as dependent on each other. Social exchange theory in general states that all social interactions depend on the exchange of resources such as money, time, love, respect, knowledge, and power. The theory explains abuse as resulting from a cost/benefit balance. As long as the abuse does not outweigh the dependency, then the elder will stay in the situation (Nadien, 1995).

For example, an elderly invalid is in need of care. A younger relative who has no place to live volunteers to take care of the older relative. Both are dependent on each other—one for care, the other for shelter. Let's say the younger relative starts to withhold the elder's Social Security check. The elder person will put up with this abuse as long as the benefit of having the younger relative living with him or her outweighs the cost of not getting the Social Security check.

Conflict theory explains elder abuse by focusing on the distribution of scarce resources. These resources often include power, money, and prestige. Those with the power tend to take advantage of or exploit those without power. Elderly persons often have few resources—wealth, power, or prestige. As a result, they may be abused by those who must take care of them.

Symbolic interactionism focuses on how the actors define the situation in terms of the level of stress. A situation can be described as "very stressful" or "not at all stressful" depending on the actors themselves. Abuse results when an actor, either the victim or the abuser, considers the situation to be too stressful (Nadien, 1995).

Role theory supposes that abuses may result when caregivers lack the skills and knowledge to adequately and appropriately care for the elderly. This theory states that abuse can be avoided by role playing. Caregivers and the elders can learn what is expected in their roles, and thus avoid victimization (Nadien, 1995).

Situational theory focuses on external factors that may lead to abuse, in particular, isolation. Those who are isolated tend to be abused more often, and the isolation of caregivers results in the abuse. Caregivers are viewed as people who have difficulty because of limited (or no) emotional and social support, and this isolation leads to abuse (Nadien, 1995).

Functionalism attributes abuse to the stereotypical understanding of what aging involves, referred to as ageism. Individuals tend to believe that the elderly are weak, foolish, and incompetent. This picture or expectation of the elderly leads to the abuse (Nadien, 1995).

POLICY IMPLICATIONS AND PROGRAMS

Crime prevention is one means of reducing both victimization and fear of crime. Particularly when addressing the elderly, crime-prevention strategies must build confidence, community, and physical security (James, 1993). Strategies focusing on the elderly may be categorized as proactive and reactive. Such crime-prevention strategies as providing security surveys of elderly residential homes, organizing community watch programs, and using crime prevention through environmental design (CPTED) are categorized as proactive. The purpose of the programs is to prevent victimization from occurring.

One example of such a crime-prevention program is neighborhood watches. Since the elderly are frequently at home they can be the "eyes and ears" of the neighborhood, looking for anything that seems out of the ordinary. Interacting with neighbors, city leaders, and law enforcement in this endeavor helps the elderly to feel more secure, and to be more comfortable in their neighborhoods. Other programs established to address elder victimization are categorized as reactive. The purpose of such programs is to help older people after victimization. In general, victim-witness assistance programs are designed to assist all victims regardless of age. However, because the elderly have special needs, some victim-witness assistance programs have specific programs designed for the elderly.

Roberts (1990) conducted extensive research on victim-witness assistance programs. When specifically addressing the elderly and their concerns, Roberts (1990, 78) found that 38 agencies (70% of the agencies surveyed) offered assistance to the elderly. The services provided included "home visits, transportation, escorts to court, emergency home repair and replacement of broken locks and doors, and emergency monetary support" (Roberts, 1990, 78).

Crime-prevention strategies have been developed focusing primarily on educating the elderly. The best defense against any type of crime is an awareness of the crime with some commonsense ways to avoid certain behaviors that make one more vulnerable to victimization. Many senior organizations like **American Association of Retired Persons (AARP)** or **National Committee for the Prevention of Elder Abuse (NCPEA)** provide elaborate websites with lists of publications and other resources to provide information to seniors on how to avoid becoming victims of crime and also explain how to report crime, with clear and detailed information on what to do to overcome the victimization. Workshops and presentations are given to seniors in local community settings such as senior centers and club houses, where presentations focus on senior victimization and how to avoid being victimized. These educational programs usually focus on financial crimes with some consideration given to personal crimes, such as violent crimes. Most programs spend a great deal of time talking about fraud. The elderly are particularly vulnerable to acts of deception resulting in financial loss for the victim. Generally, the types of fraud discussed include home or auto repairs, overseas investments, lottery winnings, and work-at-home schemes. The elderly are especially vulnerable to telemarketing scams because this group often is the sole target of such fraud. The first line of defense to prevent these types of crime is to question the proposal—and if "it sounds too good to be true," it probably is too good, meaning that seniors should be very suspicious of the offer. When money must to be exchanged to get the "big winnings" or prize package, fraud is often involved.

Law enforcement agencies often have Senior Victim Assistance Units or some similarly named units that deal specifically with elderly crime victims. Often volunteers work in these units to assist victims. The units serve as advocates for victims over a certain age—usually 55 or above. Police departments that have such units often also have special training for the police officers, which includes empathy-training so that police officers can understand what seniors are experiencing in terms of the decline in their physical and mental abilities, in an effort to help police be more sensitive and understanding when trying to assist senior crime victims. They are also trained on the warning signs of elder abuse, including but not limited to new or unexplained bruises, broken bones, or other physical injuries; changes in routine activities—not participating in daily or route activities; sudden financial hardships; and uncared for medical conditions.

A specific law enforcement program is the National Sheriffs Association's **TRIAD** program. According to the website (National Association of Triads, 2008), the TRIAD program is a collective effort among sheriffs, police chiefs, and AARP. They work together to reduce elderly criminal victimization and fear of crime, while enhancing services provided to this group by law enforcement and ultimately increasing the quality of life for the elderly. TRIAD opens the lines of communication between law enforcement and the elderly. The TRIAD program is individually tailored to each location in order to meet the needs of that elderly population. The program is governed by a senior advisory council.

The overall goal of TRIAD is to keep seniors safe and to reduce criminal victimization and fear of crime. Almost every state (47) has at least one TRIAD program in a county. TRIAD is an agreement between the agencies listed above to keep seniors safe, and this agreement is executed though a council of seniors and law enforcement officials called SALT (Seniors and Law Enforcement Together). There have been some changes in the composition of the TRIAD and SALT programs, with the number of partners increasing. Now partnerships in addition to law enforcement include fire services, EMS, faith organizations, senior volunteer organizations, prosecutors, Attorneys General, social service agencies, hospitals, and banking institutions. The increases in the partnerships are reflective of the community need, as TRIAD is individually tailored for each community.

Another specific example of a crime-prevention program geared towards the elderly can be found on the National Crime Prevention Council website (1995). The National Crime Prevention Council advocates for elderly by designing crime-prevention strategies to thwart crime and violence against the elderly. They also provide services to victims of such crime. The objective is to reduce victimization and fear of crime that is associated with higher levels of vulnerability. The key components of the effort include communication, training, services, and prevention. The lines of communication are open with a communication network that alerts senior citizens to potential crime. Training is provided to help seniors learn what is criminal behavior and how to report it to the police. Services are available to support seniors when they are victimized with special attention given to the physical, emotional, and financial hardships that result from criminal victimization. Finally, crime-prevention products, training, and other services are provided to prevent victimization.

The common thread between these two programs and among all crime-prevention programs for the elderly is a clear line of communication where information flows easily between law enforcement and the elderly. Knowledge is power, and the elderly can be empowered through educational programs sponsored by local law enforcement. Many local communities have excellent awareness programs for the elderly concerning economic victimization. These programs are discussed in detail in Chapter 11.

CONCLUSION

Elderly victimization is something that should cause concern. The elderly are the fastest growing age group in the United States, and thus need to be protected from all types of victimization. The gamut of behaviors that fall into elderly victimization include physical abuse, psychological abuse, psychological mistreatment, medical abuse, financial abuse, material abuse, social and environmental abuse, passive neglect, active neglect, self-neglect, plus any violent and/or property crime victimization. The common physical signs that indicate physical abuse include, to name but a few, bruises, swelling, broken bones, sores, cuts, and sprains. Sexual abuse is harder to discern only because the bodily areas affected may not be visible to the average person. However, caretakers can easily see such signs when caring for the elderly. It is even harder to recognize emotional and psychological abuse unless a person is very familiar with the elderly person. For example, such signs include the elderly becoming nervous, or avoiding talking or responding to questions—however, it is not the signs per se as much as it is a change in behavior. Therefore, it is important to know the elderly person to recognize such warning signs.

The most perplexing type of neglect is self-neglect. Some elderly just do not take care of themselves. They often do not care, are tired, and do not want to live. The aging process is sometimes a double-edged sword. We often hear people say "as long as I have my health and mental acuity, aging is no problem." However, we know that this is not often the case, and thus, the elderly themselves find it difficult to carry on—and often neglect themselves.

Study Questions

1. How do we reconcile the fact that the elderly are the most fearful of crime yet their victimization risk is relatively low?
2. Review the myths and facts about elderly abuse, why do you think we have such misconceptions about elderly abuse?
3. Describe the theoretical explanations for elderly abuse and how they are similar or different from general theories of victimization that were presented in Chapter 2. How might routine activities theory be applied to the explanation of elderly abuse and elderly criminal victimization?
4. The elderly are the fastest growing age group in the United States. How has the criminal justice system reacted to their victimization? What are the programs currently used and what programs are still necessary to deal with elderly victimization?

Key Terms

- American Association of Retired Persons (AARP)   199
- active neglect   187
- conflict theory   198
- elder abuse   194
- fear of crime   192
- financial abuse/material abuse   187
- functionalism   198
- medical abuse   187
- National Center on Elder Abuse (NCEA)   190
- Adult Protective Service (APS)   190
- National Committee for the Prevention of Elder Abuse (NCPEA)   199
- neglect   200
- passive neglect   187
- physical abuse   187
- psychoanalysis   196
- psychological abuse/mistreatment   187
- role theory   198
- self-neglect   187
- situational theory   198
- social and environmental abuse   187
- social exchange theory   197
- social learning theory   197
- symbolic interactionism   198
- TRIAD   199

SECTION IV

Stranger Victimization

CHAPTER

11

Economic Victimizations

INTRODUCTION

Historically, the notion of "let the buyer beware" made it the individuals' responsibility to know what they were getting into when they entered into business deals. People who lost money to "scam artists" were considered responsible for their own victimization due to greediness. Society thought very little of people who, they believed, were ripped off because of their own greed. These were not real crime victims; it was their own fault for getting swindled.

Criminologists rarely study economic victimizations (Moore and Millsap, 1990; Shichor, Gaines, and Ball, 2002). The traditional focus has always been on street crime. The impact of economic victimization was not even considered on par with the impact of street victimization. Economic victimization was not even considered criminal until Edwin Sutherland coined the term *white-collar crime*. In 1940, Edwin Sutherland put forth the notion that criminal behavior is not limited to street crime but can be found in the behavior of businesses, corporations, and professionals (Schuessler, 1973). The actions of monopolies, the advent of organized crime, and the expansion of fraudulent products started to change how citizens viewed the actions of individuals and businesses when engaged in economic transactions.

DEFINING ECONOMIC VICTIMIZATION

The traditional measures of criminality continue to ignore **economic victimization**. What is meant by economic crime victimization? This category encompasses a wide range of victimizations. Economic victimization can include the loss of retirement savings because of corporate fraud or the ruination of someone's credit rating due to identity theft. Families may lose their homes in confidence games. Businesses may go bankrupt, tax monies may be wasted, and the environment may suffer permanent damage. The elderly, or anyone for that matter, may lose substantial amounts of money due to telemarketing schemes. For our examination of economic victimization, we will define the phenomenon as victimization that occurs as a result of illegal activities by individuals, institutions, and public officials using seemingly legal means for the sole purpose of profiting through deception, corruption, and fraud.

The Uniform Crime Reports (UCR) has long been criticized for failing to record acts of fraud and other economic crimes. Even the National Crime Victimization Survey (NCVS), the most comprehensive study of victimization, fails to provide information with regard to the victimization of people by fraud. It is only recently that the

National White Collar Crime Center (NW3C) and the Federal Trade Commission (FTC) have started to estimate the amount of economic victimization and its impact on individuals and businesses.

Fraud is a pervasive problem that knows no boundaries. Individuals, small businesses, corporations, and governments are all likely victims of economic fraud.

Sutherland's explanation of white-collar and corporate criminality, especially fraud, is the foundation for our examination of economic crime victimization. Economic crimes are directed at individuals, such as **identity theft**; companies, such as **embezzlement**; and societies, such as **price fixing**. Estimates are that economic victimization costs upwards of half a trillion dollars annually (National White Collar Crime Center, 2006). However, even today much is not known about economic crimes and their true impact on society. Most economic victimization does not seem to make the local or national news because, as Sutherland correctly finds, most economic victimization is not dealt with in the formal criminal justice system, but instead, if even discovered, violations are handled by the civil courts or quasi-judicial commissions, even though the impact of economic victimization on individuals, businesses, and society is as great and as important as the impact of street crimes and domestic violence (Schuessler, 1973). Additionally, since much of the economic victimization is targeted toward the middle class, the idea of traditional victims being poor, uneducated, and urban no longer holds true, because the victims of economic crimes usually have a steady income and visible assets (Moore and Millsap, 1990).

Renewed interest in economic crime victimization comes with the recognition of tremendous damage done to individuals, companies, and our economic systems from crimes such as consumer frauds, cybercrime, and corporate crime. Beginning in the 1980s, economic victimization came to the forefront. First the price-gouging actions of the oil companies in the early 1980s led many people to question the capitalist economic system. This distrust of corporations really became a national issue with the collapse of several banking institutions in what became known as the "Savings and Loan" scandal. After the taxpayer-funded bailout of the banking industry, people started to realize the immense financial and personal costs to society that economic victimizations create.

Frauds at major corporations in the 1990s cost individuals hundreds of millions of dollars in lost retirement funds, devalued stocks prices, and ruined lives. The advent of the Internet and the online marketplace has subjected millions more people to an ever-growing number of victimizations from identity theft and consumer fraud to credit card fraud. Illegal campaign contributions and bribery of public officials has shaken our trust in the operation of our government and has cost taxpayers untold sums (Ivancevich et al., 2003).

Economic victimization can come into homes through the mail, telephones, or the Internet. Economic victimization can occur anytime, anywhere. This victimization is usually orchestrated by someone you have learned to trust or by seemingly trustworthy businesses and corporations. While the statistical data on victims of economic crime victimization is scarce, it has been estimated that the monetary loss from consumer frauds far outstrips the economic losses that occur from all street crimes combined. The true effect of the psychological impact of economic victimization will never be known. This chapter will examine the economic victimization created by white-collar crimes including consumer frauds, identity theft, cyber crimes, and corporate criminality.

DESCRIBING ECONOMIC VICTIMIZATIONS

White-collar crime is the general criminal act that creates economic victimization. Federal law defines white-collar crime as "an illegal act or series of illegal acts committed by nonphysical means and by concealment or guile, to obtain money or property, to avoid the payment or loss of money or property or to obtain business or personal advantage" (U.S. Code, Title 42, Section 3791 [1999]). White-collar crimes have taken on a greater importance because of the amount of financial harm they can create.

The concept of consumer fraud falls under the definition of white-collar crime. Fraud is the use of deception to acquire money or other assets from unsuspecting victims. Fraud victimization only includes individuals who actually lose money, property, or securities. Fraud includes the theft of a person's identity; the failure to provide services or goods contracted and paid for, such as home repairs; misrepresentation of products; deceptive marketing; unauthorized billing for items the consumer did not authorize; false business opportunities; and get-rich quick schemes (Peterson and Zikmund, 2004).

Certain groups tend to be more susceptible to fraud. Depending upon the fraud, the elderly, minorities, or those in the lower social classes may be targeted. The reason for increased vulnerability is a lack of education that results in consumer inferiority (Lee and Geisfield, 1999). The lack of consumer knowledge and, in some cases, a trusting nature, can make certain individuals more likely victims of economic victimization (Pressman, 1998).

Corporate criminality or crimes by businesses is also a component of white-collar crime. Corporate crimes occur when there is a socially injurious act committed by people who control companies to further their business interests in violation of legal standards. These acts can include price fixing, anti-trust violations, tax evasion, false advertising, environmental law violations, worker-safety issues, and securities fraud. The estimate of corporate crime losses incurred by American consumers is in the hundreds of billions of dollars, and this is only one example of economic crime (Siegel, 2008).

Corporations and businesses can also be the victims of economic crimes. A survey by Price Waterhouse Coopers (2004) of global economic crime estimated that over one-third of companies who responded to their survey suffered from some type of significant economic victimization during the previous two years. Asset misappropriation was the most reported crime, at 25 percent; cybercrime followed at 8 percent. The average loss per company was over $2 million.

The invasion of homes through the telephone is a major source of economic victimization. **Telemarketing fraud** has cost U.S. citizens incalculable amounts of money. The average loss to victims of telemarketing fraud was almost $2,000 in 2004, a nearly 33 percent increase from 2003 (National Fraud Information Center, 2005a). The elderly are often targeted by telemarketing fraud because of their lifestyles. Many elderly live alone, which makes them extremely vulnerable targets. Their social isolation may make them lonely and susceptible to a friendly voice on the phone (Doerner and Lab, 2006).

Today computers have become the latest weapon to be used by criminals to victimize society. Over the last two decades, a new term has been coined: *cybercrime*. The simplest definition of cybercrime, or computer crime, is when a computer is directly or significantly an instrument or object of a crime. Cybercrime against businesses can be internal or external. Crimes of theft, such as embezzlement, fraud, and propriety information are usually committed by current employees; attacks on the company computers such as using viruses and worms are usually external. Over the last decade, cybercrime has become one of the most common economic victimizations. Major fraud has become high tech, and the cost of cybercrime to businesses and individuals is immense. It has been estimated that the average American company loses 6 percent of its revenue to crime, fraud, and theft—most of it by electronic means. This does not count the expense businesses go through to protect their computer systems. In 2003, the *CSO Magazine* eCrime Watch Survey estimated the cost of cybercrime to U.S. organizations to be $666 million. Included in this amount are losses incurred due to viruses, hacking, identity theft, and embezzlement (Council of Better Business Bureaus, 2005). Other estimates of the total amount of computer crime run into billions of dollars (Conly and McEwen, 1990).

It is difficult to completely estimate the extent and amount of economic victimization because victims of these crimes receive little attention in the criminological or victimological literature (see generally Karmen, 2003; Doerner and Lab, 2006). Additionally, many victims may not even realize they have been victimized until well after a crime has occurred, or they may not want to report the victimization because they feel partially responsible or embarrassed that the crime happened to them.

Economic crime victimization is handled by the regular criminal justice process, governmental regulatory agencies, and the civil justice system. The laws governing behaviors that encompass these actions and fall under economic victimization include embezzlement, price fixing, bribery, environmental crimes, theft, fraud, false pretense, forgery, and counterfeiting.

Financially, hundreds of billions of dollars are lost every year due to corporate criminality, cybercrimes, and consumer frauds. Greater than direct financial costs to victims, economic criminality can destroy businesses, individual lives, and in some cases, contribute to someone's death (Curtin, 2003). Beyond direct costs of economic victimizations, additional impact can be seen with higher taxes, increased insurance premiums, and increased cost of goods and services purchased. These victimizations corrupt our free market system and can destroy the public trust. These crimes directly impact individuals and society as a whole by destroying individual lives and the faith citizens have in their governments and representatives, the businesses they depend upon every day, and their fellow citizens. Specific types of economic victimizations covered in this chapter are corporate fraud, consumer fraud, identity theft, and cybercrime.

ECONOMIC CRIME TODAY

Between 2001 and 2005, the Federal Bureau of Investigation (FBI) recorded an increase of 300 percent in the number of corporate fraud cases reported to them (Ashley, 2005). The increases in corporate fraud are not the only concerns of victimologists and the criminal justice system. With the advent of worldwide use of the Internet and web commerce, the destructive effects of economic victimization are reaching into every household and business in the nation. The most recent estimates of losses from economic victimization include illegal credit card purchases of almost $800 million (*Business Week Online*, 2005), losses from identity theft of almost $50 billion (Federal Trade Commission, 2003b), and healthcare fraud costing taxpayers up to an estimated $170 billion (National Health Care Anti-Fraud Association, 2002). Combining these economic crimes with other types of economic victimizations, the FBI has estimated the annual cost of white-collar crime to be between $300 billion and $660 billion (Association of Certified Fraud Examiners, 2005). Annual losses due to economic victimization put a strain on individuals, the economy, and the country.

The National White Collar Crime Center conducted a survey in 2005 to assess the impact of white-collar crime on individuals and households (2006). The purpose of the 2005 survey was to assess the quantity of victimization, the reporting behaviors of victims, and the perceived seriousness of the type of victimization taking place, focusing on individuals' experiences with white-collar crime. This survey was a follow-up to the 1999 survey (National White Collar Crime Center, 2000), which found that approximately 36 percent of individuals and households surveyed were victims of white-collar crime. These estimates are considered low given the poor reporting behavior of those who are victimized by white-collar crimes.

In telephone interviews, over 1,600 adult respondents were asked about any experiences they had concerning white-collar crime within the last 12 months as well as within their lifetime (National White Collar Crime Center, 2006). The survey inquired about product pricing fraud, credit card fraud, existing account fraud, new account fraud, unnecessary object repair, unnecessary home repair, and losses occurring due to false stockbroker information, fraudulent business ventures, and national corporate scandals. Additionally, participants were also asked about experiences with fraud involving the Internet, including experiences of monetary loss due to an Internet transaction or illegitimate emails. The current study found:

- 46.5 percent of households and 36 percent of individuals reported experiencing at least one form of these victimizations within the previous year.
- 62.5 percent of individuals reported experiencing at least one form of victimization within their lifetimes.
- Respondents reported victimization most often as a result of product pricing fraud, credit card fraud, unnecessary object repairs, and being directly affected by national corporate scandals (National White Collar Crime Center, 2006, 1–2).

The results represent an increase in victimization relative to the original survey: 36 percent of households victimized in 1999 and 46.5 percent in 2005.

The 2006 survey (National White Collar Crime Center) also found that the likelihood of becoming a victim of white-collar crime over the past year was closely associated with utilizing the Internet and living in an urban environment. Additionally, the demographic features associated with victimization during one's lifetime were being male, being Caucasian, having a higher income, and using the Internet (see Table 11.1). These factors associated with the likelihood of white-collar crime victimization differ greatly from those associated with the likelihood of street victimization (see Chapter 2). Yet, the survey also found that respondents believed white-collar crime to be as serious as traditional street crime without physical harm and they also believed more resources need to be allocated by governmental agencies to combat these types of crime. However, data show that only a small minority of victimizations are actually being reported to agencies with the legal authority to investigate and bring offenders to justice. The following are the responses to the 2006 survey (See Table 11.1).

As can be seen by the data, credit card frauds, account frauds, and monetary losses over the Internet have the greatest chance of being reported, but they are not being

TABLE 11.1 Reporting of Economic Victimization

Offense (Households May Be Victimized by More Than One Crime Type)	Total Number of Victimizations	Percentage of Victimizations Reported	Percentage of Reported Victimization Made to Crime-Control Agencies
Unnecessary repairs (home)	87	37.4	38.2
Affected by national corporate scandal	158	59.3	36.5
New account fraud	60	84.3	34.8
False stockbroker information	33	30.0	33.3
Fraudulent business venture	44	40.1	31.9
Monetary loss (Internet)	92	70.8	28.0
Existing account fraud	94	87.0	23.3
Credit card fraud	182	94.8	22.5
Unnecessary repairs (object)	154	45.8	16.1
Price lie	268	49.1	14.3
Illegitimate email	41	24.3	8.9

Source: Adapted from National White Collar Crime Center (2006).

reported to the law enforcement agencies which are charged with the responsibility to investigate those crimes.

Corporate Fraud

Economic victimization by corporations has only been recognized since the early part of the twentieth century, with the advent of the corporate world. Today the estimated losses to victims of **corporate fraud** have reached hundreds of millions of dollars (Corporate Fraud Task Force, 2004). Acts considered under the umbrella of corporate fraud include price fixing, illegal restraint of trade, false advertising, misleading investors, accounting fraud, securities fraud, and falsifying business records. In the United States, there are many examples of major frauds beginning in the 1930s (see Table 11.2).

One of the earliest examples of corporate fraud on a national level was the case of Samuel Insull, one of the cofounders of the company that would become General Electric (Curry and Shibut, 2000). In an effort to build his chain of Midwestern utility companies, he employed fraudulent financial data and reports to attract investors and customers. The companies finally collapsed and it left thousands of investors with losses of approximately one billion dollars.

Another national corporate corruption case began right after World War II. During the 1940s and 1950s, most major electrical manufacturing companies engaged in a price-fixing scheme in order to keep electrical rates and equipment prices artificially high. Major expansion was occurring in the nation as new communities and towns established

TABLE 11.2   Major Economic Victimizations

Time Period	Individuals or Companies Involved	Type of Victimization	Losses Incurred
1930s	Samuel insull	False financial data	$1 billion +
1940s–1950s	Electrical conspiracy	Price fixing	$160 million
1970s	Equity life insurance	False financial data	$2–$3 billion
1980s	Oil company price fixing	Price fixing	$4.1 billion
1980s–1990s	Savings and loan scandal	Corporate corruption	$1.7 trillion
1990s–2000s	Adelphia	Corporate corruption	$715 million
1990s–2000s	WorldCom	False financial data	$750 million
1990s–2000s	Tyco international	False financial data	$600 million
1990s–2000s	IPO scandal	False financial data	$1.4 billion
1990s–2000s	Marsh and McLennan	False financial data	$850 million
1990s–2000s	AIG	False financial data	$1.64 billion
1990s–2000s	Enron	Corporate corruption	$47 billion

to meet the needs of the baby-boom generation. Companies got together and set artificially high prices in their sealed bids for government contracts, school districts, and utilities. The companies met before the sealed bids were to be submitted to decide who would win the bid, and how much they would bid, with the winners rotating so that every company received huge profits. This price-fixing scheme cost consumers and the government an untold amount of money in overcharges (Curry and Shibut, 2000).

In 1975, officials of the Equity Life Insurance Company were indicted and later convicted of investment fraud (Curry and Shibut, 2000). In one of the largest frauds uncovered to date, the company officials were found to be inflating the value of the company. Company officials manipulated their stock value by inventing thousands of insurance policies that did not exist. With nonexistent policies counted as corporate capital, the economic wealth of the corporation became greatly inflated, which created immense interest in the stock, thereby inflating the stock price. When the existence of these fake policies came to light, investors lost between two and three billion dollars in their stock valuation.

In the late 1980s and early 1990s, one of the greatest losses ever suffered by U.S. taxpayers occurred because of what became known as the "Savings and Loan" (S and L) scandal (Jameson, 2002). During the 1980s, regulations on the banking industry were relaxed, which allowed banks, especially savings and loans, to engage in risky business ventures. The lack of regulation also encouraged fraud and corruption by the executives of many of the banks. Results of the lack of regulation and corruption occurred between 1986 and 1995 when the underwriting of failed U.S. thrifts by the financial industry and the U.S. taxpayer cost an extraordinary $153 billion (Curry and Shibut, 2000). The extent of the disaster turned into a major threat to the U.S. financial system and one of the most expensive sector crises the world had ever seen. While much of the losses were not deemed to be criminal, out-and-out corruption played its part, both in terms of direct economic losses and in bank foreclosures—it is estimated to account for at least

15 percent of the total S and L loss. Lack of government oversight is thought to be responsible for setting the scene for reckless decision making, misevaluation, and deliberately obscuring financial reporting and documentation. While the industry began to stabilize in the mid 1990s, the economic loss to taxpayers and the economy would never be recovered.

Corporate victimization uncovered since the beginning of the new millennium is estimated to have cost the American economy over $200 billion and the loss of 1 million jobs (Simon, 2006). Many of the victimizations were committed by well-known corporations such as Tyco, WorldCom, AIG, and Enron. These cases are only the tip of the iceberg. Numerous other corporations settled legal disputes with consent decrees and fines. Many more victimizations were settled out of court, rather than within the criminal justice system. In most cases of corporate victimization, no one person can be held accountable. Corporations are seen as entities unto themselves and they pay fines, agree to change their practices, may pay restitution, and continue with their operations. More recently, however, individual officers of corporations are being held directly responsible for the economic victimizations of their corporations.

The case against former Chief Executive Officer L. Dennis Kozlowski and Chief Financial Officer Mark Swartz of Tyco International LTTD provides a perfect example of individuals being held responsible (Laufer, 2006). The pair was accused of conspiring to defraud Tyco and its stockholders of millions of dollars to fund their extravagant lifestyles. They were charged with misappropriating $170 million in company funds by hiding unauthorized bonuses and secretly forgiving loans to themselves. They were also accused of making over $400 million by lying about Tyco's financial condition in order to inflate the value of their stock. They both were convicted of securities fraud, grand larceny, conspiracy, and falsifying business records. The exact amount of the victimization ran into hundreds of millions of dollars.

At WorldCom, the former head of the telecom giant, Bernard Ebbers, was charged with falsifying his company's financial statements by more than $9 billion (Hays, 2006). The true extent of the fraud was realized when the company admitted to overstating profits by over $70 billion between 2000 and 2001. Ebbers was found guilty of fraud in the company's accounting scandal. As a result of the fraud, WorldCom was forced to file for the largest bankruptcy in U.S. history. This cost stockholders and other investors well over a billion dollars, but the civil fines and restitution associated with this case only came to $750 million.

American International Group Inc. (AIG) is one of the world's largest insurance companies. In May, 2005, New York Attorney General Eliot Spitzer filed a civil lawsuit charging that the company used deceptive accounting practices to mislead investors and regulatory agencies. Additionally, the Securities and Exchange Commission (SEC), which regulates the operation of the stock market, filed and settled allegations of accounting fraud with the company. The company has agreed to pay $1.64 billion to resolve the allegations. Under the settlement, $800 million will be awarded to investors who were deceived by AIG's accounting practices, $375 million to AIG policyholders, $344 million to states harmed by the company's practices, and fines to the state of New York and the federal government. This agreement spares the company criminal prosecution.

Probably the most famous case of corporate criminality was the Enron scandal. The Enron Corporation, which was based in Texas, affected about 50,000 Enron stock and bond holders, including many individuals who worked for the company. Many of the Enron employees lost their life savings, and many institutions also lost their investments. Total losses were estimated to be $47 billion (Hays, 2006). This economic victimization involved several Enron officials and auditors at Arthur Andersen, a major accounting firm at the time. The corporate officials and their auditors are suspected of, or have plead guilty to, deluding investors into believing Enron was a growing company when it was not. They are also implicated in the manipulation of electrical prices and supplies during 2000 that victimized millions of Californians, cheated the state out of millions of dollars, and caused significant power outages. All the while Kenneth Lay, the former Chairman of Enron, and Jeffrey Skilling, former Enron CEO, were making hundreds of millions of dollars in salary, bonuses, and stock options. The trial for federal fraud and conspiracy charges of Lay, Skilling, and former top accountant Richard Causey resulted in guilty verdicts.

Congress reacted strongly to the tremendous amount of corporate criminality with the passage of the 2002 Sarbanes-Oxley Act (Hays, 2006). The Act allows the Securities and Exchange Commission to use civil fines, disgorgement of ill-gotten gains, and interest to pay back victims. The main thrust of the Sarbanes-Oxley Act is the establishment of new accounting regulations and practices corporations and their officers must follow. The Act also imposes hefty criminal penalties, including 10–20 year jail terms, for management and directors who knowingly engage in fraud (Telberg, 2004).

Even with new laws and greater attention paid to victims harmed by corporate criminality, they still face many obstacles in order to recover from their victimizations. If the corporations declare bankruptcy, the individual victim must get in line with all other victims (banks, governments, other companies, large investment groups, etc.) to try to recover what they have lost. Often there is very little left. Employees of bankrupt firms who had their retirement accounts tied to the economic health of their companies have lost almost everything. Individual corporate officers may have squandered their ill-gotten gains and have very little left to attach. But a growing sentiment in the business community that the controls attached to businesses have gone too far and are impacting legitimate business practices could result in a rollback of regulations and leave the victims of corporate criminality out in the cold again (Hays, 2006).

Consumer Fraud

Consumer frauds usually target individuals and employ some type of deception for the purpose of obtaining financial gain. This type of fraud victimization can result in the loss of money, property, or securities. Consumer fraud includes various schemes such as telemarketing fraud, fraudulent financial and investment advice, the failure to provide services or goods contracted and paid for, such as home repairs, misrepresentation of products, deceptive marketing, unauthorized billing for items the consumer did not authorize, false business opportunities, and get-rich quick schemes (Titus, Heinzelmann, and Boyle, 1995).

The consumer fraud currently known as a *Ponzi scheme* can be traced back to the 1920s. Charles Ponzi promised a 50 percent return on an investment idea he had come up with. He was able to convince numerous individuals to invest with him. The fraud occurred when early investors were initially paid with funds received from later investors. Ponzi then convinced the initial investors to reinvest and he fled with everyone's investments. His actions lead to the theft of $15 million from some 40,000 investors (Anderson, 2004).

TABLE 11.3 Vast Majority of Frauds Reported

Paid an advance fee to obtain a loan or credit card that you were promised or guaranteed you would receive.

Billed for buyers' club memberships you did not agree to purchase.

Purchased credit card insurance.

Purchased credit repair.

Paid money or made a purchase to receive a promised prize and did not receive the prize or prize was not as promised.

Billed for Internet services you did not agree to purchase.

Purchased a membership in a pyramid scheme.

Billed for information services provided either over the Internet or by pay-per-call that you had not agreed to purchase.

Made a payment to someone who represented that you would receive a government job.

Purchased a business opportunity where promised earnings were not realized or promised assistance was not provided.

Source: Adapted from Anderson (2004).

During the 1960s, Robert Vesco, a friend of future president Richard Nixon, devised a scheme to entice investors to purchase a tax-exempt fund he was in charge of. When a downturn in the stock market caused the investors to lose much of their money, Vesco took over $200 million from the company and fled to Cuba (Hays, 2006).

Currently, consumer fraud is an extensive problem in the United States. This type of fraud impacts individuals and the economy as a whole. Consumer fraud can occur over the Internet, through the mail, or even in the media. A 2004 report by the Federal Trade Commission (FTC) estimates there are more than 24 million victims of certain types of fraud in the United States alone. This translates into over 11 percent of the adult population in the United States. According to the FTC, 10 specific frauds make up the vast majority of fraud reported to authorities (See Table 11.3).

Telemarketing Frauds

Many legitimate companies and charities solicit consumers by telephone. Unfortunately, con artists use the telephone, too. According to the National Consumers League's national fraud information center (http://www.fraud.org), nearly a third of all telemarketing fraud victims are age 60 or older. Studies by AARP show that most older telemarketing fraud victims do not realize that the voice on the telephone could belong to someone trying to steal their money (National Fraud Information Center, 2005a). The FBI says there are thousands of fraudulent telemarketing companies operating in the United States. There are also an increasing number of illegal telemarketers who target U.S. residents from locations in Canada and other countries. In 2004, foreigners made up 26 percent of telemarketing fraud offenders, 40 percent more than just the year before. Many victims are even reluctant to admit they have been cheated or robbed by illegal telemarketers, blaming themselves for the victimization (National Fraud Information Center, 2005a).

The average loss to victims of telemarketing can be broken down into five categories, which are listed in Table 11.4.

TABLE 11.4 Average Loss to Victims	
Telemarketing Fraud Categories	*Average Loss*
Lotteries/lottery clubs	$5,194
Prize/sweepstakes	$3,135
Advance fee loans	$1,721
Travel/vacations	$1,268
Work-at-home plans	$1,085

Source: Based on National Fraud Information Center (2005a).

There are many tell-tale signs to indicate a telephone call is actually a fraud waiting to happen. Some of them are:

- A promise to win money, make money, or borrow money easily.
- A demand to act immediately or miss out on this great opportunity.
- A refusal to send written information before you agree to buy or donate.
- An attempt to scare a potential victim into buying something.
- Insistence that someone wire money or have a courier pick up a payment, and
- A refusal to stop calling (National Fraud Information Center, 2005a).

The common thread that runs through all telemarketing scams is the demand for payment up front. According to the National Fraud Information Center (2005a), what victims, or potential victims, of telemarketing fraud need to understand is that: (1) Fraudulent telemarketers understand human nature. People all want to believe that it's their lucky day, that they can get a great deal, or that they can solve their problems. (2) Older people are disproportionately targeted compared to other age groups by fraudulent telemarketers. That is because they are home to get calls, they have money saved that can be robbed, and they are too polite to hang up (National Fraud Information Center, 2005a). (3) It is important for potential victims to know who they are dealing with. If a company or charity is unfamiliar, check it out with a state or local consumer agency and the Better Business Bureau. Fraudulent operators open and close quickly, so the fact that no one has made a complaint yet doesn't guarantee the company or charity is legitimate.

Some telemarketing pitches are blatantly fraudulent, and potential victims should know the signs. It is illegal for telemarketers to ask for a fee up front. If they promise or claim that they will get someone a credit card or loan, or to "repair" someone's credit for a fee, they are violating the law. It is also illegal for any company to ask anyone to pay for or buy something to win a prize or to claim that paying will increase your chances of winning. It is also illegal to buy and sell tickets to foreign lotteries by phone or mail.

Other danger signs of fraud may be harder to recognize. They include: pressure to act immediately, refusal to send written information, use of scare tactics, demands to send payment by wire or courier, demands for payment of taxes or customs' fees to claim a prize, requests for financial account numbers, promises to recover money lost in other scams, for a fee; claims that lots of money can be made working from home; and a refusal to stop calling (National Fraud Information Center, 2005a).

There are various types of telemarketing scams, all with the same purpose: to get money or personal information. One of the most frequent types of telemarketing fraud is carried out by the companies themselves (National Fraud Information Center, 2005a). Currently, there are many competing companies who offer telephone service. Unfortunately, so have the chances of being "slammed." **Slamming** occurs when telephone service is switched from one company to another without permission. Long-distance service is the most common target of slamming, but it can also affect local service. In addition to "plain old telephone service," a consumer can buy extra services such as voice mail, paging, and Internet access from many different companies. But when charges show up on the phone bill for services never agreed to, the victim has been "crammed." **Cramming** is when a company charges extra services that were never agreed to appear on a telephone bill. Pay-per-call services are another type of telemarketing scam. These "900" or even "800" numbers provide live or recorded information and entertainment—everything from sports scores and weather forecasts to psychic readings and chat lines. Unfortunately, charges for these services may appear on phone bills even if consumers never agreed to pay for them or didn't understand the cost.

One way to protect potential victims from these scams is to know the cost of dialing. Services provided through 900 numbers must state the cost clearly in their ads. If the cost is more than a total of $2, it must also be disclosed at the start of the call, before the charges begin.

Some people fall victim to telemarketing schemes when they are desperate. Many citizens want to help people in need, but they need to be sure that charitable donations are not going straight into a crook's pocket. Often criminal telemarketers will pose as legitimate charities to rip people off. Most states require charities to register with them and file annual reports showing how they use donations. State or local consumer protection agencies have this information. The Better Business Bureau (BBB) Wise Giving Alliance also offers information about national charities (National Fraud Information Center, 2005b).

Calls or letters stating that there are millions for the taking in foreign lotteries are scams. Crooks take advantage of the natural desire to win. State lotteries and other contests are advertising all the time, but it is illegal to use the mail or telephone to play lotteries across borders. U.S. law prohibits it, not only across national borders, but state lines as well. So victims could end up being accused of illegal activities just by participating. Additionally, no matter how official these solicitations look or sound, they are not real. Sometimes the lotteries actually exist, but invitations to play do not come from governments that operate legitimate lotteries or anyone connected to them (National Fraud Information Center, 2005b).

Telemarketing Fraud Prevention
In fighting telemarketing fraud there are ways to reduce the number of unwanted sales calls and mailings received, and how to deal effectively with telemarketers (National Fraud Information Center, 2005b). The National Fraud Information Center lists five strategies:

- ***Avoid getting on sucker lists.***   Don't fill out contest entry forms at fairs or malls—they are a common source of "leads" for con artists. Companies should be asked not to share personal information with other marketers.
- ***"Do-Not-Call" rights.***   Under federal law, anyone can tell a telemarketer not to call again. State attorney generals' offices or consumer affairs department have information on "Do-Not-Call" laws.

- ***Screen calls.*** Use an answering machine, caller ID, or other services that are available from telephone companies.
- ***Develop a plan*** for speaking to telemarketers. Know what questions to ask or what to say. Be polite, but firm. Hang up if someone refuses to answer questions.
- ***Be aware that charges for many types of services can appear on phone bills.*** In addition to billing for its own services, phone companies may bill on behalf of other companies for services they sell such as voice mail, paging, or Internet access—even for club memberships and other types of services.

Identity Theft

Identity theft occurs when someone uses personal information without the victim's knowledge to commit fraud or a crime. A single victim of identity fraud might be victimized in dozens of ways. Often, unsuspecting victims learn of the crime with a telephone call or a letter from a creditor or a collection agency concerning bills they did not incur. Perpetrators steal victims' identifying information and sell it or use it illegally for their own benefit. Identifying information can include a victim's name, social security number, address, driver's license number, employee identification number, bank account numbers, credit card numbers, or even computer password identification. With this information, criminals can attack a person's assets or use his or her credit rating to acquire goods and services in the victim's name without ever paying for them. Anyone can be the victim of identity theft: rich or poor, black or white, male or female, young or old, identity theft affects people of all demographics in the United States.

According to the FTC, in 2003, nearly 10 million people had their identities compromised, and it took an average of 33 hours of a victim's time and $500–$1,200 out-of-pocket expense to recover from identity theft. Even then there was no guarantee that their credit rating would be the same as it was before the event happened. In 2003, the average loss incurred per case was over $5,000. The estimated losses due to identity theft in 2003 were $50 billion for businesses and $5 billion for individual victims. In 2004, the estimated number of victims fell to 8.9 million, but the dollar losses rose and victims spent more time trying to restore their good names. A survey by the Council of Better Business Bureaus found that the average loss per case of ID theft rose to over $6,300 (2005).

Identity theft is presently one of the fastest growing crimes in the United States, and one of the hardest to get a complete picture of (see Newman and McNally, 2005). It is believed that every citizen will either be or at least know one victim of identity theft in his or her lifetime (Federal Trade Commission, 2001, 2003a; Pollock and May, 2002). Most victims of identity theft do not report the crime to criminal authorities. According to a recent national survey, about 25 percent of victims said they reported the crime to local police (Synovate, 2003). One of the worst parts of identity fraud is that all too often victims are treated as though they are the criminals. Victims may have to spend countless hours defending themselves against creditors and proving they did not purchase the disputed goods themselves.

It wasn't until 1998 that identity theft received the national attention it deserved. In 1998, the United States Congress passed the Identity Theft and Assumption Deterrence Act, which made it a violation of federal law to steal a person's identity. By 2001, 37 states had enacted identity theft legislation, with ten of the states doing so during the previous year (Victim Policy Pipeline, 2001). Today, every state has some type of identity theft law, and the federal government passed an enhanced Identity Theft Penalty Act in 2005. However, there are inconsistencies in the perceived seriousness of the victimization with some states treating the offense as a misdemeanor and others classifying it as a felony.

The Federal Trade Commission has found that "credit card fraud (28%) was the most common form of reported identity theft followed by phone or utilities fraud (19%), bank fraud (18%), and employment fraud (13%). Other significant categories of identity theft reported by victims were government documents/benefits fraud and loan fraud" (2005, 3).

In spring 2003, the FTC sponsored a survey on the topic of identity theft and the resulting experiences of victims in the past year. The study involved 4,057 telephone interviews with U.S. adults. Findings of the study include:

- "1.5 percent of survey participants reported that in the last year they had discovered that their personal information had been misused to open new credit accounts, take out new loans, or engage in other types of fraud, such as misuse of the victim's name and identifying information when someone is charged with a crime, when renting an apartment, or when obtaining medical care. This result suggests that almost 3.25 million Americans discovered that their personal information had been misused in this kind of fraud in the past year."
- "12.7% of survey respondents reported that within the last five years they had discovered that they were victims of one of the three types of Identity Theft. This implies that approximately 27 million American adults have been victims in this period."
- "Victims reported that they spent 30 hours, on average, resolving their problems." Furthermore, "victims estimated that they had spent $500 on average to deal with their ID Theft experience."
- "Approximately 25 percent of victims who participated in the survey said that they had reported the crime to local police. Reporting to police increased to 43 percent with the more serious "New Accounts and Other Frauds" form of ID Theft (National Field Sellers Association, 2006 Retrieved from: http://www.nfsa.com/pdf/nfsa_nws_0106.pdf).

The problem of identity theft continues to grow. In 2005, the Federal Identity Theft Data Clearinghouse reported that 38 percent of all fraud claims in 2004.approximately 500,000, were related to identity theft (Federal Trade Commission, 2005). This is a major increase from just a few years earlier. In 2001, there were 86,212 identity theft complaints; in 2002, 161,836; and in 2003, 214,905. The more than doubling of actual complaints not only shows greater victim awareness of the crimes but also illustrates that the victimization is not going away.

The distribution of ages can be understood by examining some of the factors associated with ID theft. Identity theft is a crime of the information age. Contrary to popular belief, the elderly are not being victimized by this type of fraud as much as other types of fraud. Table 11.5 reveals that the percentage of victim complaints received by FTC from persons aged 60 and above is only nine percent.

According to the U.S. Federal Trade Commission report, identity thieves use a variety of methods to gain access to personal information. For example, they get information from businesses or other institutions by:

- stealing records from their employer,
- bribing an employee who has access to these records, or
- hacking into the organization's computers,
- rummaging through your trash or the trash of businesses or dumps in a practice known as dumpster diving,

TABLE 11.5 Age of Identity Theft Victims

Percentage of Victim Complaints to the FTC Based on Age

Under 18	5%
18–29	29%
30–39	24%
40–49	20%
50–59	13%
60+	9%

Source: Based on Federal Trade Commission (2006).

- obtaining credit reports by abusing their employer's authorized access to credit reports or by posing as a landlord, employer, or someone else who may have a legal right to the information,
- stealing credit and debit card numbers as your card is processed by using a special information storage device in a practice known as skimming,
- stealing wallets and purses containing identification, credit and bank cards,
- stealing mail, including bank and credit card statements, pre-approved credit offers, new checks, or tax information,
- completing a "change of address form" to divert your mail to another location,
- stealing personal information from your home,
- scamming information from posing as a legitimate business person or government official (ID Theft: What's It All About, 2003a, 1).

Another avenue for obtaining personal information is online resume-posting sites. Identity thieves use these sites as a springboard for obtaining personal information. Posing as employers, the thieves are able to con prospective employees into giving out additional private information, such as Social Security numbers.

Identity Theft Prevention
There are many steps potential victims of identity theft can take to make victimization less likely. First, firewalls can be used to protect computer information. Also, shredding utility bills and other personal information stops thieves from retrieving it from the trash. Other simple steps include not leaving wallets or purses in cars where they can be stolen and watching how much personal information is posted on the Internet or given out to unknown individuals (National Fraud Information Center, 2005b).

What to do if identity theft happens? The following are from a leading identity theft prevention site:

- Obtain a police report specific to identity theft.
- Notify one of the three major credit bureaus of fraudulent activity. When one is notified it must notify the other two.
- Check with your state's department of motor vehicles to see if any fraudulent IDs or driver's licenses have been issued in your name.
- Obtain a copy of your work history from the Social Security Administration and notify them if there are any errors (www.idfraud.org)

CYBERCRIME

Cybercrime is synonymous with computer crime. There are two types of computer crimes: one where the computer is the instrument used to commit a criminal offense and one in which a computer is the target of a criminal act. To better understand cybercrime, it is important to classify the various groups of crime that can occur. According to Conly and McEwen (1990), there are five major categories of computer crime: (1) internal computer crimes, such as viruses; (2) telecommunication crimes, such as hacking; (3) computer manipulation crimes, such as frauds and embezzlement; (4) supporting criminal enterprises, such as child pornography; and (5) the theft of hardware and software (p. 3).

Internet Frauds

An increasingly prevalent cybercrime is the fraudulent use of the Internet marketplace. The advent of the Internet has created a virtual marketplace where every product known to mankind can be purchased. E-commerce has provided a new, expansive arena for economic victimization. U.S. consumers lodged over 200,000 complaints of online fraud in 2004, a 66 percent increase from 2003 (National White Collar Crime Center, 2005).

One of the places to file a complaint is the Internet Crime Complaint Center (http://www.ic3.gov). The Complaint Center is a partnership between the Bureau of Justice Assistance, the National White Collar Crime Center and the Federal Bureau of Investigation. The mission of the Complaint Center is to receive Internet-related criminal complaints and to further research, develop, and refer criminal complaints to federal, state, local, or international law enforcement and regulatory agencies for any investigation they deem appropriate. In 2004, the IC3 website received over 207,000 complaints.

Internet frauds can be found intertwined with legitimate Internet commerce. Increasingly, emails are becoming a growing method of contact used by Internet fraud perpetrators. In 2004, 22 percent of Internet fraud offenders initiated contact with the victim through email, a 340 percent increase from 2003. The average loss to victims of Internet fraud was $895 in 2004, a 70 percent increase from 2003 (National Fraud Information Center, 2005a). The most common fraud occurs using Internet auction sites. The fraud that causes the most dollar loss per incident is check fraud, and the type of fraud that is least likely to cost victims money is computer fraud (see Table 11.6). **The Internet Crime Complaint Center** provides the most comprehensive explanation of various forms of Internet frauds and schemes. Some of the most common schemes are explained below:

Auction Fraud

Auction fraud involves the misrepresentation of a product advertised for sale or the non-delivery of products purchased through an Internet auction site. Internet auction fraud was, by far, the most reported Internet fraud complaint. Popular websites such as eBay and Overstock.com are the major auction sites. Frauds can occur because the item purchased is not what was described, the item is not in working order, the item is never received by the buyer and/or the item is stolen.

TABLE 11.6 Average Loss by Type of Fraud

Type of Fraud	Percentage of Complainants Who Lost Money(%)	Average Dollar Loss per Complaint
Auction fraud	87	$200.00
Nondelivery of goods	82	$264.95
Credit/debit card fraud	82	$240.00
Investment fraud	75	$625.57
Financial institutional fraud	67	$968.00
Nigerian letter fraud	52	$3,000.00
Check fraud	52	$3,600.00
Confidence fraud	46	$1,000.00
Identity theft	30	$907.30
Computer fraud	6	$391.20

Source: Adapted from National White Collar Crime Center (2005).

Counterfeit Cashier's Check

The counterfeit cashier's check scheme can impact anyone who uses the Internet to conduct business. The scheme works this way: the criminal usually located outside of the United States contacts the would-be victims and tells them he or she is interested in renting their property, buying their goods, or contracting their services. They state that they will have a friend of theirs in the United States send them a cashier's check or postal money order. When the would-be victim receives the funds the checks are for much more than the original amount agreed upon. The criminal apologizes and tells the would-be victim to deposit the checks and send him a bank check for the difference. Since the original checks are fakes, and it takes banks a number of days to discover this, the now victim has sent the criminal funds they will never see and may have to pay bank fees for depositing fraudulent checks.

Debt Elimination

Debt elimination schemes seek to victimize people who are already having serious financial problems. The scheme using a website or other means tells people that they can reduce or eliminate most of their debt from credit cards or loans by paying a set fee and sending them all of their information. This scheme not only victimizes someone by getting them to pay a fee for services not provided, but the criminals may also get valuable personal information which they can use to steal a person's identity.

Employment/Business Opportunities

Employment/business opportunity schemes are impacting numerous job seekers. Criminals contact individuals using on-line employment search websites (Monster.com, etc.). They are offered lucrative employment overseas or work-at-home jobs that will provide them with large salaries. The fraud can happen in two different ways. First, the victim is told to send all of their personal information, as you would give any normal employer. This information can be then used to steal the victims' identities. Second, the victims could be sent bogus checks similar to the counterfeit check scheme and be required to return excess funds as a condition of further employment.

Lotteries

The lottery scheme deals with criminals contacting potential victims and telling them that they have been the lucky winner of a foreign lottery. The notice promises would-be victim hundreds of thousands, even millions of dollars. A contact name or organization follows this announcement and provides the victim with a phone number, fax number, and an email address that they need to contact to receive their winnings. Once contacted, they are indeed informed that they have won and that the organization will process their winnings for a fee, pay all legal fees and any other taxes that may occur. If the victim does pay then there are additional fee or tax payment requests made without the victim even receiving a dime.

Nigerian Letter or "419"

Originating in the African country of Nigeria and named for the violation of Section 419 of the Nigerian Criminal Code, the Nigerian letter scam combines the threat of impersonation fraud with a variation of an advance fee scheme. Would-be victims are contacted mostly by email from an individual, traditionally Nigerian (but now all nationalities are represented), or foreign government officials, which offers the recipient the "opportunity" to share in a percentage of millions of dollars. The criminal is asking for help in placing large sums of money in overseas bank accounts. The would-be victim is asked to make the payment of taxes, bribes to government officials, and legal fees for which they will be reimbursed as soon as the funds are out of the country. Once the victim has started to make the payments, the victim is asked to keep sending money to eliminate various problems that have occurred which are preventing the funds from being sent out of the country.

Phishing/Spoofing

Phishing and spoofing are another way criminals try to access personal information of potential crime victims. Spoofing refers to forged emails and phishing uses fictious websites. These schemes use legitimate companies such as banks or auction sites as the foundation for their frauds. Fake emails are sent telling potential victims that there is a problem with their bank account, credit card account, or other account and they are directed to the fictious website to have their problem fixed. The website looks exactly like a legitimate website for the company. The victim is then asked for account numbers, credit card numbers, passwords, bank account information, social security number, etc., which is used to steal their accounts and their identity.

Ponzi/Pyramid

An investment scam which has been around for many years is Ponzi or pyramid schemes. Investors are promised high profits on their investments whether it is in a special stock transaction, real estate, or some other investment opportunity. When the funds are given to the criminal no investment is actually made. What does occur is that the early investors are paid minimal returns with the investment money received from the later investors who are then encouraged to bring in additional investors. The early investors receive a small percentage of what they invested and the later investors do not receive any dividends and lose their initial investment.

Spam

Spam is unsolicited bulk email. Spam is now a widely used medium for committing traditional economic crimes including bank fraud, credit card fraud, and identity theft. Spam can also be used to access computers and servers without authorization and transmit viruses. Once personal information is accessed, the criminals who sent this spam often provide services that sell this personnel information, including credit card information, social security numbers, and other information. Those sending this spam are violating the Controlling the Assault of Non-Solicited Pornography and Marketing (CAN SPAM) Act, Title 18, U.S.C., Section 1037. (The information of Internet fraud has been adapted from the Internet Crime Complaint Center, 2008.)

INTERNET FRAUD PREVENTION

The Internet Crime Complaint Center (IC3) suggests the following steps be taken to ensure you protect your personal information when using the Internet:

- Ensure websites are secure prior to submitting your credit card number.
- Do your homework to ensure the business or website is legitimate.
- Attempt to obtain a physical address, rather than a P.O. box or mail drop.
- Never throw away credit card or bank statements in usable form.
- Be aware of missed bills which could indicate your account has been taken over.
- Be cautious of scams requiring you to provide your personal information.
- Never give your credit card number over the phone unless you make the call.
- Monitor your credit statements monthly for any fraudulent activity.
- Report unauthorized transactions to your bank, or credit card company, as soon as possible.
- Review a copy of your credit report at least once a year. Internet Crime Complaint Center (2008) http://www.ic3.gov/crimeschemes.aspx;http://www.smallbusinesscomputing.com/news/article.php/3498156. Retrieved Feburary 14, 2008.

CONCLUSION

Economic victimization is a major problem facing victims, the criminal justice system, the regulatory agencies, and society. The harm caused by economic victimization is immeasurable in terms of dollars, livelihoods, emotional harm, and societal impact. Economic victimizations can take place on an individual level such as when home owners are caught up in a home repair scam. Economic victimizations can impact groups such as investors who are lured into investment schemes where all of their investments may be lost. Economic victimization can also do immeasurable damage to our nation's economy as well as occurred with the Savings and Loan frauds. There are so many intangibles when trying to understand the impact economic crimes have on people. Enforcement is mostly left up to regulatory agencies in the case of corporate criminality, and the likelihood of obtaining justice for individual frauds is almost nonexistent. In many ways, the old notion of "buyer beware" is still very present today.

Study Questions

1. Describe what is meant by economic victimization. How widespread is the problem, and what is its impact on individuals and economies? What trends do you see in economic victimization?
2. Why does corporate fraud occur, and what kind of impact has it had on the economy in the last two decades? What can be done to reduce the amount of economic victimization due to corporate fraud?
3. What is identity theft? What types of additional crimes can victims of identity theft be affected by? What resources are there to help victims of identity theft to recover?
4. What are the various types of fraud being engaged in over the Internet? What role does economic victimization play in e-commerce? What should consumers watch out for when engaging in e-commerce? What are some of the protections potential victims can employ to reduce their chances of becoming victims of economic crimes?

Key Terms

- auction fraud   217
- consumer fraud   219
- corporate crime   204
- corporate fraud   207
- cramming   213
- cybercrime   204
- economic victimization   202
- embezzlement   203

- fraud   203
- identity theft   203
- National White Collar Crime Center   203
- Nigerian Letter   219
- phishing   219
- Ponzi scheme   210
- price fixing   203

- pyramid scheme   219
- slamming   213
- spam   220
- telemarketing fraud   204
- The Internet Crime Complaint Center   217
- white-collar crime   204

CHAPTER 12

Hate Crimes and Special Populations

INTRODUCTION

Hate crimes are crimes that are directed at specific groups because of an identifiable characteristic. This characteristic may be known to the assailant or it may be presumed. The crime is a result of the offender's bigotry or prejudice, and oftentimes this bigotry can only be determined by the kind of speech the offender uses. The term *hate crime* was coined by three U.S. Representatives, John Conyers (D-Mich), Barbara Kennelly (D-Conn), and Mario Biaggi (D-NY), when they cosponsored a bill in the U.S. House of Representatives in 1985 titled, "Hate Crime Statistics Act" (Jacobs and Potter, 1998, 4). This bill sought to publish the nature and number of crimes motivated by racial, religious, and ethnic prejudice. The term *hate crime* began to be used in earnest after this bill was introduced. In the early 1990s, scholars started to use the words *hate crimes* and *biased crimes* interchangeably (Jacobs and Potter, 1998).

Hate crimes can be conceptualized in a variety of ways. What is perhaps most difficult is proving that a crime is indeed a hate crime and that hate crime or the ensuing cause, prejudice, can be eradicated with criminal law. As Jacobs and Potter (1989) point out, it is difficult to attribute crimes to a prejudiced motivation because of the complexity of defining prejudice and establishing motivation for individual crimes. Legislation has been written to help define the term and to help enforce it. Nevertheless, there is still debate about whether the legislation is too narrow in its approach to defining hate crimes.

Although hate crime seems like it should be an easy term to define, there is not a great deal of consensus on the definition of this term. However' Richard Berk provides a good starting point defining a hate crime as "an illegal act [which] is perpetrated because of what a victim represents" (Berk 1994, V). Examples of some of the different statuses include racial or ethnic groups, nationalities, sexual orientation, and gender. The crime can be of any type, but most often it is assaultive behavior that is committed specifically because of what the victim represents.

According to the latest FBI publication on hate crimes, actions "motivated by a bias against a race, religion, disability, ethnicity, or sexual orientation" are considered hate crimes (Hate Crime Statistics 2006)). This definition has evolved from the one first provided in 1990, which only included protected classes of race, religion, sexual orientation, and ethnicity. Physical and mental disabilities were added in 1997 (Federal Bureau of Investigation, 2005). The FBI UCR only includes the protected classes listed above.

All states have some hate crime legislation; however, state-by-state variations make it difficult to estimate the actual quantity of hate crime. There are other problems associated with the accuracy of the estimates (see Manzi and Dunn, 2007), but it is safe to say that hate crime is underreported, with the primary problem being differences in which protected classes are included in individual state-level hate crime legislation.

It is important to remember out that it is difficult for law enforcement to know if a crime is really a hate crime. Some incidents may appear to be hate crimes, but upon further examination it might turn out that they were not motivated by hate. The motivation of offenders is often difficult to assess, even though it is the key to defining a crime as a hate crime. As a result, statistics are difficult to collect. Some law enforcement agencies have begun to collect hate crime statistics. However, while some collect them under the rubric of "hate crimes," others collect them under the heading of "domestic terrorist acts."

Some researchers have set up criteria to assess crimes to determine if they are hate crimes. Levin and McDevitt (1993) constructed a typology of hate crimes after reviewing data collected from the Boston Police Department. They found that most of the hate crimes reported had similar characteristics: (1) they are excessively brutal, (2) they are senseless crimes committed at random against total strangers, and (3) they are committed by multiple offenders.

McDevitt, Levin, and Bennett (2002, 304) state that, "In the most horrendous of cases, bias intent may be obvious; in less severe incidents, however, detecting and identifying bias motivation becomes more complex and often goes undocumented." There often are indications at the scene of a crime that suggest it was motivated by hate. Because motivation is often hard to ascertain, it is useful for law enforcement and others to be familiar with a list of indications of hate crimes (Sherry 2000). Such a list would include:

- Signs, words, or symbols typically linked to groups that promote hate, like the KKK, or words or symbols associated with groups hated: the "N" word, "Jew," or burning crosses.
- Distasteful, rude, or insulting jokes.
- Vandalizing or ruining group symbols.
- Similar acts against others in the same group.
- Victimization occurs after group meets or after conflict within the group.
- Victims believe the acts were motivated by hate.
- Belittling victims' groups while praising offenders' groups.
- Pamphlets, brochures, or fliers found at the scene describing the groups (e.g., KKK propaganda).
- Community has experienced previous hate crimes.

McDevitt, Levin, and Bennett (2002, 304) also point out that "one indicator police officers use to determine bias intent is the lack of other motivation." If it appears that a crime results in no gain for the offender, no money or possessions are taken, and if there is no prior relationship to the victim, things of this nature, then perhaps the crime is motivated by bias. It is difficult to sort out, and as such, difficult to keep accurate statistics on the annual number of hate crimes.

WHY IS HATE CRIME LEGISLATION NEEDED?

According to Herek, Gillis, and Cogan (1999, 946) "hate crimes represent a special case because of their more serious impact on both the crime victim and the larger group to which she or he belongs." This is why hate crime legislation is needed. We often hear the argument that all crime must be hate crime, because acts against another person represent hate in our minds. In other words, who sexually assaults a person or beats someone up because they love that person? But in a hate crime, the wider ramification extends to the group that the person represents or to the identity (i.e., attribute) that caused the person to be attacked in the first place. Consequently, there are two sets of victims—the individual or individuals who were attacked based on their identification and the larger group in general.

With an understanding of this perspective, it is perhaps a bit easier to comprehend why hate crime legislation is statutorily limited to certain groups. Although the legislation may be too narrow, it may be done so purposefully to rely on what is currently protected under the law. The reason for this reliance on civil rights and protected classes may be to give more flexibility and wider inclusion of other groups at the state level.

One example that comes quickly to mind is the homeless. While homelessness is not a recognized category of hate crime, there is still a group with this characteristic that is affected when victimization occurs against an individual. The crime is motivated by the characteristic, and the group that shares that characteristic is affected as well. Thus, it should be considered a hate crime: Although you probably will never find "homelessness" as a protected class.

HATE CRIMES STATISTICS

The FBI releases a report in January of each year that contains hate crime data collected from various law enforcement agencies. As reported in Table 12.1, there were over 9,000 incidents of hate crimes in 2001 reported to the police. In the subsequent years, the number of hate crimes has dropped and increased annually but the overall numbers remain relatively stable with some 7,000 plus incidents of hate crime reported annually to the police (see Table 12.1).

The NIJ special report *Hate Crimes Reported by Victims and Police* (Harlow, 2005) reveals a great deal of information about hate crimes. The numbers reported in Table 12.1 do not give a very detailed account of the problem. The information found in the NIJ report provides a much more informative picture of hate crime.

Some of the more interesting highlights from the report are presented below in order to better explain what is known about hate crime (Harlow, 2005).

- Most hate crimes are violent crimes, with a smaller percentage being property crimes. In 84 percent of hate crimes, violent crimes like rape, robbery, and assaults occurred.
- Thirty-three percent of the crimes are major violent crimes where a weapon was used. These crimes include rape, robbery, and assault.

TABLE 12.1   Number of Hate Crimes by Year

Year	2000	2001	2002	2003	2004	2005	2006
Number of Hate Crimes	8,063	9,730	7,462	7,489	7,649	7,163	7,732

- Victims of hate crimes are threatened and assaulted in about one-half of hate crimes.
- The NCVS reports about 3 percent of the reported violent crime to be hate crime.
- On an annual basis, about 22,000 households are victimized by hate vandalism. Less than one-half (44%) of bias crime is reported to law enforcement.
- The motivations for victims reporting incidents to the police are to prevent further victimization and to get help from the police.
- When a police call is made, the response time is within 10 min.
- Bias victimization varies little by race or ethnicity.
- Offenders are more likely to be men, strangers to the victims, and operating alone.

This report also points out that hate crimes most often occur in public places. "About 62 percent of violent hate crimes took place in a public area, primarily a commercial establishment, parking area, or a school. By comparison, 51 percent of violent offenses not hate related occurred in public space" (Harlow, 2005, 9). Violent hate crimes were also less likely than nonbias crimes to take place in the victim's home.

HATE CRIME FACTS

There are many civil rights websites that provide current information about hate crimes. Sometimes the sheer number of incidents does not tell the complete story about a specific crime. According to Bias Crimes in America: The Nature and Magnitude of the Problem located at http://www.civilrights.org/publications/reports/cause_for_concern_2004/, www.civilrights.org

- Offenders commit hate crimes based on dislike or fear of someone's identity, whether real or perceived. Data from 2003 reveal the motivation for hate crime in that year in rank order: racial bias (52%), religious intolerance (18%), sexual orientation bias (17%), ethnicity/national origin bias (14%), and disability bias (.4%)
- Victims are targeted at school, with 12 percent of students indicating that they had been victimized by hate-related insults while at school. Verbal abuse focuses on race, religion, ethnicity, disability, gender, or sexual orientation.
- Hate crime victimization has increased significantly since 9–11. Crimes against Muslims have dramatically increased, by over 1,600 percent.
- Nationally, hate crimes against sexual orientation are increasing. Since beginning to collect such data, the number of hate crime victimizations based on sexual orientation has tripled.
- Almost half of all the hate crime in the United States is found in five states: California, New York, New Jersey, Michigan, and Massachusetts.
- Many states do not report hate crime statistics, and some that do report do so incompletely.

CHARACTERISTICS OF OFFENDERS

Some researchers have focused on offenders and their reasons for committing such crimes. Haiman lists economic insecurity, lack of education, political powerlessness, and the "implicit approval of group prejudice by people of influence" as possible explanations for hate crimes (1993, 26).

Berk (1994, 341) lists some characteristics or attributes of hate-motivated crimes. He observed that hate crimes are committed most frequently by males in their late

TABLE 12.2 Hate Crime Offender Typology

Offender Type	Motivation to Attack
Thrill	Offenders who commit their crimes for excitement or the thrill (p. 305). The offender is set off by a desire for excitement or power (p. 306).
Defensive	Offenders who saw themselves as defending their turf (p. 305). Offenders are provoked by feeling a need to protect their resources under conditions they consider to be threatening (p. 306).
Retaliatory	Offenders are inspired by a desire to avenge a perceived degradation or assault on their group (p. 306).
Mission	Offenders whose life's mission had become to rid the world of groups they considered to be evil or inferior (p. 305). Offenders perceive themselves as crusaders who hope to cleanse the earth of evil (p. 306).

Source: Based on McDevitt, Levin, and Bennett (2002, 306).

teens to early twenties, with multiple offenders. They are usually strangers to or sometimes distant acquaintances with the victims. The attacks usually take place outside the victims' residences in the evenings or on the weekends.

Information gathered about who commits violence against lesbians and gay men further substantiates these conclusions. Most of these offenders are young males (usually adolescents or in their early twenties) who operate in groups (Harry, 1990).

The National Coalition for the Homeless provides some information about the offenders who victimize homeless people. Their presentation is based on the work of McDevitt and Levin. And while they change the headings of the categories somewhat, the information provided is consistent with the work of McDevitt and Levin. The Coalition website reports that most offenses are committed by "individuals who harbor strong resentment against a certain group of people" (2006). From this statement, they then categorize offenders into three types including mission offenders, scapegoat offenders, and thrill seekers. Levin and McDevitt first identified a typology that consisted of three offender types. They later revised their typology to include a fourth category. The typology presented by McDevitt, Levin, and Bennett is based upon the motivation of the offender and is presented in Table 12.2.

THEORIES OR EXPLANATIONS FOR HATE CRIMES

There have been many documented cases where violence against gays and lesbians has been the result of hate. When violence of this type occurs, some suggest that it can be explained in terms of the offenders' doubts about their own sexuality. Questioning one's sexuality, especially during adolescence, can be disconcerting, even if the doubts being experienced are quite normal. People, particularly young males, confronted with someone who represents what they are confused about sometimes overreact in violent ways in order to demonstrate that they are not one of the detested group: gays. Some researchers refer to people who exhibit this tendency as **homophobic**.

Others have expanded on this concept of homophobia and labeled it **heterosexism**, an "ideological system that denies, denigrates, and stigmatizes any nonheterosexual form of behavior, identity, relationship, or community" (Herek, 1990, 316). According to this perspective, members of society should be heterosexual; all cues in society (customs and institutions) point toward heterosexuality, and those who deviate from this are considered aberrant. The belief that those who are not heterosexual are aberrant can lead to the feeling that it is okay to abuse such individuals. This is one reason why hate crimes against lesbians and gay men are tolerated in today's society.

Another way to explain hate crimes is to focus on the "intolerance of differences." Many hate crimes are the result of the victims being different from the offenders. Offenders make negative judgments: they believe that those who are different are not as good, and therefore justify their actions.

One way to begin to resolve such a problem is to increase the acceptance of all diversity within society. This is called **multiculturalism**. Many colleges have courses designed to expose individuals to different cultures within society in an effort to influence people to be more accepting of what is different. After all, no two people are exactly the same. Exposure to different types of people with different backgrounds and experiences will begin to reduce hate crimes. Many police departments also sponsor courses in diversity training for law enforcement professionals.

HATE CRIME LAWS

The Anti-Defamation League (ADL) has recommended model legislation for all states to use in developing their own hate crime laws. The purpose of hate crime laws is to deter bias-motivated criminal activity. The ADL states that laws of this nature are needed because failure to recognize crimes as hate crimes (bias crimes against certain groups) could "cause an isolated incident to fester and explode into widespread community tension, perhaps leading to an escalating cycle of reprisals" (Anti-Defamation League of B'nai B'rith, 1994, 1).

At the core of the ADL's recommendations is the "penalty enhancement" concept, which imposes harsher sentences on defendants who engage in criminal acts because of bias or bigotry. The purpose of these harsher penalties is to deter criminals from committing such crimes and also to severely punish those who do.

The reporting of such crimes is often under the auspices of the state police. The unit collecting the data on hate crimes may be labeled the "hate crime" or "domestic terrorism" unit. Once the state has identified where the repository of hate crime statistics will be maintained, the state must also "monitor, record, classify, and analyze information relating to crimes apparently directed against individuals or groups" (Anti-Defamation League of B'nai B'rith, 1994, 3). The agency in charge of collecting the statistics must present the procedure used for collecting the data to the state legislature for its approval.

Federal law, in particular, the **Hate Crime Statistics Act** (HCSA) enacted in 1990, requires the U.S. Justice Department to collect data on crimes that "manifest prejudice based on race, religion, sexual orientation, or ethnicity" (Anti-Defamation League of B'nai B'rith, 1994, 24). With the Federal Bureau of Investigation collecting such data, comprehensive and comparable statistics are available to assess the "number, location, and types of hate crimes" (p. 24).

SPECIAL NEEDS FOR HATE CRIME VICTIMS

As Herek, Gillis, and Cogan (1999) explain the psychological ramifications from hate crime victimization are especially egregious when we focus on how victims recover and deal with the victimization. They studied victimization attributed to sexual orientation; however, the results found in their study could be special issues that need to be considered when addressing the needs of victims of other hate crimes.

For lesbians and gay men, in particular, Herek and colleagues observe that a person's positive self-concept has a great deal to do with how effective his or her coping skills will be in addressing the victimization. The authors further warn, "If experiencing a hate crime causes a victim's core identity to become directly linked to the heightened sense of vulnerability that normally follows victimization (Kaniasty and Norris, 1992), being gay or bisexual may subsequently be experienced as a source of danger, pain, and punishment rather than intimacy, love, and community. . . . Consequently, the impact of a hate crime would extend beyond the trauma routinely associated with criminal victimization, challenging the victim's sense of self as a gay man, lesbian, or bisexual" (Herek, Gillis, and Cogan, 1999, 946).

They further discuss why lesbians, gays, and bisexuals might be more vulnerable to the negative psychological effects of hate crime victimization. They point out that sexual prejudice is still acceptable in many parts of the United States, and there are many places where antigay discrimination remains legal (Herek, Gillis, and Cogan, 1999).

To complicate recovery even further, sometimes the message sent from society is that these individuals *deserved* their victimization, and they often do not have the solid community support system readily found with heterosexuals because "one's identity as gay, lesbian, or bisexual usually develops outside of—often in opposition to—one's family and community of origin" (Herek, Gillis, and Cogan, 1999, 946). And while this all makes intuitive sense, few have tested these relationships.

Herek, Gillis, and Cogan (1999, 946) hypothesized that hate crime victims, especially victims of sexual orientation hate crimes, "would report more symptoms of depression and traumatic stress, would be more anxious and angry; and would display less positive affect." The overall findings support the hypotheses, and as the authors point out, have importance in recognizing that hate crime survivors have special needs that must be addressed in both the clinical setting and in public policy. Victims of hate crime based on sexual orientation feel they are at an increased risk of victimization because of their sexuality. They feel as if they have little control over the events that happen to them, and that most negative events are due to their sexual orientation. Victimizations bring out the realization that they are insecure and vulnerable to attack, which causes more stress and anxiety as the self-made illusion of personal invulnerability is shattered. As such, intervention strategies must address this issue and attempt to restore balance in the victims' lives by realistically recounting the dangers found in society based on bias towards gays, but without causing the victims to be "overwhelmed by a sense of personal vulnerability or powerlessness" (Herek, Gillis, and Cogan, 1999, 950).

There are public policy implications as well. From this research, the authors argue that, "The findings presented here indicate that laws and policies that differentiate hate crimes from non-bias crimes are justified in identifying hate crimes for special attention in the criminal justice system because hate crimes appear to have a more serious impact on the victim than other crimes" (Herek, Gillis, and Cogan, 1999, 950–951). Further, the impact of the crime is experienced by the individual and the larger group—thus making these biased crimes particularly egregious.

HOW DOES LAW ENFORCEMENT ADDRESS HATE CRIMES?

The Center for the Study and Prevention of Hate Crime Violence at the University of Southern Maine provides six law enforcement and prosecutorial initiatives that are underway to address hate crimes (Wessler, 2000). The monograph was written by Stephen Wessler, Director of the Center, and it was sponsored by the Bureau of Justice Assistance (BJA).

As first responders to criminal activity, law enforcement must remember that their actions at crime scenes can affect the outcome of hate crime investigations, as well as influence how the community views and responds to the crime. Law enforcement, then, has a crucial role in the investigation, prosecution, and prevention of hate crimes. They, along with other key criminal justice players, must be trained to recognize and investigate such crimes. There should be clear protocols and operating procedures about how to react and respond to hate crimes. Programs designed to prevent such crimes must be planned and implemented (Wessler, 2000, 1).

Specifically, the six initiatives include (1) the International Association of Chiefs of Police (IACP) Summit: Hate Crime in America; (2) DOJ's National Hate Crime Training Initiative; (3) BJA's Roll Call Video: Responding to Hate Crimes; (4) IACP's Responding to Hate Crimes: A Police Officer's Guide to Investigation and Prevention; (5) The American Prosecutors Research Institute's (APRI's) Resource Guide; and (6) The Maine Department of the Attorney General's Designated Civil Rights Officers Project (Wessler, 2000, 2).

There is a clear relationship between training law enforcement and prosecutors and the reporting of hate crimes. The statistics reported earlier are believed to be under-representative of the actual amounts of hate crimes. More training so that law enforcement can both recognize hate crimes and also provide adequate services to victims of hate crime will hopefully provide a more accurate picture of hate crimes.

VICTIMIZATION OF THE HOMELESS

Another "special population" concerns **victimization of the homeless**. On January 12, 2006, the nation was shocked as videotapes released to national news media showed that two young boys viciously attacked two homeless men in Fort Lauderdale, Florida, for no apparent reason except that the men were homeless (Fantz, 2006). Although only two men were shown on the videotape, three homeless men were attacked, and one of the men, Norris Gaynor, died. The young men beat the homeless men with baseball bats, paintballs, golf clubs, and sticks. The videotape showed that the homeless men were defenseless against the brutal attacks. The surviving victims, Jacques Pierre, 58, and Raymond Perez, 49, both suffered from broken bones, lacerations, and deep bruises.

Brian Hooks, Tom Daugherty, and William "Billy" Ammons were charged with aggravated assault, and Ammons with Gaynor's murder. A *Miami Herald* reporter, Ashley

Fantz, spoke to friends of the teenagers to get some understanding of the senseless crime. Fantz (2006, 1) reported, " 'There are kids who beat up bums on the weekend—they just do it' said one boy who knew the suspects. He also said, 'I don't think they ever intended to kill anybody.' Another young man who knew the boys said that 'beating up homeless people was "the thing to do" for a certain element at the school. It's hate,' he said."

This is just one example of the many incidents of victimization against the homeless. The National Coalition for the Homeless has identified 123 homeless people across the nation who were murdered by nonhomeless people between 1999 and 2002. During the same time period, there were 212 nonlethal assaults. The methods of killing the homeless included beating, stabbing, shooting, and setting on fire (Gonser, 2004).

The Coalition is lobbying several states and the Federal Government to study these violent crimes against the homeless and to designate such crimes as "hate crimes" so that heavier penalties can result upon conviction (Gonser, 2004). Stiffer penalties are seen as a deterrent to this type of crime.

Some researchers who have focused on explaining victimization among the homeless have done so by comparing male and female victimization (Wenzel, Koegel, and Gelbert, 2000). As these authors assert, "homeless women experience extensive health risks including physical and sexual victimization" (p. 367). They posit the theoretical explanation for this extensive health risk lies in the structural-choice model of victimization risk. (This theory is presented in Chapter 2.) Their study reports the following:

> Homeless women and men require comprehensive assistance in establishing and maintaining safe and permanent residences, many require assessment and ongoing intervention to deal with mental and substance use disorder, *and* they need appropriate educational and training opportunities to protect them from victimization and support exits from homelessness (p. 385; emphasis in original).

The **National Coalition for the Homeless** collects data annually reporting the number of deaths and violent attacks against people who are homeless. Since 1999, they have attempted to aggregate these data so that a more accurate picture of victimization against the homeless could be drawn. According to their annual report, the total number of deaths occurring from 1999 to 2005 is 169, with the most deaths occurring in the first year that statistics were collected, that is, 1999. Non-lethal victimization over the same time period was 303. Thus, the total number of victimizations of the homeless between 1999 and 2005 was 472 acts.

When looking at 2005 alone, it appears as if things have not gotten any better for the homeless. The total number of violent acts was 86, making it one of the worst years for violent victimization since the data have been collected. The number of deaths was 13 (National Coalition for the Homeless, 2006b).

Using the McDevitt, Levin, and Bennett (2002) typology to explain homeless victimization and focusing on the specific example of the teenage boys who beat the homeless men, they could easily be viewed as examples of "thrill" offenders, possibly that the offenders are "mission" types. (However, the latter is doubtful because of the offenders' ages—having a "life's mission" implies being older than a teenager.)

Mission offenders engage in the victimization of the homeless because they feel that it is their personal mission to rid the world of this particular evil. In this case, homelessness is equated with evil, and people who commit violence against the homeless do so to purify society.

EXAMPLES OF HATE CRIMES

Those who write about hate crimes use vignettes to describe situations that may or may not be considered hate crimes. They take readers through the maze of a crime and at the end determine whether it was indeed a hate crime. The authors also try to isolate the victim characteristics that are offensive to the perpetrator. For example, the Central Park jogger who was brutally beaten, raped, and left for dead is used as an example in one book (Levin and McDevitt, 1993). The authors discuss the case in great detail and ponder whether the attack was based on the gender of the jogger, her race, a combination of these factors, or neither of these factors.

It is also valuable to present information from newspapers on crimes that appear to be hate crimes. Some of the crimes have resulted in conviction, while others are still pending. The purpose of presenting these cases is to raise awareness of such crimes and to begin a discussion about how to categorize such incidents. As stated earlier, hate crimes are particularly difficult to define, because the offenders' motivations determine their classification as such.

Howard Beach, New York

On December 20, 1986, an incident in **Howard Beach**, New York, rocked the nation. Three African American men were driving in their car when it broke down in predominately white Howard Beach. As they tried to find their way to a train to take them back to Brooklyn, several white teenagers yelled racial epithets at the three African American males. Since they could not find a way back to the city, they decided to eat dinner and stopped at a pizzeria.

John Lester, a white teenage native of Howard Beach, was upset by the fact that the three African American males were in his town. He raced through a birthday party of white teenagers, pumping them up to confront the African American males. As the African American males ate their dinner, John Lester organized a group of outraged white teenagers to drive them out of town.

They armed themselves with baseball bats, a tire iron, and a tree stump. The 12 white teenagers, enraged in hatred, went in three cars to find and remove the undesirables.

It was very late, almost one o'clock in the morning. The three African American men had finished their dinner and were wandering around Cross Bay Boulevard (a major street in Howard Beach). They noticed the group of white teenagers moving up the street. All three tried to escape, but only one managed to do so. He had a knife, which distracted the group and allowed him enough time in the confusion to run up the street away from the crowd.

The other two were not so lucky. Michael Griffith, who was 23 years old, was chased through the vacant streets by the group of white teenagers. He was beaten severely. In an attempt to escape, he jumped over a concrete barricade across three lanes of traffic. He was struck by a car and his body shot 15 feet in the air before landing on the ground, where Griffith died immediately.

Michael Griffith's stepfather, Cedric Sandiford, was surrounded by the group of white teenagers. The angry mob assaulted him and beat him with the weapons they carried. After being severely beaten, Sandiford pretended to be unconscious and dead in order to survive the ordeal.

Four defendants were charged in some fashion and tried in courts of law. John Lester avoided a murder conviction. He was found guilty of having "recklessly caused the death of another." The trials for all the defendants spanned 4 years. The last set of defendants charged in the Howard Beach racial attack case agreed not to appeal their riot convictions in return for sentences of probation, community service, and no jail time (Fried, 1990). The three defendants were not charged with any crime stemming from the death of Michael Griffith or the beating of Cedric Sandiford. They were charged with rioting, for having been part of the group that yelled racial epithets, and confronting the victims before the attack.

This case was clearly a hate crime. The motivation of the white teenagers was purely racial hatred. It is unfortunate that Michael Griffith, his stepfather, and his friend were in the wrong place at the wrong time. This is how many hate crimes develop. They are not systematically planned. They are random, spur-of-the-moment acts with brutal violence perpetrated by multiple offenders.

The Case of Rodney King

In the infamous **Rodney King** beating, law enforcement officers beat an African American man who they said was avoiding arrest. Los Angeles police officers chased Rodney King until he finally stopped his car. When he stepped out of the car, more than 15 police officers began taking turns beating him with billy clubs and zapping him with stun guns. It was reported that Mr. King was struck as many as 56 times and kicked seven times by three officers while a dozen or more watched (Stevenson, 1992). A two-minute videotape of the incident hit the airwaves and was broadcast around the world.

The African American community in Los Angeles was outraged, stating that the officers, all white, were reacting to the color of Rodney King's skin and not to his alleged crimes. Mr. King's doctor reported that he suffered from a fractured eye socket, broken cheekbone, broken leg, bruises, facial nerve damage, severe concussion, and burns from a stun gun. The three officers and one sergeant who were primarily responsible for the savage beating were tried, but acquitted. Whether the law enforcement officers' reactions were motivated by hate and consequently can be categorized as a hate crime is debatable. Some have argued that the officers were only doing their jobs. Others see their behavior as excessive and indeed motivated by hate.

Following the verdict in the case of the four Los Angeles police officers, a riot erupted, with African American citizens beating up whites for no apparent reason except for the color of their skin. Los Angeles was virtually under siege. Racial crimes were being committed everywhere. It did not matter who you were; this time, if you were white you were going to be victimized. Reginald Denny was a white truck driver who was dragged out of his truck and savagely beaten by a group of African Americans. As he lay in his own blood, several people threw rocks at him and robbed him. He was able to get back into his truck and with some assistance made it to the hospital. He arrived unconscious and was in critical condition for several days.

Those who beat Reginald Denny did not know him. All they knew was what he represented. He was a white male, and he represented the injustices found in the criminal justice system. Because the officers who beat Rodney King were white and they got away with beating an African American male (or so the general public believed), all whites had to pay. This incident has the elements of a hate crime—it was a random act, excessively brutal, and accomplished by multiple offenders.

Religious Hate Crimes

To find an example of a **religious hate crime**, a newspaper and library search under the term *hate crime and religion* was conducted. Nine hundred matches were found, with about 400 of these addressing separate religious hate crimes.

Religious hate crimes fall into two categories: (1) crimes against a religious facility and (2) crimes against individuals who represent certain faiths. The example included here focuses on a hate crime where the institution was the "victim."

Florida's Tampa Bay area has a large Jewish population, with a number of synagogues and Jewish community centers. The West Pasco Jewish Community Center is one such establishment that has been vandalized by offenders motivated by hate. In the past, a burning cross was left on the front lawn by the Ku Klux Klan. More recently, in a drive-by shooting, bullets pierced two metal doors and a concrete wall before being embedded in the synagogue's holy ark.

On April 29, 1996, the religious center was again vandalized. The center was "desecrated with feces, spray painted [with] swastikas, iron crosses, [and] other Aryan symbols and slogans of white power [were written on the building] in blue and red" (Thalji, 1996). The sign near the entrance, Jewish Community Center, was spray painted. The word *Jewish* was crossed out and replaced with the word *Nazi*. This was the fourth attack on a Jewish center in the Tampa Bay area in a two-year period.

These acts are considered hate crimes. The vandalism is a direct result of the hatred the offenders have for the Jewish faith. When analyzing this crime in comparison to the Levin and McDevitt typology, it is not as easily recognized as a hate crime as the other examples. The missing element is excessive violence. Depending on how one defines the term, the desecrations listed above may or may not be considered as such.

African American churches in the South have also been the target of hate crime (Bacque, 1996). In an 18-month period in 1996, fires destroyed or damaged at least 30 African American churches in the South. Although multi-state initiatives were enacted to attempt to solve these crimes, no suspects were ever found.

As recently as February 2006, another series of fires of churches in the South raised the same questions about whether these crimes were hate crimes (Fox News, 2006). Nine church fires in rural Alabama had been linked to two suspects. Of the nine church fires, four had all–African American congregations and another four had all-white congregations (Reeves, 2006). Alabama Governor Bob Riley said that the authorities had linked the church fires, but that he saw "no evidence of a grand conspiracy against religion or Baptist churches" (Reeves, 2006, 1). An ATF investigator said that the crimes were motivated by thrill-seeking rather than any racial motivation. Nevertheless, it's hard to imagine the deliberate destruction of houses of worship as something less than hate crime.

Violence Against Lesbians and Gay Men

Berrill and Herek (1990) list seven specific examples of **violence against lesbians and gay men**. Included here are the three most recent victimizations from their list, and two other examples.

- Five men were shot in an adult bookstore in 1987. Three of them died. The offenders said they shot and killed these men because "they were avenging God and his stand against homosexuals" (Berrill and Herek, 1990, 260).

- A gay and lesbian Christian church was burned in 1988, causing a great amount of damage to the structure. The particular church was known as a place of worship that gays attended (Berrill and Herek, 1990, 260).
- A lone assailant stalked two lesbian women in 1988. One was subsequently killed and the other critically wounded (Berrill and Herek, 1990, 260).
- Paul Broussard was a victim of "gay bashing" in 1991. After leaving a Texas bar with two friends, Broussard was attacked by 8–10 high school– and college-aged males using wooden beams with exposed nails. Broussard and one of his friends were savagely beaten; the other escaped. Broussard eventually died from the attack. Seven of 10 offenders were tried and convicted of murder (either first degree or second degree). They received varying sentences from incarceration, boot camp, community service, to probation (Hatecrime.org, 2000).
- "Murder on the Mountain" was a nationally heard recount of the brutal slayings of two lesbian women. In 1996, Julianne Williams and Lollie Winans went hiking in the Shenandoah National Park. Park Rangers found their bodies with their wrists bound and their throats slit. This case is not yet resolved, but it is believed to be a hate crime (Yeoman, 1996).

On January 1, 1993, at approximately 4:00 a.m., a 22-year-old marine was murdered near the intersection of North Jefferson and West Frederick Streets in Staunton, Virginia (Williams, 1996). Staunton is a small town with a population of 24,000 where murder is a rare occurrence (less than one per year for the past 10 years). Property crimes account for better than 96 percent of all reported crimes. Making the crime even more unusual was the fact that it was a hate crime, as the victim was attacked because he was believed (by the suspect) to be gay. While there was no evidence to indicate that the victim was in fact gay, this was perceived to be the motive for the unprovoked attack.

According to a number of witnesses, the victim was returning home from a New Year's Eve party with a few of his friends. One of his friends, another marine, was intoxicated. The victim was trying to hold up his friend while walking him to another friend's home. As they walked down the street, they were noticed by the participants of a party. One of the subjects, Samuel Eugene "Bo" Benson, looked at the two marines and started yelling at them. He called them "queers" and "faggots." The victim told Benson to leave them alone and go back to his party. But Benson jumped off the porch and attacked the two marines.

Benson kicked and hit them both and knocked them down to the ground. He was interrupted by a female friend of the victim. With one blow, Benson broke the female friend's arm. Benson produced a knife and stabbed the victim a few times before stabbing him once in the abdomen. Hearing sirens, Benson ran away from the scene.

The first police units arrived shortly thereafter and secured the scene. The victim was transferred to the hospital emergency room where he was pronounced dead a short time later. The stab wounds caused massive internal bleeding, which caused his death.

This crime represents a hate crime at its worst. The assault was excessively violent and a direct result of the offender's perception that the victim was gay. The only departure from the Levin and McDevitt typology was that the offender acted alone.

Matthew Shepard

On October 6, 1998, **Matthew W. Shepard**, a student at the University of Wyoming, was brutally attacked, pistol-whipped, beaten, and left to die on a fence post. Although understanding of the events of the evening leading up to Mr. Shepard's death has changed on three different occasions, what is thought to be true is the following: Matthew Shepard was in a bar and two other men, Russell Henderson and Aaron McKinney, were also in the same bar. Henderson and McKinney gave Shepard a ride home, but he never made it there. Henderson and McKinney instead took Shepard to a deserted area, beat him, and left him on a fence post because he was gay.

At first, Henderson and McKinney's attorneys attempted to use the **homosexual panic defense** (Reasons and Hughson, 2000), arguing that McKinney went into a blind rage after Shepard made an unwanted pass at him. Then, they argued that they only wanted to rob Shepard, but things had gone bad. Finally, they tried to argue that they had been in a drug- and alcohol-induced rage that resulted in Shepard's death.

Henderson entered into a plea bargain in order to avoid the death penalty, and ultimately testified against McKinney. For his part in the crime, Henderson received two consecutive life terms without the possibility of parole. The jury found McKinney guilty of first-degree murder. Death-penalty cases have a bifurcated process, meaning that a first trial determines guilt or innocence, and a second trial determines if the sentence for the conviction should be death. As the jury began its deliberations about the death sentence, Shepard's parents requested that McKinney receive the same sentence as Henderson instead of a death sentence. The judge agreed, in part because there was a local uproar about Roman Catholic clerics coming out against the death penalty for McKinney.

This case is included in our discussion of hate crimes; however, only 21 states currently list sexual orientation as a category of protection under their hate crimes statutes. President Clinton urged Congress to add sexual orientation to federal hate crime laws shortly after the Shepard case was publicized (CNN.com, 2000). The measure was defeated then and still has not been approved.

The Shepards have a website (http://www.matthewshepard.org/site/PageServer) to keep the public informed about the progress or lack of progress being made to include sexual orientation in hate crime legislation. The site has other important information and details celebrity involvement in the cause. Some celebrities including Cyndi Lauper, Melissa Etheridge, and Elton John have lent their support in various ways in order to educate the public about Matthew Shepard's story and to encourage support to include crimes based on sexual orientation to be considered hate crimes.

Hate Crimes Against Those With Disabilities

Hate crime legislation clearly indicates that crimes committed against the disabled because of their disability are clearly hate crimes. However, the first prosecution of such a case did not occur until 1999. According to an article by Mark Sherry (2003), the facts of the case are as follows:

Eric Krochmaluk, a cognitively disabled man, was kidnapped and savagely beaten on January 30, 1999, in Middletown, New Jersey. Krochmaluk was lured away from his home by a group of individuals who promised that he would meet a pretty girl at a party if he went with the group. Krochmaluk agreed to go, and his torture began once he got to the party: he was hit, punched, choked, slapped, burned with cigarettes, taped to a chair, had his eyebrows shaven, beaten with objects, and abandoned in a forest (Reynolds, 2000).

Eight people were subsequently indicted for this hate crime. Similar attacks had occurred on two previous occasions. The leaders of the assault were Jennifer Dowell,

Brandon Cruz, and Jessica Fry. They entered into a plea bargain, pleading guilty to charges of conspiracy, kidnapping, and aggravated assault. Dowell and Cruz received sentences of 20 years, while Fry was sentenced to 15 years. The others, Daniel Vistad, David Allen, William MacKay, and Christal Lavery, also entered into plea bargains, pleading guilty to charges of conspiracy and bias assault. Their sentences ranged from five to eight years in prison.

Monmouth County Prosecutor John Kaye said, "They tormented this mentally disabled man because of his disability. . . . They did it to him because they could—because they could manipulate him, and because they believed he could not tell on them, which was almost true" (Sherry, 2003).

CONCLUSION

Hate and special populations crimes are especially egregious given that offenders specifically target their victims based upon some real or perceived characteristic that the victim embodies or possesses. The offender action is based in pure hate—for there is no rationale or excuse.

Advocating for tolerance and acceptability of differences, and to even experience cultural differences is the mark of an educated person. Broad exposure through courses, studying abroad, and traveling leads to a greater understanding and appreciation of differences. It is through these experiences that empathy is formed. Empathy, compassion, and tolerance are the keys to getting along with others who are not like you. The real challenge is moving past the victimization and finding ways to decrease hate by increasing tolerance on all dimensions.

Study Questions

1. Why do you think that so many states, and even the federal government, do not include sexual orientation as a protected class in hate crime statutes? Do you think that this is a mistake?
2. What can be done to address the problem of homelessness in the United States? How has society ignored the problem with the victimization of the homeless? Why?
3. Describe what is meant by hate crime legislation. How does hate crime legislation differ from other types of crime legislation? Given this, what do you think we should do to deter future hate crimes?
4. Select any category of hate crime victimization. See if you can find a recent newspaper article that describes an incident of a hate crime. In this specific example, how do you think the victimization could have been avoided?

Key Terms

- defensive   226
- hate crime   222
- Hate Crime Statistics Act (HCSA)   227
- heterosexism   227
- homophobic   226
- homosexual panic defense   235
- Howard Beach   231
- Matthew W. Shepard   234
- mission   226
- multiculturalism   227
- National Coalition for the Homeless   230
- religious hate crime   233
- retaliatory   226
- Rodney King   232
- Thrill   226
- violence against lesbians and gay men   233
- victimization of the homeless   229

CHAPTER 13

Mass Violence

INTRODUCTION

Mass violence covers many different topics. The topics include domestic terrorism, mass murder, serial killing, school violence, workplace violence, and drunk driving. Each area is included because of the common element that most often the victims and offenders are strangers or if the offenders and victims do know each other, their relationship is little more than "familiar." And the number of victims most often is more than one, especially if we look at the crime in the aggregate, thereby falling into the category of mass violence. These types of crimes are rare (with the noted exception of drunk driving), yet the public is very fearful of them. The reason for this paradox may result from the media attention given to these events, making the general public feel much more vulnerable, and the carnage resulting from these crimes often is devastating, resulting in the belief that no one can survive such an attack, and thereby producing heightened fear levels.

For example, the media attention given to campus shootings makes them appear to be widespread and a "common" occurrence. Students and their parents want to be safe on campus and routinely ask for ways to ensure that students, faculty, and staff are safe while attending class. Their focus seems to be more on the extreme cases like the Virginia Tech or Northern Illinois University shooting incidents, while administrators and student life counselors try to give a more balanced approach to safety on campus advocating for common sense approaches to being safe. Nevertheless, we have seen websites, videos, and criminal justice pundits promoting the protection of oneself in such incidents by detailing how students can be safe by not staying still and moving about, blocking doorways, locking doors, and so on as ways to address such incidents. A recent article in the *Chronicle of Higher Education* reports on a DVD made by a company in Spokane, WA, titled *Shots Fired on Campus*, which offers strategies for preventing and surviving gun rampages (Hoover, 2008). The article reports that about 50 campuses have already ordered the video. We are not arguing with these approaches, we just think it is better to prepare for incidents that are more likely to occur, to ensure safety by using common-sense, and then to prepare for an event that is very unlikely to occur.

Using the Virginia Tech (VA Tech) tragedy as an example of a rarely occurring mass violence event, we include in this section what the Commonwealth of Virginia is doing in the aggregate to address such violence. Governor Timothy M. Kaine set up a review panel to look at all aspects of the massacre. He did this because of the immense public pressure to figure out what went wrong with VA Tech security and to prevent it from happening again at any Virginia institution of higher education. The Virginia Tech Review Panel wrote a report summarizing what was done that day and in the subsequent days after the tragedy, providing a number of recommendations to be considered by institutions of higher education as well as by the State Legislature. Public and private institutions of higher education reviewed the recommendations and provided plans of action to address the recommendations listed within the report. The plans are internal documents with a schedule of implementation for the recommendations. The Review Panel had 43 recommendations in the report that affected higher education. The recommendations can be grouped into five areas: counseling troubled students, communication and awareness, appropriate level of security, weapons on campus, and support for victims and victims' families. Virginia institutions addressed the recommendations differently depending on the institution. However, the recommendation that seemed to affect all institutions was providing to the university community some alert system in order for students, faculty, and staff to know within a reasonable amount of time what was happening on campus. This communication system is to be used in all emergencies with most institutions exploring the idea of text messaging, while others invoked alarm systems, bull horns, or electronic messaging through monitors in student unions, dorms, classrooms, and so on. The vast majority of institutions, especially the larger institutions, agree that the communication plan must have multiple mediums for alerting their community as depending on the crisis, one or more of the ways to communicate may be ineffective. As institutions developed safety plans, they also conveyed to their constituents that these communication systems (e.g., alarms and text messaging) would most likely be used for emergencies associated with weather conditions such as tornado or hurricane warnings, or fires in buildings, or hazardous spills, which are more likely to occur, emphasizing that the VA Tech massacre is a rare occurrence; yet there are systems in place to protect the university communities if need be. The heightened awareness of these safety plans and the measures taken in Virginia and elsewhere result in both increasing the feeling of safety in students, faculty, and staff and also drawing attention to a rare event and has the unintended consequence, at times, of increasing fear in some.

This chapter explores mass violence, examining in more detail domestic terrorism, mass murder, serial killing, school violence, workplace violence, and drunk driving. The common threads in these behaviors include (1) most often the offenders and victims are strangers, and (2) the general public's knowledge about these events comes from the media—and sometimes the media blitz of reports about such incidents tends to increase fear levels even though, for the most part, these are rare events.

TERRORISM

Terrorism is associated with a tremendous loss of human life and the creation of numerous victims. Hoffman (1998) examines various definitions of terrorism and after a thorough analysis of all available data on the topic, he concludes that:

By distinguishing terrorists from other types of criminals and terrorism from other forms of crime, we come to appreciate that terrorism is

- ineluctably political in aims and motives;
- violent—or, equally important, threatens violence;
- designed to have far-reaching psychological repercussions beyond the immediate victim or target;

- conducted by an organization with an identifiable chain of command or conspiratorial cell structure (whose members wear no uniform or identifying insignia); and
- perpetrated by a subnational group or non-state entity (Hoffman, 1998, 43).

Thus, as Hoffman states, terrorism may be defined as "the deliberate creation and exploitation of fear through violence or the threat of violence in the pursuit of political change" (p. 43). It is this *fear* of violence or actual violence that creates a wider range of events that need to be included in a chapter on mass violence.

Domestic terrorism might be defined similarly to the above, with the added clarification that the act is committed by someone or some group that is part of the United States (or the country of interest). The U.S. Code provides a definition of domestic terrorism. In Section 2331 of title 18 of the U.S. Code, domestic terrorism is defined as:

activities that—

A. involve acts dangerous to human life that are a violation of the criminal laws of the United States or of any State;

B. appear to be intended—

    i. to intimidate or coerce a civilian population;

    ii. to influence the policy of a government by intimidation or coercion; or

    iii. to affect the conduct of a government by mass destruction, assassination, or kidnapping; and

C. occur primarily within the territorial jurisdiction of the United States [18 USC 2331].

The history of terrorism can be started at any point in history; however, as Henderson (2001, 98) points out, the chronology of terrorism should start with the year 1946 because it "marks the beginning of the postcolonial cold war period that shaped the environment for modern terrorism." Appendix D summarizes the chronology of domestic and international terrorism against the United States by category. The categories include **assassination attempts and murders**, racial violent groups, kidnapping, **bombings**, **product tampering**, and **mass killings**. The Chart relies on the work of Henderson with the more recent examples added by the authors. As the Chart indicates, the earliest assassination attempt by a radical group was on November 1, 1950 when Puerto Rican nationalists attempted to assassinate President Truman. Other incidents reported include assassination attempts on members of congress and the assassination of the President of American University, controversial Jewish Denver talk show host, William Buckley, and Colonel William R. Higgins.

There are many examples of **radical violent groups** protesting against political powers where violence has resulted. Such radical groups include Black Power, Black Panthers, the Black Liberation Army, Symbionese Liberation Army, Puerto Rican separatist groups (FALN), Ku Klux Klan, Weather Underground, Pablo Escobar's Medellin cartel, Earth First!, Branch Davidian sect, Islamic Fundamentalist terrorists, White Supremacist, to name but a few. These groups in themselves are not considered radical violent terrorists—this label is used when individuals or groups of individuals associated with this grouping commit a violent act in the name of it and the results being purposeful killings and/or other violence.

The next category is kidnapping, followed by bombings, and product tampering. Under domestic terrorism we include 9-11. On September 11, 2001, a coordinated attack against the United States by 19 al-Qaeda terrorists occurred. The terrorists hijacked four commercial airplanes and one by one attacked the targets. First, two planes loaded with fuel and passengers flew directly and purposefully into the twin towers of the World Trade Center in New York City. As the media immediately interrupted television programming to show the devastation that resulted from the first plane hitting the Trade Center; another plane, witnessed by many watching the live broadcast, ploughed into the second tower of the World Trade Center. The media coverage showed the buildings bursting into flames, and the ultimate collapse of both towers, and the resulting carnage as thousands were killed. At the same time that New York City was under attack, another group of terrorists flew their plane into the Pentagon headquarters of the U.S. military in Arlington, Virginia, destroying one side of the five-sided building and causing causalities. The last plane was intended to strike another target in Washington, D.C., but by this time, the passengers on the plane had realized what was happening in New York City and Arlington, and they decided to fight back. Instead of striking the intended Washington, D.C., target, this plane crashed into a field in rural Pennsylvania. The reports from the plane made to family members using cell phones, indicated that the passengers had decided to fight instead of passively going along with the plan to strike the target. It has been said that these targets were chosen by al-Qaeda because they "perfectly symbolized U.S. financial, political, and military power." These attacks in "New York and Washington constituted the first major foreign assault on the continental United States since 1814, when the British army invaded Washington, D.C., and burned the White House. More people were killed on U.S. soil on September 11 than on any day since the American Civil War" (see http://encarta.msn.com/encyclopedia_701509060/September_11_Attacks. html, retrieved June 17, 2008).

SERVICES FOR VICTIMS OF TERRORISM

The untold number of deaths at the hands of terrorists has led the Office of Victims of Crime to establish international victim units to serve victims of terrorism, mass violence, and crimes that have transnational dimensions. Moreover, OVC as part of its mission now "provides international leadership in promoting effective and sensitive victim services and rights around the world" (OVC Fact Sheet, 2001, 1). The OVC has established the **Terrorism and International Victims Unit (TIVU)** in response to the emerging issues surrounding terrorism and terrorist acts. According to the fact sheet, OVC provides services to American citizens victimized abroad and for foreign nationals victimized in the United States. As way of example, OVC lists that it is "responding to the plight of victims of terrorism, commercial exploitation, international trafficking of women and children, and international child abduction" (OVC Fact Sheet, 2001, 1). In order to improve international awareness of and responsiveness to victims' right and needs, OVC recommends that:

- Programs are designed to assist victims outside the United States. Such assistance might include traveling with victims for trials or briefings and finding out information about the court systems where the crimes occurred.

- Resources should be provided to assist victims throughout the justice process, from crisis response to posttrial proceedings.
- There should be a liaison program to help victims understand what services foreign countries provide to assist U.S. citizens. Conversely, the liaison program should also offer services to foreign victims in the United States.
- Resources should be dedicated to help in the recovery of abducted children taken outside U.S. borders (OVC Fact Sheet, 2002, 1).

TIVU also provides resources to compensate and assist victims. Moreover, there is an international terrorism victims compensation program that allows victims of terrorism abroad to apply to one single office to obtain compensation. TIVU is working with other countries to establish a directory of resources available outside the United States to assist with victims obtaining compensation. TIVU has developed guidelines to determine how to distribute compensation funds available to assist victims of terrorism and mass violence in the United States. "Funding may be used to provide a wide range of services and respond to the immediate and ongoing challenges of serving victims in the aftermath of terrorism and mass violence" (OVC Fact Sheet, 2002, 2).

Finally, TIVU is involved with other federal agencies and nonprofit organizations to improve and augment the assistance provided to these victims. TIVU's programs and initiatives include (OVC Fact Sheet, 2002, 2–3):

- Establishing protocols between federal agencies to identify how to respond to victims of terrorism.
- Providing interagency training and technical assistance to improve the response to victims of terrorism.
- Developing responses and interventions.
- Coordinating federal and nongovernmental agencies to better serve victims of terrorism.
- Establishing protocols for addressing international parental abductions. What should be done when parents kidnap children and take them outside U.S. borders?
- Developing programs that address international trafficking of women and children.
- Coordinating conferences on topics related to victims of terrorism for various groups, such as law enforcement, public, health providers, and journalists.

Very specifically, OVC has supported many victims and families of terrorist attacks. They have been very much involved with the victims of the 9-11 tragedy. As expected, OVC was there for victims and family members who resided in New York, Virginia, and Pennsylvania. Other specific services that have been developed and implemented include creating an Assistance Telephone Center, where victims can call toll-free to find out about services; developing a better navigable website to provide assistance and helpful information; and serving as a coordinating body to help victims coordinate services needed.

As way of example, for the victims of the bombing of Pan Am Flight 103, OVC established a unique partnership with the Scottish government. OVC provided assistance in getting family members to the trial of the two Libyan defendants, and they also broadcast the trial on closed-circuit TV for those who could not travel to Scotland, established a toll-free number to get updates on the proceedings, and established a secure website for the families to exchange information about the trial.

The trial, conviction, and sentencing of **Zacarias Moussaoui** for his role as the 12th terrorist in the September 11, 2001 attacks provided an opportunity for many victims' family members to present victim-impact statements to the court. Although family members had to come to terms with the sentence of life in prison without the possibility of parole for Moussaoui, they also were VERY CONCERNED AND were at the heart of the battle to prohibit razing a financial building (Deutsche Bank) in New York City that is very close to where the World Trade Center towers once stood. The building was badly damaged by the extreme heat from the burning towers. But because the massive burning of the World Trade Center spewed ashes and debris about, there were also human remains in the building. The 9-11 victims' families did not want the building razed until all bone fragments and other possible remains have been sifted through by a team of forensic experts. Construction workers had to stop the preparation to raze the building several times to sort through the debris. The razing of the building continues to be delayed because of toxic debris. However, a last report (Associated Press, 2008) stated, "hundreds of remains of Sept 11 victims were found in the last 2 years," thus it appears as if the city has taken the families' concerns into account.

MASS VIOLENCE IN CAMPUS SETTINGS: SCHOOL VIOLENCE

The U.S. Department of Education and the U.S. Department of Justice recently teamed up to produce a report entitled "Indicators of School Crime and Safety: 2004," in which the authors gauge the safety of the school environment (DeVoe et al., 2004). The report studies **school violence** and is designed to "provide an annual snapshot of specific crimes and safety indicators, covering topics such as victimization, fights, bullying, classroom disorder, teacher injury, weapons, and student perceptions of school safety" (DeVoe et al., 2004, iii). The sources of the data include surveys of students, teachers, and administrators as well as documents and files from the National Center for Education Statistics (NCES), Bureau of Justice Statistics (BJS), Federal Bureau of Investigation (FBI), and Centers for Disease Control and Prevention (CDC).

There are several indicators of campus violence. Focusing on the most egregious acts of violence at school, violent deaths, the authors found that there were 32 school-associated violent deaths in the United States between July 1, 1999, and June 30, 2000. Of these 32 incidents, 24 were homicides and 8 were suicides. Of the 24 homicides, 16 involved school-aged children. When examining homicides of children aged 5–19 in the same time period, the authors found that 2,124 children were murdered. The 16 school homicides represent about 1 percent of the total homicides of children. These statistics, and comparisons made with previous years' data, led the authors to conclude, "In each school year from July 1, 1992, to June 30, 2000, youth ages 5–19 were at least 70 times more likely to be murdered away from school than at school" (DeVoe et al., 2004, 6). This is good news, as it appears as if schools are relatively safe places.

Moving on to other indicators, we present the major conclusions made by the authors paraphrased below:

- There was a decline in the incidence of victimization both at school and away from school. The report indicated a general decline in theft, violent crime, and serious violent crime from 1992 to 2002 for students aged 12–18.
- Nonfatal victimization at school declined between 1995 and 2003. For the most recent years of the study, 2001 and 2003, there appeared to be no difference in amount of nonfatal victimizations at school.

- Male students in grades 9 through 12 were twice as likely to be threatened or injured in 2003 as were their female counterparts (12% versus 6%).
- There was a decline in the percentage of students in grades 9 through 12 who reported that they had been involved in physical fights on campus.
- Both male and female students aged 12–18 reported being bullied at school over the last six months. However, the percentage was low, 7 percent. When looking at data over the years of the study, it was found that bullying increased between 1999 and 2001, but no difference was found between 2001 and 2003. Still, more than one-quarter (29%) of the schools reported daily or weekly student bullying.
- Seventy-one percent of the schools in the study reported experiencing one or more violent incidents on school property between 1999 and 2000. However, only 36 percent of the incidents were reported to the police.
- In 1999–2000, more than one-half of the public schools surveyed reported taking some kind of serious student disciplinary action. The range of action included suspending students for five or more days (83%), removing students permanently (expulsion, 11%), and transferring students to specialized schools (7%).
- Teachers were victimized at school as well, most frequently as victims of theft over the five-year study period. Ninety thousand violent crimes were reported by teachers. Teachers in central city schools were more likely to be threatened with injury or physical attack than were teachers working in urban fringe or rural schools.
- There was a decline in the number of students carrying weapons to school from 1993 to 2003.
- Students reporting that they were afraid of being attacked at or on the way to school declined, with a decrease of 12 percent in 1995 and a decrease of 6 percent in 2003. There was no difference found in the years 2001 and 2003.
- Students reported avoiding certain places at school to avoid victimization. More avoidance behavior was reported at urban schools than at rural or suburban ones.
- Hate-related speech and graffiti were found in public schools. Some students reported having someone use a hate-related word against them (12%), and more than one-third had seen hate-related graffiti at school.
- Gang presence at school was reported more often in urban schools than rural or suburban schools.
- Alcohol and drug usage among the students in grades 9–12 is relatively common; however, usage at school is less common. Almost one-half of the students (45%) reported having at least one drink of alcohol in the last 30 days, while 5 percent had had at least one drink on school property. A smaller yet sizable percentage, 22 percent, reported having used marijuana in the last 30 days, with 6 percent using it on campus. Furthermore, 29 percent of the students reported that someone had offered, sold, or given them illegal drugs on campus.

Schools are relatively safer places; however, when violence such as a school shooting occurs, it heightens concerns about campus safety. As reported by Reddy and colleagues, school-related homicide is so rare that the widespread concern over such events occurring is unnecessary (Reddy et al., 2001). Nevertheless, the public's fear of such violence and the subsequent outcry to keep children safe led to a major study conducted in concert with the U.S. Secret Service and the U.S. Department of Education to evaluate the actual risk of violence in schools and to determine methods to prevent such attacks (Vossekuil et al., 2002). This project called the Safe Schools Initiative (SSI) looked at school shootings from 1974 to 2000 in 37 targeted schools in an attempt to identify warning signs in the offenders' behavior that might have prevented the shootings (Vossekuil et al., 2002). The shootings examined occurred in 26 states, with Arkansas, California, Kentucky, Missouri, and Tennessee reporting multiple incidents (Vossekuil et al., 2002). The results of the initiative are reported below.

Vossekuil and his colleagues paint a picture of the school shootings examined. They examined "any incident where (i) a current student or recent former student attacked someone at his or her school with lethal means (e.g., a gun or knife); and, (ii) where the student attacker purposefully chose his or her school as the location of the attack" (Vossekuil et al., 2002, 7). The common characteristics found among these incidents were reported by the authors. An interesting picture emerges (Vossekuil et al., 2002, 15–16):

- Most of the time (75%) the attackers killed just one person, while in the remaining incidents (25%) the attackers used weapons to injure at least one person.
- School shootings usually occurred during school hours (59%) rather than before (22%) or after school (16%).
- The vast majority, 95 percent, were current students when the attacks were committed. Only two of the shooters were not currently enrolled.
- Males committed all the offenses studied.
- In a large percentage of the incidents, the attackers carried out the acts alone. However, in some of the cases they had assistance in planning the crimes, and in a few incidents multiple attackers committed the offenses.
- Handguns were used in over half of the attacks (61%), followed by rifles and shotguns (49%). Most of the time, perpetrators used only one weapon (76%), but almost half of the attackers had more than one gun with them at the time of the attack.

In another Department of Education study that examined school violent crime rates, it was found that schools in urban areas with a high percentage of minority students had high violent crime rates and were considered to be areas of high social disadvantage and high residential mobility (Cantor and Wright, 2001). The study's overall conclusion was that schools are relatively safe—60 percent of all violent crimes on campus occurred in 4 percent of the schools studied. While this is a comforting finding, for those whose children have to attend the schools where most of the violence has occurred, it is a frightening realization. As an aside, this study included murder, suicide, robbery, rape, assaults, and fights with weapons as serious crimes.

EXAMPLES OF SCHOOL MASS VIOLENCE

A few examples will illustrate the violence associated with school shootings. As the first example illustrates, school shootings are not a new phenomenon; however, as reported above, they are rare occurrences. Some of these examples may be familiar; others are probably less so. The last example, VA Tech massacre, is presented in greater detail because at the time of publication the event has come full circle with most of the victims' families reaching a settlement with the state. It is important in a victimology book to demonstrate what services are available to victims' and their families, and in this case the settlement is viewed as a way to begin the healing process for the families.

Charles Whitman and the Tower Shootings

Charles Whitman is known for the infamous University of Texas at Austin Tower Shootings, where he was enrolled as an engineering student. On August 1, 1966, after killing his wife and mother the night before, Whitman made his way to the University of Texas Main Building, killing three persons to gain access to the tower. Once on the tower, Whitman began at least a 90-minute shooting spree where he killed another 11 people and wounded 32. The sniping continued until four men reached the tower deck, where Whitman was shot multiple times and killed Macleod (2006)(Court TV, 2007).

Jonesboro School Massacre

On March 24, 1998, cousins Mitchell Johnson (13) and Andrew Golden (11) fired into a crowd of their fellow students and teachers killing five and wounding 11 after a false fire alarm was activated. Johnson and Golden are among the youngest ever charged with capital murder in American history (CNN.com, 1998).

Michael Carneal/West Paducah, KY School Shooting

In late 1997, at the age of 14, Michael Carneal planned to regain his reputation with a show of power and force. He arrived at school with a shotgun and killed three people and wounded five students engaged in a prayer circle (Burgess, 2006).

Columbine High School Massacre

On April 20, 1999, two teenage students, Eric Harris and Dylan Klebold went on a shooting rampage, killing 12 students and one teacher and wounding 24 others before killing themselves. It was one of the deadliest attacks on a school in American history and had broad long-term cultural impact (CNN.com, 2000).

Red Lake High School Massacre

On March 21, 2005, Jeffrey Weise went on a shooting rampage that left 10 people dead, including Weise's grandfather and partner, a security guard and teacher, and five fellow students. At least 14 others were wounded in the shooting (ABC News, 2005).

Virginia Tech Massacre

On April 16, 2007 a lone, disgruntled, perhaps mentally ill, student killed 32 students and faculty members on the campus of Virginia Tech in Blacksburg, Virginia. The terror ended when the gunman, Seung Hui Cho, killed himself. This is the worst domestic terrorist act to date resulting in media pundits questioning the safety of all college campuses and VA Tech in particular. What could have been done to prevent or curtail the violence that occurred at VA Tech? Did campus law enforcement act appropriately? What lessons can be learned from this tragedy to make college campuses safe?

The incident: Early Monday morning, April 16, 2007, Seung Hui Cho killed a woman and man in a VA Tech dormitory, West Amber Johnston, which is a coed residence. The woman was returning to the dorm and was shot in the stairwell. Another student, a Residence Assistant (RA), left his dorm room to see what had happened and was shot and killed as well. VA Tech campus police were notified that shots were fired and that two people were dead. They assumed based upon the evidence that this was a domestic dispute, and they started to target and question the boyfriend of the female victim. They closed the dormitory as they pursued the boyfriend.

Some time later, about mid-morning, Cho continued his killing rampage in a building on campus, Norris Hall, where classes were being held. Disturbing accounts of the rampage included Cho being armed with semiautomatic weapons in each hand and extra ammunition in a vest he was wearing. He looked like he was a soldier ready to go to war. Witnesses and survivors of the attack explain that Cho did not warn anyone, did not ask anyone to lie down, he just started shooting. There were also stories of the heroic efforts of instructors and students helping each other. In particular, Professor Liviu Librescu, a professor of engineering, who also was a Holocaust survivor, blocked the classroom door with his body. He was killed but several students were able to jump from the classroom windows to safety.

Soon after the attacks, VA Tech officials closed the university. Students held prayer vigils and made decisions about whether to stay on campus or go home while the university was closed. The following Monday when the campus reopened, campus administrators, students, and staff held memorial services in honor of the victims and in an effort to reunite the campus. Officials gave students the choice to either finish out the semester, attending classes and taking final exams, or to take the grade that the students had already earned in the courses thus far. A fair amount of students took the grades but decided to stay at VA Tech. There was a sense that the campus community needed to be together and a strong spirit emerged that would not let this tragedy paralyze them.

VA Tech awarded posthumously academic degrees to those victims who would have graduated in May, 2007, and degrees for the other victims will be awarded posthumously at the time when they would have completed their degrees.

A Virginia Tech Review Panel has been established and empowered by Governor Timothy Kaine, (Virginia Governor) and another by President George Bush. The goal in both reviews was established to assess the VA Tech massacre to determine what could have been done to prevent the tragedy. Simultaneously, campus administrators throughout the Commonwealth and nation-wide examined their own safety policies and procedures. To date, there have been many meetings and discussions about threat assessment. How should we determine what level of threat exists in certain situations and then what should be done about the threat? The most vocal criticism about the VA Tech tragedy is that the campus community was not informed quickly enough about the incidents occurring on campus. Some argue that the access to the dormitory rooms was too lax; other said that classrooms should have locks, panic buttons, or phones directly to the police. These are all ideas that are being pursued by campus administrators to determine what will work at their campuses. The one consistent idea is to use text messaging to contact students. There are companies that will sell a product to universities but students must opt into it. However, text messages should only be sent in emergencies. Other universities are exploring the idea of having a bull horn (or alarm system), much like a fire or ambulance signal in small towns, that will alert faculty, students, and staff that they need to find out more information from whatever source works best for them—maybe text messaging, email, web-pages, television, or radio. For VA Tech, local news media report that text messaging went into effect in July, 2007 (Channel 12 News, Richmond, VA, May 21, 2007).

The *Chronicle of Higher Education* recently reported that "Twenty-eight of the 32 families whose relatives were killed in the shootings at VA Tech last year have reached final settlements with the Commonwealth of Virginia that preclude their filing lawsuits alleging that the state or the university is to blame" (Lipka, 2008). The settlement gives each family $100,000, provides additional funds for medical and mental-health care services, and allows for family members to meet with public officials (state-government and university officials). The settlement is seen as a way to resolve many issues for the families of the murdered victims. And while liability is denied in the settlement, it does provide for the families and "it promises to resolve many issues of the families" as reported by the victims' families' lawyer, Douglas E. Fierberg (Lipka, 2008, 1).

CHARACTERISTICS OF VICTIMS

What is known about the victims of school violence? Vossekuil and his colleagues (2002) also reported on the characteristics of the victims of the school shootings discussed above. The authors found similarities among the targets chosen in school shootings. They found that (Vossekuil et al., 2002):

- In more than one-half of the incidents examined, the offenders selected as targets at least one school administrator, faculty member, or staff member. Students were targets in less than half of the incidents.
- In about half of the cases, the attackers chose their targets beforehand, and in almost three-quarters of the incidents the attackers had grievances with the targets.
- Those targeted by the attackers were indeed harmed in almost half of the incidents. However, students, school administrators, faculty, and staff who were not targeted were also injured or killed.

While the findings above are disturbing on many levels, they should also help alleviate some of the public's fear about the randomness of school shootings. Targets, in most of the cases, were preselected by the perpetrators. The randomness of the acts seems to be less evident than it was before this study. What this study can do is help us to become aware of warning signs that would cause the average person to be concerned and to take action to deter such violence.

POSSIBLE WARNING SIGNS

The **National School Safety Center (NSSC)** provides a checklist of characteristics of youth who have caused school-associated violent deaths (National School Safety Center, 1998). The NSSC studied common characteristics of those who committed violent murders and developed a checklist from these common characteristics to serve as a *starting point* to perhaps identify youth who might harm him or herself or others. The list is reproduced below (National School Safety Center, 1998):

- Has a history of tantrums and uncontrollable angry outbursts.
- Characteristically resorts to name calling, cursing or abusive language.
- Habitually makes violent threats when angry.
- Has previously brought a weapon to school.

- Has a background of serious disciplinary problems at school and in the community.
- Has a background of drug, alcohol or other substance abuse or dependency.
- Is on the fringe of his/her peer group with few or no close friends.
- Is preoccupied with weapons, explosives or other incendiary devices.
- Has previously been truant, suspended or expelled from school.
- Displays cruelty to animals.
- Has little or no supervision and support from parents or a caring adult.
- Has witnessed or been a victim of abuse or neglect in the home.
- Has been bullied and/or bullies or intimidates peers or younger children.
- Tends to blame others for difficulties and problems she or he causes herself or himself.
- Consistently prefers TV shows, movies or music expressing violent themes and acts.
- Prefers reading materials dealing with violent themes, rituals and abuse.
- Reflects anger, frustration and the dark side of life in school essays or writing projects.
- Is involved with a gang or an antisocial group on the fringe of peer acceptance.
- Is often depressed and/or has significant mood swings.
- Has threatened or attempted suicide.

PREVENTION STRATEGIES FOR REDUCING SCHOOL VIOLENCE

The **Office of Juvenile Justice and Delinquency Prevention (OJJDP)** offers many strategies for reducing violence at schools. School violence, and the subsequent fear of being victimized at school, includes other violent acts besides school shootings. Often included in these discussions are bullying, gangs, students carrying and using weapons, and community violence that spills over into the schools. It's worth noting that bullying has serious repercussions at school: Almost 5 percent of students surveyed in a national school-based survey reported that they miss a day of school each month because they fear for their personal safety at school (Arnette and Walsleben, 1998). The primary threat is bullying.

What does the term **bullying** mean? Arnette and Walsleben (1998, 3) state that bullying is "an abusive behavior that often leads to greater and prolonged violent behavior." They further define this behavior as "**peer child abuse**." When put this way, it's hard to ignore the negative consequences of bullying. It no longer can be seen as "boys will be boys" or any other common phrase that is used to decrease the severity of the actions.

There are many strategies for mediating bullying—such as establishing rules against it, having adult mentors who assist victims and build self-esteem in those who bully, establishing buddy systems, and conducting parenting skills classes. The focus of many of these prevention strategies is to increase offender's self-esteem, to find ways for those victimized to protect themselves, most often by pairing up with another student or an adult, and to correct inappropriate behavior by focusing on "right behaviors" instead of reprimands that focus on punishing wrong behavior.

The two other areas included in the discussions about school violence and the subsequent fear of attending school center on gang activity and community violence that infiltrates schools. Gang activity can be seen as an example of community violence that affects schools. A huge amount of money has been given to support the **GREAT programs** to reduce youth violence and gang membership. GREAT stands for Gang Resistance Education and Training (GREAT). Law enforcement officers are trained though GREAT and then they deliver GREAT to students. The early indicators suggest that GREAT is having an impact on changing student behavior (Arnette and Walsleben, 1998).

Weapons carried and used at school are disturbing to the general public. As such many states have passed state and local gun-free school zones laws and other legislation that carries expulsion from school as the punishment for carrying weapons on school property. A lot of funds have been given to educate the public about this issue. There are billboards, hotlines, and videos that emphasize the lethal and injurious results of gun violence.

There are many partnerships and legislation that has been enacted to return schools to their former role as safe havens of learning. A few of those initiatives are listed below (Arnette and Walsleben, 1998, p. 12):

- Using the model of drug-free safe zones, many states have created "crime-free," "weapon-free," or "safe-school" zone statutes. Areas around schools, bus stops, and other areas where school activities take place are often included in the zones. Safe-school zone statutes advocate for zero-tolerance of weapons or drugs in protected areas.

- In 1994, federal regulations were established to mandate that school districts have drug and alcohol testing programs for bus drivers.

- Local criminal justice agencies are working with schools to share information about students who have criminal records, who are incarcerated, and who are in aftercare programs (probation).

- Crisis prevention and intervention policies are being developed to help direct individual schools to develop similar individual school-level policies as part of their safe-school plans.

- School security systems are being improved, as is the general sense of security at schools. Criminal background checks on teachers and staff are being conducted, Neighborhood Watch programs are including schools, and parents are registering their homes as "safe houses" and volunteering to monitor routes to and from school.

WHAT EXPLAINS SCHOOL MASS VIOLENCE?

Kimmel and Mahler (2003) examined random school shootings from 1982–2001 and found 28 incidents in the United States. The authors found "(a) that the shootings were not a national problem but a series of local problems that occurred in 'red states' or counties [places that voted Republican in the 2000 election]; (b) that most of the boys who opened fire were mercilessly and routinely teased and bullied and that their violence was retaliatory against the threats to manhood; (c) that White boys in particular might be more likely than African American boys to randomly open fire; and (d) that the specific content of the teasing and bullying is homophobia" (p. 1439).

The authors present a nice summary of the literature where the cause of school violence is discussed. As they point out, many scholars, pundits, and politicians have argued that school violence is the result of goth music, violent video games, the Internet, daycare, the 1960s, violence in the media, the availability of guns, psychological factors (e.g., abuse, absent fathers, or dominant mothers), to name but a few correlates (Kimmel and Mahler, 2003). These authors, however, state that the most obvious "cause" of such violence has been missed by all those weighing in on the debate. Kimmel and Mahler argue that gender—in particular being male—is the common factor found among all random school shootings. Here's what they observe:

> Most important for our argument is the fact that these studies [previously mentioned studies focusing on school violence] have all missed gender. They use such broad terminology as "teen violence," "youth violence," "gang violence," "suburban violence," and "violence in the schools" as though girls are equal participants in this violence. Conspicuously absent is any mention of just who these youth or teens are who have committed the violence. They pay little or no attention to the obvious fact that all the school shootings were committed by boys—masculinity is the single greatest risk factor in school violence. This uniformity cuts across all other differences among the shooters: Some came from intact families, others from single-parent homes; some boys had acted violently in the past, others were quiet and unsuspecting; and some boys also expressed rage at their parents (two killed their parents the same morning), whereas others seemed to live in happy families. And yet, if the killers in the schools in Littleton, Pearl, Paducah, Springfield, and Jonesboro had all been girls, gender would undoubtedly be the only story (Kimmel, 2001; see also Klein and Chancer, 2000). Someone might even blame feminism for causing girls to become violent in vain imitation of boys (2003, 1442).

The authors raise an excellent point, one that cannot be found in the literature as far as we can tell. The authors continue their discussion, further detailing who among the male gender actually shoots. Not all males are going to be shooters, and what the authors conclude is that white boys are more likely to shoot than nonwhite boys. There is also a link between bullying, masculinity, and school shootings. That is, "most of the boys who opened fire were mercilessly and routinely teased and bullied and . . . their violence was retaliatory against the threats to manhood" (p. 1439). The link between bullying and school shootings has also been supported by Ann Burgess and her colleagues (Burgess et al., 2006).

HOW CAN SCHOOLS BE MADE SAFER?

The **National School Safety Center** provides some commonsense approaches to making schools safer. Their handout, developed to encourage dialogue and participation with school stakeholders such as law enforcement, the community, faculty, and students, suggests the following practical strategies for addressing school safety (National School Safety Center, 1999):

- School safety must be part of the agenda. For students to learn, they must feel safe. To ensure safety, parents, teachers, staff, and administrators must take active roles in school safety. Developing safety plans that are district-wide in addition to individual school plans is essential. Both should have systematic procedures for dealing with crises and safety issues.
- School libraries should contain as much information as possible about safety. Information about school crime, violence, drugs, disciplinary action, attendance, and dropouts should be included and made available to anyone interested in learning more.

- Develop systematic, districtwide reporting systems to collect information on accidents, disciplinary problems, vandalism, security problems, and child abuse. These systems will allow administrators to monitor school problems to determine if school safety policies are working or need to be revamped.

- Create individual school safety brochures or develop districtwide brochures to provide parents and other interested parties with ways to help create safe havens where children can learn. Also include statistics about school safety issues (e.g., truancy rate and vandalism). Be sure to update the fact sheet regularly.

- Continue to develop and revise safety policies. Seek the help of law enforcement to make certain safety policies employ the most recent safety programs or products.

- Create an advisory group consisting of interested adults and students. Include law enforcement, social services, and other community groups who are interested in student safety.

- Become involved in **America's Safe Schools Week**. Planned for the third week in October, this time is set aside to learn more about safety ideas that might work. Support the initiative, and find out ways to participate.

- Identify individual partners in the community who can help shape community opinion. When new programs or initiatives are being tried, seek the assistance of these people in getting the word out about new initiatives, and when they succeed, in publicizing the success.

- Establish public relations committees to promote schools, teachers, staff, administration, and students. Develop a way to "brand" schools with symbols or mottos. Instill pride in schools, and their members will protect both the structures and their fellow members.

- Publish newsletters that promote schools and what is going on there, particularly new safety initiatives, for the community.

MASS VIOLENCE: MURDER

There are typically five types of murder referred to in the literature based on the number of people killed, the relationship between the victims and offenders, and the events leading up to the killings. These terms include *serial murder*, *spree murder*, *mass murder*, *classic mass murder*, and *family mass murder*. Each is conceptualized below (see Bartol, 2004; National Center for the Analysis of Violent Crime, 2005; Lacks, 2006a):

Serial murder: Incidents in which an individual kills a number of individuals (minimum of three) over time.

Spree murder: The killing of three or more individuals without any cooling off period, usually at two or more locations.

Mass murder: Murdering three or more persons at a single location with no cooling off period between murders.

Classic mass murder: A situation in which an individual barricades himself or herself inside a public building, such as a fast food restaurant, randomly killing the patrons and other individuals he or she has contact with.

Family mass murder: A situation in which at least three family members are killed (usually by another family member).

This section will focus on serial killers as a form of mass violence. Here's what we know about serial killing (National Center for the Analysis of Violent Crime, 2005; Lacks, 2006b).

- Although not every serial killer gets the same attention and notoriety as, say, a Ted Bundy, there are many serial killers in the United States and England. In a 30-year period, over 40 individuals have been identified as serial killers.

- It is difficult to know if the number of serial killers is increasing or decreasing. It certainly appears as if those known to law enforcement and then subsequently known to the public via the media are decreasing. However, this might be an artifact of the media; that is, law enforcement may not have shared new information about serial killers with them.

- Victims of serial killing are often young female prostitutes, or male or female children aged 8 to 16.

- The Child Abduction and Serial Killer Unit (CASKU) was created in the early 1990s by the FBI in response to the number of children being abducted by serial killers. Today it is known as the National Center for the Analysis of Violent Crime (NCVAC) as part of ViCAP (Violent Crime Apprehension Program). In the mid-1990s the Missing and Exploited Children's Task Force was created by Congress. Today it is known as the National Center for Missing and Exploited Children.

- Serial killers begin their killing "careers" much later in life than do typical offenders.

- Females do commit serial killings. They often kill family members or acquaintances, most often husbands, former husbands, or suitors. Their motive is financial reward. The method of killing is usually poisoning. Many female serial killers have male accomplices.

As reported above, there are some 40 serial killers including notorious ones like Ted Bundy, Henry Lee Lucas, John Wayne Gacy, Jeffery Dahmer, Kenneth Bianchi (the Hillside Strangler), Dennis Rader, the BTK (Bind, Torture, Kill) killer, the Green River Killer (Gary Leon Ridgway), Robert Pickton (Canada's most infamous serial killer), Jack the Ripper, Richard Speck, and Son of Sam (David Berkowitz), to name but a few. In this section, three serial killers are profiled. When known, information about the victims including their names is reported. The serial killers included in this section are Charles Manson, Ted Bundy, and the "Last Call" Killer.

Charles Manson

Perhaps the most notorious serial killer of all is **Charles Manson**. Manson, his family, and their violent crimes have been immortalized throughout the nation and beyond because of their reference to the Beatles' song *Helter Skelter* which they scratched on the refrigerator door in the victims' blood at the crime scene. A book by the same title details Mason's crime spree and further associates Charles Manson and his family with the phrase.

Charles Manson evoked fear throughout the nation even though his "family" and his targets were in California. Charles Manson's followers went on a killing rampage for no apparent reason beyond obliging Manson's wishes and orders. Manson and his family killed movie director Roman Polanski's pregnant wife, Sharon Tate, an up-and-coming actress, who was pregnant, and several others who were at the Tate/Polanski home. These victims included Thomas John (Jay) Sebring, Abigail Anne Folger, Wojiciech Frykowski, and Steven Earl Parent. The crime scene was one of the most brutal attacks described quite vividly in the book (see Bugliosi and Gentry, 1974). The same evening, Manson and his family also brutally attacked and killed Leo and Rosemary LaBianca (Bugliosi and Gentry, 1974).

Manson and his followers (Dianne Krenwinkel, Susan "Squeaky" Atkins, and Leslie Van Houten) were convicted seven months after the trial began, and nine days after the jury began to deliberate. They all were convicted of murder and conspiracy to commit murder. The fourth suspect, Charles "Tex" Watson, had his trial delayed for a year, but was ultimately convicted of the same charges (Bugliosi and Gentry, 1974).

Ted Bundy

Ted Bundy was born November 24, 1946, to "parents" who were really his grandparents; Ted thought that his mother was his "sister." When Ted was 4 years old, his mother married a man—Johnnie Bundy—who eventually adopted Ted as his son. Ted Bundy was a very intelligent, good-looking man who used his charms to lure in his victims.

Bundy is thought to have murdered two dozen women, including Joni Lenz, Linda Ann Healy, Donna Manson, Susan Rancourt, Kathy Parks, Brenda Ball, Georgeann Hawkins, Jane Ott, Denise Naslund, Janice Ott, Melissa Smith, Laura Aime, Carol DeRonch, Caryn Campbell, Julie Cunningham, Melanie Cooley, Lynette Culver, Susan Curtis, Shelley Robertson, Nancy Baird, Debbie Smith, Lisa Levy, Margaret Bowman, and Kimberly Ann Leach. His reign of terror sketched from 1974 to 1978, when he was finally indicted for the murder of Levy and Bowman. On November 17, 1986, Ted Bundy was supposed to be executed for murdering Levy, Bowman, and Leach. There are more than a dozen other women who Bundy is thought to have killed, but he was only tried and convicted on these three counts. Bundy's execution was stayed in 1986 and again in 1989. He was finally executed on January 17, 1989 (Larsen, 1980).

In a crime analysis of the Bundy case, it was determined that Bundy was attracted to college students who were attractive with long black hair parted in the middle. Bundy randomly selected his victims and used his good looks and false sense of helplessness to gain their trust. Bundy would pretend to be injured, wearing a cast or using crutches, and since he was on or around a college campus, he would pretend to have trouble carrying objects, usually books. Women were drawn to him and were there to help him. He took full advantage of their generosity and helping nature and ended up beating, torturing, sexually assaulting, and killing many young, unsuspecting women (Larsen, 1980).

The "Last Call" Killer (Richard W. Rogers)

Not nearly as infamous as Ted Bundy but a more current example of a serial killer is Richard W. Rogers, dubbed the **"Last Call" Killer** because he targeted his victims—gay men—at bars and usually assaulted and killed them after the bars closed. Rogers, a 55-year-old New Jersey man, has been accused of killing numerous gay men. He cut them up, put their remains in plastic bags, and dumped them on the side of roads in New Jersey and Pennsylvania. These horrific crimes were even more disturbing after it was learned that Rogers was a former nurse, a profession equated with helping others, not with butchering them (Westveer, 2006).

Rogers was convicted of two homicides on January 27, 2006, in an Ocean County, New Jersey courtroom. He received a double-life sentence for these murders, which equates to about 30 years each (Westveer, 2006). Although he was convicted of these two murders, there are other open cases that prosecutors feel Rogers is also guilty of committing. However, to date no further formal charges are pending.

FEMALE SERIAL KILLERS

Although serial killers get a great deal of media attention, such murders are rare events. It is even more infrequent when female killers are considered. However, this has not stopped criminologists from developing typologies to explain such crimes. While our interest lies in the victims, not the offenders, knowing the motivation for serial killing might shed some light on what people can do to protect themselves. Focusing on female serial killers, Moriarty and Freiberger (2003) explain that female serial killers' motives often do not match those motives found in male serial killers. They report, "The categories of motive not found in the Dietz or Holmes and DeBurger typologies but clearly the motive for some female serial killers include:"

- *Attention.* Motive for the killing is to gain attention (i.e., notice).
- *Frustration.* Stressful situations compel the woman to kill as an alternate way to solve the situation.
- *Jealousy.* The woman kills because she feels she will be supplanted in a relationship be someone else. She is afraid she will lose the affection of a significant other.
- *Cult.* Killings are part of the cult's behavior. The female is part of a cult where obsessive devotion leads to murder.
- *Revenge.* Motive for the killing is to inflict pain in return for injury or insult. The woman retaliates. (Moriarty and Frieberger, 2003, 492, 494).

Knowing the motive of an attack might help create an awareness of the crime itself: a way of learning more about a very rare event. Since it is such an infrequent crime, no specific crime-prevention activity is promoted. The same approaches used to thwart off crime in general (as discussed in Chapter 3) are recommended here as well. Commonsense approaches—avoiding unlit areas, traveling in groups, not leaving with strangers, locking doors, etc.—should be stressed here as well.

VICTIMS OF MASS VIOLENCE

What is known about victims of mass violence and what can be done to help victims of such crime and also prevent such violence? Victims of serial killers tend to be the vulnerable members in a society, those on the fringes who slip in and out of society without much notice, and those who don't have many ties, like prostitutes, the homeless, and runaway children.

Beasley (2004) conducted a study comparing seven interviewed serial killers in order to determine their similarities and differences. This article was first published in *Behavioral Sciences and the Law* and is reprinted in the FBI symposium materials (Federal Bureau of Investigation Behavioral Analysis Unit, 2005). The article is important because the authors spent a great deal of time discussing the victims in each case. The seven offenders studied were all serial killers, but there is variation in the victimology of their crimes. As reported by Beasley, variation was found among the offenders when examining the number of victims, the race and gender of the victims, the cause of death, and whether the bodies were removed. In five of the seven case studies, all the victims were white. In three of the seven cases, all the victims were female. In four of the seven cases, the method or cause of death was the same for all the victims. In other words, all the victims were strangled, shot, or stabbed. In three cases none of the bodies were moved. Beasley summarized (2004, 409), "The victims' backgrounds were diverse as well: Some were prostitutes (35%), some were elderly (15%), and some were students (19%). They were predominately White, but one was Black, two were Hispanic, and one was Asian. The methods used by the killers to perpetrate their murders were varied and included shooting, stabbing, strangulation, and blunt force with instruments and/or hands."

Some of the best-known researchers studying mass murder (Ronald Holmes, Steve Egger, Jamie Fox, and Jack Levin) have attempted to provide information about victims of such evil. However, they can only provide descriptive analysis of those who have already been victimized, and they can (and have) developed typologies where they characterize offenders and then offer some victim "preference" or common characteristics. And while this information is insightful in detailing information about known serial killers or mass murderers, it does not help determine how to avoid becoming a victim of such a crime.

Further, Egger states that, "Being a victim of a serial killer could be as simple as being in the right place at the wrong time" (cited in Holmes and Holmes, 1998, 161). Egger does further list what he finds to be the most vulnerable populations at risk for such victimization. He includes the powerless, the vulnerable, and the easily dominated. When discussing who these victims might be, Egger and others label them as "vagrants, prostitutes, migrant workers, homosexuals, missing children, and single and often elderly women" (as cited in Holmes and Holmes, 1998, 161). Others add to the list college students as well—and from the examples presented above, the victims of Ted Bundy and Richard Rogers fall into one or more of these categories.

WORKPLACE VIOLENCE

Workplace violence is any form of violence that occurs in the workplace. A more formal definition is "any act of physical violence, threats of physical violence, harassment, intimidation, or other threatening, disruptive behavior that occurs at the work site. Workplace violence can affect or involve employees, visitors, contractors, and other non-Federal employees" (USDA, 1998). When thinking of workplace violence, "**going postal**" (Molloy, 2006) comes to mind because of what appears to be the frequent killing rampages of former postal workers. The most recent incident occurred on January 30, 2006, when six people were killed in Goleta, California, by a former postal employee who then killed herself (Losey, 2006). Although it sounds as if working in the post office is a very dangerous job, the actual numbers paint a different picture. Here are some of the facts about post office workplace violence as reported by the *Herald Sun*, referring to this latest incident of postal violence (2006):

- Postal rampage killings seem to occur frequently. However, before the 2006 incident, the most recent attack was in Dallas, Texas, in 1998, when one worker fatally shot another in the heat of an argument. In the last 20 years, 19 lives have been claimed by such shootings.
- The deadliest postal shooting occurred in Edmond, Oklahoma, in 1986, when a postal employee killed himself and 14 other coworkers.
- With an employment workforce of over 700,000 individuals, the postal service claims to have a lower rate of workplace violence than the overall U.S. average.

It's clear from the post office examples that violence does occur in the workplace. But, does workplace violence have to be that severe to be considered a violent act? Not necessarily, as many employers list examples of workplace violence on company websites. Such actions include direct or implied threats, "physical conduct that results in harm to people or property, conduct which harasses, disrupts, or interferes with another individual's performance, [and] conduct that creates an intimidating, offensive, or hostile environment" (Cleveland State University n.d.).

Also listed on the website are risk factors that contribute to violence in the workplace. Places of work where there are employees who have recently had their employment terminated, who have had disciplinary actions taken against them, who have ongoing conflicts or disputes with other employees, who are involved in domestic or family violence, and who have financial problems are more at risk for workplace violence.

According to Kovacich and Halibozek (2003, 240) the causes of such violent behavior include the perception of being treated unfairly by the company, personal problems, failed relationships, job instability, pressures at work, drug or alcohol dependency, and depression. These causal factors can easily be turned into risk factors. If such conditions are observed in employees at the workplace, they should be treated as warning signs and acted upon accordingly. Other warning signs addressed by Kovacich and Halibozek include

> any changes in behavior or appearance including loud, angry outbursts in reaction to normal everyday situations; abusive verbal or physical actions toward coworkers; isolation, a decrease in social connections and support; degradation of personal appearance and hygiene; decrease in productivity; destruction of personal and company property; stalking; preoccupation with weapons; and chronic complaints and expressions of dissatisfaction with work (2003, 240–241).

Just How Much of a Problem Is Workplace Violence?

According to the Bureau of Justice Statistics, in the period from 1993 to 1999 there was an average of 1.7 million violent victimizations committed against individuals at work each year (Duhart, 2001, 1). The report also indicates that about "900 work-related homicides occurred annually" (p. 1). Finally, when focusing specifically on workplace violence versus other locations of recorded violence, Duhart found that workplace violence made up 18 percent of all reported violent crimes in the study period. Some other interesting trends and highlights of the special report include (Duhart, 2001, 1):

- As one would expect, law enforcement is a dangerous occupation in terms of workplace violence. Police officers were victims of workplace violence at higher rates than any other occupation.
- Whites were at higher risk for workplace violence than all other races combined.
- Workplace violence tended to be intraracial, with 60 percent of assailants being the same race as their victims.
- There were similar workplace violence rates for private sector and federal government employees.
- In the educational setting, junior high and high school teachers experienced more workplace violence than elementary school teachers.

- Forty percent of robberies that occurred while the victims were at work were committed against people in retail sales or transportation.
- Firearms were used in 80 percent of workplace homicides. During the study period, workplace homicides were shown to decline.

The workplace violence statistics and especially trend data reveal that some occupations are more dangerous than others. Law enforcement jobs are expected to be more dangerous than other occupations. Robbery victimization appears to be a crime that employees of certain occupations (e.g., sales and transportation) should be more concerned about than others. And while workplace homicides declined over the seven-year period, it is rather alarming that 80 percent of the homicides were committed using a firearm. A logical conclusion to this finding might be that workplace homicides are premeditated, rather than unplanned, spontaneous events, especially because it would be unlikely in most occupational settings that employees would be carrying firearms. Noted is the obvious exception of police officers, and also noted is that this occupation is the most dangerous of those examined.

PREVENTION STRATEGIES

What can be done in the workplace to prevent such violence? Kovacich and Halibozek state emphatically that "Workplace violence can be prevented" (2003, 242). They recommend managers and supervisors do the following to prevent workplace violence (2003, 242–243):

- Look for, and document, significant changes in behavior among employees.
- Pay attention to employees' work-related and personal concerns. Listen to them and be receptive to their thoughts.
- Make certain employees understand that they can talk about problems and issues in a confidential manner. Establish an environment that is conducive to candid exchanges of thoughts and issues.
- Address workplace violence immediately. Know what steps to take. Know the support systems to invoke.
- Anyone who is recognized as a potential threat should be dealt with. Seek the advice and counsel of individuals who can help address the threat. Talk with security, human resources, and employee assistance program specialists. Make certain appropriate disciplinary action is taken if need be.
- Notify Human Resources of any threats of violence or any known restraining orders against individuals.
- Investigate all threats of violence. Do not summarily dismiss any threat as not "severe enough."

DRUNK DRIVING

Drunk driving is included in this chapter because according to the National Highway Safety Administration, "Drunk driving is the nation's most frequently committed violent crime, killing someone about every 30 minutes" (see www.officer.com, retrieved June 17, 2008). Furthermore, when drunk driving fatalities involve more than one driver and perhaps several passengers it becomes a form of mass violence. The number of victims in one fatal crash can easily exceed three or more persons.

Drunk driving is among the most common types of arrest made by police (Scott et al., 2006). The statistics provided by the NHSA indicate that of all fatalities in motor vehicle traffic crashes in 2006 (n = 42,642) some 41 percent are alcohol related fatalities. This represents a decrease in the number of fatal accidents by 2 percent but it indicates an increase of 12 percent for alcohol-related fatalities (NHTSA, 2007).

Drunk driving is a social problem that has gained national attention with organizations like Mothers Against Drunk Driving (MADD), Students Against Driving Drunk (SADD which now stands for Students Against Destructive Decisions) and UMADD (for college students). These organizations promote healthy life styles and moderation in alcohol consumption. The mission statements for each found on the various websites are repeated below for clarity:

> The **mission of MADD** is to stop drunk driving, support the victims of this violent crime and prevent underage drinking (http://www.madd.org/About-Us/About-Us/Mission-Statement.aspx retrieved on June 17, 2008).
>
> Originally, the **mission of the SADD** chapter was to help young people say "No" to drinking and driving. Today, the mission has expanded. Students have told us that positive peer pressure, role models and other strategies can help them say "No" to more than drinking and driving. And that is why SADD has become a peer leadership organization dedicated to preventing destructive decisions, particularly underage drinking, other drug use, impaired driving, teen violence and teen depression and suicide (http://www.sadd.org/mission.htm retrieved on June 17, 2008).
>
> The **goals of MADD's college initiatives** are to:
>
> - Prevent alcohol use for those under the legal drinking age of 21.
> - Reduce and eliminate illegal and high-risk drinking behaviors for those of legal drinking age.
> - Activate students to engage in effective strategies by partnering them with campus and community leaders.
> - Provide resources and assistance to campus and community law enforcement, community members, faculty and staff, and parents (http://www.umadd.org/Home/MADD's-College-Initiatives.html retrieved on June 17, 2008).

There are a variety of problems associated with alcohol including underage drinking, binge drinking, and driving under the influence (or driving while drunk). Police encounter impaired and dangerous driving, not all leading to fatalities, but some of the other issues facing the police related to alcohol include driving under the influence of controlled substances, underage drinking, street racing, speeding, aggressive driving, driving with a suspended license, and hit-and-run crashes (Scott et al., 2006, 1).

Alcohol plays such a significant part in the lives of the public: we toast to happy couples, we have wine at church, we celebrate milestones with champagne and as such there is the potential for those both experienced and inexperienced to not know their limits and drive while intoxicated. The national statistics indicate that 17,602 people were killed in alcohol-related traffic accidents in 2006 (see MADD website). The irony of this tragedy is that those going out to celebrate or have a good time never once think that they will end up in an automobile accident or that they will be arrested for DUI/DWI. The impaired judgment that leads to consuming too much alcohol is the same judgment that makes an individual believe that she or he can drive after having too much to drink. This is why having the technology to prohibit people who have drunk too much from driving is a good solution; perhaps a better solution than relying on the individual to call a cab or use a designated driver.

As more traffic accidents occur, we are seeing more of these accidents being the result of drivers being impaired by alcohol. Not all impaired drivers have fatal accidents, and the number of fatal accidents is decreasing since the current campaign by Mothers Against Drunk Drivers (MADD) to eliminate drunk driving. MADD intends to eliminate drunk driving by working with law enforcement to be more visible on the highways and roadways and to establish sobriety check points, to advocate for ignition interlocks for all convicted DUI/DWI offenders, to increase the automobile technology to prevent drunk drivers from driving, and to continue to seek public support for their campaign (see MADD website, http://www.madd.org/Drunk-Driving.aspx, retrieved on June 17, 2008). According to the NHTSA, Alaska had the largest reduction in alcohol-related fatalities comparing 2005 fatalities to 2006 with a reported percent change of almost 38 percent (37.8%); Utah had the largest increase in alcohol-related fatalities with a percent change of almost 73 percent (72.5%). Perhaps MADD efforts need to focus more diligently on the states where the increases in alcohol-related fatalities are quite high.

CONCLUSION

Killing on a mass scale continues to dominate the news and strike fear into all citizens. Everyone has a chance of becoming an innocent victim of a mass killing; however, the events described in this chapter are rare. Terrorism from both domestic and international sources has greatly impacted the United States over the last two decades. In addition, mass killings in our schools have also dominated our public conscience. Even though such occurrences are rare, the media attention that follows any terrorist act, mass killing, or school shooting can evoke fear in just about anyone. The challenge is addressing the incidents in order to better understand the victimization without creating more fear in the public at large.

Discussion Questions

1. What is the definition of domestic terrorism? How does this definition differ from a general definition of terrorism or international terrorism?
2. How does emphasizing crimes that are unlikely, but extremely violent, raise the concern and fear in the general public? Do you think there is a problem with how the media focuses on such crimes?
3. How can workplace violence be prevented? What are the warning signs that indicate the chances of workplace violence occurring?
4. The media hype suggests that school violence is rampant, is it? How can we make students feel more secure in an environment that is relatively safe and where they have to spend a great deal of time?

Key Terms

- going postal 255
- "Last Call" Killer 253
- America's Safe Schools Week 251
- assassination attempts and murders 239
- attention 254
- bombings 239
- bullying 248
- Charles Manson 252
- Charles Whitman and the tower shootings 245
- classic mass murder 251
- Columbine High School massacre 245
- cult 254

- domestic terrorism 239
- drunk driving 257
- family mass murder 251
- frustration 254
- GREAT programs 248
- jealousy 254
- Jonesboro school massacre 245
- mass killings 239
- mass murder 251
- Michael Carneal 245
- National School Safety Center (NSSC) 247
- Office of Juvenile Justice and Delinquency Prevention (OJJDP) 248

- peer child abuse 248
- product tampering 239
- radical violent groups 239
- Red Lake High School massacre 245
- revenge 254
- school violence 242
- serial murder 251
- spree murder 251
- Ted Bundy 253
- terrorism 238
- Terrorism and International Victims Unit (TIVU) 240
- workplace violence 255
- Zacarias Moussaoui 241

CHAPTER

14

International Victimization, Assistance, and the Future for the Victims of Crimes

INTRODUCTION

Certain international victimizations impact the whole world. Human rights violation, war crimes, and genocide are general categories of international victimizations. The devaluing of human rights of individuals and groups continues today, creating untold numbers of victims. Beginning in 1948, the **United Nations** (UN) developed standards of treatment of individual citizens by governments throughout the world. The first standard was a Universal Declaration of Human Rights (see Appendix E) focusing on the abolishment of corporal punishments, prohibited torture, and other forms of inhumane and degrading treatment. By 1975, the UN had passed the Declaration on the Protection of All Persons from Being Subjected to Torture and Other Cruel, Inhuman or Degrading Treatment or Punishments (Waller, 2003). This document has gained worldwide acceptance and provides the foundation to many victim assistance programs throughout the world; however, human rights abuses continue to victimize hundreds of thousands. The chapter begins with an examination of the international victimizations of genocide and human trafficking, a description of various crime victims programs found throughout the world and concludes with an analysis of what the future holds for crime victims and the crime victim's movement in the United States and the rest of the world.

CRIMES AGAINST HUMANITY

Egregious human rights abuses still exist throughout the world today. Many of these abuses are carried out by governments or occur due to the failure of governments to actively try and stop the human rights abuses. Many human rights abuses can be linked to the failure to protect individuals because of their gender, ethnic orientation, or their religious beliefs. Two of the most inhuman victimizations that exist today are **genocide** and **human trafficking**.

GENOCIDE

After the horrors of the Holocaust were brought to light at the end of World War II, a number of nations came together and established an international standard for defining and dealing with genocide. The 1948 Convention on the Prevention and Punishment of the Crime of Genocide set forth that genocide is a crime under international law whether it is committed in a time of peace or a time of war. Genocide was defined as:

> Any of the following acts committed with intent to destroy, in whole or in part, a national, ethnical, racial or religious group, as such: killing members of the group; causing serious bodily or mental harm to members of the group; deliberately inflicting on the group conditions of life calculated to bring about its physical destruction in whole or in part; imposing measures intended to prevent births within the group; forcibly transferring children of the group to another group (Orentlicher, 2007, 192).

HISTORY OF GENOCIDE

While the Holocaust of World War II is the most widely known case of genocide, it was not the first and was not the last. Native cultures have been the victims of genocide, as occurred in the United States with the Native American Indians. Other native cultures such as the Mayans and Aztecs of Central and South America at the hands of the Spanish, the Aboriginals in Australia, and the natives of South Africa also faced acts of genocide when their lands were being concurred and occupied. In the twentieth century, actions such as the systematic extermination of Armenians by the Turks are generally recognized as genocide. Over one million were estimated to have been put to death (Orentlicher, 2007).

Some of the more recent genocides which have occurred since the Holocaust (see Table 14.1) are the massacre of Hutus by Tutsi in Burundi in 1972, the Khmer Rouge government in Cambodia resettlement campaign of the 1970s, the Bosnia–Herzegovina war when Bosnian Serbs sought to destroy the Bosnian Muslims (1992), the massacres that happened in Rwanda (1994), and the most recent acts of genocide occurring in the Darfur area of Sudan.

The massive amount of deaths that occur are not the only victimizations that take place in genocide. Millions of individuals are displaced and are forced to become refugees in neighboring countries, systematic rapes of women are used to disgrace and destroy ethnic identity, and mutilation of survivors is common. Those who are able to flee the killings are forced into poverty, loss of property, homelessness, and, in many cases, starvation (Genocide Watch, 2008).

TABLE 14.1   Recent Genocides

Countries and/or Responsible Group	*Estimates of the Numbers of Victims*
Burundi–Tutsi	50,000–100,000 Hutus were killed in a 3-month period
Cambodia–Khmer Rouge	1.5 million citizens out of a total of 7 million citizens killed
Bosnia-Serbia–Serbs	100,000 Bosnian Muslims killed
Rwanda–Hutus	700,000–1,000,000 Tutsi were killed by a Hutu led government
Sudan–Sudanese government	200,000–400,000 residents of Darfur

Source: Based on Orentlicher (2007).

TRAFFICKING IN PERSONS

Trafficking in persons or **human trafficking** is the equivalent of modern-day slavery. The victims of trafficking are forced, coerced, or defrauded into sexual exploitation or unpaid labor. The victims of trafficking suffer through physical and psychological violence as part of their involuntary servitude. It is estimated that approximately 600,000 to 800,000 people are trafficked across international borders each year, and millions more are enslaved in their own countries (U.S. Department of State, 2006).

The Trafficking Victims Protection Act of 2000 (Pub. L. No. 106–386) defines various forms of trafficking as:

a. **sex trafficking** in which a commercial sex act is induced by force, fraud, or coercion, or in which the person induced to perform such an act has not attained 18 years of age: or

b. the recruitment, harboring, transportation, provision, or obtaining of a person for labor or services, through the use of force, fraud, or coercion for the purpose of subjection to **involuntary servitude, peonage, debt bondage**, or **slavery** (U.S. Department of State, 2006, 25).

One of the worst forms of human trafficking is when children are being trafficked for the commercial sex trade. It is estimated that more than one million children are exploited in the commercial sex trade. These children become part of a worldwide phenomenon known as **child sex trade** (CST). Child sex trade involves adults who travel from their own country to another to engage in commercial sex acts with children (U.S. Department of State, 2006 24). Developing countries in South Asia have for many years been destinations for CST. Businessmen from Japan, the United States, and European countries would travel to South Asia and engage in sexual acts with children who were forced to work in brothels. The sexual exploitation of the children is both physically and psychologically traumatizing on the children. Not only are they sexually exploited, but many are subjected to extreme physical violence, forced abortions, drug addiction, and are likely to contract sexually transmitted infections including HIV/AIDS.

When the victim is being trafficked for forced labor, it can occur because of a debt or a bond. Victims or their families are coerced or forced into an agreement to provide their labor as a way to pay off a debt which was imposed as a condition of finding employment or providing the child an education. This debt may have been a result of monies paid to a victim's family by an employment broker. However, the debt for gaining employment is never paid off because they are told that all of the income is used to cover living expenses or they never see any income at all. Children as well as adults are victims of forced labor. In many cases, such as in South Asia, people can be enslaved from one generation to the next (U.S. Department of State, 2005).

Human trafficking can also take place when a laborer takes a position in a foreign household. What happens is that a laborer from one country takes a job in another country on the promise of a good salary and housing. Upon arriving in the new country, the servants' passports and other travel documents are confiscated and they are told if they go to authorities they will be imprisoned. The salary is never paid because the employers state that the salary only covers the housing and basic necessities or a minimal amount of money is sent back to a worker's family. The workers are required to work 6–7 days a week up to 16–20 hours each day just to have poor housing and something to eat. A recent example of this was uncovered in the United States.

A millionaire and his wife were convicted in December 2007 of keeping two Indonesian housekeepers as virtual slaves. The pair was convicted of 12 federal charges including forced labor, involuntary servitude, harboring aliens, and conspiracy. The victims, who were brought over from Indonesia, had endured years of being beaten, cut with knives, forced to work 18 or more hours per day, and were paid only $100 a month, which they never saw because it was sent to family members back in Indonesia. The husband was sentenced to 3 ½ years and fined, while his wife was sentenced to 11 years because she was seen as being primarily responsible for inflicting years of abuse on the servants (New York Times, 2008).

INTERNATIONAL CRIMINAL COURT

An effort to bring offenders to justice for a crime against humanity occurs in individual countries or in the **International Criminal Court** if it is determined that a country is unable or unwilling to bring these international criminals to justice. The International Criminal Court was created as a reaction to the atrocities committed in the former Yugoslavia and the crimes in Rwanda (Garraway, 2007). The Court was established in July 1992 through the United Nations and is located in The Hague, Netherlands. The Court has jurisdiction over the crimes of genocide, crimes against humanity, and war crimes. One Hundred and six members of the United Nations are members of the Court. However, the United States, Israel, Libya, China, Iraq, and India have not joined the Court. The Court has the power to prosecute individuals for crimes against humanity that occurred after its inception in 1992.

The victims of the crimes that the International Criminal Court investigates have many rights. The victims are guaranteed participation in the Court's proceedings. The Court has a victims unit which provides "protective measures and security arrangements, counseling and other appropriate assistance for witnesses, victims who appear before the Court, and others who are at risk on account of testimony given by such witnesses" (Rome Statute of the International Criminal Court Article 68, 2008). The Court has also established an Office of Public Counsel for Victims to provide support and assistance to victims and their legal representatives (Bottigliero, 2003).

INTERNATIONAL VICTIMIZATION SERVICE PROGRAMS

Many nations throughout the world have responded to the needs of crime victims by establishing numerous programs within their own countries. While it is impossible to do justice to each nation's programs in one chapter, an examination of various programs in New Zealand, Great Britain, the Netherlands, and Canada will be presented. The examination of the international programs provides a foundation to understanding how other countries view the importance of assisting their crime victims.

New Zealand

New Zealand developed the first national crime victims' compensation program in 1963. The **Criminal Injuries Compensation Act** was the first program in the Western world to provide compensation for victims of violent crimes. In 1974, this Act was incorporated into the Accident Compensation Insurance Act of 1972 (see Table 14.2), which mandated the state pay for all injury and rehabilitation expenses of crime victims, but prevented crime victims from suing offenders or getting compensation for noninjury-related losses. The compensation program was further revised in 1992 and now provides an "insurance-based scheme to rehabilitate and compensate, in an equitable and financially affordable manner, those persons who suffer personal injury" (Lee and Searle, 1993, 17). Crime victims are now treated the same as other accident victims. Anyone who is injured by an accident or crime victimization is covered by a national, **no-fault insurance plan**. All a person needs to do to receive compensation is to show that an injury, physical or mental, has occurred. The benefits paid by the program include a weekly allowance of $40 for

---

TABLE 14.2   Accident Compensation Insurance Act of 1972

1. Members of the police, prosecutors, judicial officers, counsel, officials, and other persons dealing with victims should treat them with courtesy, compassion, and respect for their personal dignity and privacy.

2. Victims and their families should have access to welfare, health, counseling, medical, and legal assistance that is responsive to their needs.

3a. Members of the police, officers of the court, and health and social services personnel should inform victims at the earliest practicable opportunity of the services and remedies available to them.

b. Victims should be told of available protection against unlawful intimidation.

4. The prosecuting authority or officers of the court, as the case may require, should make available to the victim information about the progress of the investigation, the charges laid or the reasons for not laying charges, the role of the victim as a witness in the prosecution, the date and place of the hearing of the proceedings, and the outcome of the proceedings, including any proceedings on appeal.

5. Law enforcement agencies and the court should return the property to its person (other than the defendant) if it is held for evidentiary purposes as promptly as possible in effort to minimize inconvenience to that person.

6a. Appropriate administrative arrangements should be made to ensure that a sentencing judge is informed about any physical or emotional harm, or any loss of or damage to property suffered by the victim through or by means of the offense, and any other effects of the offense on the victim.

b. Any such information should be conveyed to the judge either by the prosecutor orally or by means of a written statement about the victim.

7. A victim's residential address should not be disclosed in court unless excluding it would be contraryto the interests of justice.

8. On an application for bail, in respect of a charge of sexual violation or other serious assault or injury, the prosecutor should convey to the judicial officer any fears held by the victim about the release on bail of the alleged offender.

9a. The victim of an offense of sexual violation, or other serious assault or injury, should be given the opportunity to request notification of the offender's impending release or escape from penal custody.

b. When the victim makes such a request, then so long as the victim has supplied a current address and telephone number to the Secretary of Justice, the victim should be promptly notified of the offender's impending release, or escape, from penal custody.

Source: Based on Lee and Searle (1993, 2–4).

unemployed individuals and 80 percent of earnings for individuals employed at the time of the injury. All medical costs and rehabilitation services are also covered. Finally, benefits for fatal claims include surviving spouse compensation, compensation for children younger than 18 years old, a survivor's grant, and a funeral grant (Miller, 1996). Additional legislation in New Zealand has provided crime victims with extensive services. In 1982, the Domestic Protection Act was passed in an effort to provide protection to victims of family violence. This Act provides for a woman's right to get a protection order and to be protected from further abuse (Crime Prevention Action Group, 1992). The most significant legislation in New Zealand for crime victims' rights was the Victims of Offenses Act passed in 1987 (Cozens, 1994). This Act incorporated the principles laid down in the 1985 United Nations declaration of rights of crime victims. The Act set out nine principles, listed in Table 14.2.

Additionally, the Act also established the Victims Task Force for a period of 5 years. The Task Force was charged with studying the problems faced by crime victims and suggesting remedies. The result of the Task Force's work was to provide tremendous support for crime victims' rights by identifying problems with existing victims' services. One of the major initiatives of the Task Force was to provide funding to the many victims' support groups that were formed during this time. Currently, there are more than 70 victims' support groups providing services to crime victims seven days a week, 24 hours a day (Taylor, 1994). Another result of the Task Force's reports was to establish a Victims' Court Assistance project in 1993 to improve services to victims within the court system. This was similar to the American victim-witness assistance programs located in district attorneys' offices. The project's characteristics include:

- Focus on assisting victims in general, rather than witnesses.
- Emphasis on the provision of information and assisting the participation of victims involved in cases prosecuted in the criminal courts, rather than counseling or long-term support.
- Paid staff rather than volunteers.
- Victims' Court Assistants located in the courts.
- A government initiative funded by the Department of Justice, rather than a voluntary agency (Cozens, 1994).

Then in 1989, the Children, Young Persons, and Their Families Act was passed. This law provides for the needs of victims to be included when dealing with juvenile offenders. Crime victims become part of the proceeding by participating in family group conferences. Based upon the restorative justice principles (see Chapter 6), the conferences are used as a diversion program for juveniles where they, their families, social workers, court officers, and the crime victims work out what needs to be done with the juveniles to assure restoration of the crime victims and prevention of future criminal behavior by the juveniles (Brown, 1994). This active participation provides crime victims with a greater chance of being part of the justice process.

In 2002, New Zealand rewrote their laws with the enactment of the Victims Rights Act of 2002. This revision took the principles established in 1997 and made the granting of victims' rights mandatory upon governmental officials. Unlike most countries, governmental officials in New Zealand can be held accountable for failing to ensure crime victims' rights. http://www.victimsupport.org.nz/knowyourrights.htm

The rights established within the Victims Rights Act of 2002 are as follows:

Victims who have suffered any sort of harm (whether physical, emotional, or financial) as a result of an offense should be treated with courtesy and compassion and have their dignity and privacy respected. They should also receive help with meeting any of their welfare, health, counseling, medical, or legal needs which have resulted from their victimization.

Victims who have suffered physical injury or loss of or damage to property and parents or legal guardians of children who are victims are entitled to receive prompt information about the services and remedies that are available. This can include information such as:

- Medical treatment available.
- Financial or other assistance provided by the agency concerned.
- Any legal protection that may be available, for example, under the 1995 Domestic Violence Act or the 1997 Harassment Act.
- Referral to other support agencies.

The progress of any investigation including:

- Any charges laid or reasons for not laying charges.
- How the accused/offender will be dealt with.

Any court proceedings such as:

- The date and place of all court appearances, hearings, and any appeals.
- Any bail conditions that have been set.
- The victim's role as a witness.
- The result of any court proceedings (http://www.victimsupport.org.nz/knowyourrights.htm).

Great Britain

In 1964, Great Britain became the second country to establish a national scheme for compensating victims of violent crimes. While not originally established by statute, the program offered compensation to people of any nationality who were victims of violent crimes or who were injured trying to prevent one. The compensation program was incorporated into a statute under the provisions of the Criminal Justice Act of 1988 and was considered one of the most generous programs in Europe (Maguire and Shapland, 1991). In 1994, Great Britain, in an effort to save money, changed its compensation scheme to a tariff scheme. Under the tariff scheme, individuals would receive a lump sum payment based upon the physical injury incurred. The amount of payment ranged from a minimum of £1,000 (approximately $2,000) for minor injuries, such as a broken nose, to £250,000 (approximately $500,000) for injuries which resulted in complete paralysis (Crime Injuries Compensation Authority, 1994). The plan was very controversial, with victims' groups claiming that many crime victims would receive little or no compensation, and that crime victims such as children of sexual abuse would be awarded less than adults who had a tooth broken during an assault (Victim Support, 1994b).

Currently, Great Britain has an extensive and a very generous compensation program. Great Britain (including England, Scotland, and Wales) has a crime victim compensation program to provide financial compensation for victims of violent crime. Northern Ireland has a separate compensation program. The maximum award in Great Britain is £500,000 ($1,000,000). The minimum award is £1,000 ($2,000). If a death results from a crime, compensation for the suffering of a close relative may be paid. In Northern Ireland, each qualifying claimant is eligible for a bereavement support payment of £12,000 ($24,000).

The following is a list of the compensational costs victims and their survivors can request:

- Pain and suffering
- Lost wages for disabled victims
- Medical expenses (if unavailable via National Health Service or other sources)
- Mental health expenses (if unavailable via National Health Service or other sources)
- Reasonable funeral expenses
- Damage to property or equipment relied upon as a physical aid
- Provision of special equipment to aid mobility
- Adaptations to accommodation
- Travel expenses
- Rehabilitation for disabled victims (if unavailable via National Health Service or other sources)
- Bereavement
- Lost financial support for dependents of homicide victims
- Loss of parental services for qualifying claimants under 18 years of age. (U.S. Department of Justice (2007) *Directory of International Crime Victim Compensation Programs 2004–2005*. Retrieved from http://www.ojp.usdoj.gov/ovc/publications/infores/intdir2005/greatbritain.html)

Another important development for crime victims in Great Britain was the birth of the **Victim Support** organization in 1974. A single Victim Support program was set up by a committee of criminal justice and social work professionals to help victims of crime deal with the emotional and practical problems created by their victimization. The program received referrals from the police, and volunteers visited crime victims to find out what difficulties they were having due to victimization (Victim Support, 1994a). The number of programs grew to around 30 over the next five years. These programs were staffed by volunteers and funded by charitable donations.

In 1979, the programs banded together to form the National Association of Victims Support Schemes (now known as Victim Support). Over the years, Victim Support continued to grow and is now staffed with full-time employees funded by the government. In 1993, Victim Support had a budget of more than £8 million (approximately $12.4 million), used almost 12,000 volunteers, had more than 700 full-time staff, and served more than one million people. Victim Support also established a witness service to provide emotional support and information for people before, during, and after trial. The continuing legacy of Victim Support has been a campaign for greater crime victims' rights and participation in the criminal justice system in Great Britain. Proposals are in place to ensure crime victims are kept informed at every stage of the criminal justice process (Victim Support, 1994a).

Great Britain also supports national crime-prevention efforts. Crime prevention has been part of a general criminal justice policy since the 1960s. In the 1980s, a national office, the **Crime-Prevention Unit**, was established within the Home Office to coordinate state policy and crime-prevention programs and research. In 1988, the Unit developed the Safer Cities Program, which targeted 20 cities with funding and technical assistance in an effort to reduce high crime rates (Waller, 2003). Efforts on providing compensation, victim services, and crime prevention have tremendous support from the British government.

The Netherlands

In 1976, the Netherlands established a fund called the **Damage Fund for Violent Crimes** that provided state compensation to victims of serious violent crimes who suffered severe bodily injuries. Any victims of serious, violent crimes whose offenders could not afford to pay reparation could make a claim with the state. However, information concerning the fund was not widely known and the percentage of crime victims who received funds was small (Wemmers and Zeilstra, 1991).

Another policy that affected crime victims in the Netherlands was the passage of national guidelines for the treatment of victims by police and prosecutors in 1986. The initial guidelines were directed at victims of serious, violent crimes, but were later amended to include victims of all felonies. These guidelines established specific duties for both the police and the prosecution. The police were required to treat crime victims with consideration and respect, inform the victims of services available to them, refer the victims to local victim service schemes (rape crisis centers, domestic violence programs, etc.), give the victims a general description of what would happen with their cases, ask the victims if they wanted to be kept informed of the progress of their cases, and ask if they desired restitution from the offenders (Wemmers, 1996). If the victims requested further information or restitution, it was up to the police to provide those services.

Prosecutors received the cases from the police and were directed to continue to provide services to crime victims. The guidelines provided the victims of serious crimes to speak directly to the prosecutors and to be informed of the progress of their cases. Prosecutors also considered the wishes of the crime victims in each case and could only dismiss a case if the victim was satisfied that a reasonable effort to be compensated had been made. The guidelines for the police and prosecutors have been updated and expanded. Currently, both felonies and misdemeanors are covered, and both the police and prosecution are required to seek restitution from offenders at the earliest stages of the criminal justice process (Wemmers, 1996).

Compensation is also readily available in the Netherlands. Volunteers and staff of the Netherlands Victim Support Organization assist victims with submitting an application for compensation. On average, it takes about one year to close a case, but it might take longer for a crime victim to receive a decision on compensation. Victims receive compensation six weeks after notification. Benefits and awards are limited to €22,700 ($30,000) for material damage and €9,100 ($11,800) for immaterial damage (not for dependents of deceased victims).

One of the major efforts in the Netherlands to help crime victims is the importance placed upon crime prevention. In 1985, the Dutch Government launched a five-year crime-prevention program as a way to combat a rising crime rate. The program set up an organizational network to initiate and evaluate crime-prevention programs and to dispense information on effective crime-prevention methods. More than fifty projects were funded, and evaluation of the project concluded that crime prevention can be very effective under certain conditions (de Waard, 1993). In response to these findings, the **Directorate for Crime Prevention** (Directie Criminaliteitspreventie) was established in 1990, located in the Ministry of Justice. The Directorate is as important as the director of prisons or prosecutors. Additionally, more than 50 city halls have crime-prevention coordinators who work with the police and the prosecutor's office, as well as the city, to coordinate crime-prevention efforts (Waller, 1991).

Canada

Canada has had a very active victims' rights movement which has helped to establish numerous statutes supporting crime victims' rights. In Canada, over the last 30 years, victims' organizations have convinced various local governments as well as the federal government that the role of the victim is an important one that should be recognized. Changes with regard to the *Criminal Code* and victims' rights legislation is a direct result of the activism of the victims' organizations.

Their influence is not limited to ensuring that victims have their rights respected throughout the process, but as well with regard to legislation that will prevent future victims. While no one wants to return to the days when victims were judges, juries, and executioners, victims do want their role in the system recognized. They want their voices heard and opinions considered. They want the system and its players to recognize that they are important, and that they do have a stake in the outcome of the case.

Canada's long history of providing programs and services for crime victims (see Table 14.3). Starting in the late 1960s and early 1970s, Canada allowed the use of victim impact statements and provided for restitution as a sentencing option. Throughout the 1970s, programs sprang up on the local and provincial levels. In 1972, British Columbia established the Criminal Injury Board of B.C. to handle compensation claims. By the mid-1970s, compensation programs were spreading nationwide. Programs for victim assistance were also being established on the local level, including police-based programs and victim–offender reconciliation programs (Carter, 1995).

The 1980s was the decade of tremendous advancement in crime victims' programs. In the early 1980s, the government established a policy favoring crime victims' rights (Ismaili, 1992). The movement was led by the establishment of the Federal/Provincial Task Force on Justice for Victims of Crime in 1981. As a result of the Task Force's work, many crime victims' initiatives were begun. Victim assistance programs were being established with federal funds in local police departments. In 1985, Canada accepted the United Nation's Justice for Victims of Crime Act. By the end of the 1980s, Canada had in place victim assistance programs in the courts as well as police agencies, laws protecting children in sexual abuse cases, and widespread use of victim impact statements (Carter, 1995).

Greater access and input into the criminal justice system came to the forefront in the 1990s. Provisions allowing for crime victims' input into parole hearings and access to information regarding the custody status of offenders were put in place. By the mid-1990s, the Victims of Crime Act was passed, allowing victims the right to information about their cases from the investigation stage to the conviction stage. In the new millennium, Canada established a federal office for victims of crime, adopted the basic statement of principles for victims of crime, and developed a national association for victim assistance.

In Canada, crime victim compensation of violent or personal crimes is administered by the provinces, according to their own rules and standards. The following is a list of compensational costs:

- Medical expenses
- Mental health expenses
- Lost wages for incapacitated or disabled victims
- Lost support for dependents of victims
- Funeral expenses
- Rehabilitation for disabled victims
- Services to replace work in the home previously performed by the victim (http://www.ojp. usdoj.gov/ovc/publications/infores/intdir2005/canada.html)

Crime prevention has also been a high priority in Canada. Programs such as Neighborhood Watch and Crime Stoppers have become part of the social fabric. Schools have also been the focus of crime-prevention efforts. D.A.R.E. programs can be found throughout Canada; and in combination with a greater community policing effort, there is an active partnership between the community and the criminal justice system to eliminate crime. Canada has also developed a national strategy to deal with drug abuse, alcohol abuse, and domestic violence. At the regional level, many provinces have developed strong crime-prevention networks combining efforts of the community with resources of the government and its criminal justice system to combat crime problems today and into the future (Waller, 2003).

THE CRIME VICTIMS' MOVEMENT AND THE NEW MILLENNIUM

Where does the crime victims' movement go next? The rebirth of the crime victim, as a central figure in the criminal justice system and as a force in the political process, began in the 1950s with Margery Fry's call for the compensation of crime victims by the government (Schafer, 1970). During the 1960s and 1970s the crime victims' movement went from infancy to adolescence as new laws and programs were developed. In the 1980s and into the 1990s, the crime victims' movement flexed its muscles and became a fixture in the world's social fabric. As we progress through the new millennium, the crime victim's role in the criminal justice system is being solidified and strengthened not only in the United States, but throughout the world. A true "Golden Age" for crime victims may be at hand as the crime victims' movement matures and takes its rightful place in society.

The history of the crime victims' movement has been well documented (Elias, 1986; Kelly, 1990; Roberts, 1990; Jerin, 2004). As we have seen over the last 40 years, the crime victims' movement has progressed from conception to adulthood. The call of support for crime victims has moved from a few activists to an international priority. Victims have gone from the outside looking in at the operations of the criminal justice system to partners in society's attempt to achieve justice. Crime victims' voices are no longer cries in the wilderness, but have become a political force all over the world. With all of these advances, what else is there for the crime victims' movement to achieve? Plenty!

In looking forward, the crime victims' movement needs to look back to recognize there are many avenues for crime victims to still walk down in order to improve their current condition or to find new beginnings. The crime victims' movement has been affected by many different concerns over the past 40 years. The initial movement started as a reaction to the first victimization surveys, which uncovered the true extent of the amount of crime occurring, the harm it was creating, and the grass-roots concerns for disadvantaged groups. The male domination of the criminal justice system isolated women from gaining recognition for their victimization. Small groups of crime victims, concerned over specific issues, began to join together to provide for each other when no one else would. As an initial response to the new victimization information and a need for programs, grass-roots organizations started the crime victims' movement. The development of victim assistance programs, rape crisis centers, and battered women's shelters characterized this initial phase.

The next phase was the politicalization of the crime victim. During this phase, starting in the late 1960s and continuing into the 1990s, the crime victims' movement became synonymous with a governmental movement to get tough on crime. While victim advocates fought for more programs and services for crime victims, only small steps were taken on behalf of crime victims. In 1968, law and order became the political slogan of the day. In the 1970s, the Law Enforcement Assistance Administration (LEAA) provided millions of dollars to improve the effectiveness of police and other criminal justice operations with only token attention given to crime victims' programs (Elias, 1986). Most of the government funding during this time period was devoted to providing better equipment for law enforcement agencies. There was an initial amount of funds provided by the government for programs to encourage greater victim cooperation with the criminal justice system. Additionally, during this era, a conservative shift in corrections policies focused on increasing prison sentences and the resumption of the death penalty.

In the 1980s and into the 1990s, the victims' movement demanded more participation and rights within the criminal justice system and respect from criminal justice system personnel. It also demanded that issues affecting women, such as domestic violence and sexual assault, regain the importance they had when the crime victims' movement began. In many ways, the movement over the 1980s and 1990s made its greatest strides by having the government recognize that victims have issues that need to be included, instead of being used by the criminal justice system. The crime victims' movement has achieved a level of political power and respectability which was demonstrated by the fact that both candidates in the presidential election in 1996 supported the passage of a federal constitutional amendment guaranteeing crime victims' equal rights in the criminal justice system (Clinton urges Amendment, 1996).

The new millennium has provided some great challenges to the crime victims' movement. The horror of September 11, 2001, and the aftermath of major natural disasters have had a profound effect on the victims' movement. To hypothesize about the future, it is necessary to examine three areas which will impact crime victims: legislative initiatives, victim services, and criminal justice system policies.

LEGISLATIVE INITIATIVES

In the past 25 years, thousands of pieces of legislation affecting crime victims have become law (Office for Victims of Crime, 2006). Victims' compensation, victim's rights, and victim assistance programs are now available to almost all crime victims if they choose. Additionally, more than 20 states have amended their state constitutions to provide crime victims' rights (National Organization for Victim Assistance, 1995a). The next logical step in this process is to continue to build upon the legislation currently on the books and to expand the crime victims' rights now available. One area of increased legislation is to make more criminal offenses federal offenses. Changes in federal laws to allow for federal prosecution of carjackers and for women to sue in federal court under the Federal Violence Against Women Act, are just the start of nationalizing crime victims' concerns. The major effort will be to incorporate victims' rights into state and federal constitutional guarantees. With many states currently providing constitutional rights to crime victims, more are sure to follow. There have been bills in both houses of Congress which provide for a crime victims' rights constitutional amendment. This legislation has both bipartisan support and the support of the President of the United States; however, it has yet to be voted out of the Congress for the states to act upon.

Once legislation is approved, the courts have to agree that the new legislation does not violate any existing rights. Courts in recent years have shown a willingness to allow greater participation for crime victims, and this trend should continue (National Organization for Victim Assistance, 1990). Victim impact statements, use of restitution, and victim participation are now well entrenched in the criminal justice system. One area the courts will continue to evaluate is deciding what remedies will be available to crime victims if there is a failure to enforce their rights. The issue of liability of criminal justice personnel for failure to protect (Jerin, 1988a) or to provide specifically requested services, will come to the forefront in the near future. As more rights are granted to crime victims, remedies must be provided within the legal system to enforce those rights. Crime victims' litigation against the criminal justice system and its personnel should become more commonplace until the system adjusts to a new crime victims' orientation, instead of the self-serving orientation it has now.

The expansion of punitive sanctions is another area of debate. A tremendous amount of legislation mandating longer sentences, enacting the death penalty, and calling for changes in the jury system has been enacted in recent years. Many victims' rights supporters are not in favor of increasing sanctions and instead see more harm than good coming from these actions (Elias, 1993). Many victims' advocates recognize the presence of the cycle of violence and seek humane treatment for former victims and victims of unjust political and economic systems who have become offenders. The tremendous expense of being punitive will raise questions of its value to society, and efforts will be made to find cheaper and more effective methods of dealing with offenders. Courts are already questioning the viability of certain laws, such as three-strikes laws and mandatory minimum sentences for drug possession, which limits the discretion of the judiciary system. The more punitive a society becomes, the more it begins to lose its humanity. As cases of ruthless punishments become known, there is a chance of a societal backlash.

Another focus of legislation will be a greater focus on juvenile victims and offenders (Snyder and Sickmund, 1999). Laws are already being enacted establishing curfews on juveniles in an effort to reduce their opportunity to commit crime. The amount of violence on juveniles by juveniles will receive increased legislative attention as the rates of juvenile crime continue to increase and their percentage of the population increases. Child welfare and child protective services will also receive closer scrutiny in an effort to prevent the revictimization of children. Holding parents accountable for the actions of their children is another trend which most likely will continue.

A moderation of drug laws and greater attention to crimes of violence will be the central focus of legislation if we are to better utilize space and resources. Additional legislation to place greater restrictions on the accessibility of handguns and assault weapons should also continue. The destructive powers of handguns and assault weapons far outweigh their legitimate uses. If this country is serious about reducing criminal violence, a proactive approach to limit the availability of guns is necessary. Many efforts have been made on the national and state levels to restrict access to certain weapons and to keep handguns out of the hands of juveniles, ex-convicts, and others (Office of Juvenile Justice and Delinquency Prevention, 1996).

Finally, legislation and research will continue to recognize the seriousness of the crimes of domestic violence and sexual assault (Wallace, 1996). Protecting the victims of these crimes should maintain a prominent place on the legislative agenda. With the passage of the Federal Violence Against Women Act, funding for research and programs for female crime victims has increased dramatically. This makes it easier for victims to prosecute these cases and harder for offenders to get away with committing these crimes and has already started with mandatory arrest laws for domestic violence and sexual predator registration laws. As women and those sympathetic to their victimization exercise their political power, additional legislation focusing on sexual harassment, stalking, and date rape will continue to be developed.

VICTIM SERVICES

Services for victims of crime are now offered by thousands of programs, run by tens of thousands of individuals (Office for Victims of Crime, 2006). The need for more programs run by highly trained and qualified individuals will continue. As the federal government pumps more money into victim assistance programs, the number of programs and services offered should continue to expand. These funds will also call for the continuous evaluation of current and new programs to establish a sense of what works and what does not. These evaluations are already occurring and should provide a solid foundation for enhancing the quality of victim assistance programs. Programs should be found in every component of the criminal justice system as well as on the community level. Having victim assistance programs in every law enforcement agency, district attorney's office, and parole or correctional agencies could occur within the near future. Victim studies should also provide valuable information concerning which services are meeting crime victims' needs and which are the needs not being met.

When crime victim programs were first developed, they were usually staffed by former victims (Dussich, 1986). Over the past few years there has been a movement toward professionalizing victim assistance personnel (National Organization for Victim Assistance, 2006). Providing minimum educational requirements, practical experience, and training are important goals for the future. Colleges are starting to recognize the need for these new professionals and are beginning to provide curriculums to meet this need. The multifaceted role the victim assistant must play requires someone skilled in social work, psychology, and criminal justice. The professionalism of the career will be a massive undertaking well into the next century. Continual training of victim assistants is currently available and its use will need to be expanded. Currently, there are a few established academic programs offering degrees in victimology or victim services. There is a movement in the victim's field to expand these academic offerings to provide educated practitioners to assist crime victims. The development and expansion of victim organizations on the local and national levels will provide a foundation for victim assistant professionals. The World Society of Victimology, the American Society of Victimology, and The National Organization for Victim Assistance have sought to provide valuable research and assistance to the victims' field. The exchange of information between victim assistant professionals and academics will assist in establishing a body of knowledge to advance the profession for years to come. The crime victim advocate or assistant should become an established professional within the social service system and the criminal justice system in the not-too-distant future.

Crime-prevention services will receive greater attention in the years ahead. As technology continues to advance, crime-prevention methods will also advance. A greater emphasis on crime prevention as a cost-effective way to reduce criminal victimization in communities will be viewed as a necessary victim service. Incorporating better crime-prevention tools and techniques into everyday environments will become the norm. Teaching children and adults how to prevent victimization will be a major service to all citizens which will reduce the number of future crime victims. As international programs have recognized the benefits gained from preventing crime, so too is the United States beginning to do so. The 1994 Crime Bill set aside a substantial amount of funds for crime-prevention research, and the prominence of the National Crime Prevention Council should enhance the position of crime prevention in criminal justice policy decisions.

CRIMINAL JUSTICE SYSTEM POLICIES

The treating of crime victims with dignity and respect by officials of the criminal justice system will hopefully be the standard in this new century. The criminal justice system needs to recognize a new partner in the criminal justice process: the crime victim. Providing for victims' justice within the criminal justice system should become standard operating procedure. Better training of all criminal justice personnel on victims' issues and treatment should allow for a better assimilation of crime victims into the criminal justice system. Legislation and policy guidelines should establish crime victims' place in the system, and experience with this policy will expand and improve the services offered through the criminal justice system. Crime victims' addition to the criminal justice system's operation should not be seen as a threat or as a dissolution of other participants' rights or responsibilities, but as a benefit to a more efficient and effective operation of each stage of the criminal justice system.

One of the greatest changes occurring is with law enforcement agencies. Currently, policies such as mandatory arrests restrict police officers on the one hand and encourage them to be more innovative on the other. More restrictions on how police deal with crime victims should occur as victims secure more rights versus the criminal justice system. Holding criminal justice system personnel responsible, especially the police, for their interactions with crime victims should become part of standing policies. Having a victim assistant as part of every law enforcement agency should become a reality. The recognition for many crime victims that law enforcement officers are the only criminal justice representatives they come into contact with places a large responsibility upon those agencies to provide as many services or referrals as necessary.

Law enforcement agencies need to become victim service information resources so that crime victims understand their rights and those programs which are available to them. Greater cooperation by law enforcement with victim services in the private sector will need to occur. Extensive training on crime victim issues will become a major component of every law enforcement academy at all levels. The initial academy program will be supplemented with continuous in-service training programs to assure that quality victim service is delivered. Law enforcement will continue to become more involved in proactive crime-prevention programs and services, as a way to reduce criminal victimization. Continuation and expansion of community policing efforts will provide the foundation for more effective police service. Having citizenry of the community as active participants in the law enforcement function should improve service delivery, communication, and satisfaction with the police.

The courts also will see an expansion of influence of crime victims in their operations. The inclusion of crime victims in court processes will continue and expand. The continuing expansion of private and public crime victims advocates will help demystify the courts and encourage crime victims to seek out greater justice. New laws are providing greater roles for crime victims in determining what should happen to their offenders. These laws are also restricting the power of judges and prosecutors to dismiss crime victims' concerns when deciding what to do with accused or convicted offenders. The use of new technologies will transform the courts to better fact-finding operations and protectorates of crime victims' rights. The first priority of the courts will be to provide services to crime victims to allow for greater participation in the outcome of cases. More training of court personnel and others who come into contact with crime victims will be necessary, and an expansion of crime victim services will occur within the courts. Prosecutors will work with victims so that agreements as to the resolution of cases can be achieved. Judges will be required to respond to crime victims' concerns regarding bail, protection from intimidation or further victimization, and appropriate sanctions. Greater efforts to include as many victims as possible in the operation of the judiciary system will take place this century. Additionally, victims will find the courts more receptive to their civil actions against offenders. Having the courts provide protection through restraining orders, recognizing the harm created by stalking, and allowing victims to seek civil redress in the courts will continue to benefit the crime victims.

Corrections will need to focus its efforts on preventing future criminality. Victims will play a part in determining what sanctions need to be administered with the goal of being restored themselves. A greater variety of sanctions will be examined in an effort to achieve justice for crime victims. Sanctions such as restitution, community service, and rehabilitation should become the focus in a crime victims' justice system. The efforts of corrections to deal with providing for input from crime victims will be a major concern. Allowing impact statements at all crucial stages of the sanctioning process will become standard procedure. All parts of the criminal justice system will be made more responsible and become more responsive to the needs of the crime victims.

Today it is hard to recognize the crime victims' movement compared to the one that began some 40 years ago. Forty years from now, it may be hard to recognize the crime victims' movement we have today because of the dramatic changes it continues to go through. The hope for the future of the crime victims' movement is best described by the theme of the 1995 Victim Rights Week—Victims Rights: Planting Seeds: Harvesting Justice (National Organization for Victim Assistance, 1995b). In 1980, the first elocution of crime victims' rights was enacted by the State of Wisconsin. From this seed, a crop of victims' rights and remedies are growing. In order to achieve the goals of the crime victims' movement, there are still principles and services that must be provided to all crime victims. Over a decade ago the National Organization for Victim Assistance articulated the needs of crime victims, and they still hold true today:

---

1. **Protections** for victims, witnesses, and communities such as:
   - Rights to privacy.
   - Effective enforcement of protection orders.
   - Safety and security in criminal justice process.
   - Establishment of safe havens and peace zones.
   - Special protections for highly vulnerable populations.
   - Violence prevention.

2. **Information, notification, and consultation** on case status, decision-making, and sanctions. Implementation of decisions:
   - These rights should be applied and implemented in all criminal justice proceedings, including those in juvenile, military, educational, and administrative systems.
   - Effective remedies should be available should rights fail to be enforced.

3. **Participation** through a voice—not a veto—by victims, witnesses, and communities. Participation is enhanced through:Effective public education.
   - Community policing, community prosecution, community courts, and community corrections.
   - Community problem-solving and violence prevention.
   - Effective representation in the criminal justice process.

4. **Reparations** to the injured involving:
   - Full restitution ordered to be paid by the offender to all identifiable victims.
   - Restitution to the community rendered through service or money.
   - Restorative compensation by the state to the victim.
   - Recoveries for damages in civil actions as a supplement or alternative to criminal restitution.

5. **Preservation** of property and employment through innovative practices such as:
   - Preserving rights of victims to stay in their homes and communities while evicting or exiling their offenders.
   - Education and employment services for victims who, because of the crime, cannot continue in their past careers.

(continued)

(Continued)

- Emergency financial aid and intercession with creditors and landlords.
- Prompt property return or replacement.

6. Due Process for victims and communities through:

- Ensuring rights to the victim parallel to those of the accused in the criminal justice processes, as well as in juvenile, military, educational, and administrative proceedings.
- Returning justice to its community origins. Federal and state law should continue to set the definitions and boundaries of criminal law and procedures, but communities should be given significant responsibility for enforcing and monitoring the laws.

7. Treatment of victims with **dignity** and **compassion**, throughout the nation and the world, by:

- Training and education for criminal justice professionals in all aspects of victim issues and victim rights.
- Adequately funded victim assistance programs in every jurisdiction so that victims are never more than a telephone call away from help.
- Increasing public understanding of the impact of victimization and appropriate responses through educational curricula, as well as mandatory continuing education courses for lawyers, public safety officers, health and mental health professionals, the clergy, and others who respond to victims.
- Establishing ethics and standards for fair treatment of victims by the media.
- Eliciting responsibility and remorse from offenders and educating offenders on the impact of crime on its victims.
- Appropriately responding to needs and concerns of diverse population groups.
- Preventing future violence.

SOURCE: National Organization for Victim Assistance (1995a, 1–2).

On October 30, 2004, the most far-reaching victim rights bill ever considered by the U.S. Congress was signed into law. This new legislation is seen as breaking new ground in two significant ways. First, it establishes the most powerful enforcement mechanisms ever found in a federal victims' bill of rights. Second, it authorizes funding to help implement the law, including support of free legal clinics for victims. The bill includes the right to be reasonably protected, notified, present, and heard during proceedings; the rights to confer with the prosecutor, to restitution, and to proceedings free from unreasonable delay; and the right to be treated with fairness and respect.

The enactment of such a major reform in the treatment of victims was accomplished under conditions of rare consensus. This bill was first adopted by unanimous consent without debate by both houses. Then President Bush signed it, without fanfare, during the last stages of his re-election campaign. These were acts of near unanimous support across both parties and branches of government (National Victims' Constitutional Amendment Project, 2007).

CONCLUSION

A true "Golden Age" of crime victims may be closer at hand than at any other time in the history of mankind. However, with the amount of criminal victimization and the continuing violations of human rights that take place throughout the United States and the world, it may be hard to believe. The crime victims' movement is here to stay and will play an increasingly important role in making governments accountable to their citizens. Cesare Beccaria (1764) once described the role of government as having a social contract with its people. People would give up a small portion of their rights to be governed in exchange for peace and safety. The crime victims of the world are asking that the contract be enforced.

Restorative justice programs are providing crime victims a greater voice and control in the outcome of their victimization. The use of restorative justice principles has permeated justice systems from Australia and New Zealand to the United States and Canada. Crime victims and victims of other horrific acts are demanding more from their governments, and slowly, governments are responding. Crime victims have never sought to take away the rights of the accused; they simply want rights of their own. Crime victims want the state to take their needs and wants into consideration.

Being a victim of crime is a fear that everyone has at some point in their lifetime. The goal of the crime victims' movement has been to minimize the effects of victimization and help people get on with their lives and to allow crime victims to become crime *survivors* (Office for Victims of Crime, 2001). The government has started to accept more responsibility for making sure crime victims do not get revictimized by their encounter with the criminal justice system, but there is still a long way to go. As a prominent Victimologist has stated; "the greatest service a government can provide to a potential crime victim is to prevent the crime from occurring" (Waller, 1994, 2). While this goal may be unobtainable in totality, every governmental agency should have this as its primary objective. The importance of preventing victimizations and responding to the needs of those who do become victims can never be underestimated. The closer societies come to fully meeting the needs of victims of crime, the better it will be for all citizens of the world.

Study Questions

1. What is the importance of the United Nations Declaration of Basic Principles and how do the Basic Principles set the foundation for victims' rights in foreign countries?
2. What additional victims' rights or services do you feel international crime victims need to be provided with?
3. What rights do victims have in international countries that victims in the United States don't have? What can the United States learn from other foreign victims' service programs?
4. What do you see as the future of victims' rights, services, and programs in the United States?

Key Terms

- child sex trade 263
- crime-prevention unit 269
- debt bondage 263
- Directorate for Crime Prevention 270
- genocide 261
- human trafficking 261
- International Criminal Court 264
- involuntary servitude 263
- no-fault insurance plan 265
- peonage 263
- Rome Statute of the International Criminal Court 264
- sex trafficking 263
- slavery 263
- The Criminal Injuries 270
- The Damage Fund for Violent Crimes 269
- United Nations 261
- victim support 268

Chronology of the Crime Victim's Movement

To better understand the changes and important events in the crime victims' movement in the United States since the 1960s, one needs to examine the chronology of the crime victims' movement. The highlights over the last 40-plus years include the following:

1965	California establishes the first victims' compensation program.
	The first national victims' survey is conducted.
	Congress passes the Civil Rights Act, Title VII, forbidding discrimination on the basis of sex, race, national origin, and age, which becomes the foundation for sexual harassment laws.
1968	The Law Enforcement Assistance Administration (LEAA) is established.
1969	New York City establishes the Mayor's Task Force on Child Abuse and Neglect.
1972	First victim assistance programs are created. They are:
	Aid for Victims of Crime, St. Louis, Missouri.
	Bay Area Women Against Rape, San Francisco, California.
	D.C. Rape Crisis Center, Washington, D.C.
1973	First Victim Impact Statement is created by Fresno County, California.
1974	First victim/witness programs are created with funding from the federal Law Enforcement Assistance Administration (LEAA):
	In District Attorneys' offices in Brooklyn, New York, and Milwaukee, Wisconsin.
	First law enforcement–based, victim assistance programs are established in Fort Lauderdale, Florida, and Indianapolis, Indiana.
	Child Abuse Prevention and Treatment Act establishes a National Center on Child Abuse and Neglect within the federal government.
	Families and Friends of Missing Persons and Violent Crime Victims are established as the first support organizations for victims and survivors of violent crimes.
1975	First "Victim Rights Week" is organized by Philadelphia District Attorney.
1976	National Organization for Victim Assistance (NOVA) is established.
1977	First legislation mandating arrest in domestic violence cases is enacted in Oregon.
1978	National Coalition Against Sexual Assault (NCASA) is formed.
	National Coalition Against Domestic Violence (NCADV) is set up.
	Parents of Murdered Children (POMC), a self-help support group, is founded in Cincinnati, Ohio.
1980	First Bill of Rights for Crime Victims is enacted in Wisconsin.
	First National Victim Rights Week is organized by NOVA.
	Mothers Against Drunk Driving (MADD) is founded.
	National Crime Prevention Council is established.

(*continued*)

(continued)

1981   First nationally commemorated National Victim Rights Week is proclaimed by President Ronald Reagan.

A special task force to consider victim issues is recommended by the Attorney General's Force on Violent Crime.

A national public awareness campaign on child abduction is launched after the disappearance of young Adam Walsh, later declared a murder victim.

1982   Task Force on Victims of Crime is appointed by President Reagan.

Victim and Witness Protection Act is passed.

First Victim Impact Panel is organized by MADD in Rutland. Massachusetts, to get convicted drunk drivers to hear from victims of other drunk-driving crashes.

Missing Children Act insures that identifying information on a missing child is promptly entered into the FBI National Crime Information Center (NCIC) computer.

California "Victim Bill of Rights" initiative is overwhelmingly adopted by voters to provide a constitutional guarantee of restitution and other statutory reforms.

1983   International Association of Chiefs of Police's new Crime Victim's Bill of Rights stresses the needs of crime victims for law enforcement officers around the country.

First National Missing Children's Day is proclaimed by President Reagan in observance of a missing child, Etan Patz.

1984   The Victims of Crime Act (VOCA) is enacted to provide federal compensation to federal crime victims and subsidies for state victim compensation and local national service programs.

The National Center for Missing and Exploited Children is created, with a Congressional mandate in the Missing Children Assistance Act.

1985   International Declaration on the Rights of Victims of Crime and the Abuse of Power is passed by the United Nations General Assembly.

The National Victim Center (NVC) is founded.

1986   Victims are given the right to restitution, to submit victim impact statements, and to be treated with dignity and respect by Rhode Island's new constitution.

1987   Victims' Constitutional Amendment Network (Victims' CAN) is established.

1988   The Federal Drunk Driving Prevention Act is passed, raising the legal drinking age to 21.

State compensation programs are influenced to cover victims of domestic violence and drunk driving by amendments to the Victims of Crime Act.

1990   Victims' Rights and Restitution Act of 1990 is passed.

The Victims of Child Abuse Act is passed.

The Student Right-to-Know and Campus Security Act, known as the Cleary Act, is passed.

1991   First International Conference on Campus Rape is held in Orlando, FL.

California State University, Fresno, approves the first bachelor's degree program in victimology.

International Parental Child Kidnapping Act makes the act of unlawfully removing a child outside the United States a federal felony.

Victim impact evidence at a capital sentencing hearing is deemed constitutional in *Payne v. Tennessee.*

First Congressional Joint Resolution to place victim rights in the U.S. Constitution is introduced by Representative Ileana Ros-Lehtinen (R-FL).

1992   Spending cap and sunset sections are lifted from the Victims of Crime Act.

1993   Maine is the last state to enact a crime-victim compensation program. The law goes into effect on June 1993.

(continued)

(*continued*)

	The Brady Bill, requiring a waiting period to purchase handguns, is signed by President Clinton.

The World Trade Center in New York City is bombed, killing 6 and injuring over 1,000.

1994 The Violent Crime Control and Law Enforcement Act is passed.

Megan's Law is passed.

The National Crime Survey (NCS) is renamed the National Crime Victimization Survey (NCVS).

1995 The Alfred P. Murrah Federal Building in Oklahoma City is bombed, killing over 168 people and injuring over 500.

1996 The first version of a Victims' Bill of Rights Constitutional Amendment is introduced into Congress by Senators Feinstein and Kyl.

The Interstate Stalking Punishment Act of 1996 is passed.

The Antiterrorism and Effective Death Penalty Act amends the Foreign Sovereign Immunities Act.

The Mandatory Victim's Restitution Act of 1996 is passed.

The Gun Control Act of 1968 is amended. The amendment bans gun ownership by any person ever convicted of a domestic violence charge on the federal level.

1997 Passage of the Victim Rights Clarification Act of 1997 (VRCA) is enacted.

Congress enacts a federal antistalking law.

1998 Office for Victims of Crime publishes *New Directions From the Field: Victims' Rights and Services for the 21st Century.*

1999 Oregon passes a constitutional amendment that guarantees victims' rights, becoming the 32nd state to do so.

The proposed U.S. crime victims' constitutional amendment is shelved.

2000 National Violence Against Women Survey (NVAW) is published.

Victims of Trafficking and Violence Protection Act of 2000 is passed.

The Violence Against Women Act of 2000 is signed into law by President Clinton.

In *United States v. Morrison et al.,* the U.S. Supreme Court rules unconstitutional a section of the Violence Against Women Act that provided for a civil remedy in federal court for victims of gender-motivated violence.

2001 International terrorists hijack four airplanes and destroy the World Trade Center in New York City, damage the Pentagon in Washington, D.C., and crash into a field in Pennsylvania. Over 3,000 individuals are killed and thousands more are injured.

The Uniting and Strengthening America by Providing Appropriate Tools Required to Intercept and Obstruct Terrorism (USA PATRIOT) Act of 2001 is established.

The Victims of Crime Act of 1984 is amended to reallocate funds between compensation and victim assistance and to establish an emergency reserve antiterrorist fund.

Congress passes the September 11 Compensation Fund of 2001.

Congress passes the Child Abuse and Enforcement Act.

2002 The National Association of VOCA Assistance Administrators (NAVAA) is created.

Corporate reform law Sarbanes-Oxley goes into effect on July 30, 2002.

All 50 states, the District of Columbia, the U.S. Virgin Islands, Puerto Rico, and Guam established crime victim compensation programs.

2003 Congress passes the PROTECT Act of 2003, also known as the "**Amber Alert**" law.

The Office on Violence Against Women becomes a permanent independent office within the U.S. Department of Justice.

The American Society of Victimology (ASV) is established.

(*continued*)

(*continued*)

	Congress passes the Fair and Accurate Credit Transaction Act, providing new protections against identity theft.
	Congress passes enhanced identity theft legislation.
2004	Congress passes the Justice for All Act of 2004, providing substantive federal rights for crime victims and mechanisms to enforce them.
2005	Congress establishes the first ever Victims' Rights Caucus to elevate crime victim issues in Congress.
	The International Organization for Victim Assistance (IOVA) is formed.
2006	President Bush signs the Adam Walsh Child Safety and Protection Act of 2006, establishing a comprehensive federal DNA database of material collected from convicted molesters.
	Trafficking Victims Protection Reauthorization Act is signed into law.
2007	September 25, 2007, will mark the first National Day of Remembrance for Murder Victims.

Source: Dussich, 1986; National Organization for Victim Assistance, 1990, 1993, 1995a; Moriarty, 2003; Jerin, 2004; Doerner and Lab, 2006; National Center for Victims of Crime, (2007).

Appendix B

Sample Application for Crime Victim Compensation

I. Victim Information

Victim's name _____ Female _____ Male _____

Mailing address _____ Home telephone (_____) _____

City/State _____ Zip _____ Work telephone (_____)

Date of birth _____ Age at time of incident _____ SSN _____-_____-_____

II. Applicant Information (If victim is applicant, write "same"; if under 18, application must be completed by parent or guardian)

Applicant's name _____ Female _____ Male _____

Mailing address _____ Home telephone (_____)_____

City/State _____ Zip _____ Work telephone (_____) _____

Date of birth _____ Relationship to victim _____ SSN _____-_____-_____

If filing on behalf of minor dependent(s) of homicide victim, relationship to minor dependent(s)_____

III. Crime Information

Type of Crime:

☐ armed robbery ☐ arson ☐ assault ☐ child physical or sexual assault

☐ domestic violence ☐ drunk driving ☐ other vehicular crimes ☐ homicide

☐ kidnapping ☐ sexual assault ☐ stalking ☐ other _____

Exact location of crime _____

City/State _____

Date of crime _____ Date crime reported _____

(If NOT reported within 5 days, please explain why in attached statement)

Name of Police Department _____ Investigating Officer _____

Name(s) of person(s) who committed crime (if known) _____

If you have been assisted by a victim advocate in the court/district attorney's office, provide name and telephone number of advocate _____

Briefly describe the crime and any injuries which resulted _____

_____

_____

_____

_____

IV. Expenses (Check types of expenses for which you seek compensation):

☐ Medical services* ☐ lost wages (for victim only) ☐ counseling for victim*
☐ Medical supplies/pharmacy* ☐ loss of financial support ☐ counseling for family members
☐ Dental services* (for dependents of homicide victims) of homicide victim*
☐ Homemaker expenses* ☐ funeral/burial* ☐ counseling for children who witness
violence against a family member*
*attach copies of bills and/or receipts

Name and address of Funeral Home:_____

V. Lost Income (complete if seeking lost wages or loss of support)

Victim's employer _____ Contact person _____ Telephone _____
Address_____ City/State _____ Zip_____
If victim has or will return to work, estimated period of disability _____
If requesting financial support for dependent(s) of a homicide victim, provide the following
information:

Name(s) of dependent(s), Date of birth, SSN, Relationship to victim

_____

_____

VI. Other Sources of Financial Assistance (Check all potential sources of full or partial
payment of expenses):

☐ health insurance ☐ hospital-based "free care" ☐ workers compensation
☐ life/accident insurance ☐ unemployment benefits ☐ public benefits (welfare, medicare,
Medicaid, SSDI)
☐ automobile insurance ☐ disability benefits ☐ restitution
☐ other (please specify) _____
Names and addresses of applicable insurance companies: _____

_____

Have you filed or do you intend to file a civil lawsuit? Yes _____ No _____ Not Sure _____
If yes: Attorney's name _____ Telephone _____
Address _____ City/State _____ Zip _____

VII. Optional Information (For statistical purposes only)

Race/ethnicity of victim: ☐ White ☐ Black ☐ Hispanic ☐ Native American ☐ Asian/Pacific Islander ☐ Other ☐ I decline to answer this question

Who referred you to Victim Compensation? _____

Acknowledgment and Information Release

I understand that the Victim Compensation Fund is a fund of last resort. I agree to inform the Division of any funds I receive from any source for losses for which I have requested compensation, and agree to promptly reimburse the Commonwealth for any such funds awarded to me or on my behalf. I give permission to any hospital, medical facility, doctor, mental health provider, insurance company, employer, person or agency, including state and federal agencies, to give information to the Victim Compensation and Assistance Division. I understand that the information will be used to determine my claim for victim compensation benefits. I do not authorize the use or release of this information to any person or entity for any other purpose whatsoever. A photocopy of this signed release is as valid as the original. This authorization shall expire upon final determination of all requirements under G.L. c. 258C and 940 CMR 14.00. I certify, under the pains and penalties of perjury, that all information and supporting documentation contained in this application is true and accurate to the best of my knowledge and belief.

X _____ Date_____
Applicant signature (parent or guardian if victim is a minor)

(*Source:* Office of the Attorney General Tom Reilly (2006, 3–4).)

Appendix C

Restraining Order Application

| COMPLAINT FOR PROTECTION FROM ABUSE (G.L. c.209A) Page 1 of 2 | COURT USE ONLY – DOCKET NO. | TRIAL COURT OF MASSACHUSETTS |

| A | ☐ BOSTON MUNICIPAL COURT ☐ DISTRICT COURT ☐ PROBATE & FAMILY COURT ☐ SUPERIOR COURT | DIVISION |

B Name of Plaintiff (person seeking protection) | Name of Defendant (person accused of abuse)

Plaintiff's Address. DO NOT complete if the Plaintiff is asking the Court to keep it confidential. *See K. 4. below.*

C

Daytime Phone No. ( )
If the Plaintiff left a former residence to avoid abuse, write that address here:

G | Def. Date of Birth | Defendant's Alias, if any

Defendant's Address | Day Phone ( )

Sex: ☐ M ☐ F

Social Security # | Place of Birth

Defendant's Mother's Maiden Name (first & last)

Defendant's Father's Name (first & last)

D
I ☐ am over the age of eighteen.
I ☐ am under the age of eighteen, and _____
my_____(relationship to Plaintiff) has filed this complaint for me.
The Defendant ☐ is ☐ is not under the age of eighteen.

E
To my knowledge, the Defendant possesses the following guns, ammunition, firearms identification card, and/or license to carry:

H The Defendant and Plaintiff:
☐ are currently married to each other
☐ were formerly married to each other
☐ are not married but we are related to each other by blood or marriage; specifically, the Defendant is my
_____
☐ are the parents of one or more children
☐ are not related but live in the same household
☐ were formerly members of the same household
☐ are or were in a dating or engagement relationship.

F
Are there any prior or pending court actions in any state or country involving the Plaintiff and the Defendant for divorce, annulment, separate support, legal separation or abuse prevention? ☐ No ☐ Yes If Yes, give Court, type of case, date, and (if available) docket no.

I Does the Plaintiff have any children? ☐ No ☐ Yes If yes, the Plaintiff shall complete the appropriate parts of Page 2.

J
On or about (dates)_____ I suffered abuse when the Defendant:
☐ attempted to cause me physical harm   ☐ placed me in fear of imminent serious physical harm
☐ caused me physical harm   ☐ caused me to engage in sexual relations by force, threat of force or duress

THEREFORE, I ASK THE COURT TO ORDER:
☐ 1. the Defendant to stop abusing me by harming, threatening or attempting to harm me physically, or placing me in fear of imminent serious physical harm, or by using force, threat or duress to make me engage in sexual relations unwillingly.
☐ 2. the Defendant not to contact me, unless authorized to do so by the Court.
☐ 3. the Defendant to leave and remain away from my residence which is located at:
_____
If this is an apartment building or other multiple family dwelling, check here ☐
☐ 4. that my address be impounded to prevent its disclosure to the Defendant, the Defendant's attorney, or the public. *Attach Request for Address Impoundment form to this Complaint.*
☐ 5. the Defendant to leave and remain away from my workplace which is located at:
_____

K
☐ 6. the Defendant to pay me $_____ in compensation for the following losses suffered as a direct result of the abuse:
_____
You may not obtain an Order from the Boston Municipal Court or a District or Superior Court covering the following item 7 if there is a prior or pending Order for support from the Probate and Family Court.
☐ 7. the Defendant, who has a legal obligation to do so, to pay temporary support for me.
☐ 8. the relief requested on page two of this Complaint pertaining to my minor child or children.
☐ 9. the following:_____

☐ 10. the relief I have requested, except for temporary support for me and/or my child(ren) and for compensation for losses suffered, without advance notice to the Defendant because there is a substantial likelihood of immediate danger of abuse. I understand that if the Court issues such a temporary Order, the Court will schedule a hearing within 10 court business days to determine whether such a temporary Order should be continued, and I must appear in Court on that day if I wish the Order to be continued.

| DATE | PLAINTIFF'S SIGNATURE
X | Please complete affidavit on reverse of this page |

This is a request for a civil order to protect the Plaintiff from future abuse. The actions of the Defendant may also constitute a crime subject to criminal penalties. For information about filing a criminal complaint, you can talk with the District Attorney's Office for the location where the alleged abuse occurred.

FA 1 (9/95)

COURT COPY

Chronology of Terrorism Against the United States of America or Citizens of the United States

Date	Assassination Attempts and Murders
November 1, 1950	An assassination attempt is made on President Truman's life by Puerto Rican nationalists. White House police and Secret Service personnel thwart the attempt.
March 1, 1954	Members of Congress are fired upon by four Puerto Rican nationalists, wounding five representatives. All the terrorists are captured alive.
January 18, 1984	The President of American University in Beirut, Malcolm H. Kerr, is murdered by Islamic Jihad terrorists.
June 18, 1984	Controversial Jewish Denver talk show host Alen Berg is killed. The Order, a neo-Nazi white supremacist group, claims responsibility.
August–December, 1991	Islamic Jihad releases six American hostages held in Lebanon. The bodily remains of William Buckley and Colonel William R. Higgins are sent back to the United States.

Date	Radical Violent Groups
October, 1966	With Black Power on the rise in the United States, Huey Newton and Bobby Seale form the Black Panthers. The group has violent clashes with the police.
January 27, 1972	The Black Liberation Army, a new U.S. terrorist group, surfaces when two New York City police officers are murdered.
May 17, 1974	The Symbionese Liberation Army (SLA) safe house in Los Angeles is raided by police, killing one tourist and injuring more than 40.
August 3, 1977	One person is killed when FALN, a Puerto Rican separatist group, bombs two office buildings in New York.
May 26, 1979	Civil rights marchers are attacked by Ku Klux Klan (KKK) members in Decatur, Alabama, killing two civil rights workers and two Klansmen.
November 3, 1979	Five U.S. communists are killed in an attack by a KKK group in Greensboro, North Carolina.
October 20, 1981	Weather Underground fugitive Kathy Boudin is arrested and turned over to the FBI after two police officers and a security guard are killed in a botched car robbery attempt.
September 16, 1983	In West Hartford, Connecticut, a Wells Fargo armored car terminal is held up by Puerto Rican FALN separatists, netting them $7.2 million.

(continued)

(*continued*)

Date	Radical Violent Groups
December 31, 1983	Bombs are set off in New York City by FALN to attack police, FBI, and federal court facilities.
May 5, 1990	Members of Pablo Escobar's Medellin Cartel are arrested in Florida by FBI agents. The members were attempting to purchase high power missiles that could shoot down aircraft.
May 24, 1990	Two members of Earth First!, a radical environmental group, are injured by a car bomb. The police claim Earth First! was planning to use the bomb to disrupt logging procedures, but Earth First! says the bomb was planted. No charges are filed.
August 31, 1992	Randall Weaver, a white separatist charged with selling illegal guns, surrenders after a long siege in which Weaver's wife and son are killed. This event becomes the rallying cry for right-wing antigovernment extremists, when Weaver is eventually acquitted of most of the charges.
April 19, 1993	The Waco, Texas, Branch Davidian sect ends when its compound is taken over by federal agents and the main building explodes. Cult leader David Koresh and 73 others, including many children, die. Waco becomes another rallying call for the extreme right wing in America, who believe the FBI destroyed the building, not the Davidians.
August 15, 1995	$3.1 million is awarded to Randall Weaver for the wrongful death of his wife and son.
October 1, 1995	Ten Islamic fundamentalist terrorists are convicted of conspiracy to destroy public buildings and structures in the United States. This is one of the most important terrorist trials in U.S. history.
April, 1997	Larry Wayne Harris, a known white Supremacist and microbiologist, is sentenced to probation and community service for illegally obtaining Bubonic Plaque.
June 29, 1997	FBI agents arrest Mir Aimal Kansi in Pakistan. He is accused of killing two people and injuring three others outside the CIA headquarters.
October 8, 1997	U.S. officials bar 30 terrorist groups from entering the United States and prohibit U.S. citizens from contributing to them.
October 19, 1998	$12 million in property damage on Vail Mountain, Colorado, is caused by a fire deliberately set by ecoterrorists.
December 31, 1999	$400,000 in damages is caused when ecoterrorists set fire to a genetic research facility partly funded by Monsanto Corporation at Michigan State University.
February 14, 2000	Internet commerce is tied up when computer hackers launch "denial of service attacks." No terrorist group takes responsibility for the action; still, it demonstrates e-commerce's vulnerability to cyberterrorism.

Date	Kidnapping
February 4, 1974	The SLA abducts Patricia (Patty) Hearst in San Francisco.
February, 1984	Hezbollah kidnaps Frank Regier, an American University professor, in Beirut.

(*continued*)

(*continued*)

Date	Kidnapping
March 16, 1984	CIA Beirut station chief William Buckley is kidnapped. Later Islamic Jihad claims responsibility for "executing" Buckley.
March 16, 1985	Islamic Jihad kidnaps Terry A. Anderson, an Associated Press correspondent in Lebanon.
June 9, 1985	Islamic Jihad kidnaps Thomas M. Sutherland, acting Dean of Agriculture at the American University in Beirut.
January 23, 2002	*Wall Street Journal* reporter Daniel Pearl is kidnapped in Pakistan while on his way to interview an Islamic fundamentalist leader. Pearl was ultimately killed by his abductors, and the video of his death was posted across the Internet.
January 7, 2006	*Christian Science Monitor* journalist Jill Carroll is kidnapped in Baghdad when gunmen ambush her car, killing her Iraqi interpreter, Allan Enwiyah, 32 years. She is released March 30, 2006

Date	Bombings
January 29, 1975	U.S. State Department headquarters in Washington, D.C., is bombed by the Weather Underground.
December 25, 1984	In Pensacola, Florida, three abortion clinics are bombed by antiabortion terrorists.
December 11, 1985	A Sacramento, California, computer store owner is killed by a package bomb sent by the Unabomber.
December 16, 1989	Mail bombs are sent to people associated with civil rights enforcement. Judge Robert S. Vance of the 11th Circuit District and civil rights attorney Robert Robinson of Savannah, Georgia, are killed. Two other bombs are disarmed.
February 26, 1993	The World Trade Center in New York City is bombed by followers of Egyptian fundamentalist spiritual leader Sheikh Omar Abdel Rahman.
April 19, 1995	In the Oklahoma City, Alfred P. Murrah Federal Building is bombed by Timothy McVeigh and Terry Nichols, killing 168 people.
July 27, 1996	In Atlanta, Georgia's Centennial Olympic Park, a pipe bomb goes off killing one person and injuring 112 others. Richard Jewell is first thought of as a hero and then becomes a suspect in the case. Jewell is later cleared.
February 28, 1997	In Atlanta, Georgia, a gay and lesbian bar is bombed by Eric Robert Rudolph, injuring five people.
January 29, 1998	A Birmingham, Alabama abortion clinic is bombed by unknown terrorists, killing off-duty police and injuring a nurse.
October 12, 2000	In Aden harbor, Yemen, the U.S. Navy destroyer *Cole* is bombed by terrorists linked to Islamic Jihad, and possibly Osama bin Laden, killing 17 sailors.
December 22, 2002	Richard Reid, attempting to destroy American Airlines Flight 63, is subdued by passengers and flight attendants before he can detonate his shoe bomb.

(*continued*)

(*continued*)

Date	Product Tampering
September–October, 1982	Seven people in the Chicago area collapse and die suddenly after taking Tylenol capsules laced with cyanide. After the mysterious deaths are attributed to Tylenol, urgent warnings are broadcast, and the publicity causes nationwide panic. Johnson & Johnson issue an immediate nationwide alert to the public and a massive recall of millions of bottles. This is believed to be one of the worst cases of product tampering ever, and it is included in our list because of the sheer fear that was invoked.
November 17, 1984	The radical animal rights group Animal Liberation Front causes a panic when they claim to have poisoned Mars brand chocolate bars. Millions of the bars are removed from store shelves and destroyed.

Date	Domestic and International Terrorism—Mass Killings
September 2,– October 20, 2002	The I-95 Snipers, teenager John Lee Malvo and John Allen Muhammad, terrorize the I-95 corridor from Washington, D.C., to North Carolina, especially the Maryland area, sowing fear as they kill individuals at random. During their reign of terror, 10 people are killed and three are wounded.8
September 11, 2001	Four U.S. domestic commercial airlines are simultaneously hijacked in a series of suicide attacks carried out by 19 militants associated with the Islamic extremist group al-Qaeda. The attacks kill over 2,900. Osama bin Laden has been named as the primary suspect in the attacks.

Source: Henderson (2001, 98–129).

Appendix E

Declaration of Basic Principles of Justice for Victims of Crime and Abuse of Power

Adopted by General Assembly resolution 40/34 of 29 November 1985

A. Victims of Crime

1. "Victims" means persons who, individually or collectively, have suffered harm, including physical or mental injury, emotional suffering, economic loss or substantial impairment of their fundamental rights, through acts or omissions that are in violation of criminal laws operative within Member States, including those laws proscribing criminal abuse of power.

2. A person may be considered a victim, under this Declaration, regardless of whether the perpetrator is identified, apprehended, prosecuted or convicted and regardless of the familiar relationship between the perpetrator and the victim. The term "victim" also includes, where appropriate, the immediate family or dependants of the direct victim and persons who have suffered harm in intervening to assist victims in distress or to prevent victimization.

3. The provisions contained herein shall be applicable to all, without distinction of any kind, such as race, color, sex, age, language, religion, nationality, political or other opinion, cultural beliefs or practices, property, birth or family status, ethnic or social origin, and disability.

Access to Justice and Fair Treatment

4. Victims should be treated with compassion and respect for their dignity. They are entitled to access of the mechanisms of justice and to prompt redress, as provided for by national legislation, for the harm that they have suffered.

5. Judicial and administrative mechanisms should be established and strengthened, where necessary, to enable victims to obtain redress through formal or informal procedures that are expeditious, fair, inexpensive, and accessible. Victims should be informed of their rights in seeking redress through such mechanisms.

6. The responsiveness of judicial and administrative processes to the needs of victims should be facilitated by:

   (a) Informing victims of their role and the scope, timing, and progress of the proceedings and of the disposition of their cases, especially where serious crimes are involved and where they have requested such information.

   (b) Allowing the views and concerns of victims to be presented and considered at appropriate stages of the proceedings where their personal interests are affected, without prejudice to the accused and consistent with the relevant national criminal justice system.

   (c) Providing proper assistance to victims throughout the legal process.

   (d) Taking measures to minimize inconvenience to victims, protect their privacy when necessary, and ensure their safety, as well as that of their families and witnesses on their behalf, from intimidation and retaliation.

   (e) Avoiding unnecessary delay in the disposition of cases and the execution of orders or decrees granting awards to victims.

(continued)

(*continued*)

Access to Justice and Fair Treatment

7. Informal mechanisms for the resolution of disputes, including mediation, arbitration and customary justice or indigenous practices, should be utilized where appropriate to facilitate conciliation and redress for victims.

Restitution

8. Offenders or third parties responsible for their behavior should, where appropriate, make fair restitution to victims, their families, or dependents. Such restitution should include the return of property or payment for the harm or loss suffered, reimbursement of expenses incurred as a result of the victimization, the provision of services, and the restoration of rights.

9. Governments should review their practices, regulations, and laws to consider restitution as an available sentencing option in criminal cases, in addition to other criminal sanctions.

10. In cases of substantial harm to the environment restitution, if ordered should include, as far as possible, restoration of the environment, reconstruction of the infrastructure, replacement of community facilities and reimbursement of the expenses of relocation, whenever such harm results in the dislocation of a community.

11. Where public officials or other agents acting in an official or quasi-official capacity have violated national criminal laws, the victims should receive restitution from the State whose officials or agents were responsible for the harm inflicted. In cases where the Government under whose authority the victimizing act or omission occurred is no longer in existence, the State or Government successor in title should provide restitution to the victims.

Compensation

12. When compensation is not fully available from the offender or other sources, States should endeavor to provide financial compensation to:

    (a) Victims who have sustained significant bodily injury or impairment of physical or mental health as a result of serious crimes.

    (b) The family, in particular dependents of persons who have died or become physically or mentally incapacitated as a result of such victimization.

13. The establishment, strengthening, and expansion of national funds for compensation to victims should be encouraged. Where appropriate, other funds may also be established for this purpose, included in those cases where the State, of which the victim is a national, is not in a position to compensate the victim for the harm.

Assistance

14. Victims should receive the necessary material, medical, psychological, and social assistance through government, voluntary, community-based, and indigenous means.

15. Victims should be informed of the availability of health and social services, other relevant assistance, and be readily afforded access to them.

16. Police, justice, health, social services, and other personnel concerned should receive training to sensitize themselves to the needs of victims, and guidelines to ensure proper and prompt aid.

17. In providing services and assistance to victims, attention should be given to those who have special needs because of the nature of the harm inflicted or because of factors such as those mentioned in paragraph 3 above.

(*continued*)

(*continued*)

B. Victims of Abuse of Power

18. "Victims" means persons who, individually or collectively, have suffered harm including physical or mental injury, emotional suffering, economic loss, or substantial impairment of their fundamental rights, through acts or omissions that do not yet constitute violations of national criminal laws, but of internationally recognized norms relating to human rights.

19. States should consider incorporating into the national law norms proscribing abuses of power and providing remedies to victims of such abuses. In particular, such remedies should include restitution and/or compensation and necessary material, medical, psychological, social assistance, and support.

20. States should consider negotiating multi-lateral international treaties relating to victims, as defined in paragraph 18.

21. States should periodically review existing legislation and practices to ensure their responsiveness to changing circumstances. They should enact and enforce, if necessary, legislation proscribing acts that constitute serious abuses of political or economic power, as well as promoting policies and mechanisms for the prevention of such acts. Finally, they should develop, and make readily available, appropriate rights and remedies for victims of such acts.

Source: Office of the United Nations High Commissioner for Human Rights, 2008.

References

ABC News. (2005). Available at http://abcnews. go.com/US/WireStory?id=602824

Abramowitz, E., and Bohrer, B. A. (2005). White-collar crime: Supreme court review: The 2004–2005 term. *New York Law Journal, 2,* 234.

Achilles, M., and Zehr, H. (2001). Restorative justice for crime victims: The promise, the challenge. In G. Bazemore, G. Schiff, and M. Schiff (Eds.), *Restorative community justice: Repairing harm and transforming communities.* Cincinnati, OH: Anderson.

Adair, D. N. (1990). Looking at the law. *Federal Probation, 3,* 66–71.

Administration for Children and Families. (2005). Available at http://www.acf.hhs.gov/

Alexander, E. K., and Lord, J. H. (1994). *Impact statements: A victim's right to speak, a nation's responsibility to listen.* Washington, DC: U.S. Department of Justice.

Alicke, M. D., and Davis, T. L. (1989). The role of *a posteriori* victim information in judgments of blame and sanction. *Journal of Experimental Social Psychology, 25,* 362–377.

Allen, H. E., and Simonsen, C. E. (1995). *Corrections in America: An introduction* (7th ed.). Upper Saddle River, NJ: Prentice Hall.

American Bar Association Commission on Domestic Violence. (2006). *For victims.* Retrieved from http://www.abanet.org/domviol/

Houghton Mifflin Company. (2000). *American heritage dictionary of the English language* (4th ed.). Boston, MA: Houghton Mifflin.

AMT Children of Hope Foundation. (2007). Available at http://www.amtchildrenofhope.com/

Amir, M. (1971). *Patterns in forcible rape.* Chicago: University of Chicago Press.

Andersen, P. (2006, January 13). Family applauds law to help fight domestic violence by law officers. *The Associated Press.* Retrieved from http//159.54.227.3/apps/pbcs.dll/article?AID=/20060106/News06/60106012.

Anderson, J. R., and Woodard, P. L. (1985). Victim and witness assistance: New state laws and the system response. *Judicature, 68,* 221–224.

Anderson, K. B. (2004a). *Consumer fraud in the United States: An FTC survey.* Retrieved from http://www.ftc.gov/reports/consumerfraud/040805confraudrpt.pdf

Anderson, M. J. (2004b). *Understanding rape shield laws.* Retrieved from http://www.vawnet.org/SexualViolence/PublicPolicy/RapeShield.php

Anderson, S. M., Boulette, T. R., and Schwartz, A. H. (1991). Psychological maltreatment of spouses. In R. T. Ammerman, and M. Hersen (Eds.), *Case studies in family violence.* New York: Plenum.

Anti-Defamation League of B'nai B'rith. (1994). *Hate crimes laws: A comprehensive guide— 1994 hate crime statutory update.* New York: Anti-Defamation League of B'nai B'rith.

Anti-Defamation League of B'nai B'rith. (1996). *ADL concerned about incomplete 1994 FBI Hate Crime Figures.* Retrieved from http://www.adl.org/PresRele/breaking_news.asp

Antler, S. (1978). Child abuse: An emerging social priority. *Social Work, 23,* 58–61.

Arnette, J. L., and Walsleben, M. C. (1998). Combating fear and restoring safety in schools. *Juvenile Justice Bulletin, 1,* 18–24.

Associated Press. (2008, April 30). Work resumes on Deutsche bank building where firefighters died. *Daily News,* available at: http://www.nydailynews.com/news/2008/04/30/2008-04-30_work_resumes_on_deutsche_bank_building_w.html

Ashley, G. D. (2005, November 21). *Remarks by grant D. Ashley, Executive Assistant Director, Law enforcement Services, Federal bureau of Investigation.* Retrieved from http://www.fbi.gov/pressrel/speeches/ashley112105.htm

Association of Certified Fraud Examiners. (2005). *2004 report to the nation on occupational fraud and abuse.* Retrieved from http://www.acfe.com/documents/2004RttN.pdf

Bachman, R. (1992). *Elderly victims: Bureau of Justice Statistics special report.* Washington, DC: U.S. Department of Justice.

Bachman, R., and Saltzman, L. (1995). *Violence against women: Estimates from the redesigned survey.* Washington, DC: Government Printing Office.

Bachman, R., and Taylor, B. M. (1994). The measurement of family violence and rape by the redesigned national crime victimization survey. *Justice Quarterly, 11*(3), 499–512.

Bacque, P. (1996, June 11). Gilmore spearheads regional probe of hate crimes. *Richmond Times Dispatch,* p. B3.

Baker, L., and Jaffe, P. (2006). *A teachers' handbook: Understanding woman abuse and its effects on children.* Strategies for responding to students. London, ON: Centre for Children and Families in the Justice System, available at: http://www.crvawc.ca/documents/TeacherHandbook.pdf

Barnett, O. W., Miller-Perrin, C. L., and Perrin, R. (1997). *Family violence across the lifespan: An introduction.* Thousand Oaks, CA: Sage.

Barnett, O. W., Miller-Perrin, C. L., and Perrin, R. (2004). *Family violence across the lifespan: An introduction* (2nd ed.). Thousand Oaks, CA: Sage.

Barrett, J. (2006). *Hate, violence, and death on main street USA, 2005.* Retrieved from http://www.nationalhomeless.org/getinvolved/projects/hatecrimes/index.html

Bartol, C. (2004). *Criminal behavior: A psychosocial approach* (7th ed.). Upper Saddle River, NJ: Prentice Hall.

Basile, K. C. (2002). Prevalence of wife rape and other intimate partner sexual coercion in a nationally representative sample of women. *Violence and Victims, 17*(5), 511–524.

Bass, E., and Davis, L. (1994). *The courage to heal: A guide for women survivors of child sexual abuse* (4th ed.). New York: HarperCollins.

Bastian, L. (1995). *Bulletin: Criminal victimization 1993.* Washington, DC: Bureau of Justice Statistics. (Report Number NCJ-151658).

Bazemore, G., and Schiff, M. (1994, October). *Balanced and restorative justice: Program summary.* Washington, DC: U.S. Department of Justice, Office of Juvenile Justice and Delinquency Prevention.

Bazemore, G., Schiff, G., and Schiff, M. (2001). *Restorative community justice: Repairing harm and transforming communities.* Cincinnati, OH: Anderson.

Bazemore, G., and Umbreit, M. (1995). Rethinking the sanctioning functions in juvenile court: Retributive or restorative responses to youth crime. *Crime and Delinquency, 41*(3), 296–316.

Beasley, J. (2004). Serial murder in America: Case studies of seven offenders. *Behavioral Science and the Law, 22,* 395–414.

Beccaria, C. (1963[1764]). *On crimes and punishments.* Trans. H. Paolucci. Indianapolis: Bobbs-Merrill.

Beck, A., and Shipley, B. (1989). *Recidivism of prisoners released in 1983.* Washington, DC: U.S. Bureau of Justice Statistics.

Beland, K. R. (1996). A school-wide approach to violence prevention. In R. L. Hampton, P. Jenkins, and T. P. Gullotta (Eds.), *Issues in children's and families' lives: Preventing violence in America.* Thousand Oaks, CA: Sage.

Belknap, J., and Melton, H. (2005, March). In brief: Are heterosexual men also victims of intimate partner abuse? *Applied Research Forum, National Electronic Network on Violence Against Women.* Retrieved from http://new.vawnet.org/category/index_pages?category_id=10

Belsky, J. (1980). Child maltreatment: An ecological integration. *American Psychologist, 35,* 320–335.

Bergen, R. K. (1996). *Wife rape: Understanding the response of survivors and service providers.* Thousand Oaks, CA: Sage.

Bergen, R. K. (1999). In brief: Marital rape. *National resource center on domestic violence.* Retrieved from http://new.vawnet.org/category/index_pages?category_id=695.

Berk, R. A. (1994). Foreward. In M. S. Hamm (Ed.), *Hate crimes: International perspectives on causes and control.* Cincinnati, OH: Anderson and Academy of Criminal Justice Sciences.

Berliner, L. (1996). Community notification of sex offenders: A new tool or a false promise. *Journal of Interpersonal Violence, 11*(2), 294–300.

Berrill, K. T. (1990). Anti-gay violence and victimization in the United States: An overview. *Journal of Interpersonal Violence, 5*(3), 274–294.

Berrill, K. T., and Herek, G. M. (1990). Violence against lesbians and gay men: An introduction. *Journal of Interpersonal Violence, 5*(3), 269–273.

Bidinotto, R. J. (1996). *Free to kill: How America's revolving door system of justice fails to protect the innocent.* Washington, DC: Safe Streets Coalition.

Black, H. C. (2001). *Black's law dictionary* (2nd ed.). St. Paul: MN: West.

Block, M. R., and Sinnott, J. D. (1979). The battered elder syndrome: An exploratory study. In P. Decalmer, and F. Glendenning (Eds.), *The mistreatment of elderly people.* Newbury Park, CA: Sage.

Bocij, P. (2003, October). Victims of cyber stalking: An exploratory study of harassment perpetrated via the Internet. *First Monday,* p. 8, 10. Retrieved from http://firstmonday.org/issues/issue8_10/bocij/index.html

Bohm, R. M., and Haley, K. N. (1997). *Introduction to criminal justice.* New York: Glencoe.

Bohm, R. M., and Haley, K. N. (2007). *Introduction to criminal justice* (4th ed.). New York: McGraw Hill.

Bohmer, C., and Parrot, A. (1993). *Sexual assault on campus: The problem and the solution.* New York: Lexington.

Bono, A. (2006). *John Jay study reveals extent of abuse problem: Four percent of priests serving over last 50 years accused of abuse.* Retrieved from http://www.americancatholic.org/news/clergysexabuse/

Bottigliero, I. (2003, April). The International Criminal Court—Hope for the Victims, 32 *SGI Quarterly,* pp. 13–15. Retrieved June 17, 2008 from http://www.sgiquarterly.org/english/Features/quarterly/0304/perspective.htm

Brandi, S. G., and Horvath, F. (1991). Crime-victim evaluation of police investigative performance. *Journal of Criminal Justice, 19,* 293–305.

Brantingham, P. J., and Faust, F. L. (1976). A conceptual model of crime prevention. *Crime and Delinquency, 22,* 284–296.

Breckman, R. S., and Adelman, R. D. (1988). *Strategies of helping victims of elder mistreatment.* Beverly Hills, CA: Sage.

Brody, J. (2003, January 28). Personal health: Empowering children to thwart abductors. *New York Times,* p. 6.

Brown, C. G. (1993). *First get mad, then get justice: The handbook for crime victims.* New York: Carol Publishing.

Brown, M. J. (1994, August). *Empowering the victim in the New Zealand youth justice process: A strategy for healing.* Address to the 8th International Symposium on Victimology. Adelaide, S.A, Australia.

Brownmiller, S. (1975). *Against our will.* New York: Simon and Schuster.

Bryce-Rosen, C. E. (2005, March). *Identity theft and prevention.* Invited presentation and discussion for the Virginia United Methodist Women's Group. Richmond, VA.

Bugliosi, V., and Gentry, C. (1974). *Helter Skelter: The true story of the Manson murders.* New York: Norton.

Bureau of Justice Statistics. (1995). *Bureau of justice statistics fact sheet: National crime victimization survey redesign.* Retrieved April 28, 2006 from http://www.ojp.usdoj.gov/bjs/pub/pdf/redesfs.pdf

Bureau of Justice Statistics. (1996). *Criminal victimization in the United States, 1995.* Washington, DC: Government Printing Office.

Burgess, A. W. (2006, August 23). Current research in victimology. Paper presented at the World Society of Victimology 12th International Symposium on Victimology, Orlando, FL.

Burgess, A. W., Lewis-O'Connor, A., Nugent-Borakove, M. E., and Fanflik, P. (2006). SANE/SART services for sexual assault victims: Policy implications. *Victims and Offenders, 1,* 205–212.

Burgess, A. W., Garbarino, C., and Carlson, M. I. (2006). Pathological teasing and bullying turned deadly: Shooters and suicide. *Victims and Offenders, 1*(1), 1–14.

Burt, M. R. (1979). *Attitudes supportive of rape in American culture.* Washington, DC: National Institute of Mental Health, National Center for the Prevention and Control of Rape.

Burt, M. R. (1980). Cultural myths and supports for rape. *Journal of Personality and Social Psychology, 38,* 217–230.

Busby, D. M., and Inman, J. R. (1996). Physical abuse of women in marriage. In D. M. Busby (Ed.), *The impact of violence on the family.* Boston, MA: Allyn and Bacon.

Butterfield, F. (1996, May 6). Major crimes fell in '95, early data from F.B.I. indicate. *New York Times,* pp. A1, B8.

Butts, J., and Snyder, H. (1992, September). *Restitution and juvenile recidivism OJJDP update on research.* Washington, DC: U.S. Department of Justice: Office of Juvenile Justice and Delinquency Prevention.

Buzawa, E. S., and Buzawa, C. G. (1990). *Domestic violence: The criminal justice response.* Newbury Park, CA: Sage.

Buzawa, E. W., and Buzawa, C. G. (1996). *Domestic violence: The criminal justice response* (2nd ed.). Thousand Oaks, CA: Sage.

Caffaro, J. V., and Conn-Caffaro, A. (1998). *Sibling abuse trauma: Assessment and intervention strategies for children, families, and adults.* New York: Haworth Maltreatment and Trauma Press.

Cantor, D., and Wright, M. (2001). *School crime patterns: A national profile of U.S. public high schools using rates of crime reported to police: Report on the study of school violence and prevention.* Washington, DC: U.S. Department of Education, Planning and Evaluation Service.

Carrington, F. C. (1975). *The victims.* New Rochelle, NY: Arlington House.

Carrington, F., and Nicholson, G. (1984). The victim movement: An idea whose time has come. *Pepperdine Law Review, 11*, 1–14.

Carrow, D. M. (1980). *Crime victim compensation: Program model.* Washington, DC: Government Printing Office.

Carter, W. (1995). *Victims of crime: Victim service worker handbook.* British Columbia: Ministry of Attorney General.

Catalano, S. M. (2006). *National crime victimization survey, criminal victimization 2005.* Retrieved from http://www.ojp.usdoj.gov/bjs/pubalp2.htm#cv

Chen, P. N., Bell, S., Dolinsky, D., Doyle, J., and Dunn, M. (1981). Elderly abuse in domestic settings: A pilot study. *Journal of Gerontological Social Work, 4*, 3–17.

Child Welfare Project. (2003, October 21). *Update safe havens for abandoned infants.* Retrieved from http://www.ncsl.org/programs/cyf/ailaws.htm#Laws

Child Welfare Information Gateway. (2008). Recognizing signs of child abuse and neglect, available at: http://www.childwelfare.gov/can/identifying/signs_symp.cfm (Retrieved on September 17, 2008).

Clemente, F., and Kleiman, M. B. (1977). Fear of crime in the United States: A multivariate analysis. *Social Forces, 56*(2), 519–531.

Cleveland State University. (n.d.). *Workplace violence: If a workplace violence occurs.* Retrieved from http://www.csuohio.edu/riskmanagement/emergency/violence.html

Clifford, M. (1998). *Environmental crime: Enforcement, policy, and social responsibility.* Gaithersburg, MD: Aspen.

Clinton urges amendment on victims' rights. (1996, June 26). *Boston Globe*, p. A6.

CNN.com. (1998). Available at http://www.cnn.com/US/9803/24/school.shooting.folo/index.html

CNN.com. (2000). President Clinton urges congress to pass hate crimes bill: GOP aides predict legislation will pass house, but won't become law, available at: http://transcripts.cnn.com/2000/ALLPOLITICS/stories/09/13/hate.crimes/index.html

Cohen, L., and Felson, M. (1979). Social change and crime rate trends: A routine activities approach. *American Sociological Review, 44*, 588–607.

Cohn, D., and Thomas, P. (1989, February 14). Student shot at school. *Washington Post*, p. 1.

Cole, G. F. (1995). *The American system of criminal justice.* Belmont, CA: Brooks/Cole.

Cole, T. B. (2006). Rape at U.S. colleges often fueled by alcohol. *JAMA, 296*(5), 504.

College and University Personnel Association. (1986). *Sexual harassment issues and answers: A guide for education, business, and industry.* Washington, DC: Author.

Conklin, J. (1975). *The impact of fear.* New York: Macmillan.

Conly, C. H., and McEwen, J. T. (1990, January–February) Computer Crime. *NIJ Reports, 218*, 2–7.

Consumer Sentinel. (2006). *The US safe web act: Protecting consumers from spam, spyware, and fraud.* Retrieved from www.ftc.gov/reports/ussafeweb/USSAFEWEB.pdf

Comer, R.J. (1999). *Fundamentals of abnormal psychology* (2nd ed.). Worth Publishers, Inc.

Corporate Fraud Task Force. (2004). *Second year report to the President.* Washington, DC: Department of Justice.

Council of Better Business Bureaus. (2005). *New research shows that identity theft is more prevalent offline with paper than online.* Arlington, VA: Author.

Cox, S. M. (1996). *Police: Practices, perspectives, problems.* Boston, MA: Allyn and Bacon.

Cox, S. M., and Conrad, J. J. (1996). *Juvenile justice: A guide to practice and theory* (4th ed.). Dubuque, IA: Brown and Benchmark.

Cozens, J. (1994, August). *New Zealand victims court assistance pilot project.* Paper presented at the 8th International Symposium on Victimology. Adelaide, S.A, Australia.

Crawford, A. and Clear, T. (2001). Community justice: Transforming communities through restorative justice. In G. Brazemore, and M. Schiff (Eds.) *Restorative community Justice: Repairing harm and transforming communities*. Cincinnati, OH: Anderson Publishing Co.

Crime Prevention Action Group. (1992). *Strategy paper on crime prevention: Report on the preliminary stage of analysis*. Wellington, New Zealand: Department of Prime Minister and Cabinet.

Crime Injuries Compensation Authority. (1994). *Criminal injuries compensation—The tariff scheme*. Glasgow: Author.

Cromin, R. C., and Borque, B. B. (1981). *National evaluation program phase I report: Assessment of victim/witness assistance programs*. Washington, DC: U.S. Department of Justice.

Cullen, K. (1991, June 13). Effort continues to save victim aid program. *Boston Globe*, p. 40.

Cuomo, M. M. (1978). The crime victim in a system of criminal justice. *St. John's Journal of Legal Commentary, 8*, 1–20.

Curriden, M. (1990, April 26). Successful victim-witness program threatened by a lack of funding. *Atlanta Constitution*, pp. 2, 4.

Curry, T., and Shibut, L. (2000). The cost of the savings and loan crisis: Truth and consequences. *FDIC Banking Review, 13*, 26–35.

Curtin, M. (2003). Anatomy of online fraud: How thieves targeted eBay users but got stopped instead. *Interhack*. Retrieved from www.interhack.net/pubs/fraud-anatomy/fraud-anatomy.pdf

Daly, M., Wilson, M., and Salmon, C. A. (2001). Siblicide and seniority. *Homicide Studies, 5*(1), 30–45.

Davidson, W. S., Redner, R., and Amdur, R. L. (1990). *Alternative treatments for troubled youths: The case of diversion from the justice system*. New York: Plenum.

Davis, R. C., and Henley, M. (1990). Victim service programs. In A. J. Lurigio, W. G. Skogan, and R. C. Davis (Eds.), *Victims of crime: Problems, policies, and programs*. Newbury Park, CA: Sage.

DeKeseredy, W. S., and Hinch, R. (1991). *Women abuse: Sociological perspectives*. Toronto: Thompson.

Delaware State Police. (1993). *Standard operating procedure of the Delaware state police victim service unit*. Dover, DE: Author.

DeValve, E. (2007). Repeat victimization and problem-oriented policing: Surmounting crime by attending to victims' needs. In L. J. Moriarty, and R. A. Jerin (Eds.), *Current issues in victimology research* (2nd ed.). Durham: Carolina Academic Press.

DeVoe, J. F., Peter, K., Kaufman, P., Miller, A., Noonan, M., Snyder, T. D., and Baum, K. (2004). *Indicators of school crime and safety*. Washington, DC: Government Printing Office. (NCES 2005–002/NCJ 205290).

de Waard, J. (1993). *The Dutch criminal justice system*. English written information. The Hague: Ministerie van Justitie.

Dickstein, L. (1988). Spouse abuse and other domestic violence. *Psychiatric Clinics of North America, 2*, 611–625.

Dillingham, S. D. (1992). Foreword. *Elderly victims. Bureau of justice statistics special report*. Washington, DC: U.S. Department of Justice.

Doerner, W. G., and Lab, S. P. (1980). Impact of crime compensation on victim attitudes toward the criminal justice system. *Victimology, 5*(2), 61–77.

Doerner, W. G., and Lab, S. P. (2006). *Victimology* (4th ed.). Cincinnati, OH: LexisNexis.

Dubber, M. D. (2002). *Victims in the war on crime: The use and abuse of victims' rights*. New York: New York University Press.

Duhart, D. T. (2001). *Special report: Violence in the workplace, 1993–1999*. Washington, DC: U.S. Department of Justice. (NCJ 190076).

Durose, M. R., Harlow, C. W., Langan, P. A., Motivans, M., Rantala, R., and Smith, E. L. (2005). *Family violence statistics including statistics on stranger and acquaintances*. Washington, DC: U.S. Department of Justice. (NCJ 207846).

Dussich, J. P. (1976). *Development of a victim advocacy program: Police technical assistance report*. Washington DC: Public Administration Service.

Dussich, J. P. (1986). The victim assistance center: Its history and typology. In K. Miyazawa, and M. Ohya (Eds.), *Victimology in comparative perspective*. Tokyo: Seibunco Publishing.

Dwyer, D. C., Smokowski, P. R., Bricourt, J. C., and Wodarski, J. S. (1996). Domestic violence and woman battering: Theories and practice implications. In A. R. Roberts (Ed.), *Helping battered women: New perspectives and remedies*. New York: Oxford University Press.

Dziegielewski, S., and Robert, A. (1995) Stalking victims and survivors: Identification, legal remedies and crisis treatment. In A. Roberts (Ed.), *Crisis intervention and time-limited cognitive treatment* (pp. 73–90). Thousand Oaks, CA: Sage Publications.

Earthlink. (2003). Earthlink joins with FBI and kids fighting chance to provide family safety advise, available at: http://www.hostapproval.com/press_releases/604.html

Eck, J. (1997). Preventing crime at places. In L. W. Sherman, D. Gottfredson, D. MacKenzie, J. Eck, P. Reuter, and S. Bushway (Eds.), *Preventing crime: What works, what doesn't, what's promising*. A report to Congress, Prepared by the National Institute of Justice. Retrieved from National Criminal Justice Reference Service website: http://www.ncjrs.gov/works/index.htm

Edelhertz, H., and Geis, G. (1974). *Public compensation to victims of crime*. New York: Praeger.

Eigenberg, H. M. (1990). The national crime survey and rape: The case of missing question. *Justice Quarterly, 7*(3), 655–669.

Eigenberg, H. M. (2003). Victim blaming. In L. J. Moriarty (Ed.), *Controversies in Victimology* (pp. 15–24). Cincinnati, OH: Anderson.

Elias, R. (1983a). *Victims of the system: Crime victims and compensation in American politics and criminal justice*. New Brunswick, NJ: Transaction.

Elias, R. (1983b). The symbolic politics of victim compensation. *Victimology, 8*(1), 210–219.

Elias, R. (1984). Alienating the victim: Compensation and victim attitudes. *Journal of Social Issues, 40*(1), 103–116.

Elias, R. (1986). *The politics of victimization: Victims, victimology, and human rights*. New York: Oxford University Press.

Elias, R. (1993). *Victims still: The political manipulation of crime victims*. Newbury Park, CA: Sage.

Ellingworth, P., Farrell, G., and Pease, K. (1995). A victim is a victim is a victim? Chronic victimization in four sweeps of the British Crime Survey. (Symposium on Repeat Victimization). *British Journal of Criminology, 35*(3), 360–365.

Epstein, J., and Langenbahn, S. (1994). *The criminal justice and community response to rape*. Washington, DC: Government Printing Office.

Erez, E. (1990). Victim participation in sentencing: Rhetoric and reality. *Journal of Criminal Justice, 18*, 19–31.

Erez, E., and Tontodonato, P. (1992). Victim participation in sentencing and satisfaction with justice. *Justice Quarterly, 9*(3), 393–415.

Fantz, A. (2006, January 19). Details about suspects emerge. *The Miami Herald*. Retrieved from http:/Miami.com/mld/miamiherald/news/breaking_news/13658559.htm

Farrell, G. (1992). Multiple victimization: Its extent and significance. *International Review of Victimology, 2*, 85–102.

Farrell, G., and Bouloukos, A. C. (2001). International overview: A cross-national comparison of rates of repeat victimization. In G. Farrell, and K. Pease (Eds.), *Repeat victimization, crime prevention studies*, Volume 12 (pp. 5–26). Monsey, NY: Criminal Justice Press.

Farrell, G., and Pease, K. (1993). *Once bitten, twice bitten: Repeat victimization and its implications for crime prevention*. Police research group crime prevention unit series paper No. 46. London, England: Home Office Police Department.

Farrell, G., and Pease, K. (2001). Why repeat victimization matters. In G. Farrell, and K. Pease (Eds.), *Repeat victimization, crime prevention studies*, Volume 12 (pp. 1–4). Monsey, NY: Criminal Justice Press.

Fattah, E. A. (1967). Towards a criminological classification of victims. *International Criminal Police Review, 209*, 162–169.

FBI homepage. (2006). *Uniform crime reports (UCR): Summary reporting, frequently asked questions*. Retrieved from http://www.fbi.gov/ucr/ucrquest.htm

Federal Bureau of Investigation. (1996). *Crime in the United States*. Washington, DC: Government Printing Office.

Federal Bureau of Investigation Behavioral Analysis Unit. (2005). *Symposium on serial killers*. Washington, DC: Government Printing Office.

Federal Parole Commission. (2006). *Crime victims rights guidelines*. Retrieved from http://www.usdoj.gov/uspc/victim.htm

Federal Trade Commission. (2001). *Identity theft complaint data: Figures and trends. January 1–December 31, 2000.* Retrieved from http://www.consumer.gov/sentinel/pubs/top10Fraud2000.pdf

Federal Trade Commission. (2002). *Identity theft complaint data: Figures and trends. January 1–December 31, 2001.* Retrieved from http://www.consumer.gov/sentinel/pubs/top10Fraud2001.pdf

Federal Trade Commission. (2003a). *Identity theft complaint data: Figures and trends. January 1–December 31, 2002.* Retrieved from http://www.consumer.gov/sentinel/pubs/top10Fraud2002.pdf

Federal Trade Commission. (2003b). *National and state trends in fraud and identity theft: January–December 2002.* Retrieved from http://www.consumer.gov/sentinel/pubs/top10Fraud2002.pdf

Federal Trade Commission. (2004a). *National and state trends in fraud and identity theft: January–December 2003.* Retrieved from http://www.consumer.gov/sentinel/pubs/top10Fraud2003.pdf

Federal Trade Commission. (2004b). *Consumer fraud in the United States: An FTC survey.* Retrieved from http://www.ftc.gov/reports/consumerfraud/040805confraudrpt.pdf

Federal Trade Commission. (2005). *National and state trends in fraud and identity theft: January–December 2004.* Retrieved from http://www.consumer.gov/sentinel/pubs/top10Fraud2004.pdf

Field, R. P. (1991). Constitutional law-Payne v. Tennessee: The admissibility of victim impact statements—A move toward less rational sentencing. *Memphis State University Law Review, 22,* 135–156.

Felson, R. (1997). Routine activities and involvement in violence as actor, witness or target. *Violence and Victimization, 12,* 209–223.

Finkelhor, D. (2000). *Sourcebook on child sexual abuse.* Newbury Park, CA: Sage.

Finkelhor, D., Mitchell, K., and Wolak, J. (2001). *Highlights of the youth internet survey: OJJDP fact sheet # 4.* Washington, DC: U.S. Department of Justice.

Finn, P., and Lee, B. N. W. (1987). *Servicing crime victims and witnesses.* Washington, DC: National Institute of Justice.

Fisher, B. S., Cullen, F. T., and Turner, M. G. (2000). *The sexual victimization of college women.* Washington, DC: U.S. Department of Justice.

Flowers, R.B. (1987). *Women and criminality: The woman as victim, offender, and practitioner.* New York: Greenwood Press.

Fortunato, F. (2005a). *Battling fraud on eBay: Part I.* Retrieved from http://www.ecommerce-guide.com/news/trends/article.php/3495451

Fortunato, F. (2005b). *Battling fraud on eBay: Part II.* Retrieved from http://www.ecommerce-guide.com/essentials/ebay/article.php/3496021.

Fox News. (2006). *Alabama churches set ablaze.* Retrieved from www.foxnews.com

Frazier, P. A. (1993). A comparative study of male and female rape victims seen at a hospital-based rape crisis program. *Journal of Interpersonal Violence, 8*(1), 64–76.

Freivalds, P. (1996, July). *Balanced and restorative justice project (BARJ) FactsSheet.* Washington, DC: U.S. Department of Justice, Office of Juvenile Justice and Delinquency Prevention.

Fried, J. P. (1990, November 29). Prosecution ends in negotiated sentence. *New York Times,* p. B3.

Frieze, I. H. (1980, September). *Causes and consequences of marital rape.* Paper presented at the American Psychological Association, Montreal, Canada.

Fry, M. (1957, November 10). Justice for victims. London Observer, Reprinted (1959) in *Journal of Public Law, 8,* 191–194.

Gaines, L. K., and Miller, R. L. (2006). *Criminal justice in action* (4th ed.). Belmont, CA: Thomson Wadsworth.

Galaway, B., and Hudson, J. (Eds.). (1981). *Perspectives on crime victims.* St. Louis, Missouri: C. V. Mosby.

Galaway, B., and Hudson, J. (1996). *Restorative justice: International perspectives.* Mosley, NY: Criminal Justice Press.

Gamroth, B. (2006). Study reviews college sexual harassment, *Oregon Daily Emerald,* available at: http://www.dailyemerald.com

Garraway, C. (2007). *Yearbook of international humanitarian law.* Cambridge University Press.

Gardner, J., Fagan, J., and Maxwell, C. (1995). Published findings from the spouse assault replication program: A critical review. *Journal of Quantitative Criminology, 11*(1), 3–28.

Gates, L., and Rohe, W. (1987). Fear and reactions to crime: A revised model. *Urban Affairs Quarterly, 22*(3), 425–453.

Gebo, E. (2002). A contextual exploration of siblicide. *Violence and Victims, 17*(2), 157–168.

Gelles, R. J. (1977). Power, sex and violence: The case of marital rape. *Family Coordinator, 26,* 339–347.

Gelles, R. J. (1983). An exchange/social control theory. In D. Finkelhor, R. J. Gelles, G. T. Hotaling, and M. A. Straus (Eds.), *The dark side of families: Current family violence research.* Beverly Hills, CA: Sage.

Gelles, R. J. (1987). *The violent home.* Newbury Park, CA: Sage.

Gelles, R. J. (1988). Violence and pregnancy: Are pregnant women at greater risk of abuse? *Journal of Marriage and Family, 50,* 1045–1058.

Gelles, R. J. (1993a). Through a sociological lens. Social structure and family violence. In R. J. Gelles, and D. R. Loseke (Eds.), *Current controversies on family violence.* Newbury Park, CA: Sage.

Gelles, R. J. (1993b). Family violence. In R. L. Hampton, T. P. Gullotta, G. R. Adams, E. H. Potter, and R. P. Weissberg (Eds.),*Family violence: Prevention and treatment.* Newbury Park, CA: Sage.

Gelles, R. J., and Conte, J. (1990). Domestic violence and sexual abuse of children. *Journal of Marriage and the Family, 52,* 1045–1058.

Gelles, R. J., and Loseke, D. R. (Eds.). (1993). *Current controversies on family violence.* Newbury Park, CA: Sage.

Gelles, R. J., and Straus, M. A. (1988). *Intimate violence: The causes and consequences of abuse in the American family.* New York: Simon and Schuster.

Genocide Watch. (2008). Retrieved June 27, 2008 from http://genocidewatch.org/home.html

Ghose, C. S. (2006, January 12). Bishop reveals he was abused by priest. *Washington Post.* Retrieved from www.washingtonpost.com

Gil, D. G. (1970). *Violence against children.* Cambridge, MA: Harvard University Press.

Giles-Sims, J. (1983). *Wife-beating: A systems approach.* New York: Guilford.

Glendenning, F. (1993). What is elder abuse and neglect? In F. Glendenning, and P. DeCalmer (Eds.), *The mistreatment of elderly people.* Newbury Park, CA: Safe.

Goldstein, A. (1984). The victim and prosecutorial discretion: The federal victim and witness

protection act of 1982. *Law and Contemporary Problems, 47,* 225.

Goldstein, H. (1990). *Problem-oriented policing.* New York: McGraw-Hill.

Gonser, J. (2004). 4 arrested in attack on homeless man. *The Honolulu Advertiser.* Retrieved from http://the.honoluluadvertiser.com/article/2004/jan/10/in/in01a.html/?print=on

Gordon, M. T., and Riger, S. (1989). *The female fear.* New York: Free Press.

Gottfredson, D. (1997). School-based crime prevention. In L. W. Sherman, D. Gottfredson, D. MacKenzie, J. Eck, P. Reuter, and S. Bushway (Eds.), *Preventing crime: What works, what doesn't, what's promising.* Retrieved from National Criminal Justice Reference Service website: http://www.ncjrs.gov/works/index.htm

Graham-Bermann, S. A., Cutler, S. E., Litzenberger, B. W., and Schwartz, W. E. (1994). Perceived conflict and violence in childhood sibling relationships and later emotional adjustment. *Journal of Family Psychology, 8*(1), 85–97.

Graham, R. (2006). Male rape and the careful construction of the male victim. *Social & Legal Studies, 15*(2), 187–208.

Gray Panthers of Austin. (1983). *A survey of abuse of the elderly in Texas.* Austin, TX: Author.

Greenbaum, S. (1987). What can we do about school bullying? *Principal, 67,* 21–24.

Greenbery, J. (1984). The victim in historical perspective: Some aspects of the English experience. *Journal of Social Issues, 40*(1), 77–102.

Greenwood, P. B. (1983). *Selective incapacitation.* Santa Monica, CA: Rand.

Griffiths, C. T., and Hamilton, R. (1996). Spiritual renewal, community revitalization and healing: Experience in traditional aboriginal justice in Canada. *International Journal of Comparative and Applied Criminal Justice, 20*(2), 289–311.

Groth, N., Burgess, A. W., and Holmstrom, L. L. (1977). Rape: Power, anger, and sexuality. *American Journal of Psychiatry, 134*(11), 1239–1243.

Gruss, S. (2006).*Is safe haven legislation an efficacious policy response to infant abandonment?* Unpublished dissertation proposal. Virginia Commonwealth University, Richmond, VA.

Haiman, A. J. (1993). *Speech acts and the first amendment.* Carbondale: Southern Illinois University Press.

Hate Crime Statistics. (2006). Available at http://www.fbi.gov/ucr/hc2006/index.html (Retrieved on May 30, 2008).

Hatecrime.org. (2000). Available at http://www.hatecrime.org/subpages/bldebate_hrctexas.html (Retrieved on January 10, 2006).

Hammer, H., Finkelhor, D., and Sedlak, A. (2002). Runaway/thrownaway children: National estimates and characteristics. *NISMART*, available at: http://www.ncjrs.gov/html/ojjdp/nismart/04/

Hampton, R. L. (1987). Family violence and homicide in the black community: Are they linked? In R. I. Hampton (Ed.), *Violence in the black family*. Lexington, KY: Lexington Books.

Hampton, R. I., and Coner-Edwards, A. F. W. (1993). Physical and sexual violence in marriage. In R. L. Hampton, T. P. Gullotta, G. R. Adams, E. H. Potter, and R. P. Weissberg (Eds.), *Family violence: Prevention and treatment*. Newbury Park, CA: Sage.

Hannah, S. (2003). Stranger danger: Explaining women's fear of crime. *Western Criminology Review*, 4(3), available at: http://wcr.sonoma.edu/v4n3/scott.html

Harlow, C. W. (2005). *Bureau of justice statistics special report: Hate crime reported by victims and police*. Washington, DC: U.S. Department of Justice.

Harris, R. N., and Dewdney, R. (1994). *Barriers to information: How formal help systems fail battered women*. Westport, CT: Greenwood Press.

Harry, J. (1990). Conceptualizing anti-gay violence. *Journal of Interpersonal Violence*, 5(3), 350–358.

Hartmann, F. (2007). Bosnia. In R. Gutman, D. Rieff, and A. Dworkin (Eds.), *Crimes of War*. New York: W.W. Norton and Co.

Hate Crime Statistics. (2006). Available at http://www.fbi.gov/ucr/hc2006/index.html (Retrieved on May 30, 2008).

Hawkins, D. F. (1987). Devalued lives and racial stereotypes: Ideological barriers to the prevention of family violence among blacks. In R. I. Hampton (Ed.), *Violence in the black family*. Lexington, KY: Lexington.

Hayes, H. R., and Emshoff, J. G. (1993). Substance abuse and family violence. In R. L. Hampton, T. P. Gullotta, G. R. Adams, E. H. Potter, and R. P. Weissberg (Eds.), *Family violence: Prevention and treatment*. Newbury Park, CA: Sage.

Heffernan, K., Johnson, R., and Vakalahi, H. (2002). Ho'okele: A Pacific Island *approach to aging*. Paper presented at the Baccalaureate Program Directors Conference, Pittsburgh, October 23–25.

Hellerstein, D. R. (1989). The victim impact statement: Reform or reprisal? *American Criminal Law Review*, 27(Fall), 391–430.

Henderson, H. (2001). *Terrorism*. New York, NY: Facts on File.

Herek, G. M. (1990). The context of anti-gay violence: Notes of cultural and psychological heterosexism. *Journal of Interpersonal Violence*, 5(3), 316–333.

Herek, G. M., Gillis, J. R., and Cogan, J. C. (1999). Psychological sequelae of hate crime victimization among lesbian, gay, and bisexual adults. *Journal of Consulting and Clinical Psychology*, 67(6), 945–951.

Herrington, L. H. (1985). Victims of crime: Their plight, our response. *American Psychologist*, 40, 99–103.

Hess, K. M., and Wrobleski, H. M. (1992). *Introduction to private security* (3rd ed.). New York: West.

Hickey, T., and Douglass, R. L. (1981). Neglect and abuse of older family members: Professionals' perspectives and case experiences. *Gerontologist*, 21(2), 171–176.

Hill, G. D., Howell, F. M., and Driver, E. T. (1985). Gender, fear and protective handgun ownership. *Criminology*, 23(3), 541–552.

Hill, C., and Silva, E. (2005). *Drawing the line: Sexual harassment on campus*. Washington, DC: AAUW Educational Foundation, available at: http://www.aauw.org/research/upload/DTLFinal.pdf

Hindelang, M. J., Gottfredson, M. R., and Garofalo, J. (1978). *Victims of personal crime: An empirical foundation for a theory of personal victimization*. Cambridge, MA: Ballinger.

Hoffman, B. (1998). *Inside terrorism*. New York, NY: Columbia University Press.

Hoke, J. (1996, June 11). Rape case a constitutional test. *Richmond Times Dispatch*, pp. B1, B5.

Holmes, R. M., and Holmes, S. T. (1998). *Serial Murder* (2nd ed.). Thousand Oaks, Sage.

Homeless. (2006). Available at: http://www.nationalhomeless.org/getinvolved/projects/hatecrimes/history.html (Retrieved on April 17, 2006).

Horne, F. (1993). The issue is rape. In R. Muraskin, and T. Alleman, (Eds.), *It's a crime: women and justice*, (3rd ed.). (pp. 305–315), Englewood Cliffs, NJ: Prentice Hall.

Hoover, E. (2008, June 23). Colleges wade into survival training for campus shootings: A new video offers tips on how to react when shots are fired. *Chronicle of Higher Education*, available at: http://chronicle.com/weekly/v54/i42/42a00101.htm?utm_source=at&utm_medium=en

Human rights campaign special report. *The truth about hate crimes in Texas*. Retrieved from http://www.hatecrime.net/

Hurdle, D. (2002). Native Hawaiian traditional healing: Culturally-based interventions for social work practice. *Social Work, 47*(2), 183–192.

IACP. (2003, July). *Domestic violence by police officers: A policy of the IACP police response to violence against women project*. Retrieved from http://www.theiacp.org/documents/pdfs/Publications/DomViolenceModelPolicy.pdf

Inciardi, J. (1993). *Criminal Justice* (3rd ed.). San Diego, CA: Harcourt Brace Jovanovich.

Internet Crime Complaint Center. (2008). "Internet Crime Schemes". available from http://www.ic3.gov/crimeschemes.aspx (Retrieved on January 4, 2008).

Ismaili, K. (1992). *Understanding policy responses to victims of crime in Canada: A Social constructionist perspective*. Paper presented at the American Society of Criminology Meeting, New Orleans, Louisiana.

Ivancevich, J. M., Duening, T. N., Gilbert, J. A., and Konopaske, R. (2003). Deterring white-collar crime. *Academy of Management Executive, 17*(2), 114–127.

Jacobs, J. B., and Potter, K. (1998). *Hate crimes: Criminal law and identity politics*. New York: Oxford University Press.

James, M. P. (1993). *Crime prevention for older Australians*. Canberra, ACT: Australian Institute of Criminology.

Jeffery, C. R. (1977). *Crime prevention through environmental design* (2nd ed.). Beverly Hills, CA: Sage.

Jeffords, C. R. (1983). The situational relationship between age and fear of crime. *International Journal of Aging and Human Development, 17*(2), 103–111.

Jenkins, C. (2005). *Behavioral aspects of violent crime*. Paper presented at the American Criminal Justice Association, Regional Meeting. Richmond, VA, October 21.

Johnson, E. H. (1987). *Crime prevention: Approaches, practices and evaluations*. Westport, CT: Greenwood Press.

Johnson, I.M., and Sigler, R.T. (1997). *Forced sexual intercourse in intimate relationships*. Brookfield, VT: Ashgate.

Jones, D.P. (1991). Ritualism and child sexual abuse. *Child Abuse and Neglect, 15*(3), 163–170.

James, M. P. (1993). *Crime prevention for older Australians*. Canberra, ACT: Australian Institute of Criminology.

Jameson, R. (2002). *Case study: US savings and loan crisis*. Retrieved from http://www.erisk.com/Learning/Intro.asp

Jerin, R. A. (1987). *Police civil liability to crime victims for failure to provide protection*. Unpublished doctoral dissertation. Sam Houston State University, Huntsville, TX.

Jerin, R. A. (1988a). Police liability for failure to protect battered women. *American Journal of Police, 8*(1), 71–87.

Jerin, R. A. (1988b). The victim. In R. H. C. Teske (Ed.), *Crime and justice in Texas*. Huntsville, TX: Sam Houston Press.

Jerin, R. A. (1990, November). *A descriptive analysis of victim's laws: The victim's rights movement over the last 25 years*. Paper presented at the American Society of Criminology Annual meeting, Baltimore, MD.

Jerin, R. A. (2001). Victims rights legislation. In L. J. Moriarty (Ed.), *Police and Crime Victims*. Englewood Cliffs, NJ: Prentice Hall.

Jerin, R. A. (2004). The status of victimological research and victims' rights in the United States. *International Perspectives in Victimology, 1*(1), 129–149.

Jerin, R. A., and Moriarty, L. J. (1994, November). *North Carolina's victim/witness program*. Paper presented at the Annual Meeting of the American Society of Criminology, Miami, FL.

Jerin, R. A., Moriarty, L. J., and Gibson, J. (1992, November). *Victim service or self service: An analysis of victim service providers*. Paper presented at the Annual Meeting of the American Society of Criminology, New Orleans, LA.

Jerin, R. A., Moriarty, L. J., and Gibson, J. (1995). Victim service or self service: An analysis of prosecution-based victim-witness programs and providers. *Criminal Justice Policy Review, 7*(2), 142–154.

Jerin, R. A., and Moriarty, L. J. (1998). *Victims of crime*. Chicago, IL: Nelson-Hall.

Johnson, D. R. (1981). *American law enforcement: A history*. St. Louis, MO: Forum Press.

Johnson, H. A. (1988). *History of criminal justice*. Cincinnati, OH: Anderson.

Johnson, K. (1996, May 6). Homicide, rape, robbery: The numbers are fewer but crime is rising among teens. *USA Today*, p. 8A.

Kadushin, A., and Martin, J. A. (1988). *Child welfare services* (4th ed.). New York: Macmillan.

Kahaner, L. (1988). *Cults that kill*. New York: Warner.

Kansas Victim Assistance Association. (1992). *Prosecutor-based victim/witness manual*. Kansas City: Kansas County and District Attorneys Association.

Karmen, A. (1984). *Crime victims: An introduction to victimology*. Belmont, CA: Brooks/Cole.

Karmen, A. (1990). The implementation of victims' rights: A challenge for criminal justice professionals. In R. Muraskin (Ed.), *Issues in justice: Exploring policy issues in the criminal justice system*. Bristol, IN: Wyndham Hall.

Karmen, A. (1996). *Crime victims* (3rd ed.). Belmont, CA: Wadsworth.

Karmen, A. (2003). *Crime victims* (5th ed.). Belmont, CA: Wadsworth.

Karp, D. R., and Walther, L. (2001) Community reparative boards in Vermont: Theory and practice. In G. Bazemore, and M. Schiff (Eds.), *Restortive Community Justice*. Cincinnati, OH: Anderson.

Kelley, D. P. (1984). Delivering legal services to victims: An evaluation and prescription. *Justice System Journal, 9,* 62.

Kelley, L. (1988). *Surviving sexual violence*. Minneapolis: University of Minnesota Press.

Kelly, D. P. (1990). Victim participation in the criminal justice system. In A. J. Lurigio, W. G. Skogan, and R. C. Davius (Eds.), *Victims of crime: Problems, policies, and programs*. Newbury Park, CA: Sage.

Kempe, C., Silverman, F. N., Steele, B. F., Droegemueller, W., and Silver, H. K. (1962). The battered-child syndrome. *Journal of the American Medical Association, 181,* 17–24.

Kent, C. C. (1993). Ritual abuse. In R. T. Ammerman, and M. Hersen (Eds.), *Case studies in family violence*. New York: Plenum.

Kenworthy, P. C. (1997). *Virginia and North Carolina: An examination of two models of child representation*. Unpublished master's thesis.

Virginia Commonwealth University, Richmond, VA.

Kilpatrick, D. G. (1983, Summer). Rape victims: Detection, assessment and treatment. *The Clinical Psychologist, 36*(4), 92–95.

Kilpatrick, D. G. (1990, August). *Violence as a precursor of women's substance abuse*. Paper presented at the annual meeting of the American Psychological Association, Boston, Mass.

Kilpatrick, D. G., Best, C. L., Saunders, B. E., and Veronen, L. J. (1988). Rape in marriage and in dating relationships: How bad is it for mental health? *Annals of the New York Academy of Sciences, 528,* 335–344.

Kilpatrick, D., and Saunders, B. (1997). The prevalence and consequence of child victimization. *NIJ Research Preview*. Retrieved from http://www.ncjrs.org/txtfiles/ fs000179.txt

Kilpatrick, D. G., Tidwell, R. P., Walker, E., Resnick, H. S., Saunders, B. E., Paduhovich, J., and Lipovsky, J. A. (1989). *Victim rights and services in South Carolina: The dream, the law, the reality*. Charleston, SC: Crime Victims Research and Treatment Center.

Kimmel, M. (2001). Snips and snails . . . and violent urges. Newsday, Minneapolis Star-Tribune, San Francisco Examiner, p. A41.

Kimmel, M. S., and Mahler, M. (2003). Adolescent masculinity, homophobia, and violence. *American Behavioral Scientist, 46*(10), 1439–1458.

Kirkwood, M. K., and Cecil, D. K. (2001). Marital rape: A student assessment of rape laws and the marital exemption. *Violence Against Women, 7*(11), 1234–1253.

Klaus, P. A. (1994). *The costs of crime to victims*. Washington, DC: U.S. Department of Justice.

Klaus, P. A. (2005). *Crimes against persons age 65 or older, 1993–2002*. Washington, DC: U.S. Department of Justice. (NCJ 206154).

Klein, J., & Chancer, L. S. (2000). Masculinity matters: The omission of gender from high-profile school violence cases. In S. U. Spina (Ed.), *Smoke and mirrors: The hidden content of violence in schools and society*. Lanham, MD: Rowman & Littlefield.

Klotter, J. C. (2001). *Criminal law and criminal law study guide* (6th ed.). Cincinnati, OH: Anderson Publishing Company.

Kopetman, R. (1989, April 16). School erecting 10 foot wall to deflect bullets. *Los Angeles Times*, p. 1.

Koss, M. P. (1983). The scope of rape: Implications for the clinical treatment of reactions. *Clinical Psychologist, 36*, 88–91.

Koss, M. P. (1992). The underdetection of rape: Methodological choices influence incidence estimates. *Journal of Social Issues, 48*(1), 61–75.

Koss, M. P., and Harvey, M. R. (1991). *The rape victim*. Newbury Park, CA: Sage Publications.

Kovacich, G. L., and Halibozek, E. P. (2003). *The manager's handbook for corporate security: Establishing and managing a successful assets protection program*. New York: Butterworth-Heinemann.

Krummel, S. (1996). Abuse of the elderly. In D. N. Busby (Ed.), *The impact of violence on the family*. Boston: Allyn and Bacon.

Kutner, L. (1966). Crime-torts: Due process of compensation for crime victims. *Notre Dame Lawyer, 41*, 487–502.

Kurz, D. (1993). Physical assaults by husbands: A major social problem. In R. J. Gelles, and D. R. Loseke (Eds.), *Current controversies on family violence*. Newbury Park, CA: Sage.

Lab, S. P. (1992). *Crime prevention: Approaches, practices and evaluations*. Cincinnati, OH: Anderson.

Lacks, R. D. (2006a, March). *Cops and docs*. Presentation at the 4th Annual American Symposium on Victimology, Huntsville, Texas.

Lacks, R. D. (2006b, April 11–14). *Personal communication*. Richmond, VA.

Lacter, E. P. (2003). *Brief synopsis of the literature on the existence of ritualistic abuse*. Retrieved from http://truthbeknown2000.tripod.com/Truthbeknown2000/id19.html

LaFree, G. H. (1989). *Rape and criminal justice: The social construction of sexual assault*. Belmont, CA: Wadsworth.

LaGrange, R., and Ferraro, K. (1989). Assessing age and gender differences in perceived risk and fear of crime. *Criminology, 23*(3), 541–552.

Lanning, K. (1992). Satanic ritual abuse: A 1992 FBI report. Available at http://www.rickross.com/reference/satanism/satanism1.html

Larsen, R.W. (1980).
Bundy—the deliberate stranger. Prentice Hall Trade.

Laub, J. H. (1997). Patterns of criminal victimization in the United States. In A. J. Lurigio, W. G. Skogan, and R. C. Davis (Eds.), *Victims of crime: Problems, policies, and programs*. Newbury Park, CA: Sage.

Laufer, W. S. (2006) *Corporate bodies and guilty minds: The failure of corporate criminal liability*. Chicago, IL: University of Chicago Press.

Lee, J., and Geisfield, L. V. (1999). Elderly consumers' receptiveness to telemarketing fraud. *Journal of Public Policy and Marketing, 18*(2), 208–218.

Lee, A., and Searle, W. (1993). *Victims needs: An issues paper*. Wellington, New Zealand: Department of Justice.

Levin, J., and McDevitt, J. (1993). *Hate crimes: The rising tide of bigotry and bloodshed*. New York: Plenum Press.

Liebman, D. A., and Schwartz, J. A. (1973). Police programs in crisis intervention: A review. In J. R. Snibbe, and H. M. Snibbe (Eds.), *The urban policeman in transition: A psychological and sociological review*. Springfield, IL: Charles C. Thomas.

Lipka, S. (2008, June 18). 28 Families reach final settlements with Virginia Tech and the state. *Chronicle of Higher Education*, available at: http://chronicle.com/daily/2008/06/3427n.htm?utm_source=at&utm_medium=en.

Losey, S. (2006). *Six dead in Calif. postal plant shooting*. Retrieved from http://federaltimes.com/index.php?S=1502273

Lord, J. H. (1990). *Victim impact panels: A creative sentencing opportunity*. Irving, TX: Mothers Against Drunk Drivers.

Lonsway, K. A. & Fitzgerald, L. F. (1994). Rape myths: In review. *Psychology of Woman Quarterly, 18*, 133–164.

Lowe, S. (2005). *An exploration of the issues of older women who have experienced violent long-term intimate partner relationships: Listening to older women*. Unpublished doctoral dissertation proposal. November, 2005.

Luigio, A. J., Skogan, W. G., and Davis, R. C. (1990). Criminal victimization. In A. J. Lurigio, W. G. Skogan, and R. C. Davius (Eds.), *Victims of crime: Problems, policies, and programs*. Newbury Park, CA: Sage.

Luthern, J. R. (1991, March). Victim witness assistance. *FBI Law Enforcement Bulletin*, pp. 1–5.

Lystad, M.H. (1986). *Violence in the home: Interdisciplinary perspectives*. New York: Brunner/Mazel.

Mackey, V. (1990). *Restorative justice: Toward non-violence*. Louisville, KY: Presbyterian Justice Program.

Macleod, M. (2006). Charles Whitman: The Texas tower sniper, available at: http://www.trutv.com/library/crime/notorious_murders/mass/whitman/tower_6.html (Retrieved on May 3, 2006).

MacDonald, J. M. (1995). *Rape—Controversial issues: Criminal profiles, date rape, false reports, and false memories*. Springfield, IL: Charles C. Thomas.

Maguire, M., and Shapland, J. (1991). The victim movement in Europe. In A. J. Lurigio, W. G. Skogan, and R. C. Davis (Eds.), *Victims of crime: Problems, policies, and programs*. Newbury Park, NJ: Sage

Mallory, P. R. (2006). Crimes committed against homeless persons. Retrieved from http://caag.state.ca.us/cjsc/publications/misc/SR18net/preface.pdf

Manzi, S. and Dunn, K. (2007). Hate crime victimization: A legal perspective. In L. J. Moriarty and R. A. Jerin, (Eds.), *Current issues in victimology research*, (2nd Ed.) (pp. 75–86). Durham: Carolina Academic Press.

Mathew Shepard. available at: http: //en.wikipedia.org/wiki/Matthew_Shepard (Retrieved on February 1, 2008).

Mathews, D. J. (1995). Parenting groups for men who batter. In E. Peled, P. G. Jaffe, and J. L. Edleson (Eds.), *Ending the cycle of violence: Community responses to children of battered women*. Thousand Oaks, CA: Sage.

Maxwell, G.M., and Morris, A. (2001). Restorative conferencing. In G. Brazemore, and M. Schiff (eds.), *Restorative community justice: Repairing harm and transforming communities*. Cincinnati, OH: Anderson Publishing Co.

Mawby, R. I., and Walklate, S. (1993). *Critical victimology: International perspectives*. London: Sage.

McCarthy, B. R., and McCarthy, B. J. (1991). *Community-based corrections* (2nd ed.). Pacific Grove, CA: Brooks/Cole.

McCloskey, K. (2005, August). *Battered women arrested for domestic violence*. Paper presented at the meeting of American Psychological Association, Washington, DC.

McDevitt, J., Levin, J., and Bennett, S. (2002). Hate crime offenders: An expanded typology. *Journal of Social Issues, 58*(2), 303–317.

McEvoy, A. (1990). Combating gang activities in schools. *Education Digest, 56*, 31–34.

McShane, M. D., and Williams, F. P. (1992). Radical victimology: A critique of the concept of victim in traditional victimology. *Crime and Delinquency, 38*, 258–271.

Meadow, R. (1977). Munchausen syndrome by proxy: The hinterland of child abuse. *Lancet, 2*, 343–345.

Meadows, R. J. (2007). *Understanding violence and victimization* (4th ed.). Upper Saddle River, NJ: Pearson, Prentice Hall.

Melamed, J. (2008). What is mediation. available at: http://www.mediate.com/articles/what.cfm (Retrieved on September 15, 2008).

Mendel, M.P. (1995). *The male survivor: The impact of sexual abuse*. Thousand Oaks, CA: SAGE

Mendelsohn, B. (1940). Rape in criminology. Trans. and cited in S. Schafer (1968). *The Victim and His Criminal*. New York: Random House.

Mercer, D., Lorden, R., and Lord, J. H. (1999, Winter). *Victim impact panels: A healing opportunity for victims of drunk driving crashes* (pp. 8–9). MADDvocate, Dallas: Mothers Against Drunk Driving.

Miethe, T. D., and Meier, R. F. (1990). Opportunity, choice, and criminal victimization: A test of a theoretical model. *Journal of Research in Crime and Delinquency, 27*, 243–266.

Miethe, T. D., and Meier, R. F. (1994). *Crime and its social context: Toward an integrated theory of offenders, victims and situations*. Albany, NY: SUNY.

Miller, J. (1996). *Compensation crime victims within New Zealand's no fault accident compensation scheme: The advantages and disadvantages*. In C. Sumner, M. Israel, M. O'Connell, and R. Sarre (Eds.), International victimology: Selected papers from the 8th International Symposium, No 27. Canberra, ACT: Australian Institute of Criminology.

Miller, B., and Marshall, J. C. (1987, January). Coercible sex on the university campus. *Journal of College Student Personnel, 24*, 38–47.

Miller, T. R., Cohen, M. A., and Wierseman, B. (1996). *Victim costs and consequences: A new look*. Washington, DC: Government Printing Office.

Milner, J. S., and Crouch, J. L. (1993). Physical child abuse. In R. L. Hampton, T. P. Gullotta, G. R. Adams, E. H. Potter, and R. P. Weissberg (Eds.), *Family violence—Prevention and treatment*. Newbury Park, CA: Sage.

Miron, H. J., Goin, L. J., Keegan, S., and Archer, E. (1984). *The national sheriffs' association guidelines for victim assistance*. Washington, DC: U.S. Department of Justice.

Mitchell, K. J., Finkelhor, D., and Wolak, J. (2003). Exposure of youth to unwanted sexual material on the internet: A national survey of risk, impact, and prevention. *Youth & Society, 34*(3), 330–358.

Mobile phones given to victims of domestic violence. (1996, February 9). *Boston Globe*, p. 35.

Modglin, T. W., and O'Neil, J. (1989). How victim assistance supports crime prevention. *Crime Victims Digest, 6*(9), 1–5.

Moffitt, T. E. (1997). Adolescence-limited and life-course persistent offending: A complementary pair of developing theories. In T. Thornberry (Ed.), *Developmental theories of crime and delinquency* (pp. 11–54). New Brunswick, CT: Transaction Publishers.

Mokhiber, R. (2002, April). Do corporations kill? *Multinational Monitor*, p. 29.

Molloy, T. (2006). *Former postal employee kills five, commits suicide at mail-processing center*. Retrieved from http://www.nctimes.com/articles/2006/01/31/news/state/16_44_311_31_06.txt

Moore, E., and Mills, M. (1990). The neglected victims and unexamined costs of white-collar crime. *Crime and Delinquency, 9*, 1–5.

Moore, E., and Millsap, M. (1990). The neglected victims and unexamined costs of white-collar crime. *Crime and Delinquency, 36*(3), 408–419.

Moore, K. (1995). Social work's role with patients with Munchausen syndrome. *Social Work, 40*(6), 823–825.

Moriarty, L. J. (2003). *Controversies in victimology*. Cincinnati, OH: Anderson.

Moriarty, L. J., and Earl, J. (1999). An analysis of services for victims of wife rape: A case study. *Journal of Offender Rehabilitation, 29*(3/4), 171–181.

Moriarty, L. J., and Freiberger, K. L. (2003). Classifying female serial killers: An application of prominent typologies. In R. Muraskin (Ed.), *It's a crime: Women and justice*. Upper Saddle River, NJ: Prentice Hall.

Moriarty, L. J., and Freiberger, K. L. (2006). *Investigating cyberstalking: An examination of victimization patterns*. Paper presented at the World Society of Victimology 12th International Symposium on Victimology, Orlando, FL, August 23.

Moriarty, L. J., and Jerin, R. A. (1998). *Current issues in victimology research*. Durham, NC: Carolina Academic Press National Organization for Victim Assistance.

Mulford, R. (1958). Emotional neglect of children. *Child Welfare, 37*(8), 19–24.

Murphy, C. M., and Cascardi, M. (1993). Psychological aggression and abuse in marriage. In R. L. Hampton, R. P. Gullotta, G. R. Adams, E. H. Potter, and R. P. Weissberg (Eds.), *Family violence, prevention and treatment*. Newbury Park, CA: Sage.

Nadien, M. B. (1995). Elder violence (maltreatment) in domestic settings: some theory and research. In L. L. Adler, and F. L. Denmark (Eds.), *Violence and the prevention of violence*. Westport, CT: Praeger.

Nansel, T. R., Overpeck, M., Pilla, R. S., Ruan, W. J., Simons-Morton, B., and Scheidt, P. (2001). Bullying behaviors among U.S. youth: Prevalence and association with psychosocial adjustment. *Journal of the American Medical Association, 285*, 2094–2100.

National Association of Triads, (2008), available at: http://www.nationaltriad.org/resources/index.htm (Retrieved September 18, 2008)

National Archive of Criminal Justice Data. (2008a). "NCVS Data" available at: http://www.icpsr.umich.edu/NACJD/NCVS/ (Retrieved on May 30, 2008).

National Archive of Criminal Justice Data. (2008b). "About NCVS" available at: http://www.icpsr.umich.edu/NACJD/NCVS/ (Retrieved on May 30, 2008).

National Briefing South. (2006, October). Alabama: Bid for bomb files. *York Times*. Retrieved from http://query.nytimes.com/gst/fullpage.html?res=9C01EED71630F93AA15753C1A9659C8B63andn=Top%2fReference%2fTimes%20Topics%2fPeople%2fJ%2fJewell%2c%20Richard.

National Center for the Analysis of Violent Crime. (2005). *The serial murder symposium: Collected readings*. Washington, DC: Federal Bureau of Investigation.

National Center for Women & Policing. (2006). Retrieved from http://www.womenand policing.org/violenceFS.asp

National Center of Child Abuse and Neglect. (1994). *Fact sheet*. Retrieved from http://www.acf.dhhs.gov/ALFPrograms,NCCAN/abuse.txt

National Center for Disease Control. (1991). *National survey of high school behavior*. Atlanta, GA: NCDC.

National Center for Victims of Crime. (1999). *Promising practices and strategies for victim services in corrections*. Arlington, VA: U.S. Department of Justice.

National Center for Victims of Crime. (2005). Fact Sheet, available at: http://www.ncvc.org/src/AGP.Net/Components/Documentviewer/Download.aspxnz?DocumentID=40616.

National Center for Victims of Crime. (2007). *Public Policy*. Arlington, VA: National Victim Center. Available at: http://www.ncvc.org/ncvc/main.aspx?dbID=DB_PublicPolicy185 (Retrieved on May 1, 2008).

National Center for Victims of Crime. (2008). Available at: http://www.ncvc.org

National Clearinghouse on Child Abuse and Neglect Information. (1996). *Statistics desk*. Retrieved from http://www.calib.com/nccanch/services/stats.htm.

National Crime Prevention Council website. (1995). Available at http://www.ncpc.org/

National Crime Prevention Council. (1994a). *National service and public safety: partnerships for safer communities*. Washington, DC: Government Printing Office.

National Crime Prevention Council. (1994b). *Taking the offensive to prevent crime: How seven cities did it*. Washington, DC: Government Printing Office.

National Crime Prevention Institute. (1986). *Understanding crime prevention*. Boston: Butterworths.

National Crime Victim Bar Association. (2001). *Helping crime victims pursue civil justice*. Retrieved from http://www.victimbar.org/vb/Main.aspx

National Crime Victim's Center. (2006). *2006 NCVRW resource guide*. Washington, DC: Government Printing Office.

National Fraud Information Center. (2005). *Telemarketing scams January–December 2004*. Washington, DC: National Consumer League.

National Fraud Information Center. (2005). *Internet scams fraud trends 2004*. Washington, DC: National Consumer League.

National Field Sellers Association (2006) *An Identity Theft Crisis*. Philadelphia, PA, available at: http://www.nfsa.com/pdf/nfsa_nws_0106.pdf (Retrieved on August 30, 2007)

National Heath Care Anti-Fraud Association. (2002). *Estimated financial loss to fraud: Factsheet*. Retrieved from http://www.nhcaa.org.

National Institute of Justice. (1995, September). *Evaluation of violence prevention programs in middle schools, update*. Washington, DC: Government Printing Office.

National Institute of Mental Health. (2002). *Mental health and mass violence: Evidence-based early psychological intervention for victims/survivors of violence. A workshop to reach consensus on best practices*. Washington, DC: Government Printing Office. (NIH Publication No. 02–5138).

National Organization for Victim Assistance. (1984). *The victim service system: A guide to action*. Washington, DC: Author.

National Organization for Victim Assistance. (1990). *Victims' rights and services: A legislative directory 1988/1989*. Washington, DC: Author.

National Organization for Victim Assistance. (1992). Impact statement not having much effect. *Nova Newsletter, 16*, 2.

National Organization for Victim Assistance. (1993). A chronology of victims' rights. *NOVA Newsletter, 16*, 11.

National Organization for Victim Assistance. (1995a). Basic rights revisited. *NOVA Newsletter, 17*(4), 1–4.

National Organization for Victim Assistance. (1995b). Victims rights week. *NOVA Newsletter, 17*, 4.

National Organization for Victim Assistance. (2006). Victims rights week. *NOVA Newsletter, 28*, 4.

National School Safety Center. (1998). *Checklist of characteristics of youth who have caused school-associated violent deaths*. Retrieved from http://www.nssc1.org/

National Sheriffs' Association. (1984). *Victim assistance training program handbook*. Alexandria, VA: Author.

National School Safety Center. (1999). Available at http://www.schoolsafety.us/

National Victims' Constitutional Amendment Project. (2007). Recent news/chronology, available at: http://www.nvcan.org/

National Victim Center. (1997). *The 1996 victims' rights sourcebook: A compilation and comparison of victims' rights laws.* Washington, DC: U.S. Department of Justice.

National White Collar Crime Center. (2000). *National public survey on white collar crime.* Retrieved from http://www.nw3c.org/

National White Collar Crime Center. (2004). *IC3 2004 Internet fraud crime report.* Retrieved from http://www.nw3c.org/

National White Collar Crime Center. (2005). *Internet crime complaint center 2004 Internet fraud—Crime report.* Retrieved from http://www.nw3c.org/

National White Collar Crime Center. (2006). *The 2005 national public survey on white collar crime.* Retrieved from http://www.nw3c.org/.

NBC News. (2006, April 15). *The today show.*

Nelson, B. J. (1984). *Making an issue of child abuse: Political agenda setting for social problems.* Chicago: University of Chicago Press.

Neubauer, D. W. (1996). *America's courts and the criminal justice system.* New York: Wadsworth.

Newman, O. (1972). *Defensible space.* New York: Macmillan.

Newman, G. R., and McNally, M. M. (2005). *Identity theft literature review.* Washington, DC: U.S. Department of Justice.

New Jersey Department of Law and Public Safety. (1988). *Attorney General standards to ensure the rights of crime victims manual.* Trenton, NH: Department of Law and Public Safety.

New York Times. (2008, June 27). *2nd Millionaire gets prison in slavery case.* Retrieved June 27, 2008 from http://www.nytimes.com/aponline/us/AP-Forced-Labor.html?scp=2&sq=slavery&st=nyt

New Zealand government web site of Child, Youth, and Family. Retrieved from http://www.cyf.govt.nz/1254.htm

NHTSA. (2007). Traffic safety facts: Research note. "2006 Traffic Safety Annual Assessment—Alcohol-related Fatalities." National Center for Statistics and Analysis. Washington, DC: NHTSA.

Nicholson, G. (1992). Victims' rights, remedies, and resources: A maturing presence in American jurisprudence. *Pacific Law Journal, 23,* 815–841.

North Carolina Victim Assistance Network. (1994a). *The status of crime services and rights in North Carolina.* Raleigh, NC: Author.

North Carolina Victim Assistance Network. (1994b). *Newsletter, 4*(1), 1–2.

Oates, R. K. (1991). Child physical abuse. In R. T. Ammerman, and M. Hersen (Eds.), *Case studies in family violence.* New York: Plenum.

O'Donoghue, J. (1995). Violence in the schools. In L. L. Adler, and F. L. Denmark (Eds.), *Violence and the prevention of violence.* Westport, CT: Praeger.

Office of the United Nations High Commissioner for Human Rights. (2008). Declaration of basic principles of justice for victims of crime and abuse of power, available at: http://www2.ohchr.org/english/law/victims.htm (Retrieved on January 30, 2008).

Office for Victims of Crime. (1996). *The national victims resource directory.* Rockville, MD: Author.

Office for Victims of Crime. (1998). *New directions from the field: Victim's rights and service for the 21st Century.* Washington DC: U. S. Department of Justice.

Office for Victims of Crime. (2001). *First response to victims of crime.* Rockville, MD: Author.

Office for Victims of Crime. (2006). *Mandatory Victims Restitution Act of 1996.* Rockville, MD. Retrieved from http://www.ojp.usdoj.gov/ovc/help/cvr.htm

Office of Juvenile Justice and Delinquency Prevention. (1996). *Reducing youth gun violence: An overview of programs and initiatives.* Washington, DC: Government Printing Office.

Office of the Attorney General Tom Reilly. (2006). Victim*compensation.* Boston, MA: Author.

O'Leary, K. D. (1993). Through a psychological lens: Personality traits, personality disorders, and levels of violence. In R. J. Gelles, and D. R. Loseke (Eds.), *Current controversies on family violence.* Newbury Park, CA: Sage.

Ollenburger, J. C. (1981). Criminal victimization and fear of crime. *Research on Aging, 3*(1), 101–118.

O'Malley, T. A., Everitt, D. E., O'Malley, H. C., and Campion, E. W. (1983). Identifying and preventing family mediated abuse and neglect of elderly persons. *Annals of Internal Medicine, 98,* 998–1005.

Orentlicher, D. F. (2007). Genocide. In R. Gutman, D. Rieff, and A. Dworkin (Eds.), *Crimes of War.* New York: W.W. Norton and Co.

Ortega, S. T., and Myles, J. L. (1987). Race and gender effects on fear of crime: An interactive model with age. *Criminology, 25*(1), 133–152.

OVC Fact Sheet. (2001). *International activities.* Retrieved from http://www.ojp.usdoj.gov/ovc/ publications/factshts/interact.htm

OVC Fact Sheet. (2002). *Terrorism and international victims unit.* Retrieved from http://www.ojp.usdoj.gov/ovc/publications/facts hts/tivu/welcome.html

Pagelow, M. D. (1984). *Family violence.* New York: Praeger.

Pagelow, M. D. (1992). Adult victims of domestic violence: Battered women.*Journal of Interpersonal Violence, 7,* 87–120.

Pain, R. H. (1995). Elderly women and fear of violent crime: The least likely victims? A reconsideration of the extent and nature of risk. *The British Journal of Criminology, 35,* 584–598.

Parent, D., Auerbach, G. B., and Carlson, K. E. (1992). *Compensating crime victims: A summary of policies and practices.* Washington, DC: U.S. Department of Justice.

Payne, B. K. (2002). An integrated understanding of elder abuse and neglect. *Journal of Criminal Justice, 30,* 535–547.

Payne, B.K., Berg, B. and Byars, K., 1999. A qualitative examination of the similarities and differences of elder abuse definitions among four groups: nursing home directors, nursing home employees, police chiefs and students. *Journal of Elder Abuse and Neglect, 10,* 63–86.

Payne, B. K., and Cikovic, R. (1995). An empirical examination of the characteristics, consequences, and causes of elder abuse in nursing homes. *Journal of Elder Abuse and Neglect, 7*(4), 61–74.

Payne, B. K., and Gainey, R. R. (in press). Differentiating self neglect as a type of elder mistreatment: How do these cases compare to traditional types of elder abuse. *Journal of Elder Abuse and Neglect, 22*(3/4), pp. 3–20.

Payne, B. K., and Gainey, R. R. (2006). Differentiating self neglect as a type of elder mistreatment: How do these cases compare to

traditional types of elder abuse. *Journal of Elder Abuse and Neglect, 17,* 21–36.

Pazder, L. (1980). *Ritual abuse.* Paper presented at the American Psychiatric Association, New Orleans, LA, cited in Kent (1993).

Peacock, P. L. (1995). Marital rape. In V. R. Wiehe, and A. I. Richards (Eds.), *Intimate betrayal: Understanding and responding to the trauma of acquaintance rape.* Thousand Oaks, CA: Sage.

Pelfrey, W. P., Bohm, R. M., Dean, C. W., Humphrey, J. A., Moriarity, L. J., Vasu, M. L., Willis, G. W., and Zahn, M. A. (1992). *The North Carolina violent crime assessment project: A final report.* Report prepared for the North Carolina Governor's Crime Commission, Raleigh, NC.

Perkins, C. (1996). *Bulletin—Criminal victimization 1994.* Washington, DC: Bureau of Justice Statistics. (Report Number (NCJ-158022).

Pertman, A. (1996, June 21). Ruling deals blow to 3-strikes law. *The Boston Globe,* sec 1: 3.

Peters, S. D., Wyatt, G. E., and Finklehor, D. (1986). Prevalence. *Sourcebook on child sexual abuse.* Newbury Park, CA: Sage.

Peterson, B. K., and Zikmund, P. E. (2004). 10 truths you need to know about fraud. *Strategic Finance, 85*(11), 29–34.

Pfohl, S. (1977). The "discovery" of child abuse. *Social Problems, 24,* 310–323.

Pillemer, K. A., and Finkelhor, D. (1988). The prevalence of elder abuse: A random sample survey. *Gerontologist, 28*(1), 51–57.

Pillemer, K. A., and Moore, D. W. (1989). Abuse of patients in nursing homes: Findings from a survey of staff. *Gerontologist, 29*(3), 314–320.

Plass, P. S., and Straus, M. A. (1987, July). *Intrafamily homicide in the United States: Incidence, trends, and differences by region, race and gender.* Paper presented at the Third National Family Violence Conference, University of New Hampshire, Durham, NH.

Polito, K. E. (1990). The rights of crime victims in the criminal justice system: Is justice blind to the victims of crime? *Criminal and Civil Confinement, 16*(2), 241–270.

Pollock, J. N. (1994). *Ethics in crime and justice: Dilemmas and decision.* Belmont, CA: Wadsworth.

Pollock, J., and May, J. (2002). Authentication technology: Identity theft and account takeover. *FBI Law Enforcement Bulletin, 71*(6), 1–4.

President's Task Force on Victims of Crime. (1982). *Final* report. Washington, DC: Government Printing Office.

Pressman, S. (1998). On financial frauds and their causes: Investor overconfidence. *American Journal of Economics and Sociology, 5*(4), 405–422.

Putnam, F. W. (1991). The satanic ritual abuse controversy. *Child Abuse & Neglect, 15*, 175–179.

Price, Waterhouse, & Coopers. (2004, April 2004). "Information Security Breaches Survey". available at http://www.pwc.com/images/gx/eng/about/svcs/grms/2004Exec_Summ.pdf (Retrieved 2 November, 2006).

Prison Fellowship International. (2006) Restorative Justice Online. Retrieved from http://www.pfi.org/cjr

Quay, H. C., and Love, C. T. (1977). The effect of a juvenile diversion program on rearrests. *Criminal Justice and Behavior, 4*, 377–396.

Radbill, S. A. (1980). A history of child abuse and infanticide. In R. Heler, and C. Kempe (Eds.), *The battered child* (3rd ed.). Chicago: University of Chicago Press.

Ramker, G., and Meagher, M. (1982). Crime victim compensation: A survey of state programs. *Federal Probation*, 68–72.

Rand Newsletter. (2000). Retrieved from http://www.rand.org/multi/dprc/pubs/2000_newsletter/homeless.html

Rantala, R. R., and Edwards, T. J. (2000). "Effects of NIBRS on crime statistics: BJS special report". *Power point presentation*, available at: http://www.ojp.usdoj.gov/bjs/pub/pdf/enibrscs.pdf (Retrieved on May 30, 2008).

Rathbone-McCuan, E. (1980, May). Elderly victims of family violence and neglect. *Journal of Contemporary Social Work, 23*, 296–304.

Ratrbone-McCuan, E., and Voyles, B. (1982). Case detection of abused elderly parents. *American Journal of Psychiatry, 139*(2), 189–192.

Reasons, C.E. and Hughson, Q. (2000). Violence against gays and lesbians. In Race, Ethnicity, Sexual Orientation, Violent Crime: The realities and the myths, (pp. 137–159). New York: Hawthorne Press.

Reddy, M., Borum, R., Berglund, J., Vossekuil, B., Fein, R., and Modzeleski, W. (2001). Evaluating risk for targeted violence in schools: Comparing risk assessment, threat assessment, and other approaches. *Psychology in the Schools, 38*(2), 157–172.

Reeves, J. (2006). Alabama church fires appear linked, Governor says. *The Washington post.* Retrieved from www.washingtonpost.com

Regoli, R., Wilderman, E., and Pogrebin, M. (1985). Using an alternative evaluation measure for assessing juvenile diversion programs. *Children and Youth Services Review, 7*, 21–38.

Reiss, A. J., and Roth, J. A. (1993). *Understanding and preventing violence.* Washington, DC: National Academy Press.

Rennison, C. M. (2002). Rape and sexual assault: Reporting to police and medical attention, 1992–2000. Washington, DC: U.S. Department of Justice. (NCJ – 194530).

Ress, D. (2008, January 10). Richmond's first homicide of 2008: Women set on fire dies. *Richmond Times Dispatch. Metro & Business*, pp. B1, B3.

Reynolds, D. (2000). *Judge upholds anti-bias law in disabled man's torture.* Retrieved from www.inclusiondaily.com/news/crime/krochmaluk.htm

Roberts, A. R. (1990). *Helping crime victims: Research, policy, and practice.* Newbury Park, CA: Sage.

Roberts, A. R. (1996). *Helping battered women: New perspectives and remedies.* New York: Oxford University Press.

Robin, M. (1982). Historical introduction: Sheltering arms—The roots of child protection. In E. H. Newberger (Ed.), *Child abuse.* Boston: Little, Brown.

Rodgers, K., and Roberts, G. (1995). Women's non-spousal multiple victimization: A test of the routine activities theory. *Canadian Journal of Criminology, 37*(3), 361–391.

Rome Statute of the International Criminal Court Article 68. (2008). Retrieved June 17, 2008 from http://untreaty.un.org/cod/icc/statute/99_corr/cstatute.htm.

Roscoe, B., Goodwin, M., and Kennedy, D. (1987). Sibling violence and agonistic interactions experienced by early adolescents. *Journal of Family Violence, 2*, 121–138.

Rosenbaum, D. P. (1987). Coping with victimization: The effects of police intervention on victims' psychological readjustment. *Crime and Delinquency, 33*(4), 502–519.

Rosenblum, R. H., and Blew, C. H. (1979). *Victim/witness assistance.* Washington DC: U.S. Department of Justice.

Rossi, P. H., and Freeman, H. E. (1994). *Evaluation: A systematic approach* (5th ed.). Newbury Park, CA: Sage.

Roth, J. A. (1994). *Understanding and preventing violence.* Washington, DC: National Institute of Justice.

Ryan, M. G., Davis, A. A., and Oates, R. K. (1977). One hundred and eighty-seven cases of child abuse and neglect. *Medical Journal of Australia, 2,* 623–628.

Sacco, V. F., and Nakhaie, M. R. (2001). Coping with crime: An examination of elderly and non-elderly adaptations. *International Journal of Law and Psychiatry, 24*(2–3), 305–323.

Saunders, D. G., and Browne, A. (1993). Domestic homicide. In R. T. Ammerman, and M. Hersen (Eds.), *Case studies in family violence.* New York: Plenum Press.

Schafer, S. (1968). *The victim and his criminal.* New York: Random House.

Schaefer, S. (1970). *Compensation and restitution to victims of crime.* Montclair, NH: Patterson Smith.

Schafer, S. (1977).*Victimology: The victim and his criminal.* Reston, VA: Reston.

Schafer, S. (1981). The beginning of victimology. In B. Galaway, and J. Hudson (Eds.), *Perspectives on crime victims.* St. Louis, MO: C.V. Mosby.

Schuessler, K. ed. (1973) *Edwin H. Sutherland: On analyzing crime.* Chicago, IL: University of Chicago Press.

Schmalleger, F. (1995). *Criminal justice today: An introductory text for the twenty first century.* Englewood Cliffs, NH: PrenticeHall.

Schmidt, H. (2004). Rape myths. In M. D. Smith (ed.), *Encyclopedia of rape.* Westport, CT: Greenwood Press.

Schnaps, Y., Frong, M., Rand, Y., and Tirosh, M. (1981). The chemically abused child. *Pediatrics, 68,* 119–121.

Schuessler, K. (1956). *Edwin H. Sutherland: On analyzing crime.* Chicago, IL: University of Chicago Press.

Schur, E. M. (1971). *Labeling deviant behavior: Its sociological implications.* New York: Harper and Row.

Schwartz, M. (2006, April 25). *How can these strategies be adopted? A panel response to Ed McGuire's presentation entitled, "Police Research and Practice: Key findings and the issue of trust.* Panel presentation at the Science and Crime Prevention: Providing the Foundation for Change Two-Day Workshop, Richmond, VA.

Scott, M. S., Emerson, N. J., Antonacci, L. B., and Plant, J. B. (2006). *Drunk driving.* Problem-oriented guides for police, Problem-specific guides series, No. 36. U.S. Department of Justice. Washington, DC: Office of Community Oriented Policing Services.

Seligman, M. E. P. (1992). *Helplessness: On depression, development and death.* New York: W.H. Freeman and Company.

Senate Document Number 17. (1993). Second report on sexual assault and rape on Virginia's campuses. Sexual assault on Virginia's campuses. A report of the State Council of Higher Education and the Task Force on Campus Rape. State document number 19. Commonwealth of Virginia.

Seper, J. (1997, June 3). Reports of major offenses fall for fifth year running FBI says. *Washington Times,* p. A6.

Shakeshaft, C. (2004). Educator sexual misconduct: A synthesis of existing literature, available at: http://www.ed.gov/rschstat/research/pubs/miscon ductreview/report.pdf

Sherry, M. (2000). Hate crimes against people with disabilities, available at: http://www. wwda.org.au/hate.htm

Sherman, L. (1984). *Domestic violence: Crime file series.* Washington, DC: National Institute of Justice.

Sherman, L. W., and Berk, R. (1984). The specific deterrent effects of arrest for domestic assault. *American Sociological Review, 49,* 261–272.

Sherman, L. W., Gottfredson, D., MacKenzie, D., Eck, J., Reuter, P., and Bushway, S. (1997). *Preventing crime: What works, what doesn't, what's promising.* Retrieved from National Criminal Justice Reference Service website: http://www.ncjrs.gov/works/index.htm works

Sherry, M. (2003). *Don't ask, tell or respond: Silent acceptance of disability hate crimes.* Retrieved from http://dawn.thot.net/ disability_hate_crimes.html

Shichor, D. Gaines, L.K. and Ball, R (2002) *White collar crime.* Prospect Heights, IL: Waveland Press.

Simon, D. R. (2006). *Elite deviance* (8th ed.). Boston, MA: Allyn and Bacon.

Siegel, L. J. (1989). *Criminology* (3rd ed.). St. Paul, MN: West.

Siegel, L. J. (2006). *Criminology* (9th ed.). Belmont, CA: Thomson Wadsworth.

Skogan, W. G., and Maxfield, M. G. (1981). *Coping with crime: Individual and neighborhood differences*. Beverly Hills, CA: Sage.

Smith, B. L. (1988). Victims and victim rights activists: Attitudes toward criminal justice officials and victim-related issues. *Criminal Justice Review, 13*, 21–27.

Smith, L. N., and Hill, G. D. (1991a). Victimization and fear of crime. *Criminal justice and behavior, 18*(2), 217–239.

Smith, L. M., and Hill, J. D. (1991b). Victimization and fear of crime. *Criminal Justice and Behavior. 18*(2), 217–239.

Smith, M. S. (2005). Identity theft: The internet connection. Washington DC: Congressional Research Service Report for Congress.

Snarr, R. W. (1996). *Introduction to corrections* (3rd. ed.). Dubuque, IA: Brown and Benchmark.

Snyder, H. N., and Sickmund, M. (1999). *Juvenile offenders and victims: 1999 national report*. Washington, D.C.: Office of Juvenile Justice and Delinquency Prevention.

Snyder, H. N., and Sickmund, M. (2006). *Juvenile offenders and victims: 2006 national report*. Washington, DC: Office of Justice Programs, available at: http://ojjdp.ncjrs.gov/ojstatbb/nr2006/downloads/NR2006.pdf

Sperry, W. E. (1992). Victim impact evidence within a retributive system of justice. *Creighton Law Review, 25*, 1275–1310.

Stafford, M., and Galle, O. (1984). Victimization rates, exposure to risk, and fear of crime. *Criminology, 22*(2), 173–185.

Stalking Resource Center. (2006). Stalking fact sheet. Retrieved from www.ncvc.org/src

Stanko, B. (1992). Sexual harassment and the criminological profession. *The Criminologist, 17*, 1, 3–5.

Starkweather, D. A. (1992). The retributive theory of "just deserts" and victim participation in plea bargaining. *Indiana Law Journal, 67*, 853–878.

State of Connecticut Judicial Branch. (2006). *Article XXIX: Rights of Victims of Crime*. Retrieved from http://www.jud.state.ct.us/crimevictim/crime-const-rights.htm

State of Massachusetts. (1995). *Annual report on the state of Massachusetts court system, 1995*. Boston: Supreme Judicial Court.

Stein, J. H. (1977). *Better services for crime victims: Prescriptive package*. Washington DC: The Blackstone Institute.

Steinberg, J. (2006). Study says college sexual harassment up. *Daily Pennsylvanian*, available at: http://www.dailypennsylvanian.com

Steinmetz, S. K. (1977). *The cycle of violence: Assertive, aggressive and abusive family interaction*. New York: Praeger.

Stevenson, R. W. (1992, April 30). Riots in Los Angeles: Moments of terror; Blacks beat white truck driver as TV cameras record the scene. *New York Times*, p. A21.

Straus, M. A. (1973). A general systems approach to a theory of violence between family members. *Social Science Information, 12*, 105–125.

Straus, M. A. (1993). Physical assaults by wives: A major social problem. In R. J. Gelles, and D. R. Loseke (Eds.), *Current controversies on family violence*. Newbury Park, CA: Sage.

Straus, M. A. (2000a). *Beating the Devil out of them: Corporal punishments in American families and its effects on children* (2nd ed.). New Brunswick, NJ: Transaction Publishers.

Straus, M. A. (2000b). Corporal punishment and primary prevention of physical abuse. *Child Abuse and Neglect, 24*(9), 1109–1114.

Straus, M. A., and Gelles, R. J. (1986). Societal change and change in family violence from 1975–1985 as revealed by two national studies. *Journal of Marriage and the Family, 48*, 465–479.

Straus, M. A., and Gelles, R. J. (Eds.). (1990). *Physical violence in American families: Risk factors and adaptations in 8.145 families*. New Brunswick, NH: Transaction Books.

Straus, J. A., Gelles, R. J., and Steinmetz, S. K. (1980). *Behind closed doors: Violence in American families*. Beverly Hills, CA: Sage.

Stuart, B. (1996). Circle sentencing in yukon territory, Canada: A partnership of the community and the criminal justice system. *International Journal of Comparative and Applied Criminal Justice, 20*(1 & 2), 291–309.

Stuart, B. (2006). *Building community justice partnerships: Community peacemaking circles*. Ottawa, ON, Canada: Aboriginal Justice Section, Department of Justice of Canada.

Student Right to Know and Campus Security Act. (1990). Public Law No. 101–542 (1990). Amended by Public Law No. 102–26,10(e). (1991). 20 USC 1092(f).

Sutton, R.M., and Farrall, S. (2005). Gender, socially desirable responding, and the fear of crime. Are women really more anxious about crime? *British Journal of Criminology, 45,* 212–224.

Sutherland, E. H. (1924). *Criminology.* Philadelphia: J. B. Lippincott.

Synovate. (2003). *Identity theft survey report.* Washington, DC: Federal Trade Commission.

Taylor, J. J. (1994). *Support to community by victim support groups in New Zealand.* Paper presented at the 8th International Symposium on Victimology, Adelaide, S.A, Australia.

Taylor, R. B., and Hale, M. (1986). Testing alternative models of fear of crime. *Journal of Criminal Law and Criminology, 77*(1), 151–189.

Teaser, P. B., Dugar, T. A., Mendiondo, M. S., Abner, E. L., Cecil, K. A., and Otto, J. M. (2006). *The 2004 Survey of state adult protective services: Abuses of adults 60 years of age and older.* Retrieved from http://www.ncea aoa.gov/ncearoot/Main_Site/index.aspx

Telberg, R. (2004). A joint effort to fight corporate fraud. *Journal of Accountancy, 197*(4), 53–56.

Thalji, J. (1996, April 29). Jewish center bears the mark of vandals. *St. Petersburg Times*, p. 1.

Thorvaldson, S. (1990). Restitution and Victim Participation at Sentencing. In B. Galaway, and J. Hudson (Eds.), *Criminal justice, restitution and reconciliation.* Monsey, NY: Criminal Justice Press.

The Truth About Credit-Card Fraud. (2005, June 21). *Business Week Online.* Retrieved from http://www.businessweek.com/technology/

The National Center on Shaken Baby Syndrome, 2008. "What is shaken baby syndrome?" available at: http://www.dontshake.com/Audience.aspx?categoryID=8&PageName=MedicalFactsAnswers.htm#WhatIsSBS (Retrieved on September 17, 2008).

Thornhill, R., and Palmer, C. (2000). A *natural history of rape.* Cambridge, MA: The MIT press.

Titus, R. M., Heinzelmann, F., and Boyle, J. M. (1995). Victimization of person by fraud. *Crime and Delinquency, 41,* 54–75.

Tjaden, P., and Thoennes, N. (1998). *Stalking in America: Findings from the national violence against women survey.* Washington, DC: U.S. Department of Justice.

Tjaden, P., and Thoennes, N. (2000). *Full report of the prevalence, incidence, and consequences of violence against women: Findings from the National violence against women survey.* Washington, DC: U.S. Department of Justice.

Tomz, J. E., and McGillis, D. (1997). *Serving crime victims and witnesses* (2nd ed.). Washington, DC: U.S. Department of Justice.

Troup-Leasure, K., and Synder, H. N. (2005). *Statutory rape known to law enforcement.* Washington, DC: U.S. Department of Justice.

Turman, K. M., and Pover, K. L. (1998). *Children victims and witnesses: A handbook for criminal justice professionals.* Washington, DC: U.S. Department of Justice.

Uniform Crime Reports. (1993). Washington, DC: Department of Justice, Federal Bureau of Investigation.

Uniform Crime Reports. (1994). Washington, DC: Department of Justice, Federal Bureau of Investigation.

Uniform Crime Reports. (1995). Washington, DC: Department of Justice, Federal Bureau of Investigation.

Uniform Crime Reports. (1996). Washington, DC: Department of Justice, Federal Bureau of Investigation.

United States Parole Commission. (2002). *Participation of victims and witnesses in parole commission proceedings.* Washington, DC: United States Department of Justice.

University of Michigan Health System. (2007). Available at http://www.med.umich.edu/

USDA. (1998). *Handbook on workplace violence.* Retrieved from http://www.usda.gov/news/pubs/violence/wpv.htm

U.S. Capital Police. (1990). *Victim-witness assistance manual.* Washington, DC: Government Printing Office.

U.S. Department of Justice. (1985). *Justice assistance news.* Washington, DC: Government Printing Office.

U.S. Department of Justice (1988). *Report to the nation on crime and justice* (2nd ed.). Washington, DC: Government Printing Office.

U.S. Department of Justice. (1993). *Highlights from 20 Years of surveying crime victims: The national crime victimization survey, 1973–92.* Washington, DC: U.S. Department of Justice.

U.S. Department of Justice. (1996). *Criminal victimization 1994.* Washington, DC: Government Printing Office.

U.S. Department of Justice. (1997). *Serving crime victims and witnesses* (2nd ed.). Washington, DC: Government Printing Office.

U.S. Department of Justice. (2007). Uniform Crime Report, Crime in the United States, 2006. "Expanded Homicide Data" available at: http://www.fbi.gov/ucr/cius2006/documents/expandedhomicidemain.pdf (Retrieved on May 30, 2008).

U.S. Department of Justice, Bureau of Justice Statistics. (1994). *Criminal victimization in the United States, 1992.* Washington, DC: Government Printing Office.

U.S. Department of Justice, Bureau of Justice Statistics. (1995). *Fact sheet.* Washington, DC: U.S. Department of Justice.

U.S. Department of Justice, District of Massachusetts. (2006.). *Victim/witness assistance program.* Retrieved from http://www.usdoj.gov/usao/ma/vicwit.html.

U.S. Department of Justice, Office of the United States Attorney General. (2006). *Guidelines for victim and witness assistance.* Washington, DC: Government Printing Office.

U.S. Department of State. (2006, June). *Trafficking in persons report.* Washington, DC: U.S. Department of State.

U.S. Department of Heath and Human Services. (2008). Date Rape Drugs, available at: http://www.4woman.gov/FAQ/rohypnol.htm#3 (Retrieved on September 17, 2008).

U.S. Equal Employment Opportunity Commission. (2007). Sexual Harassment. http://www.de2.psu.edu/harassment/legal/

Van Ness, D., and Strong, K. H. (1997). *Restoring Justice.* Cincinnati, OH: Anderson.

Vasu, M. L., Moriarty, L. J., and Pelfrey, W. P. (1995). Measuring violent crime in North Carolina utilizing mail and telephone surveys simultaneously: Does method matter? *Criminal Justice Review, 20*(1), 34–43.

Viano, E. (1983). Victimology: The development of a new perspective. *Victimology, 8*(1–2), 17–30.

Viano, E. C. (1992). Violence among intimates: Major issues and approaches. In E. Viano (Ed.), *Intimate violence: Interdisciplinary perspectives.* Oxford, UK: Taylor and Francis.

Victim Policy Pipeline. (2001). Congress Responds Quickly to Victims of September 11 Terrorist Attacks.

Victim Support. (1994a). *Annual Report 1994.* London: Author.

Victim Support. (1994b, November 14). Compensation crisis for crime victims. *News Release.*

Virginia Commonwealth University, Campus Resources. (2006). available at: http://www.resourcecenter.vcu.edu/campus.resources.html (Retrieved on April 30, 2006).

Volpone, L. J. N. (1995). *Cooperation among agencies involved in Virginia's domestic violence mandatory and pro-arrest protocols: A descriptive study.* Unpublished master's thesis. Virginia Commonwealth University, Richmond, VA.

Von Hentig, H. (1941). Remarks on the interaction of perpetrator and victim. *Journal of the American Institute of Criminal Law and Criminology, 31,* 303–309.

Von Hentig, H. (1948). *The criminal and his victim: Studies in the sociobiology of crime.* New Haven, CT: Yale University Press.

Von Hirsch, A. (1976). *Doing justice: The choice of punishments.* New York: Hill and Wang.

Vossekuil, B., Fein, R., Reddy, M., Borum, R., and Modzeleski, W. (2002). *The final report and findings of the safe schools initiative: Implications for the prevention of school attacks in the United States.* Washington, DC: United States Secret Service and United States Department of Education. Retrieved from http://www.schoolsafety.us/

Walker, L. (1979). *The battered woman.* New York: Harper and Row.

Walker, L. (2000). *Battered woman syndrome* (2nd ed.). New York: Springer Publishing Company.

Walker, L., Price, R. L., Wilk, D., and Rogers, S. (2008). Domestic Violence and the Courtroom: Understanding the Problem ... Knowing the Victim. American Judges Foundation Inc. Available at: http://aja.ncsc.dni.us/domviol/booklet.html (Retrieved on June 4, 2008).

Walker, S. (1980). *Popular justice: A history of American criminal justice.* New York: Oxford University Press.

Wallace, H. (1996). *Family violence: Legal, medical, and social perspectives.* Boston, MA: Allyn and Bacon.

Wallace, H. (1998). *Victimology: Legal, psychological, and social perspectives.* Boston: Allyn and Bacon.

Waller, I. (1991). *Putting crime prevention on the map.* Paris: European Forum for Urban Safety.

Waller, I. (1994). *Effective policies to prevent crime: The right of victims to national investment in what works internationally.* Paper presented at the 8th International Symposium on Victimology, Adelaide, S.A, Australia.

Waller, I. (2003). *Crime victims: Doing justice to their support and protection.* Helsinki Finland: European Institute for Crime Prevention and Control.

Warr, M. (1984). Fear of victimization: Why are women and the elderly more afraid? *Social Science Quarterly, 65*(3), 681–702.

Warr, M., and Stafford, J. (1983). Fear of victimization: A look at the proximate causes. *Social Forces, 61*(4), 1033–1043.

Warshaw, R. (1994). *I never called it rape.* New York: HarperPerennial.

Watkins, S. A. (1990). The Mary Ellen myth: Correcting child welfare history. *Social Work, 35*(6), 500–503.

Weihe, V.R. (1997). *Sibling abuse: Hidden physical, emotional, and sexual trauma.* (2nd ed.). Thousand Oaks, CA: Sage.

Weisheit, R., and Mahan, S. (1988). *Women, crime, and criminal justice.* Cincinnati: Anderson.

Weed, F. J. (1995). *Certainty of justice: Reform in the crime victim movement.* New York: Aldine de Gruyter.

Weedon, M. A. (1996). *The implementation of the student right to know and campus security act of 1990: An analysis of the dissemination of the annual security report in Virginia's fifteen senior public institutions of higher education.* An unpublished master's thesis. Virginia Commonwealth University. Richmond, VA.

Wemmers, J. M. (1996) *Victims in the Criminal Justice System.* WODC/Kugler Publications, Den Haag/Amsterdam/New York: Kugler Pubns B V.

Wemmers, J. M., and Canuto, M. (2002). *Victims' experiences with, expectations and perceptions of restorative justice: A critical review of the Literature.* Montreal, CAN: International Centre for Comparative Criminology, University of Montreal.

Wemmers, J. M., and Zeilstra, M. I. (1991). *Dutch penal law and policy: Notes on criminological research.* The Hague, The Netherlands: Ministry of Justice.

Wenzel, S. L., Koegel, P., and Gelberg, L. (2000). Antecedents of physical and sexual victimization among homeless women: A comparison to homeless men. *American Journal of Community Psychology, 28*(3), 367–390.

Wessler, S. (2000). *Addressing hate crimes—Six initiatives that are enhancing the efforts of criminal justice practitioners. Center for the Study and Prevention of Hate Violence. University of Southern Maine.* Washington, DC: Bureau of Justice Assistance. (NIJ report #: 179559).

Westveer, A. (2006, April 14). *Personal communication.* Richmond, VA.

Whitcombe, D. (1988). *Guardian ad litems in criminal court.* Washington, DC: National Institute of Justice.

WHOA. (2006). Working to Halt Online Abuse, available at: http://www.haltabuse.org/.

Wiehe, V. R., and Richards, A. L. (1995). *Intimate Betrayal: Understanding and responding to the trauma of acquaintance rape.* Newbury Park, CA: Sage.

Williams, J. (1996, May 23). *Personal communication.* Richmond, VA.

Williams-Mbengue, N. (2001). Analysis of state actions on important issues – Safe havens for abandoned infants. NCSL State Legislative Report, 26, 8, available at: http://www.ncsl.org/programs/cyf/slr268.htm

Williams, F. P., and McShane, M. D. (1994). *Criminological theory.* Englewood Cliffs, NJ: Prentice Hall.

Williams, F. P., and McShane, M. D. (1999). *Criminological Theory* (3rd ed.). Upper Saddle River, NJ: Prentice Hall.

Winfield, I., George, L. K., Swartz, M., and Blazer, D. G. (1990). Sexual assault and psychiatric disorders among a community sample of women. *American Journal of Psychiatry, 147*, 335–341.

Wolfgang, M. (1958). *Patterns in criminal homicide.* Philadelphia: University of Pennsylvania Press.

Wolfgang, M., and Ferrracuti, F. (1967). *The subculture of violence.* London: Tavistock.

Wolfgang, M., and Ferracuti, F. (1982). *The subculture of violence* (2nd ed.). London: Tavistock.

Women's Rural Advocacy Programs. (2006). Available at: http://www.letswrap.com/

Wood, E. F. (2006). *The availability and utility of interdisciplinary data on elder abuse: A white paper for the national center on elder abuse.* Retrieved April 29, 2006 from http://www.ncea.aoa.gov/ncearoot/Main_Site/index.aspx

Wright, M. (1995). Victims, mediation and criminal justice. *Criminal Law Review, 32,* 187–199.

Wrobleski, H. M., and Hess, K. M. (1990). *Introduction to law enforcement and criminal justice* (3rd ed.). New York: West.

Wrobleski, H. M., and Hess, K. M. (1993). *Introduction to law enforcement and criminal justice* (4th ed.). New York: West.

Yeoman, B. (2006). *Murder on the mountain.* Retrieved January 10, 2006 from www.barryyeoman.com/articles/murderon-mountain.html

Yeoman, B. (2006) Murder on the mountain: The double slaying of lesbian hikers along the Appalachian Trail remains unsolved. Beyond the murder mystery is the tragic story of two women in love, available at: www.barryyeoman.com/articles/murderonmountain.html (Retrieved on January 10, 2006).

Yllo, K. A. (1993). Through a feminist lens: Gender, power, and violence. In R. J. Gelles, and D. R. Loseke (Eds.), *Current controversies on family violence.* Newbury Park, CA: Sage.

Yorburg, B. (1982). *Introduction to sociology.* New York: Harper and Row.

York County (VA) website. Property crime. Retrieved June 26, 2008 from http://www.yorkcounty.gov/vw/property/property_who.htm

Young, M. A. (1992). Victim services as a profession. *NOVA Newsletter, 16*(11), 1–10.

Young, M. A. (1993). *Victim assistance: Frontiers and fundamentals.* Washington, DC: National Organization for Victim Assistance.

Young, M. A. (1996). Victim services: Towards a new millennium in victim assistance. In C. Sumner, M. Israel, M. O'Connell, and R. Sarre (Eds.), *International victimology: Selected papers presented at the 8th International Symposium on Victimology, No 27.* Canberra, ACT: Australian Institute of Criminology.

Zehr, H. (1990). *Changing lenses.* Scottdale, PA: Herald Press.

Zehr, H. (2002). *The little book of restorative justice.* Intercourse, PA: Good Books.

Zehr, H., and Toews, B. (Eds.). (2004). *Critical issues in restorative justice.* Monsey, NY: Criminal Justice Press.

Statutes, Laws, and Cases

Booth v. Maryland, 482 U.S. 496.

Bundy v. Jackson, 641 F.2d 934 (D.C. Cir. 1981).

Chronological List of Legislation Enacted by the 107th Congress. Public Law No. 107–56. 10/26/01 Signed by President George Bush. Retrieved February 6, 2006 from http://www.uscis.gov/portal/site/uscis

Code of Virginia §18.2–60.3.

Moire V. Temple University School of Medicine, 613 F. Supp. 1360, 1366 (D.C.Pa1985).

Omnibus Consolidated Appropriations Act of 1997 (H.R. 3610 [104th]).

Payne v. Tennessee, 111 S.Ct. 2597.

S.C. code Annotated 16-3-1550 (b).

South Carolina v. Gathers, 490 U.S. 805.

Thurman v. City of Torrington, CT, 595 F. Supp. 1521 (D.C. CT 1984).

United States Code, Title 18, part I, chapter 113B, Section 2331. Definition of Domestic Terrorism. 18 USC 2331.

Violence Against Women Act of 1994 (H.R. 3355, Title VI—Violence Against Women).

Index